DISPLACING BLACKNESS

Power, Planning, and Race in Twentieth-Century Halifax

In this book Ted Rutland argues that although improving the quality of human life has long been a central goal of city planning, the process ultimately works to undermine the welfare of citizens living on the margins. Using twentieth-century Halifax as a case study, Rutland positions anti-blackness at the heart of contemporary city-making. Through a close examination of a series of important planning initiatives, from a social housing project concerned with the moral and physical health of working-class residents to a sustainability-focused regional plan, he shows how race – specifically blackness – has both guided and defined the boundaries of urban planning, with grave consequences for Halifax's Black residents.

Drawing connections between the history of planning and emerging scholarship in Black studies, *Displacing Blackness* develops an ambitious critique of urban planning by focusing not on its subservience to economic or political elites, but rather on its possibilities – and limitations – in bettering people's lives.

TED RUTLAND is an associate professor in the Department of Geography, Planning, and Environment at Concordia University.

TED RUTLAND

Displacing Blackness

Planning, Power, and Race in Twentieth-Century Halifax

UNIVERSITY OF TORONTO PRESS
Toronto Buffalo London

Toronto Buffalo London
utorontopress.com

ISBN 978-1-4875-0356-7 (cloth) ISBN 978-1-4875-2272-8 (paper)

Library and Archives Canada Cataloguing in Publication

Rutland, Ted. 1977 – , author
Displacing blackness: planning, power, and race in twentieth-century Halifax / Ted Rutland.

Includes bibiliographical references and index.
ISBN 978-1-4875-0356-7 (cloth), – ISBN 978-1-4875-2272-8 (paper)

1. City planning – Social Aspects – Noya Scotia – Halifax – History – 20th century. 2. Blacks Nova Scotia – Halifax – History – 20th century. 3. Power(Social sciences) – Nova Scotia . – Halifax – History – 20th century. 4. Halifax(N.S.) – Race relations – History – 20th century. I. Title

HT169.C32H35 2018 307.1'216097162250904 c2018-901014-2

This book has been published with the help of a grant from the Federation for the Humanities and Social Sciences, through the Awards to Scholarly Publications Program, using funds provided by the Social Sciences and Humanities Research Council of Canada.

University of Toronto Press acknowledges the financial assistance to its publishing program of the Canada Council for the Arts and the Ontario Arts Council, an agency of the Government of Ontario.

Canada Council for the Arts Conseil des Arts du Canada

Funded by the Government of Canada Financé par le gouvernement du Canada

Contents

Figures

Acknowledgments

This book was composed in three cities, and among many communities. Like all things, it was a collective achievement, and I am deeply grateful for the support, guidance, and inspiration I have received along the way. The Department of Geography at the University of British Columbia, where I completed my doctoral studies, was an incredibly vibrant and stimulating intellectual milieu. In various classrooms, over food and drinks, and in the midst of walks along the water, I picked up insights and inspiration from Haida Antolick, Alex Aylett, Emilie Cameron, Camerin Cobb, Rosemary Collard, Matt Dyce, Jess Dempsey, Jamie Doucette, Aftab Erfan, Fiona Jeffries, Jim Glassman, Calli Haggis, Chris Harker, Sara Koopman, Liz Lee, Pablo Mendez, Jeremy Murphy, Tyler Pearce, Joanna Reid, Andrew Shmuely, Juanita Sundberg, and Luna Vives. Gerry Pratt and Geoff Mann were exemplary mentors, offering guidance and asking questions that disrupted my early (too-easy) conclusions and continually pushed my thinking further. The support of Trevor Barnes and Elvin Wyly was also invaluable. Their suggestions and critical readings of my work while at UBC made visible the strengths and the weaknesses of my analysis, and taught me how to develop a more incisive and persuasive critique of urban planning.

Halifax was a part-time home during my doctoral years, and I returned many times thereafter to conduct research for this book. It is a city in which communities and categories have a habit of folding into one another, and it is hard for me to identify an intellectual community that is distinct from any other community that sustained me as this book developed. For colleagueship and comradeship, I extend particular gratitude to Denise Allen, Megan Best, Henry Bishop, David Black, Sue

Campbell, Afua Cooper, Tim Crabtree, Candace Daye, Michael Doan, Trish Glazebrook, Jill Grant, Ami Harbin, Max Haiven, Yuill Herbert, El Jones, Lynn Jones, Karin Kronstal, Shannon Lynch, Darryl Leroux, Hillary Lindsay, Amy Lounder, Catherine MacLellan, Leslie Oliver, Sylvia Parris, Jane Parpart, Moira Peters, LaMeia Reddick, Isaac Saney, Ben Sichel, Douglas Sparks, Ed Sturgeon, Ingrid Waldron, and Dennis Wright. In nearby Sackville, New Brunswick, I offer the same thanks to Andrew Nurse, Tim Reiffenstein, Anna Sheridan-Jonah, and Brad Walters. The written and political work of three elder African Nova Scotians – Rocky Jones, Sylvia Hamilton, and George Elliott Clarke – was a constant and essential companion during my time in Halifax. I thank them for leaving legacies, recorded and vividly remembered, that a person like me could pick up and learn from.

Montreal allowed me at last to plant my feet, and there is nowhere I would have rather planted them. Concordia University has been a very special place to work, and I feel fortunate to be surrounded by faculty and students that continue to challenge and teach me. For their colleagueship, however brief or sustained, thank you to Samah Affan, Aaron Barcant, Rachel Berger, Hannah Brais, Rosemary Collard, Shannon Gittens, Jess Glavina, Kiley Goyette, Kevin Gould, Steven High, Nasrin Himada, Bojana Kojic, Estraven Lupino-Smith, Pierce Nettling, Gada Mahrouse, Mireille Paquet, Kelly Pennington, Norma Rantisi, Elena Razlogova, Sophia Sahrane, Sujitha Sugen, Amy Twigge, and Aaron Tyree. To write in Montreal is to be sustained by an incredibly vibrant intellectual, political, and cultural community. In addition to the Concordia community, I thank the following Montreal colleagues, comrades, and conspirators: Claire Abraham, Stéphane Alix, Leila Bdeir, Hélène Bélanger, Leila Benhadjoudja, Didier Berry, Sirma Bilge, Martin Blanchard, Julien Caffin, Stefan Christoff, Amy Darwish, Nydia Dauphin, Tanya Davis, Fabien Desage, Gabriel Faveau, Louis Gaudreau, James Goddard, Renaud Goyer, rosalind hampton, Mostafa Henaway, Dru Jay, Radney Jean-Claude, Joana Joachim, Violaine Jolivet, Yuseph Katiya, Ricardo Lamour, Anne Latendresse, Marie Le Ray, Anne-Marie Livingstone, Jess MacCormack, Isabel MacDonald, Rina Mackereth, Caroline Martel, Bianca Mugyenyi, Bev Mullings, Charmaine Nelson, Natalie Oswin, Alex Popovic, Will Prosper, Lillian Radovac, Maya Rolbin-Ghanie, Jaggi Singh, Lib Spry, and Elena Stoodley.

The most important influence on this book came from a remarkable reading group, serendipitously formed in Montreal in 2013 and active ever since. The group, focused on the Black intellectual tradition, provided a sustained venue in which to work through recent Black scholarship and to consider its implications for places in Canada (seldom explicitly examined in this scholarship). The arguments in this book took shape, more than anywhere else, in our monthly meetings and the conversations that carried on between them. All of this helped to break the intellectual isolation that *can* characterize the research and writing process, and gave my work the feeling of a conversational, collective project. For all of this, I thank the group's core members, Val Bah, Nathalie Batraville, Amal Kenshil, Samiha Khalil, Nènè Konaté, Robyn Maynard, Anthony Mclachlin, Délice Mugabo, Valérie Simon, Fab Yoboua, and Rachel Zellars.

And here, my focus on physical places encounters its limit. Friends and colleagues who supported me along the way, despite the challenges of physical distance, include Jaime Alves, Justin Bigos, Bruno Cornellier, Deb Cowen, Chris Dixon, Andreas Elpidorou, Patrick Falby, Matt Farish, Carole Ferrari, Lauren Freeman, Kanishka Goonewardena, Emily Gilbert, Christina Heatherton, Brady Heiner, Joy James, Nithya John, Dalton Anthony Jones, Stefan Kipfer, Jenna Loyd, Graeme Moffat, Sean Mills, Shiri Pasternak, Jesse Proudfoot, Jacob Remes, Jen Ridgley, Elise Roche, Judah Schept, Rashad Shabazz, Anna Shea, Alexis Shotwell, Chad Smith, Joanna Smith, Erin Stalcup, Brett Story, Amy Wood, Joel Wood, and Jenny Wills. Thanks also to my family and the very particular support they unfailingly provided long before and throughout the writing of this book: Beth, Marcia, and Peter.

Thank you to University of Toronto Press, and particularly Douglas Hildebrand, for their interest in this book and the considerable work that brought it into existence. The three anonymous reviewers selected by the press provided extensive, encouraging, and yet critical comments on earlier drafts of this book. It is a much better book because of their efforts, and I am grateful for their work. Tyler Peace edited and commented on the entire first draft, providing valuable advice and sturdy confidence in the text's basic worth, at a time when both were sorely needed. Thank you, Tyler. Susan McClure and Kerry Mogg at the Halifax municipal archives were great company and great help on the many days I spent in their little cloister in the industrial park – and, in the case of Susan, on the many occasions I have needed assistance from a distance. Valuable help with archival research was also provided by Hugh Pouliot, Veronica Simmonds, Daniel Rotsztain, and Hillary Lindsay. Maps were graciously created by Julia Gregory and Eric Leinberger. Financial support was provided by a Social Sciences and Humanities Research Council (SSHRC) doctoral fellowship and an Awards to Scholarly Publications Program (ASPP) publications grant. An earlier, different, and substantially abridged version of chapter 4 appeared as "Enjoyable life: Planning, amenity, and the contested terrain of urban biopolitics," *Environment and Planning D: Society and Space* 33, no. 5 (2015): 850–68. Thank you all, *mille fois*.

Abbreviations

BLM	Black Lives Matter
BUF	Black United Front
CAP	Canada Assistance Plan
CMHC	Central Mortgage and Housing Corporation
COINTELPROs	Counterintelligence Programs
CORE	Congress for Racial Equality
CRA	Central Redevelopment Area
DREE	Department of Regional Economic Expansion
DUA	Dalhousie University Archives
FBI	Federal Bureau of Investigation
GHP	Greater Halifax Partnership
HCW	Halifax Local Council of Women
HDBA	Halifax Downtown Business Association
HDI	Halifax Developments Incorporated
HRM	Halifax Regional Municipality
HRMA	Halifax Regional Municipality Archives
HTNS	Heritage Trust of Nova Scotia
IAND	Indian Affairs and Northern Development
LIP	Local Involvement Program
MAPC	Metropolitan Area Planning Commission
MOVE	Movement for Citizens' Voice and Action
NCWC	National Council of Women of Canada
NHA	National Housing Act
NSAACP	Nova Scotia Association for the Advancement of Coloured People
NSARM	Nova Scotia Archives and Records Management

NSPS	Nova Scotia Planning Secretariat
NSVPB	Nova Scotia Voluntary Planning Board
RCMP	Royal Canadian Mounted Police
RSC	Royal Securities Company
SIDLC	Society for Improving the Dwellings of the Labouring Classes
URA	Uniacke Redevelopment Area
VON	Victorian Order of Nurses

1 Introduction

Urban planning in Halifax is, and has always been, a world-altering instrument of power and race.

The city's founding dates to 1749, when the British state moved to fortify its control over the province of Nova Scotia by building a new military settlement on the banks of an Atlantic-coast inlet known by the native Mi'kmaq as K'jipuktuk. Between 21 June and 1 July of Halifax's first year, Colonel Edward Cornwallis and a coterie of 2,575 would-be settlers reached shore at K'jipuktuk after a two-month Atlantic crossing. For the next month and a half, the newcomers huddled in a compact, makeshift camp while a pair of military engineers prepared territorial surveys and settlement plans. As elsewhere in the British Empire, the surveys and plans were essential to the seizure, control, and administration of land. The surveys disclosed the precise boundaries of ostensibly sovereign British territory, while the plans ensured a distribution of people across the territory that would allow both people and the territory to be administered by the colonial state. Expressing the designs of empire, the plans for Halifax outlined a compact, defendable settlement and a mosaic of discrete, contiguous property allotments. On 8 August, with the surveys and plans completed, 464 households were allotted to the new city's 464 lots and could finally begin the task of felling trees, levelling the ground, and building the houses in which they would endure their first Halifax winter.[1]

Establishing the new city required more than meticulous plans and arduous labour, however. The territory claimed by Britain and allotted to the settlers traditionally belonged to the Mi'kmaq, and British aspirations in the area contravened the "Peace and Friendship" Treaties of 1713 and 1745. The founding of Halifax, as Mi'kmaw scholar

Daniel Paul suggests, was effectively an act of war and could therefore be expected to provoke a reprisal.[2] Sure enough, the Mi'kmaq soon made their continued presence felt, striking at the very machinery of city making. On 30 September, they descended upon Major Jarmon's sawmill on the Halifax harbour and killed four workmen as they prepared planks for the building of Halifax homes. British blood spilled on the ground and mixed with sawdust: one of the first explicit signs that Halifax would be a racially divided city, and that its development would both provoke and occur through racialized violence.

Cornwallis's response to the attack was neither retreat nor negotiation, but a violent reassertion of an illegal territoriality. On 2 October, the colonel issued the so-called Scalping Proclamation. Claiming that Halifax and the province of Nova Scotia were under threat from a band of "Ruffians" who refused to recognize British rule, Cornwallis called on military and civilian subjects alike to "annoy, distress, take or destroy the Savage commonly called Micmac [*sic*]." A volunteer band of fifty men was ordered to "scour the wood all around the Town [of Halifax]." A further band of one hundred men was sent to hunt the Mi'kmaq "over the whole province," and all British settlers, military and civilian, were offered a bounty of ten guineas for every Mi'kmaw captured or killed. The bounty would be paid upon the delivery of evidence – either the "Savage taken" or "his scalp" – to one of three military command posts in the province (including Halifax).[3]

In colonial Halifax, the imbrication of planning, power, and race could scarcely be more clear: planning outlines a state of affairs that only through racialized subjugation and violence can be brought into being. Planners drew up a settlement that was meant to fit beneath the sovereignty of the colonial state, and that was meant to be inhabited exclusively by colonial settlers. There was no place in this plan for the Mi'kmaq, even as the plan pertained to territory that they had occupied and claimed for millennia. In relation to planning's objectives, therefore, the Mi'kmaq were positioned as an "external enemy," and only by "root[ing] them [out] entirely" could these planning objectives be realized.[4] The violence inflicted upon the Mi'kmaq eventually had its intended effect. Between 1749 and 1752, soldiers and mercenaries heeded Cornwallis's call and delivered scalps "by the bagful." The Mi'kmaw population was decimated, and although the war on the Mi'kmaq would continue – and though it continues, albeit less gruesomely, to this day – no further attacks would be experienced in Halifax. To suggest that planning is an instrument of power and race, at this point, is simply to acknowledge the gory violence that enabled the city to exist. It is to see the first official plan for the city and the Scalping Proclamation as intertwined: the two-volume founding documents of the new city.

The passing of time has altered, but not severed, these initial affiliations between planning, power, and race. In the second half of the nineteenth century, city leaders in Halifax began to introduce a set of techniques, forms of knowledge, and objectives that they described as "modern." A new form of planning, consequently, came to operate alongside the older, colonial form. This newer, "modern" form of planning would tend to be concerned less with securing physical territory than with producing and regulating material conditions in such a way that human life is protected and improved.[5] Whereas Halifax's first planners sought to establish a territory that could be controlled and administered by the colonial state, an exemplary modern planning initiative would seek to protect the "physical and moral health" of city residents (1906), make the city "a more agreeable place to live in" (1908), or improve the "general welfare" of the population (1945).[6] The pursuit of such objectives from the mid-nineteenth century onward has reworked and rearranged the ground of colonized territory. Especially significant planning initiatives in twentieth-century Halifax have included the development of sewer and water systems, the establishment of building codes and property development regulations, the demolition of impoverished "slums," and the redesign of the city's public spaces. In these and other interventions, the remaking of physical spaces is meant to act upon individuals and populations, to protect and improve people's lives according to period-specific conceptions of human flourishing.

The arrival of these new planning ambitions was accompanied by new and complex forms of subjugation. As I will elaborate in this book, modern planning's attention to human flourishing has gone hand-in-hand with various forms of physical displacement, political exclusion, sanctioned exposure to dangerous living conditions, imposed impediments to good health or welfare, and enforced restrictions on people's movement and daily activities. In some cases, effects like these are traceable to the exemption of certain lives from the sphere of planning's concerns. The forms of life that planning seeks to safeguard simply do not extend this far. In other cases, adverse effects are more intimately connected to the operation of modern planning. Here, it is precisely through targeted degradation and subjugation that planning seeks to promote a better form of life, either for the broader population or for the adversely affected residents themselves. In all cases, the line between lives improved and lives degraded is written most clearly and indelibly in the font of race. From the late nineteenth century to the present, evolving conceptions of race have shaped the meaning of the "life" that planning has sought to secure and nurture, and have contributed to planning outcomes that are racialized in both self-evident and surreptitious ways. While Halifax planners' horrific overt war against the Mi'kmaq has ceased, the city's significant and long-standing Black population – descendants, for the most part, of people enslaved in Nova Scotia or the United States – has experienced modern planning as an unyielding source of imperilment and plunder.

Modern urban planning is formed by particular entanglements with power and race. The power of modern planning is expressed less in the creation of sovereign territory than in the creation of material conditions that act upon individuals and populations: the creation, through spatial means, of tangible improvements in human health, happiness, and welfare. The results of modern planning are often impressive and sometimes salutary, but they are other things as well. The paradox of modern planning is that its seemingly benevolent aims are structured by evolving, normative conceptions of what it means to be human. Many social groups have, at one time or another, found themselves expelled from the conception of human life that planning seeks to secure and nurture. Among those expelled from the sphere of normative humanity in twentieth-century Halifax are countless residents who would identify as "white," people dehumanized or pathologized on the basis of social class (for example) rather than race. But life's pathological outside has been defined and populated most enduringly by the city's Black residents, and a deep-rooted structure of anti-blackness has shaped planning's dealings with all city residents, Black and non-Black. This book, while attending to diverse forms of planning-induced subjugation over time, argues that anti-blackness is fundamental to the operation of modern planning. The moves of modern planning, its attempts to create a life-improving urban terrain, are rendered conceivable and achievable by the displacement of blackness – sometimes physically (physical displacement) and sometimes symbolically (displacement from the field of planning's concerns). Displacing blackness, physically and symbolically, is the unending work of modern planning.

Planning, Power, and Race in Twentieth-Century Halifax

This book traces the imbrication of planning, power, and race across more than a century of history in the city of Halifax, Nova Scotia. The time period that I examine begins slightly before the twentieth century (around 1890) and finishes somewhat after it (around 2010). During this period, the aims of urban planning entailed a series of subtle variations on a consistent modern objective: the promotion, through spatial means, of a better form of human life in the city. Seeking to illuminate both constants and variations, each chapter of this book traces the emergence and consequences of a particular planning vision or project, a particular instantiation of modern planning's more general commitment to the fostering of life. In each chapter, I explore a series of questions: What did planning hope to achieve? How was the protection or improvement of life imagined? What forms of knowledge (e.g., studies, theories, expert advice) rendered people and spaces intelligible, assessable, and ostensibly improvable? How did social or spatial norms ultimately divide up the terrain of life and adjudicate the differential treatment of various individuals and populations? How, finally, did anti-blackness structure these normative divisions and thereby orient planning's conception, assessment, and management of human life (including non-Black life)? All of these questions require a careful routing of the damage inflicted by modern planning back to its larger and seemingly more gentle aims. Accordingly, *Displacing Blackness* is concerned with the complex entanglements of damage and protection, with the forms of harm produced in the interest of securing and nurturing of life, normatively conceived.

Though pointedly focused on modern urban planning, the scope of this book is somewhat broader than the usual scholarly treatment of the subject. It is broader, first of all, in its attention not simply to what planning does – the decisions it makes, the actions it carries out, and so on – but also to the ways that planning conceives of what it does and the ways in which these conceptions come into place. Following scholars like Michel Foucault, I am interested in how modern planning operates as a technology of power within worlds disclosed and rendered intelligible through particular forms of knowledge. The essential assumption here is that the same worldly conditions can be made intelligible in many different ways and that the fixing of a particular intelligibility, a particular rendering of the world, provides a terrain in which power can operate and (potentially) achieve its desired effects. Especially important to modern planning, I will show, are period-specific conceptions of human beings and urban spaces. It is on the basis of such forms of knowledge, such renderings of people and spaces, that planning has been able to establish its authority, calibrate its interventions and noninterventions, and seek to achieve its social and spatial objectives. Norms, and anti-blackness, find a practical entry point and discursive utility in these conceptions. Indeed, they limn the contours of the "human" and thus secure its intelligibility. Accordingly, my inquiry aims to identify and track the historical emergence of particular, normatively structured conceptions of people and spaces that have most significantly shaped modern planning and its efforts to protect and improve human life in Halifax.[7]

My inquiry is broadened also in its attention to planning as an activity rather than just a profession or job title. In other words, I am interested not simply in the practices of recognized urban planners and official urban planning departments, but also in a very wide array of institutions and actors that seek to shape the collective management of urban space. Long before a certified urban planner was hired in Halifax, urban spaces were studied, planned, and regulated in the expectation of achieving a specified outcome. The actors involved included engineers, medical doctors, philanthropists, clergymen, social reformers, and many others. The planning initiatives of these actors included the layout of streets, the establishment and enforcement of building codes, the construction of sewers and water systems, the regulation of land use, and much more. Even after the founding of an official urban planning department in the 1950s, moreover, some of the most significant planning ideas and practices continued to emerge from elsewhere, most notably from activists, economists, social workers, and property developers. In this book, then, I focus on professional planners, as well as the broader activity of planning, an activity that I understand to encompass collective efforts to coordinate, manage, and regulate the form and use of urban space in the interest of specified objectives. As I have suggested, the objective that interests me in this book is the one that modern planning has most often been expected to fulfil: that of protecting, improving, or otherwise optimizing human life.[8]

Tracking these concerns across the twentieth century requires a wide-ranging collection and analysis of research sources. The archives of the Halifax planning department provide many useful insights, but they pertain only to the period in which an official planning department existed. More importantly, these sources are limited to the actions of designated planning officials and committees, and are likely to miss the broader sources of power and knowledge that shape planning practices. Seeking a broader perspective, this book assembles and assesses a wide range of sources, including the minutes and reports of Halifax City Council and other city institutions; the records of provincial and federal institutions; the minutes and reports of Halifax-based civil-society organizations; newspapers, magazines, and documentary films; the records of the provincial land-registry office; telephone directories; and, when it comes to later periods, interviews with key actors.

In all cases, my reading of these sources seeks to map an effective nexus of knowledge and power. It seeks to identify the group of actors that devised, advocated, or otherwise supported important planning initiatives, as well as the set of knowledges that made it possible for these initiatives to be imagined and legitimated. In most cases, the relevant actors included people and institutions located well beyond the offices of the municipal planning department, while the pertinent forms of knowledge emerged beyond and before the planning initiatives they informed. My reading of these sources, importantly, also pursues planning's various institutional and intellectual "outsides." It aims to locate the actors who were not involved in devising planning initiatives (but could have been) and the forms of knowledge that were ignored or unknown (but should not have been). Tracking these outsides is a challenging but essential task. Doing this work makes it possible to recognize the social consequences of implemented planning initiatives and to identify planning possibilities, ignored in the past, that could still be mobilized in the present to guide city making to a much better future.

In examining planning's efforts to protect and improve human life, *Displacing Blackness* stakes out a very specific position within relevant literatures and discussions. That modern planning is devoted to the nurturing of life is a relatively common (though certainly disputed) observation. Also well recognized is planning's penchant for wrecking lives, particularly the lives of racialized populations. And yet, these two observations are seldom brought into the same analytical frame. Planning's dreadful effects, perhaps because they are so difficult to square with its professed concern for life, are typically treated as an aberration or mistake. They are seen as a deviation from planning's proper role, a deviation most often attributed either to prevailing economic exigencies (e.g., the need for planning to facilitate capital accumulation) or to a flawed political epistemology (e.g., a "modernist" rationality too confident in its comprehension of the city and its capacity to bring about a substantially better order of things). Planning's concern for "life," in this literature, appears unblemished and unassailable. Indeed, because it is not planning's concern for life but deviations from this objective that are deemed responsible for the worst effects of modern planning, the documentation of adverse effects becomes an occasion to insist, yet again, on the capacity and responsibility of planning to protect and improve life. For the dominant literature, in fact, one of the foremost reasons to overcome capitalism or to replace planning's faulty epistemology is to enable urban planning to assume its proper role unhindered.[9]

From a contrasting perspective, a range of critical scholarship has called into question modern conceptions of the human being, or simply "the human." This scholarship, discussed in detail below, falls into two groups. The first group examines the emergence of new conceptions of human individuals and populations in Europe and North America, and shows how practices like urban planning have sought to manage human beings, so conceived. Conceptions of the human, this work shows, have continually been structured by social norms that array "normal" life against its "pathological" variants and have provided orientation to social practices that imagine human flourishing to entail the proliferation of normal life and the diminution, disciplining, or subjugation of the pathological. The second group shares this attention to the conception and management of human life but brings the question of "race" more squarely and incisively into the analysis. This group of studies shows, in particular, how enslaved and colonized Black populations were cast outside of Euro-American conceptions of the human from the beginning, and how these conceptions of always-already pathological populations opened up a spectrum into which human variants *within* Europe could be slotted. Reading these two literatures together elicits a question that animates the present book and that is skirted in all existing scholarship: if planning is concerned with "the human," and blackness constitutes the horizon or outside of "the human," then how could planning be anything *other* than anti-Black?

Halifax is an opportune place to explore questions of planning and anti-blackness. More than any other Canadian city, Halifax is widely known for a particular example of anti-Black urban planning: the destruction of a community called Africville in the 1960s. Africville, at the time, was a community of four hundred Black residents on the northern edge of the city. Founded at least a century earlier, the community was routinely labelled a slum by twentieth-century planners, politicians, and white Haligonians. These earlier conceptions prepared the ground for the targeting and destruction of the community as part of a broader slum-clearance program between 1964 and 1969, despite clear and vocal resistance of Africville residents themselves. In the years since, the destruction of Africville has been documented in an ever-expanding collection of books, articles, book chapters, master's and doctoral theses, films, plays, stories, and poems. Through this work, the destruction of Africville has become relatively well known in Halifax and across the country, and it has become one of the stories most often cited in critical scholarship that seeks to show that Canada, despite its pretensions to multicultural innocence, has a deeply racist history.[10]

These discussions are important and generative. For myself, a white man from Northern Ontario, the story of Africville helped to expose my own ignorance about Canadian racism and the role of racism in shaping (advantageously) the circumstances of my own life. When I moved to Halifax in 2004 to begin a master's program at Dalhousie University, the story also helped me to make sense of my new home. I thought of the destruction of Africville often as I walked and biked the city's streets, participated in its politics, and observed forms of political and spatial segregation everywhere in the city. It also led me, soon enough, to the intellectual and political work of African Nova Scotians. This important work, from the writing of Sylvia Hamilton and George Elliott Clarke to the activism of Rocky Jones, Denise Allen, and Dennis Wright, provided an entry point to the long history of anti-blackness and Black resistance in Nova Scotia.[11] In time, this work transformed the way I saw the city and the world, compelling me to look beyond what Clarke calls Nova Scotia's "great beautiful landscape" to discern the "history of ... great pain and tragedy" that its beauty conceals.[12] All of this sparked a more focused interest in the history of urban planning, a history that encircles the story of Africville and seems to demand the kind of two-way seeing that Clarke advises. The present book would certainly not have been written without the questions and intellectual work that the story of Africville compelled me to contemplate.

This is not, however, a book about Africville. Though I discuss the community at certain points in the book (especially chapter 3), my project takes this well-known story as an entry point to larger and less explored concerns. I aim to bring attention, for one thing, to the operation of urban planning in other Halifax-area Black communities, including parts of the Halifax North End and a series of outlying Black communities like Beechville, Upper Hammonds Plains, and North Preston. Black people, enslaved by white settlers, were among Halifax's first inhabitants. This early Black population was augmented, massively, by three major migrations of formerly enslaved people from the United States and Jamaica between 1783 and 1834. The result is that the greater Halifax region had the largest Black population of any Canadian city until the 1970s, when the dewhitening of federal immigration policy began to alter the demographics of cities like Toronto and Montréal.[13] These Black Haligonians, like those of Africville, experienced and struggled against the imperatives of modern planning throughout the twentieth century, and these experiences and struggles reveal important aspects of the broader, anti-Black structure of planning practice. To examine the larger reach of anti-Black planning, as I do in this book, is not to diminish the significance of Africville, but rather to convey its significance in the terms of many Black Haligonians. Africville is important, in this view, partly because of what happened to this place and the people who lived there, but also because of the broader structure of power that it symbolizes: the centuries-long neglect, plunder, and subjugation of Black people in Halifax and across Nova Scotia by the state (in general) and planning (in particular).

The book, while focused on the Halifax region, develops an analysis of modern planning that exceeds the boundaries of any particular city or region. The planning initiatives that I examine were, in every case, linked to similar initiatives elsewhere. Indeed, these initiatives were typically conceived within a network of actors and ideas that linked Halifax to cities elsewhere and that helped to install similar initiatives in a range of locations in Canada, the United States, and around the world. Accordingly, my analysis of particular initiatives pays attention to the wider networks that made them possible and, in so doing, points towards a broader analysis of planning practice. These networks of planning ideas and actors, more importantly, were themselves part of a broader (not just planning-focused) structure of knowledge and power: a world-spanning effort to manage human life and an equally vast, anti-Black conception of what human life entails. Broad-based structures, as critical geographers have long argued, are bound to exhibit context-specific particularities, and there are certainly particularities specific to Halifax in the following analysis.[14] These particularities, however, need to be seen not as a departure from broader phenomena but as the attributes of phenomena that are necessarily broad based *and* particular, phenomena that can be qualified *as* broad based precisely because they exist, in modestly different forms, in different places. I approach planning in Halifax, then, as a city-specific instantiation of world-spanning relations of power, and I invite others to examine how the form of planning that I describe in this book plays out in other contexts.

Tracing these relations of power, in Halifax or anywhere else, ultimately requires that the experiences of Black people be placed alongside the experiences of other mistreated and subjugated populations. As I noted above, the wreckage of twentieth-century planning in Halifax included the damaged lives and living conditions of thousands of non-Black residents, including over four thousand poor and working-class white residents displaced and dishoused as part of the same slum-clearance program that ploughed through Africville. This book seeks to bring attention to outcomes like these. It does so, in part, to provide a broader view of twentieth-century planning, but also to put research on planning and racism on a stronger footing. In many existing studies, planning is shown to be detrimental to racialized populations, but its effect on oppressed white populations is never analysed. As a result, this work appears to document racial subjugation but actually skirts the issue at hand. It is unable to explain what is specifically racial about the subjugation it observes – how it differs, for example, from class subjugation. Other studies exhibit a different problem. This work helpfully brings planning's mistreatment of oppressed white and racialized populations into view but then concludes that the same structure of power determined the experiences of both groups. The basis of these groups' mistreatment, it is claimed, is their common position in a hierarchical class structure.[15]

While there are important insights in these studies, they fail to provide an analysis of planning and racism. The first set of studies documents racial subjugation but fails to explain why it should be understood as racial, while the second set documents class subjugation but fails to explain why it should *not* be understood as racial (when it implicates people of colour). I am perhaps most wary of the second set. This work, part of a broader pattern in socio-political analysis, either ignores the effects of racism entirely or else confines its effects to processes and institutions external to urban planning, as if racism exists in places like the job market or political system and enters urban planning strictly through the class characteristics (e.g., poverty and lack of political power) that its operation elsewhere produces. One of the aims of this book, therefore, is to clarify the meaning and consequences of anti-Black racism and to show how it exists alongside (and shapes) other forms of oppression *within* the realm of urban planning. This is best achieved, I believe, by situating the experiences of Black Haligonians within a city-wide planning apparatus and carefully comparing planning's conception, assessment, and treatment of various nonnormative populations, Black and non-Black. Although Black people are not the only ones whose lives have been neglected or damaged by modern planning, there is a particularity and often a gravity to it that needs to be illuminated. It is only by taking a wider view, by studying urban planning in Black communities and outside them, that the specificities of anti-blackness can be fully recognized, analysed, and combated.

One of the challenges in this work is to keep anti-Indigenous or settler-colonial oppression in view during a period (the twentieth century) when relatively few Indigenous people resided in Halifax. The Mi'kmaq, the historical inhabitants of K'jipuktuk, were reduced to just one resident in Halifax and 130 residents in the broader Halifax region in 1901. A century later, their population had grown to the still-modest figure of 3,525 in the city-region. These relatively low numbers were owed, in part, to the early effects of European colonization and Indigenous elimination, actions that reduced the Mi'kmaw population of the maritime region from thirty-five thousand to one hundred thousand in 1500 to a mere two thousand in 1700.[16] They were also owed, however, to a range of state policies in the nineteenth and twentieth centuries that sought to confine Mi'kmaw and other Indigenous people to specific nonurban locations. These policies, beginning in earnest with the federal Indian Act of 1876, regarded nonurban "reserves" as the proper places for Indigenous people, places where they could be observed, trained, and eventually transformed into Canadian citizens like any other (i.e., citizens without sovereign claims to territory or nationhood). In Nova Scotia, the fulfilment of this strategy involved the relocation of Mi'kmaw people to an ever-smaller set of reserves located ever farther from white cities like Halifax and Sydney. It also involved a set of policies, including restrictions on marriage, education, and employment, that made it extremely difficult, if not criminal, for Mi'kmaw people to depart the reserves and make their lives in urban areas.[17]

Small in number, the Mi'kmaq attracted almost no attention in twentieth-century discussions of urban planning in Halifax – in stark contrast, clearly, to the discussions that surround the founding of the city. It is difficult, consequently, to make substantial claims about how the Mi'kmaq fit into twentieth-century planning visions. And yet, there are certain connections that can be drawn. All of the initiatives that I examine, for one thing, start from the unstated premise that the terrain of the city falls under settler-state control, that this terrain, though never ceded by the Mi'kmaq, is the state's to plan and manage. Settler colonialism is reproduced in this premise, this non-effort to recognize or deal with continuing Indigenous sovereignty. There are salient connections, moreover, between urban planning in Halifax and the ongoing management of Indigenous lives and spaces elsewhere. These two forms of socio-spatial intervention have often involved similar objectives and relied on similar (but not identical) racial discourses. Throughout the book, accordingly, I make a point to mention the most relevant overlaps in thought and practice between urban planning and nonurban colonial management. A full analysis of these overlaps, to be clear, would require another book. It would require, among other things, a patient analysis of the relationship between nominally distinct state institutions and subtly different racial discourses. Though I cannot undertake it here, I hope to have provided some small insights towards such a project and emphasized its potential intellectual and political importance.

The effects of planning as a whole, of course, are not limited simply to abandoned, wrecked, or subjugated lives. For many people, perhaps even the majority of people, planning is indeed the life-improving operation that it claims to be. I make this point not to concede that planning has "done some good things" or that it has aided "the population in general." These are the kinds of claims that planning ritually makes about itself, and it is precisely my aim to examine whose lives disappear and disintegrate behind such generalizing statements. My point is meant, rather, to illustrate the connections between the lives secured and the lives subjugated by modern planning, to show, as Joy James puts it, how "the white civic body" has been strengthened through a kind of "social parasitism" organized by urban planning.[18] Analytically, this means showing how a better life has been produced for some people (especially white people) at the expense of other people (especially Black people). It means detailing how anti-blackness is woven through both of these effects, how it inheres in lives upgraded and lives degraded, in spaces that sustain life and those that imperil it – in the production, at last, of politically sustained white life and politically enforced Black vulnerability and (sometimes) death. To the extent that planning has taken the urban terrain under its charge and organized this terrain in the service of an anti-Black conception of human life, there is nowhere in the city and no *one* in the city that is unaffected.

All of this means that, for a white person like me, the injustices of anti-Black planning are located rather close to home. They are inscribed not just in unjustly higher levels of white wealth or unjustly better white housing conditions but in the very make-up of our bodies and our experiences of the world. It is important, I think, to acknowledge these effects, the intimate privileges provided to white people in contexts produced and organized by anti-Black urban planning. And yet, I also reject the idea that a life of narrowly conferred and violently defended privileges is indeed a better life – better, that is, than the form of life that could exist in the absence of unjustly configured planning practices. The actual benefits of modern planning, in other words, need to be gauged in terms other than those provided by planning itself. While planning has certainly provided its own conception of the good life to some people, it has also rendered impossible and almost unthinkable the much better life that could be created in a context of interhuman care and solidarity. Modern planning, in this sense, has actually degraded life in general. It has foreclosed a form of life that is better, not because it has escaped subjugation, but because everyone has escaped subjugation – a form of life in which the categories "privileged" and "subjugated" no longer apply. This conviction subtends the scholarly and political aims of this book.

The scholarly aim of this book is to bring new insights to discussions of planning, power, and race. I aim, in particular, to bring these discussions closer to emerging work on anti-blackness and detail how anti-blackness is fundamental not simply to modern conceptions of "the human" but also to a significant activity (planning) that continually enlists conceptions of the human and seeks to produce material conditions conducive to human flourishing. My central argument is that anti-blackness structures planning's conception of human life, that it brings into being the always-already pathological pole of a normality/pathology spectrum into which various individuals and populations can be slotted. Displacing blackness from the field of planning's concerns and (sometimes) from the physical terrain itself is thus the opening and continually repeated move of modern planning. My political aim, quite clearly, is to bring an end to this form of planning. This book contains certain lessons for urban planners and city officials, should they wish to receive them. However, it locates the possibility of substantial social change elsewhere: among the many people who will be, or are already, involved in grass-roots movements that place Black lives at the centre of efforts to eradicate all forms of oppression and, indeed, all forms of privilege. The filaments of such movements, I will show, have always existed in Halifax. I offer this book in the hopes that they expand and proliferate.

Planning and the Cultivation of Life

In pursuing a critical analysis of modern planning, this book participates in a long-standing intellectual project that stretches across several disciplines in the social sciences and humanities. Until recently, this project was dominated by a pair of long-standing approaches. The first, centring on the work of Marxist geographer David Harvey, approaches urban planning as an expression of specifically capitalist social relations. Beginning from a careful delineation of the spatial requirements that capital (or simply "business") cannot fulfil on its own, this approach shows how urban planning takes on the tasks of providing the infrastructure, amenities, and spatial "order" that continued capital accumulation requires. Planning, this work shows, operates as an aid to capital accumulation. It does so not necessarily because planners have no other objectives, or because they are duped or lobbied into playing this role, but because cities must attract, retain, and therefore please footloose capital in order to sustain local employment, solicit tax revenues, and achieve a panoply of other (nonprofit-oriented) objectives.[19] The second approach, centring on the work of anthropologist James Scott, views planning as the expression of a particular state rationality. This rationality, sometimes termed "modernist," seeks to render the world intelligible and governable through various simplifications, especially the representation of phenomena in simple quantitative terms (e.g., land values, demographics, traffic volumes). Conducive to state governance, this rationality also effaces much of the real world and renders vulnerable to violence and destruction any phenomena that elude planning's simplified world view.[20]

While drawing insights from these two approaches, this book engages primarily with a third approach to urban planning. Less developed than the other two, this approach builds upon the work of Michel Foucault, especially his analysis of the discourses and practices affixed to "the human" in modern societies. As Foucault explains, the nature of the human being came to the centre of European intellectual and political reflections in the second half of the eighteenth century. In fields like biology, political economy, and linguistics, the centring of the human resulted in a profound epistemological break. Understanding the nature of the human – its behaviours, motivations, capacities, and so on – was now essential to the study of natural, economic, and social processes. Entirely new fields, such as the humanities and social sciences, also came into being alongside the figure of the human. The raison d'être of these fields was precisely to reflect upon, investigate, and theorize the lives of human individuals and populations. What makes these intellectual transformations important is the new terrain of practical intervention that they opened up. Knowledge of the human, Foucault argues, became a precondition and product of various forms of modern power (the broadest of which he calls "biopower"). These forms of power, exercised by the state, capital, and an array of other institutions, take the human as their primary object; seek to protect, improve, or otherwise manage human existence; and accumulate authority or "surplus power" through these efforts. Analysing these forms of knowledge and power – their coming into being, their consequences, and their historical and geographical variation – is the central aim of the broad intellectual and political project that Foucault sometimes terms "critical ontology."[21]

The political purchase of Foucault's project lies primarily in its attention to the role of norms in the management of human beings. From the beginning, Foucault claims, the human attained legibility in relation to particular biological and social norms. In domains ranging from public health to psychology, ostensibly "normal" human functioning was conceived alongside its opposite ("pathological" functioning). The discursive space opened up between the opposed poles of normality and pathology provided the essential foundation of human-centred knowledge and power as such.[22] Enfolded into the exercise of modern power, the apparent distinction between normality and pathology has been extremely consequential. Efforts to produce a healthier or more secure population, in many cases, have assumed a particular, normative human subject as the constituent of this population and have offered protection and care strictly to those who exhibit this assumed normality. In other cases, producing an optimal population focuses squarely on the pathological. Targeted efforts are made, here, to modify pathological lives, to render them normal, or to eliminate their degrading taint from the overall population. In all of these cases, the distinction between normality and pathology provides an orientation to the exercise of power. It gives meaning to life-fostering projects and produces vastly different trajectories of human existence. Many lives are, in fact, improved; they are rendered healthier, happier, or more secure. Other lives are undermined in either relative or absolute terms; their fate becomes a kind of living death: an enforced exclusion from the protections and qualities of life that modern power proliferates.[23]

The relevance of these insights to the analysis of urban planning has only begun to be explored. Foucault himself discusses urban planning in a few places and hints at its broader significance in his claim that the management of urban space is the "primary technique" of biopolitical power (a form of power that seeks to manage human populations or "aggregates").[24] Later work, influenced by Foucault, has tracked the management of human beings across a variety of contexts and planning initiatives. The development of public housing, sanitary infrastructure, transportation systems, recreational spaces, and pollution-curtailing initiatives have all been shown to be linked to particular conceptions of human flourishing (especially optimal human health, morality, and security).[25] In the seminal contribution to this work, Paul Rabinow's *French Modern* examines how planning conceived, assessed, and managed human beings across a century of spatial interventions in metropolitan France. Essential to these efforts, he shows, was the emergence of conceptions of the human in the early nineteenth century that posited an essential connection between living beings (or "forms of life") and their material environment (or "conditions of life"). The assessment of human beings, consequently, was now accompanied by an assessment of their material conditions, and any problems (i.e., pathologies) identified among the former were believed to be remediable (in part) through alterations to the latter. Changing the city, in effect, became a way of changing people, and the power of planning came to be founded in its capacity to operate upon the lives of individuals and populations.[26]

This still-nascent approach to urban planning provides an essential opening to the concerns of this book. As I have suggested, the planning initiatives that I seek to understand in this book are those that aim to produce a better form of human life, initiatives that invoke a particular image of human flourishing and that seek to remould individuals or populations in this image through spatial interventions. In some cases, such as the provision of sewers and running water (chapter 3) and the adoption of property development controls (chapter 7), these initiatives were targeted towards a normative human subject. Upholding and enlivening normal life – to the exclusion and detriment of pathological lives – was the adopted means of improving and strengthening the overall population. In other cases, such as the regulation and development of working-class housing (chapters 2 and 4), these initiatives were oriented towards pathological subjects. Altering pathological lives, remaking them in the image of the normal, was believed to be beneficial to the city and the targeted individuals alike. In all cases, the power of modern planning was constituted and exercised through its operation upon human beings, and its destructiveness to particular people and communities was connected to its fundamentally normative conception of what it means to be human. Twentieth-century planning in Halifax, I argue in this book, has been allied to a form of power that seeks to protect, nurture, and bolster life, and that produces violence and subjugation in the pursuit of these noble ends.

None of this is to suggest that the planning imperatives identified by David Harvey and James Scott have been absent or unimportant. The attraction of capital has been an ever-present concern in twentieth-century Halifax, and the (seeming) dependence of local employment, housing, tax revenues, and social expenditures on continued private investment has clearly placed limits on the field of planning possibilities that could be reasonably contemplated. The attraction of capital, however, has never been planning's only priority, and it has been planning's *foremost* priority only for a relatively small (albeit influential) group of actors. Perhaps more importantly, the interests of capital have often been pursued in Halifax through precisely the kind of spatial practices analysed by Foucault and Rabinow: practices that aim to remake individuals and populations, and thereby fulfil a variety of objectives (including profit making). The modernist rationality described by Scott, meanwhile, has certainly been significant to urban planning during certain periods. The initiatives of post-World War II urban renewal, in particular, were informed by an almost obsessive quantitative analysis of human and spatial conditions, and the resulting veneer of scientific objectivity undoubtedly bolstered the authority and destructiveness of the postwar planning regime. Earlier and later periods, however, were informed by quite different forms of analysis, including quasi-literary accounts of slum housing in the early 1900s and the outputs of planning-focused citizen participation in the post-1960s period. The forms of state power, subjugation, and violence that Scott allies to a particular rationality coursed unabated through this succession of other rationalities. These effects are not isolatable to modernist simplifications alone.

The biggest advantage of a Foucauldian or critical ontological approach to urban planning lies less in its identification of planning objectives than in its critique of these objectives. The promotion of a better "quality of life," critiqued by Foucault, is almost universally described in other critical work as the aim that planning should pursue, or else the aim that it *could* pursue in a radically different, revolutionized society. Harvey, for example, argues that the interests of capital have historically hemmed in the achievement of "well-intended and benevolent" planning ambitions. One of the merits of a progressive transformation of society, he claims, is that it would unblock planning's "capacities to create a new species of human being."[27] The possibility that destruction, violence, and subjugation might occur partly *through* well-intended initiatives and various efforts to create "new species of human being" is never entertained. For Scott and his followers, meanwhile, the problem with modernist rationalities is their failure to properly improve the "human condition." Thus, a range of ostensibly nonmodernist forms of knowledge making, from storytelling to participatory map making and decision making, are suggested in this work as the means through which this same objective could be achieved.[28] Though I am sympathetic to these political projects, I would urge closer attention to the perceived make-up of "the human" whose condition is to be improved through these new knowledge-making practices.

Though invaluable as a starting point, the work of Foucault, Rabinow, and other exponents of a critical ontology of urban planning is not without limitations or problems. For the most part, this work has focused on rather isolated planning initiatives, initiatives that are relatively narrow in their objectives and relatively specific in their temporal and spatial application. With the exception of Rabinow's book-length treatise, this work lacks the broader historical perspective that would allow the subtle variations of human-centred planning practices across a succession of interventions and time periods to be assessed. The present book, covering more than a century of significant planning initiatives, seeks to address this limitation and extend this line of work. A related limitation concerns the existing Foucauldian literature's narrow conception of the human characteristics or qualities that planning seeks to comprehend and manage. The efforts of planning, in existing work, are consistently directed towards the most basic biomedical and (sometimes) moral dimensions of existence: the health, morality, and physical security of individuals; the longevity, growth, and decline of populations; and so on. In contrast, the present book assesses and critiques planning's attention to the broader "qualitative" elements of human existence, including feelings of "enjoyment" and "pleasure," that have been essential to the endeavours of twentieth-century planning in Halifax and elsewhere.

The most serious problem in the existing Foucauldian literature is its limited and usually nonexistent attention to the role of race in the conception and management of human beings. Foucault's attention to race is famously short-sighted. His analysis of modernizing France strangely brackets the networks of knowledge and power that extended beyond the metropole, including extensive practices of slave trading, slave holding, external colonialism, territorial occupation, and Indigenous elimination across the so-called French Atlantic. Foucault's sole discussion of race, moreover, is confined to a set of lectures that were never published in his lifetime and that problematically describe European racism as a reformulation of a prior class discourse – a development, that is, entirely confined to continental European history.[29] Subsequent Foucauldian work on urban planning largely sidesteps these essential problems, ignoring questions of race entirely instead of retracing and rethinking the significance of race to modern forms of urban planning. The problem is not just that an analytical gap surrounds the treatment of racialized individuals and subpopulations within modern planning regimes. The more important problem is that the treatment of any individual or population by modern planning – which is to say, the operation of modern planning in general – remains inadequately understood to the extent that the role of race in the delineation of the human is unobserved. To make sense of urban planning, then, it is useful to read the work of Foucault, Rabinow, and like-minded critics of urban planning alongside the work of scholars who examine how race is involved in the conception of the human.

Race-focused work on the conception of the human is increasingly abundant. Particularly important to this book is a line of work that traces the historical and present relationship between Western conceptions of the human and global anti-blackness. Beginning with Frantz Fanon's interrogation of Eurocentric ontologies in *Black Skin, White Masks*, this line of analysis includes the work of Katherine McKittrick, Rinaldo Walcott, Sylvia Wynter, Saidiya Hartman, and the collection of scholars who have adopted the term Afro-pessimism to describe their intellectual project.[30] In slightly different and sometimes conflicting ways, these scholars have each excavated the historical and ongoing co-constitution of blackness and humanity within Euro-American discourses and practices – the constitution, more precisely, of blackness as the boundary or outside of humanity as such. Blackness, for these scholars, is not synonymous with Black people, for the critical task is to explain the process through which blackness acquires its meaning and certain people are identified with it. Blackness, instead, refers to a subordinate structural position within a set of spatially and temporally differentiated relations, discourses, and practices that continually constitute gradations of the human. How these relations, discourses, and practices are reproduced and how people are relegated to the structural positions they constitute is a question for research.[31] This work, it must be recognized, has seldom broached questions of urban planning, but it does develop a compelling and race-centred critical ontology that I think can be brought together with the Foucauldian analysis of planning discussed above.

Historically, the co-constitution of blackness and humanity was rooted in the world-spanning relations of European colonialism and enslavement. Very early in this history, new conceptions of the human began to appear in European social and political thought. These conceptions, novel in their secular rather than religious foundation, centred on a series of attributes or qualities (e.g., reason, conscience, sentiment) that were presented as unique to the human species and yet unequally distributed among the world's various societies. Europeans, or at least the most privileged among them, were believed to embody these qualities in their most perfect and advanced form. The very meaning of these qualities, however, depended on the identification of their absence, or most "beastly" expression. It was the latter, the expression of nonhumanity or not-quite-humanity, that was most consistently sited in sub-Saharan Africa. The effect of the emerging ontology was thus to constitute a pair of interdependent categories: "the human" and "the Black." The former category was taken to express the essence of the secular human being. Indexed to the people of Western Europe, now discussable as "European" or "white," the category also applied to a lesser and varying extent to the world's non-European societies. The latter category, in contrast, expressed the horizon or outside of the human. Indexed to the people of sub-Saharan Africa, now discussable as "African" or "Black," this category signified the absence or near-absence of the qualities that now defined the human being and the forever questionable, if not annulled, humanity of the people it included.[32]

The forms of anti-Black subjugation sustained by this new ontology have varied over the last five centuries. The most important of these was chattel slavery, a status that was essential to the making of the New World (including Halifax) and that was eventually reserved exclusively for Black people. As many scholars have demonstrated, it was human qualities (in their absence) that underwrote the European-wide consensus on Black enslavability, just as it was the assumed possession of these qualities by non-Black people that shielded them from enslavement. Though slavery was formally abolished in Europe and North America in the course of the nineteenth century, it is far from clear that the ontology and social structure interlinked with it has disappeared. Indeed, distinctly modern and scientific conceptions of race emerged precisely as the system of formal slavery withered, transferring the meaning of blackness from a legal register (enslavable) to a series of biological, cultural, and political discourses that reasserted and sustained slavery-era conceptions of Black inferiority and inhumanity. As Rinaldo Walcott argues, the "global anti-black condition" produced in the era of racial slavery has persisted in the form of "a perverse relationship to the category of the Human in which our [Black people's] existence as human beings remains constantly in question and mostly outside the category of *a life*." Black existence, Walcott claims, is "*marked* as social death," even as Black people consistently create social lives that exceed and sometimes thwart this deathly imposition.[33]

These insights allow us to return to Foucault's critical ontology and nuance some of its central claims. It allows us to recognize, above all, that the emergence of a normal / pathological bipolarity within Europe (and among European people) occurred against the backdrop of the prior eviction of African-descended people from the category of the human. The distinction between "the normal" and "the pathological" outlined by Foucault established a differentiation internal to the European or "human" population, with Black people positioned somewhere beyond the pathological extreme. The point is not that Europeans are always or necessarily recognized as full humans. As Sylvia Wynter and others make clear, many European populations – women, the insane, the delinquent, the homosexual, the indigent, and so on – have been denied full human standing in certain contexts and have only conditionally and through great struggle obtained access to the status accorded sui generis to the bourgeois, able-bodied, heterosexual, cisgendered man. The point, instead, is that these European lesser humans and not-fully-humans remain some distance from the "ultimate zero-degree category" of "the Black," the figure against which all measures of humanness, normality, and pathology are established.[34] As Lewis Gordon argues, Black people cannot be pathologized (as others can). In an anti-Black world, he argues, they *are* pathology; their existence defines the "pathology" that is subsequently and contingently attributed to (some) non-Blacks.[35]

What, then, of urban planning? The literature on anti-blackness itself seldom mentions urban planning, and it discusses the related issue of spatiality primarily through the familiar examples of Black containment:

the enforced segregation of Black people within the plantation, the ghetto, and the penitentiary.[36] And yet, the anti-blackness literature's careful distinction between the "pathologized" and the always-already "pathological" provides an analytical lens through which much more significant insights about urban planning can be glimpsed. For one thing, it can help to make sense of the subtle distinctions between the subjugation of Black Haligonians and marginalized white populations. As this book demonstrates, poor and working-class white populations have often been described in planning discussions as pathological and have endured various forms of planning-induced subjugation. Black populations, however, have consistently been seen as still *more* pathological, and it is difficult to identify a single example in which planning sought to understand, sustain, or improve the specific circumstances of Black people. None of this should serve to dismiss or discount the subjugation of certain white populations. It should, however, raise questions about how different forms of subjugation are related and what it might take to eliminate all of them. It is hard, for example, to imagine an end to the subjugation of poor and working-class white populations that does not involve the dissolution of a concept of pathology that, although defined by blackness, has always been available to dehumanize non-Black populations as well.

This literature, in its analysis of anti-Black conceptions of the human, also makes it possible to locate racism (anti-Black or otherwise) much closer to the heart of modern planning discourse and practice. Planning's negative effects on Black populations, in this view, are not the mere echo of racism elsewhere in society. The problem is not simply that Black people encounter racism elsewhere (e.g., in the job market) and therefore experience conditions like poverty and lack of political power that render them vulnerable to the predations of urban planning. The problem, anti-Black racism, is also internal to urban planning. Nor are these effects explainable simply in terms of the limited resources, knowledge, or adaptability available to urban planning. Planning, at times, has certainly lacked the resources to serve all populations equally or has been required to expropriate resources like land from particular locations (i.e., from particular people). But then, it needs to be asked why the expenditure or expropriation of resources so consistently harms Black populations – why planning's shortcomings, in effect, are not more racially diverse. Similarly, planning has often lacked sufficient knowledge of existing socio-spatial conditions, and it has often lacked the adaptability required to address the different conditions and requirements of different populations. But then, it needs to be asked why better knowledge of Black conditions has so seldom been sought; why this knowledge, when it is explicitly provided by Black communities, has so consistently been ignored; and why planning policies and programs, ostensibly lacking adaptability, are so often *tailored* to white living conditions and only appear maladapted when they encounter non-white conditions.

Nor, finally, can these negative effects simply be attributed to planners' individual racial prejudices. Racial prejudices abound in modernity, and planners have never been immune from them. But racism also exceeds the realm of individual dispositions, and its effects are observable in at least one planning initiative that I examine (in chapter 5), where the actors involved made an explicit effort to rid themselves and others of prevailing racial prejudices. The sources of planning's shortcomings, including its relationship to racial injustice, are no doubt multiple and evolving. It makes the most sense, however, to locate these sources within the larger ontological field staked out by the Black scholars cited above. The consistent negation of Black life in modern planning is most cleary traceable, in other words, to the originary and persistent eviction of blackness from the object ("the human" or simply "life") that planning professes to serve. In the face of planning's avowed efforts to sustain human life, Black lives have registered, if they have registered at all, as a condition to be transcended.

Understood in this way, anti-blackness can be seen to shape urban planning in its relationship not only to Black people and spaces but everywhere else as well. It is significant, for example, that planning's mistreatment of poor white individuals in the early twentieth century was sometimes meant to normalize these individuals, where normality was explicitly understood as a certain distance from the "ultimate zero-degree category" of blackness. In a later context, planning's efforts to produce "enjoyable" urban spaces were directed towards an area that had recently been cleared of Black residents and that was maintained as non-Black through the racism of the area's employers, shopkeepers, and landlords. What needs to be apprehended, these examples suggest, is the persistent and expansive role of anti-blackness in the making of urban spaces and the nurturing of urban lives – not just Black spaces but also white spaces, and not just Black lives but also non-Black lives. A project of this kind is pursued neither in Foucault-inspired critical ontologies of planning (which largely bracket race) nor in current work on anti-blackness (which largely brackets urban planning), but is suggested when these two literatures are pulled together. To displace blackness from the category of the human, I argue in this book, is also to displace blackness from the positive effects of urban planning. Urban planning is, among other things, an anti-Black operation. The result of this operation is an anti-Black city.

Recognizing the constitutive anti-blackness of modern planning necessarily re-routes intellectual and political efforts to transform planning in the present. As I discuss in the book's second half, the most common move to address planning-induced injustices from the 1960s onward has been to offer inclusion in planning discussions to populations that have been ignored or maltreated. There is no reason to oppose this response as such. A socially just and nonracist approach to urban planning, however, requires something more than the inclusion of Black people within a regime of thought and practice that was historically constituted through their denigration and subjugation. A more substantive transformation would involve a rejection of urban planning as it is presently constituted and a reconception of the object (the human) that it professes to serve. While this is undoubtedly a massive and uncertain project, it is also a project that Black communities have essentially pursued, with little or no outside support, for centuries. It is a project, manifest in countless acts of Black refusal and mutual aid, as well as in the actions of high-profile organizations like the Black United Front (chapter 7), that traverses the history of anti-Black planning and that renders *actual* Black lives something other than the pathological mirror image of white vitality, co-creating, in effect, another "genre" of human being.[37] Planning-related struggles in the present, I argue in the book's final chapter, would do well to recognize and support the resistance of Black communities, creating actions and movements that centre Black lives while struggling to end all forms of planning-induced subjugation.

Outline

The book opens with a treatment of the emergence of a distinctly modern form of urban planning in late nineteenth-century Halifax. Modern planning, as I have suggested, is distinguished by its efforts to produce and organize material conditions that are believed to promote particular conceptions of human flourishing. Aims of this kind emerged in Halifax in two parallel forms: one focused on lives and living conditions of particular individuals, the other focused on the characteristics of the city or population as a whole. Chapter 2 focuses on the first form. The emergence of planning-related concerns about particular individuals, the chapter shows, was connected to the social and physical transformations of the Canada-wide "reform era" (roughly 1880 to 1920) and the development of a vibrant and internationally connected reform movement grounded in the city's expanding middle classes. For many middle-class reformers, the gravest problems of the time were to be found in the city's various low-income slum districts. Observing, surveying, and publicizing the world of the Halifax slums, the reformers drew public attention to a dramatic amalgam of biomedical, moral, and spatial pathologies: a collection of individuals who, the reformers argued, were abnormally unhealthy and prone to disease, whose behaviours were a moral "disgrace," and whose degraded and overcrowded living conditions not only paralleled the slum residents' pathological health and morality but also *produced* the latter.

In attributing medical and moral pathologies to aberrant material conditions, the reformers effectively opened up a new vocation and terrain of anchorage for urban planning. Through a whole series of proposed interventions, from the adoption of a new building code to the (never-fulfilled) razing and rebuilding of an area known as the "upper streets," the reformers popularized a form of action that sought to remake and normalize individuals through the remaking of their material conditions. These interventions sometimes benefited people in certain respects, but they also introduced new forms of surveillance, new threats (and acts) of displacement, and a form of unaccountable power that some slum residents spoke against and resisted. The consistent ignoring of slum residents' own words and actions, I argue, was essential to the emerging form of urban planning: a form of spatial practice that, through pathologization, cast poor residents beyond the realm of political subjecthood, while giving over their lives and living conditions to the calculated interventions of others.

Chapter 3 traces the emergence of slightly different planning concerns and interventions. While reformers busied themselves in the Halifax slums, certain city councillors and bureaucrats were evaluating the conditions of the overall population and proposing extensive spatial interventions, from sewers to street lights, that were expected to improve overall health, welfare, and prosperity. Noticeably excluded from these improvements were the residents of Africville, a community located within city limits but evidently outside the sphere of planning's concerns. As I detail in this chapter, new forms of infrastructure uplifted people's health and convenience elsewhere in the city but were denied to Africville; new zoning protocols protected "public health" by shifting health-impairing land uses to Africville; and new concerns about "efficient" land use (an aid to overall prosperity) led to the city's first plan to seize and redevelop the entirety of Africville. As this suggests, modern planning found in Black lives and spaces a kind of refuse: people whose lives could be damaged to save the lives of others, spaces that could liberated and redeveloped in order to improve others' welfare and prosperity. The negation of Africville was thus essential to the broader, ostensibly "caring" planning regime. Backed by an ascendant "scientific" anti-Black racism (in Halifax and across Canada), planning would nurture "overall" life alongside and through the decimation of Black life. It would lay claim to the urban terrain and put this terrain at the service of human flourishing through the displacement of Black people's claims to any part of it. Anti-blackness, in other words, helped to bring modern planning into being.

Chapter 4 moves forward in time to examine the unprecedented social and spatial interventions of the twenty-five years following World War II. Planning in this period was guided largely by long-established ideas and ambitions but was enabled by new sources of state funding and expertise arranged under the heading of nation-wide "urban renewal." Throughout the urban renewal period, planners approached the city through a normatively structured gaze, assessing people and spaces in relation to assumed norms and devising normalizing interventions that were supposed to augment population-wide "health, happiness, and welfare." The major planning initiatives of this period included widespread slum clearance, the construction of public housing, and the improvement of the city's transportation systems. Those most negatively affected by these initiatives were the roughly four thousand poor and working-class residents, white and Black, who were removed from their homes and only sometimes offered alternative city-provided lodgings. Though both white and Black residents were adversely affected, the anti-blackness of postwar renewal is observable, I argue, in the model of improvement it forced upon displaced slum residents. This model, premised on the provision of better *rental* housing, was ultimately disastrous to the forms of survival that Black Haligonians had constituted on the basis of almost population-wide home ownership. The anti-blackness of urban renewal, then, lies less in the racialization of its displacees (most of whom were white) than in the racialization of the improvement it offered: an improvement that took the situation of poor white people, nearly always tenants, as it baseline.

While chapters 2 through 4 examine the emergence and consequences of a relatively consistent planning program, the next three chapters trace the introduction of subtle modifications to this program in the post-1960s period. Chapter 5 examines the most successful grass-roots effort to transform modern planning in Halifax. By the mid-1960s, the chapter shows, the damaging effects of postwar renewal on the physical and social landscape of the city had become more apparent, and a range of new activist groups and renegade bureaucrats began to combat the prevailing planning regime. Among the new planning priorities supported by anti-renewal activists was the creation of a more "lively" and "enjoyable" urban experience, and the promotion of organized "citizen involvement" in planning decisions. The achievements of these new activist currents were significant and often laudatory, including the annulment of a proposed expressway project in 1972 that brought an end to urban renewal in Halifax. The new priorities that they forced upon the city, however, tended to re-adorn an enduring anti-Black planning program. The creation of more enjoyable urban experiences was ultimately directed towards an area of the city (the downtown) that had recently been cleared of poor and racialized residents and that was known to be distinctly off-limits to Black residents. The promotion of citizen involvement, meanwhile, entailed adherence to a political model that effectively normalized the political actions and demands of privileged white activists. The potential influence of subordinate groups on the new planning priorities, including the racially restrictive conception of urban enjoyment, was therefore isolated and nullified.

The entanglements of planning and anti-blackness, ignored by most white activists, was central to the activism of a new Black organization – the Black United Front (BUF) – formed in the same period. Chapter 6 focuses on BUF and its early engagements with planning in Halifax. Formed in 1968, BUF carried forward a long-standing tradition of Black resistance in Nova Scotia but also drew upon principles and strategies prevalent within the burgeoning Black Power movement in the United States and elsewhere. One of these principles was "self-determination." Adhering to this principle, BUF criticized city planners for dismissing the lives and agency of Black communities; promoted alternative, Black-created programs in areas like housing, recreation, and infrastructure; and provided a strong basis for creating and living new genres of human existence. BUF's emphasis on Black self-determination was not without limitations. As studies of other contexts have noted, this principle risks collapsing the diverse experiences of Black people into a universal Black norm and risks constituting Black organizations as the representatives of an ostensibly unified Black community. BUF, in the early years, largely avoided these pitfalls. The Canadian state, however, could only tolerate a more limited, representational role for BUF, and substantial efforts were made by the federal, provincial, and municipal levels of the state to transform the organization into a passive intermediary between Black people and state institutions. In 1974, when a major BUF operating grant expired, these efforts had their intended effect. BUF's activities were duly contained and the short-lived possibility of planning that centred Black lives and decisions was extinguished.

Chapter 7 turns its eye to the early years of the twenty-first century and examines how contemporary planning has responded to the various challenges and changes of the post-1960s period. Modified by the activism of the 1960s, urban planning has also adapted to the wider (regional) scope of property development, the perceived need to attract nonlocal residents and investment capital, and the ascendancy of "neoliberal" ideologies and practices. These new realities were clearly expressed in the signature planning projects of this period: a downtown-focused design project called HRM by Design (2006–9), and a new metropolitan-scale development framework called the Regional Plan (2001–6). Different in certain ways, these two projects were united in their conception of human subjectivity and flourishing, a conception that emphasized the "rational" economic behaviours of individuals and households. Supporting people's economic lives would now be planning's foremost priority, and vast changes to region-wide urban design, property development regulations, and infrastructure provision were introduced to address this priority. Though local heritage activists were the most visibly incensed by these changes, outlying Black communities were the most adversely affected. Post-1960s development had already encircled these communities, wrecked community amenities, and displaced hundreds of residents. The planning protocols instituted by the Regional Plan would ultimately assist this damaging form of development, direct public spending and infrastructure away from Black communities, and regulate against ostensibly uneconomic Black practices of property development. Planning in the new century, I conclude, reworks the discursive and material terrain of the old, promoting a subtly different form of human flourishing with an enduring anti-Black framework.

The final chapter recapitulates the book's major arguments and considers their implications for ongoing scholarship and political struggle.

Modern planning, the book argues, is an enterprise founded on the protection and improvement of human life, where distinctions between "normal" and "pathological" determine which lives are nurtured, which are forcibly normalized, and which are abandoned and wrecked. Throughout the twentieth century, "blackness" has constituted the always-already pathological pole of a normal/pathological continuum. Black people, consequently, have rarely been aided by planning without a fight and have frequently been imperiled by it. At the same time, the benefits actually provided by modern planning – provided, that is, to normative individuals and populations – have been derived from the symbolic and physical displacement of blackness. The ostensible nonhumanity of Black people brings the human into focus; it makes it possible to define what being human means. The wrecking of Black lives and spaces, meanwhile, produces much of the security and vitality delivered to the lives of others. Anti-blackness, therefore, is neither a characteristic of particular projects nor the experience of particular people, but rather an enduring element of modern planning as such. Re-routing planning in the present, I conclude, requires attention to the constitutive limits of its object and the more promising genres of human being that have been created outside and against these limits. Any meaningful change in urban planning must begin not from the polite inclusion of people within an unchanged and enduringly anti-Black enterprise but from the resolute centring and prioritization of Black lives – and, thus, the development of planning practices and forms of life that have never before existed.

2 "Higher Living through Environment": The Reformers, the Slums, and the Emergence of Modern Urban Planning

Modern urban planning emerged in Halifax with a series of interrelated initiatives in the late nineteenth and early twentieth centuries. In this period, dubbed the "reform era" by many historians, a small network of self-described reformers began to express concerns about the living conditions of local residents. The reformers were particularly concerned with the living conditions of the city's poor and working-class residents, the inhabitants of tight-packed urban areas that began, in this period, to be called "slums." Present in the slums, the reformers argued, were a host of social and spatial problems, including immoral behaviours, high rates of illness, absent sanitary facilities, and overcrowded conditions. Not simply co-present, these problems appeared (to the reformers) to be causally linked. More precisely, the problems of individuals (e.g., ill health and immorality) were believed to be both subtended and caused by the problematic environment in which these individuals lived. Putting this particular diagnosis to work, the reformers developed, borrowed, and promoted a series of new initiatives that promised to improve individuals through the improvement of their housing conditions. These efforts culminated in a plan, announced in 1905, that called for a twelve-block area of slum housing in the downtown to be demolished and a set of "model tenements" to be erected in their place. An unprecedented spatial intervention, the model tenements plan was meant to achieve its primary effect on the lives of individuals – "educat[ing] the people," as one proponent put it, "into a higher form of living through better environment."[1]

The reformers' efforts to improve living conditions in Halifax were part of a larger movement in reform-era cities in Canada, the United States, and Western Europe. At the centre of these reform movements were a host of new problems linked to the rapid growth, industrialization, and stratification of urban societies, as well as new forms of knowledge produced and circulated within an expanding range of middle-class professions, voluntary organizations, and institutions. While seeking to diagnose and address particular problems, the reformers ultimately articulated a new and ambitious vision of collective life: a vision in which human failings like ill health and immorality could be systematically identified among individuals, and an ostensibly "higher" form of life could be brought into being, in part, through targeted spatial interventions. Underwriting these efforts was an essential and historically novel doctrine, often dubbed "environmentalism," that attributed the condition of individuals to the condition of their material environment and believed that better environments would produce better individuals. The ascendancy of this doctrine in the mid- to late nineteenth century, it is often noted, constituted a reversal of the perspective that had prevailed in the first half of the century (a perspective that attributed problematic environments to problematic individuals). Seldom noted, however, is the new form of urban planning that this perspective brought into being. Planning, always concerned with the material environment, would now be responsible for the environmentally influenced condition of human beings. Planning's target would become "life" itself; its aim would be to take hold of life, to improve its condition, through calculated spatial interventions.[2]

In this new form of planning, the role of "norms" would be fundamental. The reformers' understanding of individual life, for one thing, was premised upon medical and behavioural norms that individuals were perceived to either exhibit or betray. It was these norms that allowed the reformers to describe individuals' lives, to diagnose these lives, and to propose interventions that would "improve" these lives – an improvement imagined, quite explicitly, as a form of normalization. Norms were fundamental, as well, to the reformers' assessment of the material environment. It was spatial norms, especially "normal" qualities and configurations of domestic space, that guided the reformers' examination of material conditions and their practical efforts to improve these conditions. More than just framing the reformers' assessment of people and spaces, however, norms served to adjudicate the boundaries of proper knowledge and political subjectivity. The reformers' embodiment of ascendant norms, in effect, elevated their own political position, while diminishing the position of norm-betraying slum residents – precisely the individuals the reformers claimed to be aiding. The reformers' vision of improvement and the new form of planning that it enabled gained purchase in modern cities through political-ontological fractures like these, fractures whose specific relationship to prevailing class-based and racial hierarchies requires close and patient attention.[3]

The reformers' efforts to diagnose and address the problems of the Halifax slums helped to establish some of the defining elements of twentieth-century planning. Operating amid the tumult of late nineteenth-century urban change, the reformers gave voice and energy to newly established institutions like the municipal board of health, the newly reform-focused St Paul's Church, and new voluntary organizations like the Halifax Local Council of Women. Focused initially on the problem of public health, the scope of reform efforts gradually widened onto "moral" terrain. Attributing the gravest problems of "physical and moral health" to the city's slums, the reformers promoted a range of actions between 1890 and 1912 that promised to improve pathological housing conditions and pathological individuals in tandem. The model tenements plan, though never finally carried through, was supported by a wide range of Halifax reformers and provided the clearest expression of the exigencies and social coordinates of the nascent planning regime. Earmarked for an impoverished and largely white district known as the "upper streets," the plan shows how the attribution of pathologies to particular lives and spaces provides a vocation for modern planning, how it renders conceivable a program of "improvement" while barring the recipients of this improvement any role in devising or approving it. And yet, the very prospect of improvement – something never envisioned in this period for the city's Black-majority areas – expresses the racial specificities of pathologization and the racial limits of the "higher life" that modern planning was constituted to provide.

The Reformers, the Slums, and the Problem of Public Health

The problem of the slums came to the attention of the Halifax public in a period of far-reaching social transformation. Halifax, like other North American cities, became a markedly different city in the second half of the nineteenth century as a result of rapid population growth, industrialization, and social stratification. In this period, the Halifax population nearly doubled in size, expanding from 20,749 in 1850 to 40,832 in 1900. Part of this growth was caused by high local birth rates, while another part was due to immigration from rural parts of Nova Scotia and New Brunswick. Immigrants from overseas, though they arrived at the Halifax port in great numbers in this period, seldom settled in the city for good. Among the nearly 500,000 people who fled the Irish famine of the

1840s to settle in Canada, for example, only a few hundred elected to stay in Halifax. Immigrants to Canada from non-British countries, more numerous in this period, were similarly unlikely to make their home in Halifax. As a result, population growth in this period tended to swell the ranks of the city's existing ethnic groups, with only slight alterations to the overall ethnic composition. In 1871, the city's largest ethnic groups were Irish (39%), English (32%), and Scottish (16%), while the next largest groups were German (4%), African (3%), and French (2%). In 1901, though the population had doubled, the same six ethnic groups predominated: English (46%), Irish (24%), Scottish (14%), German (8%), French (3%), and African (2%).[4]

Accompanying the city's surge in population in this period was a somewhat erratic process of industrialization. The Halifax civilian economy, long centred on maritime trade with the British West Indies, endured a series of painful setbacks in the mid-nineteenth century. These included the collapse of the West Indies sugar trade (following the abolition of slavery in 1834) and Britain's abandonment of colony-favouring import tariffs and trade relations in favour of "free trade" in the 1850s. John A. MacDonald's National Policy, adopted in 1879, entailed further setbacks for maritime trade (as it erected stiff tariffs on imports to Canada) but also enabled the development of relatively new forms of production and profit making. Buoyed by protective tariffs and the construction of the nation-spanning Intercolonial Railway, modest industrial development began to occur in Halifax and across the region. The Halifax Sugar Refinery, established in 1880, eventually produced five hundred barrels of sugar a day and employed 120 workers in two rotations (day and night). The Nova Scotia Cotton Manufacturing Company, established in 1882, produced plain cloth and employed three hundred workers (mostly young women and girls) in its best year of operation. The period's largest new industry, the Halifax Graving Dock, began operation in 1889 and eventually employed hundreds of local men in the repair of steel-hulled ships. Other new companies, smaller in scale but collectively significant, included industrial firms devoted to the production of candy, boots, rope, nails, and ice skates.[5]

The most significant industrial expansion in this period occurred not in Halifax but in the peripheral coal and steel towns of Pictou, New Glasgow, and Sydney. This development, though it made some Halifax entrepreneurs jealous, soon provided profitable new opportunities for local businesses as well. Halifax-based banks and investment houses were active across the Maritime region, securing deposits and investment dollars from far-flung cities and towns and channelling them into the region's most promising enterprises. Companies like the Bank of Nova Scotia and the Royal Securities Company (RSC), both headquartered in Halifax, played the leading role in the capitalization of the Halifax Sugar Refinery and Nova Scotia Cotton, as well as the broader region's coal, iron, and steel industries. These activities helped to establish Halifax as the financial centre of the Maritime region and as an important centre in the larger Canadian financial landscape as well.[6] Halifax-based merchants, meanwhile, found in the region's booming industrial towns a tantalizing alternative to the now-restricted overseas trade in processed foods, clothing, and hardware. By 1899, the profits of local merchants had improved to such an extent that the Halifax Board of Trade could announce that "never in her history has [Halifax] occupied a more promising position than at present."[7] Intertwined with all of these developments was the emergence of an increasingly significant and Halifax-based professional class, including lawyers, accountants, doctors, and engineers. Though these individuals were often trained in other cities (especially Montréal), the establishment of Dalhousie Medical School in 1868 and the Nova Scotia Technical College in 1907 eventually provided the bases of local professional training and regional-scale professional expertise.

As in other North American cities, the increasing prosperity of this period was not widely shared in Halifax. As the Board of Trade heralded a time of great promise, the situation of the city's poor and working-class residents either remained unchanged or worsened (especially in relative terms). Along the harbourfront, longshoremen earned twenty cents for a gruelling hour of work in 1900, precisely the same wage they had received two decades earlier. Unable to support a family on their own, longshoremen often worked the docks alongside their lesser-paid and barefoot children.[8] Working-class women, especially young women and girls, laboured in the city's new textile, tobacco, and confectionery industries, where they were paid half the wages (or less) than men and were excluded from labour unions. Women, always a much smaller segment of the industrial workforce than men, were also the fastest growing segment of the workforce in the late nineteenth century.[9] Regular employment, for workers of any gender, was difficult to secure. Casual work, in most sectors, was the norm. "No man who depends upon labouring work," reported a local newspaper in 1884, "can hope to become a settled ... member of the community, because he has no regular work."[10] Two decades later, casual work remained the norm in many sectors, and industrial wages continued to tail the prevailing cost of living, even when multiple members of a household laboured outside the home.[11]

Perhaps the clearest sign of the diverging fortunes of Halifax residents was visible in the residential developments of this period. As the thriving middle class was constructing impressive Georgian homes in the city's South End, the poor and working class were relegated to cramped, two-story "saltboxes" in the North End. The homes of the North End were often badly constructed and lacked indoor plumbing, proper insulation, and reliable heating well into the twentieth century. These problems seem to have been especially acute in a few areas of the city, including the twelve-block area known as the "upper streets." Located just north of the downtown, this area was the closest residential district to the Halifax harbour and the most easily affordable to the harbour's workforce. The area's economic situation, as a result, tended to be closely tied to the working conditions on the docks and the ethnic composition of its population tended to change in tandem with that of the docks' workforce. At the end of the nineteenth century, the area was majority Irish Catholic, with smaller populations of Black, English, French, and Chinese residents – all of them struggling to sustain themselves in a fast-changing and socially divided city.[12]

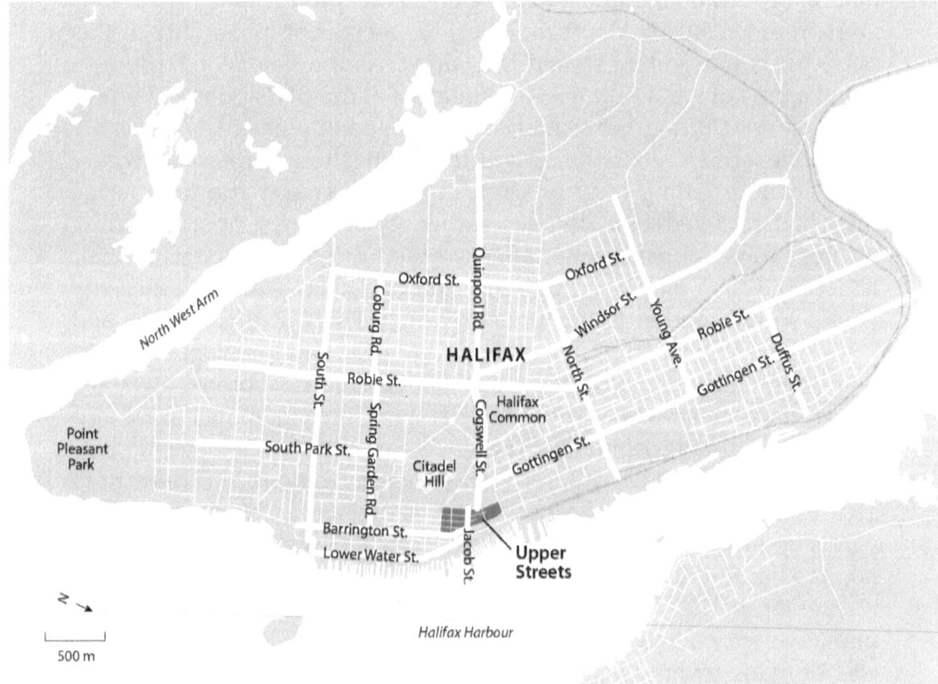

Figure 2.1 Map showing "upper streets," 1910. Map created by Eric Leinberger.

Late nineteenth-century population growth and industrial development had important effects on the political life of the city. In Halifax, as in other North American cities, this period saw the emergence of a multifaceted urban reform movement that greatly expanded the breadth and vitality of organized civil society and eventually reshaped the programs and policies of the municipal state. Members of the reform movements were, in virtually all cases, members of the city's expanding merchant, financial, and professional middle classes. Working-class Haligonians, while they might have been involved with local trade unions or the Halifax Trade and Labour Council, were entirely absent from the leading reform-oriented organizations of this period. The Halifax Board of Trade, founded over a century earlier, was the city's most active and influential proponent of reform. Expressing the core interests of Halifax merchants, industrialists, and financiers, the board's urban reform efforts centred on the promotion of changes to municipal taxation and political representation that would enable local businesses to outcompete their nonlocal rivals in a fast-changing and increasingly nationally integrated economy. Alongside these self-interested reforms, however, the board also supported a wide range of social policies and programs, including the model tenements, that promised to improve the living conditions of the working classes and therefore produce more productive, reliable, and "moral" employees.[13]

Other reform efforts were driven by more recently established organizations, as well as by esteemed private citizens. Local doctors, often speaking through institutions like the Medical Society of Nova Scotia, were high-profile proponents of expanded public health initiatives, including state-provided vaccinations, infrastructure like sewers and water mains, and health-oriented housing reforms. Other Halifax professionals, including lawyers and engineers, contributed to the urban reform movement as well, lending their expert credentials to particular reform initiatives while simultaneously enhancing the prestige of their nascent profession. Local clergy, meanwhile, sometimes moved beyond the traditional charity orientation of their community engagements to place themselves and their parishioners in the fray of politically oriented reform campaigns. Especially significant in this respect were the efforts of Rev. William Armitage, the long-time pastor of St Paul's Church in downtown Halifax. Armitage, a major proponent of the reform-oriented "social gospel" that reshaped the political life of cities across North America and Europe in this period, contributed to all the reform efforts that I discuss in this chapter.[14]

Perhaps the most instructive example of the reform movement's elite character was the Halifax Local Council of Women (HCW). Founded in 1894, the HCW either launched or actively supported a whole range of charitable and reform initiatives in this period, including several related to local housing conditions. Like the city's male-headed reform organizations, the HCW's membership was drawn exclusively from the city's thriving and expanding middle class. The HCW's first president, Edith Archibald, was married to a prominent mining-industry executive and eventual head of the Bank of Nova Scotia. The group's subsequent president, Agnes Dennis, was married to the publisher of the local daily newspaper, *The Evening Mail*. Eliza Ritchie, an active and influential member of the HCW, was married to a prominent local physician, and she herself had earned a doctorate in philosophy from Cornell University. Demonstrative of the elite circles in which HCW members travelled, one of the city's wealthiest residents, George Wright, frequently offered his support to the organization's reform projects. When, in 1912, Wright perished on the infamous maiden voyage of the Titanic, his enormous South End mansion was willed to the HCW and has served as its headquarters ever since.[15]

The relatively elite character of the HCW was often heralded by the organization itself, and it testified to the particular privileges of elite and middle-class lives. Middle-class women, unlike their poorer counterparts, typically did not labour outside of the home in this period and often had the benefit of significant paid help within the home. The labour of domestic workers, roughly half of the Halifax female workforce in 1911, was thus an aid to the public activities of more privileged women, as well as a clear restriction on their own ability to undertake these activities. These class divisions gave a particular character to the organization's conception and pursuit of urban reforms. The HCW, like other contemporary reform organizations in Halifax and elsewhere, tended to see the social and spatial norms of middle-class lives as a potentially universalizable ideal. Thus, as I show below, the task of reform was often to remake the aberrant lives and living conditions of the city's less privileged in the image of these norms – without, of course, disrupting the inequalities in wealth and power that *could* have been seen as the primary causes of these aberrations. There is no question, of course, that the impoverished residents of areas like the "upper streets" faced a range of severe problems, including horrific housing conditions. These problems, however, could be understood in a variety of ways, and it remains to be seen what, if anything, the diagnoses of these problems produced within exclusively middle-class organizations offered to the task of solving them.[16]

The living conditions of the city's poor and working-class residents entered the sphere of urban reform, initially, as a public-health concern. In Halifax, as in other North Atlantic cities, concerns about public health in general intensified in the second half of the nineteenth century, as unparalleled population growth and industrialization produced new and ill-understood threats to bodily health and survival. Cholera struck the city several times, including a major outbreak in 1881. Tuberculosis, a smaller but more constant threat, killed up to two hundred people a year in this period, while diphtheria killed nearly the same number each year (including 192 people in 1890).[17] The threat of disease was clearly unsettling to Halifax residents and civic leaders, and it ultimately created new opportunities for the city's expanding class of doctors and health professionals to play a vaunted public role in the community. Guided by medical expertise, the city introduced an infectious diseases hospital in 1870, invested increasing sums in infrastructure like sewers and water mains from 1880 onward, and established an important municipal institution, the Halifax Board of Health, in 1889. The problem of ill health, though it existed to some extent throughout the city, tended nevertheless to shine considerable attention on the upper streets and other impoverished areas. It was in these areas that doctors and board of health inspectors found the most alarming incidents of disease and ill health, as well as the greatest potential for health-related reforms.[18]

As doctors and health inspectors made their way through the slums, they became the vehicle of a new form of expert knowledge that was then radically transforming how cities and their problems were understood. This new knowledge was derived, to a great extent, from the scientific examinations of the human body conducted in the European medical clinics of the late eighteenth century. In these spaces, doctors and other researchers tracked various causes of premature death to visible markers on (and inside) the human cadavers they studied and thereby brought death and its ostensible causes into visibility for the first time. Death, for the first time, could be read from the body of the deceased, and the spectre of death (i.e., life-threatening illness) could be observed upon the body of the living. The effects of this new perspective were significant. Life and death, or health and morbidity, came to constitute a pair of opposite poles between which the lives of individuals could be situated. Assessed between these two poles, an individual could be seen either as healthy (a "normal" state of being) or as unhealthy (a departure from the normal state). Once established, importantly, this new medical bipolarity provided a framework through which many other aspects of human existence could be assessed as well. Questions of morality, in particular, appeared increasingly alongside those of physical health from the early nineteenth century onward, such that "physical and moral health" became a composite condition that could be apprehended in relation to the assumed norms that a given individual might either exhibit or betray.[19]

This new bipolar structure of knowledge became integral to the conception and management of urban problems in the course of the nineteenth century. A major cholera outbreak in 1832, an occurrence in most industrial cities of the North Atlantic, was a particularly important moment in the spread of this new knowledge. In Paris, hard hit by the outbreak, a major public-health inquiry found not only that the contraction of cholera was concentrated in particular locations in the city (i.e., the slums), but also that it seemed to be nurtured by these areas' particular socio-physical conditions. On the one hand, then, slum residents were found to be abnormally diseased, unhealthy, and immoral. On the other hand, these abnormalities were found to be caused by the abnormal *conditions* in which people lived (including, especially, the high number of people per slum housing unit and the low quality and dampness of the units themselves). As Paul Rabinow suggests, the diagnosis of the 1832 cholera outbreak marked the entry of "norms" – or rather a normal/pathological bipolarity – into the study and regulation of urban spaces.[20] To know this city, from this perspective, was to assess people and spaces in relation to assumed norms, while to *improve* the city was to identify and normalize its ostensibly pathological elements. Essential to the Paris context, the same general perspective appeared in a long series of post-1832 public-health inquiries in European and North American cities, and became the dominant perspective on public-health concerns by the second half of the nineteenth century.[21]

In Halifax, the most important purveyor of a bipolar medical perspective on the city was the municipal board of health, an institution formed just before a major diphtheria outbreak in 1890 and shaped in its outlook and approach by the assumed causes of this outbreak. The outbreak, an official city inquiry revealed, had spread unevenly across the urban terrain and induced its gravest effects in the city's poorest areas (see *figure* 2.2). In one particularly hard-hit area, the disease appeared to be attributable to the existence of an open pit, several feet deep, into which untreated sewage had been poured and stagnated.

The soil in the area, the inquiry found, was "very foul and apparently saturated with old sewage," resulting in high rates of "sickness and death in the quarters of it's [*sic*] immediate neighbourhood."[22] Emerging in this context, the board embodied the spatially attuned perspective on ill health and disease that I discussed above. While its mandate included actions like the distribution of vaccines and the regulation of food supplies, its most important initiatives pertained to the identification and containment of the threats to public health that lurked within the material conditions of local businesses, residences, public spaces, and backyards. To this end, the board's early actions included ordering the closure of certain businesses, circumscribing certain economic activities (e.g., the slaughtering of animals), and overseeing the demolition or substantial renovation of several local residences (most of them in the upper streets).[23]

The board's regulation of material conditions intensified in 1904, when it was provided a larger budget and a mandate to send inspectors around the city in search of potential threats to public health. These inspections began, as might be expected, in the city's poorest areas. For the first three years, the inspectors had no specific program to apply in their inquiries. Their task was simply to identify housing conditions they deemed to be "unsanitary" and prepare an official report to that effect. In 1907, the unstructured nature of the inspection process was called into question, and a detailed inspection framework was introduced. From that point forward, inspectors were expected to evaluate particular characteristics of the home environment, including the number of rooms, the number of resident adults and children, as well as the condition of the home's drainage system, plumbing, cellar, water closet, and backyard. Oriented towards these characteristics, the inspection process became not only more structured but also more normative. The process involved assessing inspected premises in relation to assumed norms (a normal residential density, a normal process of drainage, and so on) and would render premises intelligible as a series of characteristics that either exhibited or violated these norms. Much like the public-health inquiries discussed above, importantly, the existence of abnormal housing conditions was regarded as a problem irrespective of the health issues that may or may not have afflicted the inhabitants and that, in any case, were not recorded in the inspection report. Consistent with the dominant medical perspective, the imperative was simply to chart the prevailing normalities and pathologies of the material environment and thereby illuminate potential targets of intervention.[24]

Figure 2.2 Map showing diphtheria incidents, 1890. Halifax, Engineering and Works Department records, RG 102-39P E-6-542, HRMA. Image courtesy of HRMA.

Adding to the knowledge produced by the housing inspectors were the perspectives and information expressed at official board of health meetings. Overseen by a three-person board, the meetings functioned as a kind of public trial on allegedly flagrant housing conditions: a contest in which inspectors' reports of unsanitary housing were taken up, where property owners (and sometimes tenants) were allowed to provide counterevidence, and where the board would finally decide on the fate of the targeted dwelling. In many cases, substantial repairs or upgrades to local buildings were mandated. In other cases, the dwelling was condemned and its inhabitants ordered to vacate. The proceedings and resulting decisions were consistently covered in the local press, and it would be hard to believe that public concern about housing conditions was the only reason. Coverage of the meetings provided the newspapers' middle-class readers with a rare and sometimes tantalizing look at the homes and domestic lives of the city's poorest residents. People's homes, in this coverage, were presented in all their shocking squalor, with colourful language often substituted for the technical diagnoses of health inspectors. Conditions that inspectors might dryly describe as "unsanitary" were revealed at the board meetings to be "unfit for human habitation," "disgraceful," or "fit only for the housing of rats."[25] Cramped living conditions were also described at times (leaving room for readers' imagination), and the alleged dysfunctions of poor and working-class people were sometimes conveyed alongside descriptions of their living conditions.[26]

The most alarming descriptions of housing conditions generally came not from the participants at board meetings but from the observing journalists themselves. The author of an *Evening Mail* article in 1911, for example, provided a suitably dramatic rendering of the board of health's apparent findings in a recent tour of the upper streets:

> A few days ago the Board of Health of the city had their inspector make a house to house inspection of Albemarle and Grafton streets and he found A PRETTY BAD STATE OF AFFAIRS. The Albemarle street report showed that only fourteen water closets exist on this street between Jabob and Blowers streets. Of sixty-eight outside privy vaults only six are in good condition. Nine houses on Albemarle street were reported as UNFIT FOR HUMAN HABITATION ... Some houses have NO WATER CONNECTIONS AT ALL. IN ONE OR MORE INSTANCES SO MUCH DIRT AND FILTH WAS IN EVIDENCE THAT THE INSPECTION COULD NOT BE CONCLUDED. Some were described as MOST FILTHY. Some

> were described as FILTHY BEYOND DESCRIPTION, and some as MOST FILTHY. Some cellar floors were covered with sewage, some walls and ceilings were covered with filth.[27]

The author's description, though certainly dramatic, is nevertheless consistent with the bipolar perspective of contemporary public-health expertise. What appears in the author's description is a long series of norms, either exhibited or betrayed. Privies are either in "good condition" or they are not. Water connections are either present or they are not. Cleanliness, an assumed norm, is either present or tarnished by "filth" of varying levels of intensity. It was through normatively structured assessments like these that the slums were rendered intelligible and described to the Halifax public.

The board's attention to the Halifax slums was thorough in its diagnosis, but relatively limited in its prescribed treatment. Expected to deal with housing on a case-by-case basis, the board's interventions never surpassed the condemnation of a few buildings in a single month. The slums, in their entirety, were always beyond its reach. More expansive health-related interventions were ultimately advanced by the city's medical doctors, especially doctors affiliated with the board of health (but not constrained its mandate). The most influential public-health doctor in this period was William Hattie. A graduate of McGill Medical School in Montréal, Hattie moved to Halifax in 1891 and quickly established himself within the leadership of several medical institutions and reform-minded organizations.[28] Consistent with his training, Hattie described the city's overall health in relation to a presumed normal functioning, a functioning that he believed the city had failed to achieve. In a high-profile intervention, Hattie announced to the public in 1906 that the city's death rate was "higher than it should be in this favoured locality."[29] The city, Hattie suggested, was not just unhealthy but abnormally so. Its problem was not so much death itself but superfluous death. By Hattie's calculations, roughly four hundred too many Haligonians were dying each year, and *this* was the problem to be addressed.

From this city-wide assessment, Hattie's attention turned concertedly towards the slums: the assumed source of the city's superfluous deaths. The slums, for Hattie, were a festering landscape of disease, a concentration of the "pest spots" and "revolting dens" that local doctors were "so often called on to enter."[30] While emphasizing the slums' ill health, Hattie also brought attention to their apparent moral problems. Alluding to the behaviours he had witnessed on house calls, Hattie described the slums as "a disgrace to the citizens," and he frequently described ill health and immorality (in general) as pathologies that tended to coexist in the same individuals and that needed to be treated in tandem. The proper treatment, for Hattie, was usually a spatial one. In the first decade of the twentieth century, Hattie offered expert support to the emerging argument that individual pathologies were spatially caused and became a key advocate of the 1905 "model tenements" plan. Replacing the slums with model tenements, Hattie argued in 1906, would "tend to improve the health of the city, and thus lower [the] death rate." Indeed, he continued, the people of Halifax "should be ashamed" to have allowed the medical and moral problem of the slums to have existed for so long when a concrete solution like the tenements plan was possible.[31]

"Race" rarely appeared in the public statements of Halifax medical authorities like William Hattie and the board of health. To be sure, the areas that most concerned these authorities (including the upper streets) contained a handful of racialized residents. Building inspections, moreover, were conducted across the central-city landscape, and the housing conditions of at least one Black household were brought before a meeting of the board of health.[32] And yet, areas of higher Black inhabitance, like Africville and sections of the North End, never garnered the same level of attention as white areas, and the board's only *action* in these areas (as I discuss in detail in the next chapter) was to make conditions dramatically worse. In such a way, race appears in these health-oriented actions only through its nonappearance. It appears as a kind of silence with respect to living conditions that, if they had affected white residents, would have attracted more attention and called for remedial action. As much as the lives of poor and working-class white residents were pathologized by health authorities, then, they remained within a certain sphere of humanity and extant public concern. These lives, though degraded, could be improved. They could, in effect, be normalized. Indeed, one of the major effects of the housing-related initiatives supported by the board of health and Dr Hattie would be to bring pathologized white individuals closer to bourgeois whiteness / normality and ever further from the pathology present, perhaps untreatably, among Black individuals.

The Problem of "Moral Health"

As time passed, other reformers developed an interest in the Halifax slums. Particularly important was Rev. William Armitage and his parishioners at the Evangelical St Paul's Church.[33] The church, in addition to being the oldest religious institution in Halifax, was distinguished by its location in the northern part of the downtown core, just two blocks from the edge of the upper streets. Many people who attended the church, consequently, were poor. Many who were *not* poor, moreover, became involved in church-based efforts to bring relief, both material and spiritual, to poor individuals and families living in the vicinity. Through such efforts, the parishioners were offered an intimate and privileged view of the homes and habits of the poor, and many of this city's foremost champions of reform projects, including the model tenements, were parishioners of St Paul's.[34] The foremost authority on the slums, however, was undoubtedly the church's rector. As rector of the church from 1897 to 1929, Armitage made an astonishing ten thousand house calls in Halifax, allowing the Halifax *Evening Mail* to describe him in 1905 as "better posted on the subject [of the slums] than any other man in the city."[35] Armitage's diagnosis of the slums differed somewhat from that of the local medical community. He was more likely to emphasize the moral or spiritual aspects of the slums, for example, and his perspective drew more on theology than on medical science. Like other Evangelicals, however, Armitage was able to work alongside medical officials in the struggle for housing reform, and these collaborations had much to do with the compatibility of their perspectives on the slum environment.

The faith of Armitage and other Evangelicals lent itself amicably to the pursuit of social reforms in general, and housing reforms in particular. For late nineteenth-century Evangelicals, social reforms were an extension of their more formal commitment to "saving" individuals, and housing reform was consistent with the particular way that they understood the process of salvation. Salvation, in their view, was not a matter of attending church or reciting prayers per se; rather, it was a result of acknowledging one's own unworthiness with respect to God's love and accepting that Christ's "atonement" had created a perpetual "hereafter" for all those who put their faith in it. One of the consequences of this emphasis on spiritual realization was to shift or extend the setting of the spiritual life from the environment of the church to the environment of the home (the place where contemplation, and potential realization, would tend to occur). It tended to matter, in other words, whether the home environment was suited or ill suited to spiritual realization. But it was not just the condition or suitability of Evangelicals' own homes that concerned them. Importantly, Evangelicals believed that ensuring others' salvation, and thus the material conditions of that salvation, was their unending duty. The project of housing reform generally entered the concerns of Evangelicals on this basis: as a project that promised to remove the material obstacles to others' salvation and therefore fulfil the other-directed duty of already-realized individuals.[36]

To the extent that the homes of the unsaved were seen as an obstacle to salvation, the mission of Evangelicals would tend to carry them enthusiastically into the orbit of existing housing-reform efforts. Indeed, Evangelicals were among the leading figures of the early housing-reform and model tenements movements in Britain, the United States, and Canada. In Britain, Lord Shaftesbury (an Evangelical) worked alongside influential public-health doctors on the creation of two major model tenements companies, as well as several public inquiries and regulatory projects related to working-class housing.[37] The affinities between Evangelical and medical perspectives on slum housing, essential to these collaborations, is demonstrated quite clearly in the private reflections of Lord Shaftesbury. After spending three days touring the slums of Manchester in the company of James Kay-Shuttleworth, a leading English public-health doctor and housing reformer, Shaftesbury reflected in his journal that the two men had "conversed from morning till night, and scarcely ever touched on a subject unconnected with the moral and physical condition of the poor, and the means of repairing it."[38] Although Shuttleworth was not an Evangelical, moreover, Shaftesbury felt that he had nevertheless been touched by "the grace of God" and found "his whole pleasure in [the pursuit of] moral good."[39] If the two men differed somewhat in their ultimate aims, they could clearly agree that the "moral and physical condition" of the poor needed to be improved, and that a transformation in the home environment of the latter was the best means of achieving this.

Armitage's perspective on the connection between Evangelicalism and housing reform is spelled out in his 1908 book, *Cities of Refuge*. Although the title is a metaphor – Jesus Christ, in fact, is the only "city of refuge" – the book offers instructions for physical, earthly cities as well. A city, for Armitage, ought to be administered in such a way that it "point[s] to Christ as the sinner's refuge."[40] Principally, such an administration would involve purging the "environment" of exterior pleasures, the "things of sense and time," so that city dwellers might turn inward and find deeper enjoyment in their cultivated connection with God.[41] Like the local medical officials with whom he collaborated, Armitage clearly apprehended the city through the lens of a particular norm or ideal. For Armitage, the proper state of an individual was a "realized" state; the proper environment was one that enabled, rather than impeded, the attainment of this proper state. With "realized" individuals and pleasure-purged environments as the assumed norm, the city's other individuals and environments would seem to contain irregularities or pathologies, and it is clear that creating a "city of refuge" would require the identification and removal of these socio-spatial pathologies no matter where they happened to appear.

Indeed, gazing across the Halifax landscape, Armitage and his reform-minded parishioners certainly found some areas of the city to be "pointing to Christ" and others, improperly, pointing in the opposite direction. The Evangelicals described the slums, in various ways, as a veritable den of sin, a breeding place, as one parishioner put it, "of sloth, poverty, and immorality."[42] Their descriptions of the slums seldom ignored the problem of ill health and disease. Echoing the medical arithmetic of Dr Hattie, Armitage repeatedly claimed that "the death rate" was "astonishingly high in Halifax, largely [due] to the existence of the slums."[43] Much more than local doctors, however, Armitage and his parishioners described the slums as a grave and glaring moral problem, an ever-present "menace to the morals" of the community and an enduring "curse to the city."[44] Though most middle-class Haligonians would not need to be convinced that there were problems of "sloth" and moral deviance in the city's slums, they would not necessarily diagnose these problems as Armitage did. It was common in Halifax, as elsewhere, to see pathological living conditions as a consequence, rather than cause, of individuals' moral failings. The "pig," as the saying went, created the "sty." For Armitage and his parishioners, in contrast, it was incontrovertibly the "sty" that created the "pig," and it was this causal connection between immoral individuals and their material surroundings that they sought to promulgate in Halifax.

Clearly contending with the belief that slum dwellers were inherently immoral, Armitage and his parish continually stressed the connection between "the habits of the people" and "the indescribable character of the places in which they live."[45] As Armitage explained, "the home" needed to be seen as "the cradle in which the morals of men are formed." The effect of unsuitable homes, he argued, was to produce "bad tendencies" in people. In contrast, proper, well-built homes would produce a range of "good tendencies."[46] According to this framework, the city of Halifax could be divided into two segments: good tendencies and good environments, on one hand, and bad tendencies and bad environments, on the other. This essentially bipolar perspective, though grounded in Evangelical theology, clearly mirrored the medically based perspective of Dr Hattie and the board of health, and it tended to suggest very similar modes of action. Armitage was a strong supporter of efforts, both incremental and immense, to improve housing conditions in the Halifax slums, and he eventually became the city's foremost proponent of the proposed "model tenements." For Armitage, as I discuss below, the model tenements plan would achieve what no small-scale intervention ever could: the total elimination of the "squalid conditions" that prevailed in the slums and the creation, in the same place, of "decently constructed" and morally uplifting "dwelling places." The end result, achieved spatially, would be to "stamp out vice" in the city and summon forth a contrasting moral and spiritual condition in the same place. The tenements, as one of Armitage's consorts put it, would "educate the people into a higher form of living by better environment."[47]

Armitage's attention to the supposed moral problems of the slums was amplified by the efforts of another group of reformers, the HCW. Founded in 1894, the HCW provided an important venue for the city's privileged (white and middle-class) women to network and collaborate around the public issues that concerned them. Most of the city's existing women-headed organizations became members of the HCW upon its formation, while the group itself spawned a series of important new initiatives and affiliated organizations. Among member organizations and HCW initiatives, the city's slums frequently registered as a major concern and terrain of intervention. One HCW member, Bessie Egan, had managed a women's shelter in the slums since 1892 and had the opportunity, beginning in 1902, to visit the homes of many poor families as a representative of the provincial child protection agency. Egan was also a parishioner at St Paul's, and she provided a key link between the reforms efforts of Rev. Armitage and those of the HCW. In 1902, the HCW deepened its connection to the slums when it created a local branch of the Victorian Order of Nurses (VON). In the next five years, VON nurses would conduct over three thousand home visits per year, many of them in what VON head (and HCW member) Agnes Dennis referred to as the city's most "wretched" areas.[48]

Though influenced by Evangelical theology and medical science, the HCW's analysis and activities were more explicitly informed by the thinking of the broader Canadian and international women's movement of the time. As its name suggests, the group was a local branch of a larger organization, the National Council of Women of Canada (NCWC). The larger council was established in 1893 under the leadership of the British émigré Lady Ishbel Aberdeen, who had been active in the women's movement in Britain before moving to Canada and carried the ideology of British feminism into her new activities. It was an ideology, often called "maternal feminism," that envisioned the advancement of women's interests occurring within the prevailing patriarchal division of life into "separate spheres." In practice, this tended to mean reaffirming women's responsibilities and aptitudes within the home (the so-called private sphere), while staking out new sites and tasks *outside* of the home (the so-called public sphere) in which these ostensibly private, feminine qualities could be marshalled. Such an approach, as many have argued, was partly a strategic choice. It helped to carve out a small niche for women in the public sphere without overtly threatening the territory of men. While other feminist strategies certainly existed in this period, the creation of the NCWC provided a powerful vehicle for the transmission and activation of maternal feminism in cities across Canada. Linked together through NCWC publications and annual meetings, local councils like the HCW became the nodes of a strengthening, interconnected, and ideologically consistent women's movement.[49]

The Halifax branch was an important contributor to the NCWC's aims, both locally and across the country. Locally, the HCW was active on a variety of issues, nearly all of them related in some way to the lives of children. A focus on children, common to NCWC chapters, was the group's primary gateway into the city's public life in the first two decades of its operation. Focusing on children allowed the group to mobilize then-traditional ideas about women's specific responsibilities and aptitudes – including their "maternal instinct" and "insider knowledge" of children's lives – while taking on recognizably "public" tasks.[50] The key to this move was the group's cunning and ultimately fraught rescripting of the relevant space of the mother-child relation. Women's responsibilities to children, the HCW conceded, were synonymous with the home. The latter, however, needed to be seen as encompassing "not merely the four walls of the house, but [rather] the whole atmosphere in which the little life unfolds, develops, and comes to maturity."[51] Extending the home in this way opened up a whole network of sites in which the HCW could exert an influence, including local schools, churches, parks, factories, and retail establishments. At the same time, it put the group into a potential conflict with the city's unaffiliated and inevitably less privileged women. It was largely these women's children, rather than their own, that ultimately preoccupied HCW members and allowed them to play a public role in the city.

The HCW's activities, like those of Dr Hattie and Rev. Armitage, were structured by assumed social and spatial norms. A child, for the HCW, was naturally and inherently good. Moral conduct was the child's normal behaviour. Bad or immoral behaviour was thus a pathology, a sign that "the good in [a child's] character" had somehow been "perverted" or "crushed out."[52] Observing the city's children through this lens, the HCW noticed a whole array of bad and therefore pathological behaviours: swearing, rude manners, rowdiness, sexual promiscuity, and unspecified "hoodlum things."[53] Casting these behaviours as pathological was essential to the HCW's activities. Not only did it give the group a problem to solve, but it also licensed their otherwise questionable interventions in the lives of other people's children. For if the good in a child's character had been "crushed out," it was ultimately the fault of the child's parents, and the HCW could assume an ostensibly public role here in providing the kind of parenting that these children lacked. In some cases, this work involved taking direct control over aberrant children. Among the HCW's earliest initiatives was the formation of a local Children's Aid Society, an institution that visited the homes of poor families and removed children whose parents had failed to provide "a home, worthy of the home, to their offspring."[54] More often, however, the HCW sought to repair the damage of poor parenting through "environmental" means, through the creation of a city-wide "home" that would refurbish the inherent good in children's character.

The HCW's belief in the moral effects of the material environment brought the group into the realm of housing reform. Certain environments, the group suggested, had a corrupting rather than nurturing influence on the moral character of children. For many years, this belief was expressed in the HCW's efforts to remove the lives of poor children from the corrupting environment of "the streets" – the veritable "recruiting ground[s]," as one member put it, "for Satan's armies of evil."[55] Combating these moral effects, for the HCW, was less a matter of stamping out street life itself than creating a series of more wholesome alternatives, like supervised children's playgrounds. The latter, for the HCW, provided normative "counter-attractions" to the streets and acted as "mighty agents in the mental and moral well-being of the children in our congested districts."[56] In addition to the environment of the streets, the homes of poor and working-class children were an obvious concern. One of the HCW's efforts on this issue, begun in 1905, involved the preparation of the city's first "systematic" survey of slum housing. Like earlier surveys in France and Britain, the results of the HCW's work represented the domestic spaces of the slums as a series of worrying departures from assumed spatial norms. Sanitary conditions, the survey found, were "bad," buildings were "dilapidated," plumbing was "poor," and homes were "overcrowded." Acting upon these pathologies, the report concluded, was an urgent moral task. The proposed model tenements plan, in particular, "would be a good investment morally and financially."[57]

The HCW's most important contribution to housing reform came in 1906, when two of its members led an *Evening Mail* reporter through the upper streets and enabled him to write a gripping three-part exposé of the city's "other half."[58] Together, the articles reiterated the pathologizing perspective of Hattie, Armitage, and the HCW, while contributing some of the dramatic and voyeuristic conventions of contemporary journalistic slumology. Like journalistic exposés in other cities, the articles took the narrative form of a quasi-colonial exploration of unknown and exotic territories, with the newspaper's white and middle-class readers addressed as "you" and invited to follow along. "As you entered the door, you saw to the left …," began one article. "Imagine to yourself, if you have ever seen one," invited another article, "the most squalid peasant hut in Ireland, and you may then do justice to this place." In terms of content, the articles echoed the reports of the board of health and the HCW in their enumeration of a vast series of social and spatial pathologies, but also offered readers a uniquely sensory perspective on these problems. People's homes were not just "unsanitary" but also "dark," "damp," "cold," and "foul smelling." Furnishings and personal effects were not simply "inadequate" but also "chil[ling] to the heart," "wretched," and "miserable."[59]

As in other depictions of the slums, the *Evening Mail* articles linked prevailing housing conditions to the physical and moral health of the inhabitants. Not only immoral and unhealthy, slum residents were depicted in the articles as something less than full human beings. Their lives were recognized as *lives* only within scare quotes (people "lived" rather than simply lived in the slums), and their existence was described as something close to that of nonhuman animals. Adhering to the reformers' environmentalist perspective, however, the articles attributed the residents' alleged animality to the material condition of their homes. It was slum housing, variously described as "unfit for human habitation" or unfit to "kennel a dog," that had effectively produced a collection of less-than-human residents. The "sty," to invoke the famous metaphor, had created the "pig." Formulating the relationship in this way provided a potential escape to the residents' degraded status, as well as an opportunity for middle-class Haligonians to lift them graciously through it – not through moral exhortation but through *spatial* normalization. "We may preach to the people and exhaust our energies in seeking to uplift them morally," one article concluded, "but while they continue to occupy such places as these, we may confidently count upon failure." Like Armitage and the HCW, the *Evening Mail* articles brought the problem of immorality into the previously health-focused discussions of the Halifax slums, accentuating the argument for housing reform. Ill health and immorality could now be seen as interrelated afflictions that manifested in the bodies and behaviours of the poor but originated in their material surroundings.

The role of race in the HCW's conception of housing reform was complex. On the one hand, the HCW's discussion of lacklustre housing conditions often mentioned the racial background of the afflicted residents (when these residents were non-white), and it is clear that the group found the living conditions of Black Haligonians worrying. Indeed, one of the *Evening Mail* articles on the slums that the HCW orchestrated began with a lengthy and horrifying description of the home of a "coloured" family, a five-person household forced to live in "wretched[ness]," "confusion," and "dirt." Immediately thereafter, however, the article introduces readers to the living conditions of nearby white residents with the aforementioned comparator of an imagined "peasant hut in Ireland." Why Ireland? Why this explicitly racio-ethnic transition? It is as if the article wanted to put Black and white pathologies next to one another, to put them in sequence, while enforcing a certain space between them. White pathologies are *like* those of Black residents, the article implies, but they are still white (Irish) pathologies. This suggested proximity of white and Black pathologies would tend to motivate support for housing reform on the part of white middle-class residents, who were not yet fully secure in their racial-ethnic supremacy in Halifax or elsewhere in Canada.[60] It would compel action, that is, to retrieve poor white residents from their apparent closeness to blackness, their still-remediable embodiment of the pathologies embodied more fully and fundamentally by the Black poor.

Indeed, the HCW's approach to many reform issues presumed racially distinct forms of pathology and advocated racially distinct programs of improvement. It went without saying for the HCW, for example, that neglected children would be removed from their families and placed in an institution or family that matched their race. Thus, when it was discovered in the 1910s that most Black families were "too poor to take a [neglected] child and provide a home and training for it," the HCW advocated for the creation of a segregated "home for neglected coloured children," rather than have these children placed in existing white orphanages. The HCW also supported the segregation of other social institutions, including the free-lunch counters operated by the city. Here, impoverished white residents were served a daily meal in a room furnished with tables and chairs, while Black residents were relegated to a stand-up counter in a separate room. One HCW member, in a 1916 meeting, called this arrangement into question. She was quickly informed by another member, however, that the separate lunch rooms did not represent "any discrimination as to colour," and the issue was immediately dropped. One effect of the HCW's support for segregated social services was to ensure that the improvement of white lives and behaviours was never impeded by their physical proximity to Black lives. Another effect, plainly evident in some cases, was the provision of lower-quality services to Black recipients.[61]

In the end, the HCW's proposed actions on housing reform reflected this racialized vision of pathology and improvement. No substantial housing reforms were ever proposed by the HCW for Black-majority areas of the city. Nothing like the model tenements project, to be sure, was ever proposed in this period for Black slums like Africville and the Black-majority sections of the North End. More importantly, it would have been radically incompatible with the segregated perspective of the HCW to advocate or accept that the model tenements provide occupancy to both white and Black residents. The improvement brought into being by the model tenements' environment would, in the HCW's view, have been impaired by the presence of Black tenants and the graver form of pathology they embodied. The HCW's discussion of Black living conditions in this period, then, tended to serve a purpose other than building support for the improvement of these conditions. Its primary effect was to underscore the depravity of white conditions. It was to demonstrate how very low impoverished white residents had been allowed to fall. The aim of housing reform, consequently, was to improve the living conditions of white residents, while those of Black residents (as I show in chapter 3) were either left unimproved or rendered much worse.

The Making of a Dominant Perspective

The affinities between the perspectives of Halifax medical doctors, Evangelicals, and maternal feminists provided a sturdy basis for reform-minded interventions in the slums. Active on a variety of fronts in this period, these groups were important participants in public discussions, and their views were widely respected in the city. Yet their ability to implement changes to the slum environment still requires some explanation. There were, after all, competing perspectives on the slums and their problems at this time (discussed below), and there is nothing inherently truthful or otherwise superior about the views of Hattie, Armitage, or the HCW. The argument that the environment was the major determinant of slum residents' physical and moral condition, in fact, could fall apart rather easily at times. An HCW member, for example, delivered a near-absurd response in 1910 to the question of whether disparities in wealth might have some effect upon children's health and behaviour. Having conceded that some children were born with "silver spoons" in their mouths and others were not, the member proceeded to reaffirm the importance of the environment – as if the latter were not, like "silver spoons," a product of a household's wealth. A "silver spoon," she explained, "is but an item, [and] silver spoons amount to but very little in the race of life. What does count – overwhelmingly – is ENVIRONMENT."[62]

As the above suggests, the attribution of ill health and immorality to the environment requires that the latter stand apart from any surrounding social or economic process. As the *cause* of evident pathologies, the environment itself is treated as uncaused. It simply exists, causelessly, and influences other things. This perspective, the perspective of the Halifax reformers, is thus a highly questionable one. More plausible perspectives, moreover, were routinely developed and circulated in the industrializing cities of the nineteenth and early twentieth century. Friedrich Engels, for example, famously developed an analysis of the industrial slums of England that rejected either configuration of the "pigsty" equation. Rather than following contemporary progressives in attributing social ills to the material environment, Engels sought to provide an explanation for this environment, as well as for the forces that had compelled poor people to live in such environments.[63] In a somewhat different analysis, W.E.B. DuBois tangled with the white slumologists of Philadelphia, describing the African American slum as a "symptom" rather than a problem in itself. To understand the racialized slum, DuBois claimed, one needed to understand the history of slavery, the (unwelcome) arrival of freed slaves in Northern cities, the racism of employers and landlords, and other social factors.[64] While there was no recognized equivalent to Engels or DuBois in early twentieth-century Halifax, there were certainly other people who assumed to know something about the slums and whose analysis differed, sometimes dramatically, from that of the reformers. How, then, did the reformers become the city's experts on the slums?

One of the vaunted merits of the reformers' knowledge vis-à-vis that of other Haligonians was its connection to first-hand, visual observation. What the reformers knew about the slums, they claimed, stemmed from what they had seen first-hand, and this particular form of knowledge acquisition was alleged to be more authoritative than any other. Hattie, for one, explicitly linked his knowledge of the slums to the house calls that he (and others) had performed as a doctor. When, in 1906, he claimed that "medical men" had had "better opportunities than any other class of people to know the conditions in the poorer parts of the city," he was referring less to their knowledge of medical science than to their comprehensive, first-hand observations of the "hovels" that "physicians are so frequently called upon to enter."[65] Rev. Armitage also regularly emphasized his first-hand knowledge of the slums. Even more explicitly than Hattie, moreover, Armitage asserted that it was the faculty of vision, the act of seeing for oneself, that underpinned the credibility of his knowledge: "I have personally *seen* enough to convince me," he proclaimed in 1905, "that it is the duty of the community both from the standpoint of self interest and of ethics ... to do something to secure for its deserving poor, places to live in [that] are constructed with at least a moderate regard for sanitary principles."[66] For Armitage, to see the slums was both to know them and to know what to *do* with them.

The HCW was perhaps the most explicit proponent of first-hand, visual knowledge. Some members, like Bessie Egan, had acquired direct experience in the slums through their existing voluntary activities, while others gained experience through their involvement with the HCW and its various initiatives. The HCW-established VON was a particularly important vehicle of first-hand knowledge production and circulation. VON nurses, as noted above, conducted over three thousand home visits per year between 1903 and 1908, many of which occurred in the slums. These visits, Dennis claimed in 1908, gave VON nurses an understanding of the slums that other people, people with little or no first-hand knowledge, generally lacked. Unlike other Haligonians, Dennis announced at the 1908 annual meeting, VON nurses had "*actual contact* with poverty, filth, and disease in ... wretched tenement[s]."[67] Anyone who might dispute the nurses' knowledge of the slums, Dennis implied, would have to demonstrate that they had an equal amount of contact with their residents and living conditions. No one, aside from Armitage, would be able to do so.

This emphasis on first-hand, visual observation was a common feature of the reform campaigns of the nineteenth and early twentieth centuries. Housing reformers on both sides of the North Atlantic routinely grounded their perspectives and propositions on the basis of their having personally seen the slums, and they often expended great efforts to survey the slums in as many cities as possible.[68] While first-hand observation might seem a rather obvious and sturdy source of knowledge, it should not immediately be regarded as such. In other times, authority would tend to be linked to the comprehension of distinctly unobservable phenomena, such as the abstract processes and statistical quantities ostensibly understood by economists, while first-hand experience has quite often signalled personal bias and untrustworthy knowledge rather than the bolster of credible knowledge claims. Indeed, changes instituted in this period to the city's system of property assessment were founded on precisely opposite premises. The aims of these changes were explicitly to base assessments on an abstract and mathematical derivation of property value's distribution across the urban landscape, as well as to remove the distorting influence of the assessors' first-hand experience by subjecting their work to a system of rule-bound procedures. The output of the reformed assessment system – "scientifically" estimated property values – would soon provide essential guidance to urban planners and partially displace the kinds of knowledge produced by Hattie and the other housing reformers.[69]

The connection between the reformers' knowledge claims and first-hand observation is more complicated and fragile than it might seem. Most of what the reformers claimed to see in the slums was, in fact, fundamentally unseeable. A building can be described as dilapidated, an apartment as overcrowded, only through reference to some abstract conception of normal upkeep and normal density – and these conceptions appear nowhere within the visual field. As Mary Poovey suggests, abstract or theorized norms were an essential part of the slum surveys of reformers like James Kay-Shuttleworth; they rendered the description of slum conditions possible even as they contradicted the alleged source of these descriptions (first-hand observation).[70] The credibility accorded to the reformers' perspectives in Halifax, therefore, was due less to their inherent truthfulness than to their accordance with a broad and long-established structure of knowledge: a patterned way of surveilling and diagnosing human beings that informed reform campaigns in many North Atlantic cities and that the Halifax reformers brought forcefully to bear upon the city's slums.

A further and rather important characteristic of the reformers' knowledge was its ostensible nontransferability. As passionately as the reformers tried to communicate their knowledge to the Halifax public, there was always something missing from the act – something that they could not convey and that would thus remain knowable only to *them*. The limits of words and images to convey the reformers' knowledge to others was underlined in various ways. In many cases, the reformers would simply assert that conditions in the slums were "beyond description," "beggared description," or were "indescribable."[71] Similarly, the 1905 *Evening Mail* articles that so eagerly entreated readers to imagine themselves in the place of the reporter also acknowledged the impossibility of actually doing so. "It would be difficult," an article claimed, "for anyone who had not seen this place to understand in how serious a degree it is unfit for habitation by any living creature."[72] In 1910, the British housing reformer Henry Vivian reprised and reinforced this position during a visit to Halifax. Vivian was toured through the slums by George Wright, a wealthy businessman and close associate of Armitage and the HCW. His comments to the local press, after the tour, convey his near-total incapacity to represent what he had seen. The houses were "unspeakable in their filthiness," he said. "They were pigsties – too dark even for that."[73] The force of Vivian's description seems to be derived partly from what it cannot accomplish, from its gesture towards a reality that ostensibly eludes the words that might but ultimately cannot convey it to others.

Rather than undermining the reformers' authority, these admissions of representational failure were essential to its constitution. It was partly because of these failures or limits that the reformers could inform people about the slums without making other people experts in their own right. The reformers' words were always inadequate. For others to know the slums as the reformers did, they would have to reproduce the originary act of cognition. They would have to see for themselves. And since few Haligonians seem to have had the time or inclination to undertake such a task, the opinions of a vast segment of the Halifax public could essentially be consigned to the category of nonknowledge or (at best) secondary knowledge. This hierarchical categorization of knowledge claims was invoked by the reformers on various occasions and filtered into public and media discussions of housing reform as well. In a characteristic move, an *Evening Mail* reporter distinguished between the comprehensive, credible knowledge of the housing reformers and the "superficial" knowledge of those who opposed their propositions. People who had only minimal contact with the poor often "doubt as to their needs," the report explained. However, "if the superficial observers would accompany the city missionary [i.e., Armitage] into the homes, they would ... *see sights which speak forcibly for themselves* of the need for liberal support [for the poor]."[74] People who believed no reforms were necessary or merited, therefore, were fundamentally ignorant. If these opponents were to acquire actual knowledge, which would mean seeing the slums comprehensively and first-hand, they would come to the very same conclusions as Armitage and his collaborators on the question of reform.

Of course, there were *some* other Haligonians who had seen the slums first-hand – namely, the slum residents themselves. Yet the slum residents' perspectives on their own living conditions was never explicitly mentioned in the local media or in the pronouncements of the reformers. Perhaps it was taken for granted that the residents would support the reformers' propositions, or perhaps their opinions simply did not matter. In any case, the residents' perspectives were evidently inessential to the discussion of housing reform and left no clear trace in the public record. However, some faint indications of poor and working-class perspectives on the reform initiatives did exist. Some working-class mothers, for example, refused to send their children to the supervised playgrounds that the HCW had introduced, despite the persistent outreach and coaxing of the HCW to participate in what could potentially be seen as free daycare. An exhibit that the HCW and other reformers had set up on Gottingen Street to instruct the neighbourhood on the proper upkeep of homes and yards was also vandalized, and a middle-class couple that was admiring the exhibit one afternoon had sheets of cardboard and other trash thrown at them by a group of Black teenagers (who were, it might be imputed, less than impressed by the forthright moral of the exhibit). On some occasions, finally, poor residents contested the official designation of their homes as unsanitary and refused to leave their homes when the board of health ordered a condemnation.[75]

In one of the only records in which a slum resident's verbal response to a housing-reform initiative can be clearly discerned, the tenants of a home on Buckingham Street contested the conclusions of the board of health. The home was rented by the Orton family and was represented at the hearing by Mrs Orton. After denying the Board's assertion that their home was "filthy," Mrs Orton explained that "the rooms were as clean as they could be made."[76] Mrs Orton and her family had evidently defied earlier orders to vacate their home, staying put even after an authority had removed the home's windows in the still-frigid month of March. Having refused to leave a windowless Halifax home in the enduring winter season, it is unlikely that the Ortons would respond any differently to the board's renewed call for their eviction (which the article recounts). It is impossible to know precisely why the Ortons wished to stay put. Perhaps their expectations in the realm of housing were somewhat different than those of the board of health, and they were puzzled to be informed that their home was filthy. Perhaps they simply knew better than the board that their meagre income could not bring them any better lodgings in Halifax's recognizably tight, privately controlled housing market. Whatever their reasons, however, it is safe to say that the Ortons would be reluctant to be forcibly uprooted and moved into someone else's idea of proper housing. The model tenements plan, which targeted their street, would have been opposed with vigour.

The discounting of poor residents' perspectives on their own living conditions was an important effect of the reformers' structure of knowledge, as well as a fundamental condition of that structure's coherence. As should now be apparent, the social and spatial norms that structured the reformers' observations about the slums did more than simply render this area intelligible and improvable. They also cast the area's residents, the "nonnormal," beyond the realm of subjecthood. Lacking the characteristics of normal individuals, the residents were accorded no part in prevailing discussions of housing reforms, even when these discussions dealt squarely with their own homes and their own lives. "People trained to think," as HCW members described themselves, could participate as subjects in the development and discussion of reforms; the "unthinking," as the HCW described less privileged residents, could appear as objects (at best) in someone else's project of reform.[77] This bifurcated configuration of subjects and objects was clearly essential to the reformers' activities. It enabled them to construct an entire area and its people as an object of knowledge. It enabled them to speak as authorities on other people's lives and living conditions, with no requirement that these people agree with them. It enabled, more than anything, a new form of planning to take hold of the city and its people: a form of planning that would install itself in the spaces of epistemically displaced human beings, people whose pathologies qualified them for improvement and disqualified them from any say in the matter. This is what planning centred on the fostering of life, the basis of modern planning itself, unerringly looks like.

The Model Tenements Plan

In 1905, the reformers proposed their most ambitious solution to the ostensible problems of the slums. The upper streets' existing homes, in this plan, would be entirely demolished, and a set of "model tenements" would be constructed in their place. The tenements plan, while it exceeded the scope of any previous housing action, drew significantly on the preceding fifteen years of housing studies, campaigns, and interventions. When Armitage described material conditions in the area targeted by the plan as "squalid" and "miserable," he was reminding Haligonians of something that, by that point, they had heard many times before. When he proposed, moreover, that the removal of these squalid conditions would have beneficial effects on the area's inhabitants, he was reprising the environmentalist logic of a whole series of prior housing interventions. The logic of the plan, "educat[ing] the people into a higher form of living by better environment," was thus a familiar rather than outlandish proposition, a proposition that had already grounded smaller-scale interventions for years. And yet, the model tenements plan also entailed something more, something bigger, than the initiatives that preceded it. Transcending prevailing conceptions of what spatial interventions could reasonably achieve, the plan entailed the wholesale demolition and calculated reconstruction of an entire neighbourhood, the creation of a wholly new and normal environment from the wreckage of the old and pathological. Unveiled at the start of the twentieth century, the plan was a gripping outline of things yet to come: the harbinger of a new form of urban planning and a new, strategically planned city.

The inspiration for the model tenements plan was rooted in Britain, where a major experiment in working-class housing had been underway for over seventy years. The public-health crises of the 1830s had spawned the first experiments. Having linked ill health and disease to abnormal material conditions, as happened in Paris and other major cities, reformers began the task of imagining and modelling the material conditions that ought to exist, conditions that would be healthy, wholesome, and yet affordable to working-class residents. In the 1830s, the first model tenements projects made their appearance in Edinburgh, Glasgow, and London. Thereafter, the construction of model tenements intensified and spread to other cities. A signature model tenement erected at the 1851 World's Fair in London brought new attention to the possibilities of better working-class housing, while the formation of large-scale model tenements companies, like the Society for Improving the Dwellings of the Labouring Classes (SIDLC) and Peabody Trust, freighted a vast expansion of tenement construction. By the end of the century, Britain's five largest model tenements companies had constructed over one hundred thousand model housing units across the country.[78] The British experiments eventually proved attractive to at least a few housing reformers on the other side of the Atlantic. Significant model tenements were constructed in New York and Boston in the second half of the nineteenth century, while Toronto and Halifax seemed poised to follow suit at the beginning of the next century. Having heard of the British experiments, Rev. Armitage travelled to England and Scotland in 1904 to tour several model tenements projects and to meet with prominent housing reformers. He and his collaborators in Halifax also read the available literature on the tenements, including published blueprints.[79]

One of the most distinctive features of the model tenements was their reliance on private, profit-seeking investors. Backed entirely by private (rather than state) capital, the tenements and the companies that constructed them inevitably brought new individuals and objectives into the broader project of nineteenth-century housing reform. Indeed, the approach of model tenements companies has sometimes been described as "capitalist philanthropy" or "five per cent philanthropy" in recognition of the two worlds that they brought together and the two objectives, social and financial, that they sought to fulfil. The companies' financial objective was plainly to provide an attractive profit to their investors. This profit, as in any other rental housing scheme, was ultimately drawn from the buildings' tenants, who were expected to pay rent and thus to work for a wage. The established *rate* of profit, however, was always a relatively low one, typically set at 5 per cent per year. This lower rate of profit sometimes made it difficult for the tenements companies to attract investors, but it was also essential to the overall operation. The difference between the profit rate accepted by the tenements companies' investors and those of conventional landlords created space for the pursuit of other, nonfinancial objectives – namely, the improvement of cities' poor and working-class inhabitants.

The tenement companies' vision of improvement was consistent with a whole series of eighteenth- and nineteenth-century initiatives that sought to rid individuals of the pathologies that new forms of knowledge rendered apparent. As Foucault suggests, the bipolar perspective of late eighteenth-century doctors and other experts provided an impetus and framework for the development of new, normalizing interventions in the lives of individuals. These new interventions, examples of what Foucault calls disciplinary power, aimed to subject pathological individuals to a near-constant process of evaluation, correction, and alteration. Through this process, people's lives were remade, their habits altered, and the forces of their bodies brought into closer alignment with the imperatives of power. Essential to this process, in many cases, was the construction of new environments, new normalizing spaces that would render the lives of individuals visible and "carry the effects of power right to them."[80] Foucault's most well-known example is the panopticon, a model prison, proposed by Jeremy Bentham in 1843, meant to enable a more persistent process of surveillance and ultimately induce forms of self-surveillance among the inmates. The effects of the panopticon, for Bentham, would be extensive: "Moral reformed – health preserved – industry invigorated – instruction diffused – public burdens lightened ... all by a simple idea in architecture!"[81] The panopticon, never constructed, embodied at least three spatial tactics that would eventually infuse a host of actually constructed normalizing environments, including the model tenements: partitioning, enclosure, and surveillance.[82]

These three spatial tactics can be understood by looking closely at one of the signature British model tenements, the 1850 "Model Houses for Families" building in Bloomsbury, London (see *figure* 2.3). A project of the SIDLC, the building stood five storeys tall and was meant to accommodate fifty-three families. The first spatial tactic, partitioning, is evident in the layout of the building's domestic spaces. Each housing unit in the building was clearly separated from the others, creating clear lines around the lives of particular "nuclear" families that did not always exist in prevailing (nonmodel) poor and working-class housing at the time. Each unit, moreover, was subdivided into a series of smaller spaces, each of them devoted to one or more specific domestic activities. Through this layout, a clear departure from the relatively open space of most "slum" housing, certain activities were drawn together, while others were kept apart. Activities like undressing, sleeping, and having sex, in particular, were spatialized in walled-off bedroom spaces, and the bedroom-appropriate activities of parents (in the case of family units) were clearly walled off from those of their children. The layout, in effect, tended to suppress tenants' old domestic habits and encourage, if not enforce, the adoption of new ones. The tenants, the tenements' supporters hoped, would be taught to live like upstanding middle-class individuals through spatial means, through their removal from the depraved environment of the slums and their insertion into a well-ordered, morally conducive environment. Partitioning was an important tactic in this endeavour.[83]

The second spatial tactic, "enclosure," is observable in the configuration of the building's exterior walls. Consistent with other model tenements, the building's outer walls constituted a fortress-like barrier between the normalizing environment of the tenement and the still-pathological world outside, and could be crossed over strictly through a particular, well-designated point of passage. For tenants, leaving their home now meant exiting their housing unit *not* onto a city street but onto a shared corridor and then transiting this corridor towards a common exit. Returning home entailed a similar passage, a discernible crossing of a barrier between their new home and the outside world they once inhabited. In the new world, living conditions were better, more normal. Expectations in terms of behaviour were similarly elevated, and the tenants were expected to read these expectations, in part, from the form of the environment they now shared. From the tenements companies' perspective, the creation of an enclosed environment allowed the effects of the overall project to be assessed. Individuals subjected to normalizing processes (i.e., the buildings' tenants) were clearly distinguishable. The effects of these processes could thus be observed in the habits of the buildings' tenants and especially in the gap between *these* habits and those prevailing in the world outside. This gap was expected to be a significant one, a kind of frontier (as one company described it) between manicured "plots of civilization" and the "wide swath of barbarism" that characterized the unimproved slums.[84] The tactic of enclosure allowed categorical differences like these to be discerned and, ideally, widened.

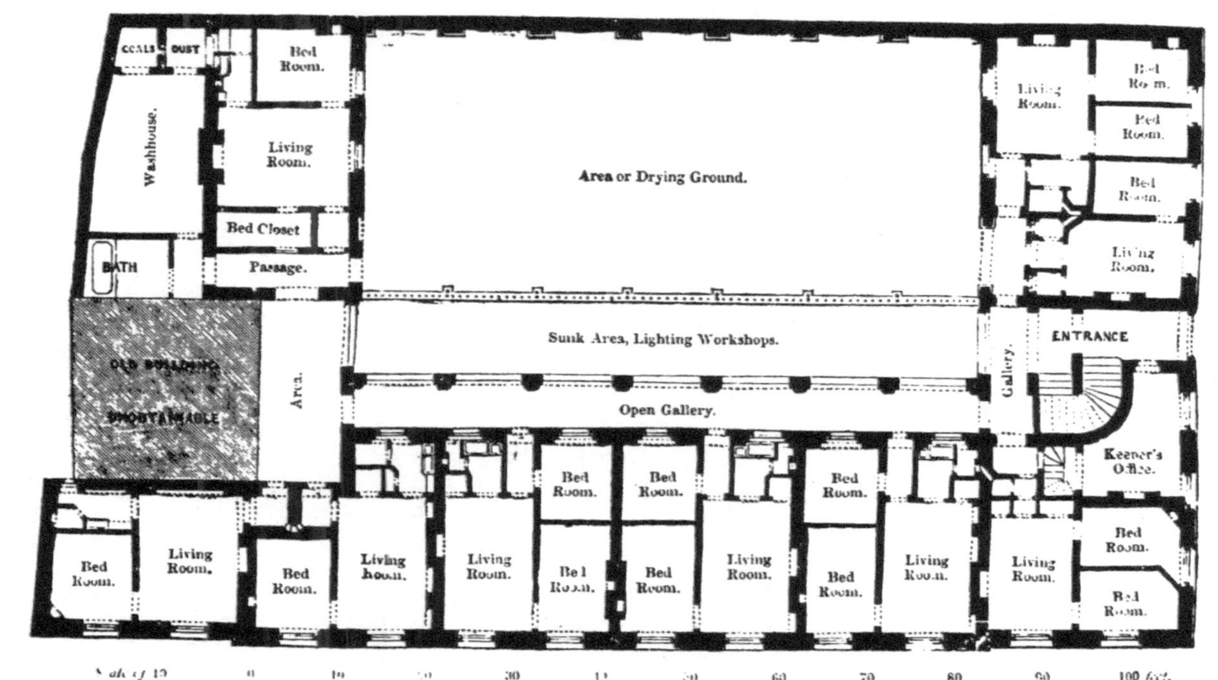

Figure 2.3 Model Houses for Families, Bloomsbury, 1850. From John Tarn, *Five Per Cent Philanthropy: An Account of Housing in Urban Areas Between 1840 and 1914* (Cambridge: Cambridge University Press, 1973), 19. Image courtesy of Cambridge University Press.

The final tactic, surveillance, involves the creation of ongoing, built-in processes of observation. The possibility of surveillance, so defined, was most pronounced at the building's point of entry. Located next to the building's entrance was the office and living quarters of the superintendent. From this location, the superintendent could easily observe the comings and goings of the tenants, and continually evaluate (and potentially correct) their behaviours as they passed. A somewhat different process was enabled by the building's inner courtyard, the intended play space of the residents' children. In contrast to the streets and alleyways in which most poor and working-class children played in this period, the open space of the courtyard put the children's activities on display from the hallways that surrounded it. This arrangement, while it would certainly enable the building's superintendent to conduct an inspection, was expected to create surveillance through a kind of relay: the building's mothers were expected to oversee the children, assess their behaviour, and impart any required discipline. The occasional inspection of the superintendent, in this case, was meant to act upon the mothers, to ensure that the latter were playing their proper maternal role. The tactic of surveillance, built into the space of the tenements, was the surest means of "carrying the effects of power right to [the tenants]." It helped to constitute a process in which the tenants would ultimately become self-surveilling and self-normalizing. Surveillance would help to fulfil the tenements' purpose (it was hoped) without heavy-handed instruction, coercion, or repression.

These forms of built-in normalization were essential to the British model tenements that so inspired North American housing reformers like Rev. Armitage. When, in 1905, Rev. Armitage announced a model tenements plan for central Halifax, he was drawing upon a long history of housing experiments like Model Houses for Families and the particular configuration of capitalist financing and normalizing social reform that they embodied. Like its British predecessors, the Halifax tenements would rely on the profit-motivated support of wealthy merchants and financiers. "The most purely philanthropic of movements," Rev. Armitage announced in 1906, "cannot be carried on without money."[85] Concretely, Armitage hoped to secure $200,000 of private capital for the initiative and would reward investors with a modest return of 7 per cent per year. With the requisite "philanthropic capital" in hand, the venture would begin the most ambitious and thorough spatial intervention since the city's founding. The upper streets, an area that was now synonymous with ill health and immorality, would be comprehensively bought up, torn down, and rebuilt. In the now-vacated space of (in)human squalor would be erected a large-scale, modern tenement "identical" to a particular project in Liverpool, completed in 1888 (see *figure* 2.4). The overall project would be massive in scale, 480 feet long by 180 feet wide, with a large courtyard in the centre serving as a supervised playground for children. It would comprise 550 individual units, ranging from three-bedroom to single-room dwellings – housing units suitable, collectively, "for almost every condition of family life."[86]

Unmentioned by Armitage and his associates but certainly essential to the overall initiative was the tenements' incorporation of the three normalizing design elements discussed above. The individual housing units would be divided from one another and carefully partitioned into a series of smaller spaces. In many units, the ideal of three bedrooms – one for the adults and one for the children of each gender – would indeed

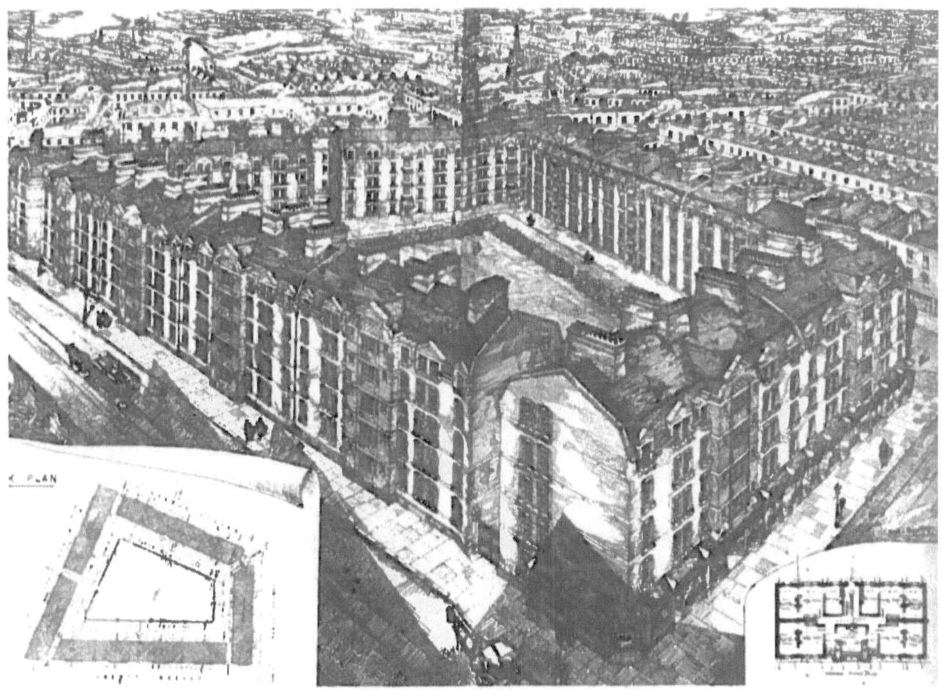

Figure 2.4 Victoria Buildings, Liverpool, 1885, the model that Armitage hoped to construct in Halifax. From John Tarn, *Five Per Cent Philanthropy: An Account of Housing in Urban Areas Between 1840 and 1914* (Cambridge: Cambridge University Press, 1973), 90. Image courtesy of Cambridge University Press.

be provided, and domestic activities like bathing, cleaning, cooking, and sleeping would certainly be kept apart. The overall project, moreover, would discernibly enclose and isolate the inner world of the tenements from the surrounding neighbourhood. The external walls of the buildings would create a distinctive and imposing barrier: a geometric series of a long, straight walls, the height of which would exceed nearby homes by at least three stories. The design of the buildings, finally, would provide built-in platforms and relays for ongoing practices of surveillance. In a feature that would certainly have pleased the HCW, an open courtyard would be available for the amusement of the building's children, a wholesome and surveillable "counterattraction" to the much-vilified "streets." It was through measures like these that the model tenements would not only eliminate the pathology-causing environment of the Halifax slums but also provide a positive counterenvironment: a normalizing enclosure that its proponents claimed would "educate the people into a higher form of living."

Progress on the tenements plan was slow but steady between 1905 and 1908. In 1906, Armitage was able to reveal that several major investors had been secured for the project and two years later announced that "a large strip of property" on two intersecting streets had been purchased.[87] While the area encompassed by the overall project was enormous, its ambitions were tempered by the desire to ensure that the area's residents were actually rehoused. Thus, before any building was torn down, the residents of the area were counted, their weekly rents were recorded, and meticulous calculations were carried out. Based on careful calculations, Armitage estimated that the housing units provided by his venture would be "within the reach of every working man" in the city. The residents of the model tenements – 1,800 in total – would obtain a higher quality of housing in the model tenements "without any additional expense."[88] The process of rehousing, moreover, would proceed gradually: one block of homes would be demolished and a new tenement block erected in their place *before* proceeding to the next block of homes. It is unclear whether the residents of a targeted block would have anywhere to live in the interval between the demolition of their home and the completion of a new tenement. Nevertheless, the decision to proceed "block by block" was at least intended to minimize displacement, and even the Board of Trade premised its support for the model tenements plan on Armitage's assurances that the current tenants of the area would be rehoused.[89]

By 1908, the fulfilment of the model tenements plan seemed all but inevitable, and the local media had already begun to celebrate the elimination of the long-reviled downtown slum. The *Evening Mail*, noting that major properties had been purchased in the upper-streets district, proclaimed in 1908 that "one of the greatest forward movements for the betterment of the workingman was ... sure to materialize."[90] It was at this point, however, that the plan began to fall apart. The first public sign of trouble was registered in 1907, when Armitage complained in a public lecture that "it would be easier to move the Citadel [military fortress] than to move the people of Halifax to have these [slums] torn down and replaced by proper and modern tenements."[91] Two years later, Armitage was forced to admit that the venture's initial investors had backed out and chanelled their capital elsewhere. The reason for the investors' withdrawal was never stated, but Armitage offered an important hint in 1912 when he lamented that Haligonians were willing to invest their money in Cuba or Mexico "but not on Brunswick Street (one of the so-called upper streets)."[92]

This was indeed a time of massive capital flight out of Halifax. Especially significant was the trajectory of RSC, an initially Halifax-based firm. Founded in 1903, RSC was devoted initially to selling securities for Scotia Group, a Halifax-based conglomerate of Maritime-based steel, coal, and financial concerns. However, it soon turned its attention to more lucrative opportunities in Western Canada, the Caribbean, and Latin America. By 1907, the firm's leadership had reached the conclusion that there was little future in Maritime-based industry and moved its operations to Montréal.[93] In enlisting local capital, sending it elsewhere, and then leaving the city entirely, RSC was taking part in a broad and well-documented migration of capital out of the Maritime region in the early part of the twentieth century.[94] As capital moved eastward, the prospects for model tenements in Halifax were certainly impacted. Of the tenements company's five initial investors, four were heavily involved with RSC and the Scotia Group, while the other was president of the increasingly Toronto-centred Bank of Nova Scotia.[95] The flight of financial capital, therefore, was also a flight of "philanthropic capital." The money that was to be invested in the model tenements was quickly leaving town, whether its owners physically moved with it or not. By 1909, it would be clear to Armitage and his associates that the model tenements could not proceed as originally planned.

Armitage did not abandon the tenements project right away. In 1909, he asked city council for support, suggesting that the city could either fulfil the project itself as a municipal enterprise or else guarantee a $150,000 bond issue that would allow Armitage to proceed. Council agreed to study the issue, but replied two months later that neither of the options outlined by Armitage was tenable.[96] It was unlikely, the councillors reasoned, that the city would be able to develop and operate the tenements project any more successfully than the businessmen who had recently abandoned it. The *social* proposition of the tenements, the councillors added, was also dubious. Similar projects in Britain and the United States, they argued, had often failed to rehouse the populations that they aimed to benefit, largely because the rents in the model tenements were unaffordably high. The results of the British model tenements were indeed rather mixed. In many cases, they were able to rehouse only the highest strata of the working class – the "artisan" rather than the "labourer" – and they made little effort at all to rehouse the urban poor. In the end, then, the model tenements companies displaced more poor and working-class residents than they ultimately rehoused or "improved."[97] Council's entry point to this history was the 1906 book, *On Municipal and National Trading,* from which it lifted Lord Rosebury's polemical message to housing reformers in Britain: "You build admirable buildings, but the inhabitants of these new dwellings are not the people you dispossessed."[98] It was this message that most clearly convinced council not to support Armitage's proposal.

The prospect of mass displacement, never mentioned in the discussion of the tenements until now, would clearly be devastating to the tenements plan. Having premised the plan on the idea that it would transform and "educate" people into a higher form of living, the reformers' cause was undercut by the newly raised possibility that it might instead evict people from their existing homes and throw them into an uncertain and risky situation. There might be other reasons to tear down the slums and build something different, and other reasons would indeed be put forward in time. This particular reason, however, could expect little public support in the face of the evidence the city had unearthed. The city's decision in 1909 dashed the last real hope of the tenements campaign. Armitage and his associates would continue to advocate for the tenements for a few more years, but with much less intensity and to no ultimate avail. After 1912, public discussion of the proposal ceased entirely, and the reformers' energies were finally dissipated – or rather, chanelled in other directions.[99]

The model tenements campaign, in its successes and its failures, offers important insights about the form of knowledge and power that was expressed through it. The campaign's failure was not the result of insufficient public support for its specific *aims.* To the contrary, Armitage and his associates succeeded in tapping into pre-existing public concerns about the ill health and immorality of the slums, and they worked to amplify and broaden such concerns to a remarkable extent. From the local press to the Trades and Labour Council, from city council to the Board of Trade, the most vocal and influential constituents of Halifax public life concurred with the reformers that "educating the people into a higher form of life" was a worthy pursuit. Normalizing poor and working-class people, altering their environment in order to improve their lives, was seen as a legitimate project, if not a necessary one. Where the disagreement occurred, in the end, was on the affiliated and vexed question of means – specifically, whether a project that aimed to transform the environment of the poor while simultaneously providing a profit to the project's investors could indeed be fulfilled. Reservations about the project were ultimately expressed from both sides of the model tenements' proposition. From one side, the profitability of the tenements project seemed suspect. From the other, the prospect of social reform – the normalization rather than displacement of slum residents – seemed doubtful. Profits might be surely achieved without reforms, or reforms without profit, but the likelihood of achieving both goals simultaneously was seen as highly doubtful.

Part of the problem lay in the particular scope of the proposed transformation: the complete and total normalization of a relatively small part of the city. To achieve this aim, the slums would need to be completely bought up and demolished. A totally different environment, a middle-class environment in miniature, would then need to be created, and the former residents of the slums installed within it. All of this was to occur, moreover, without altering any *other* aspect of urban life, including the wages earned by poor and working class individuals, and thus the rent these individuals were able to pay in their new home. This form of intervention, the total transformation of a relatively small part of urban life, ultimately proved infeasible, or at least too costly. The total rectification of total pathology would involve a level of expense that neither the business class nor civil society nor the state was willing to cover. The failure of the model tenements campaign would thus make way for different forms of intervention, less focused and less totalizing in their scope – forms of intervention, gathered under the heading "comprehensive planning," that I discuss in the next chapter. The prospect of a total transformation of the slums, a prospect nurtured and coveted by Rev. Armitage and his reform-minded associates, would lie dormant in the interim. It was not until the end of World War II, with a wealthier and more ambitious welfare state in place, that the ambitious and costly transformation envisioned in the model tenements would finally become achievable.[100]

Conclusion

From 1890 to 1912, the Halifax slums were an unequalled site of new ideas, new practices, and new visions of modern life. Emerging from epoch-defining processes of population growth, industrialization, and social stratification, a small network of middle-class reformers brought new forms of knowledge to bear upon the living conditions of the city's poor and working-class residents, especially the densely packed inhabitants of the city's slums. Working together and separately, the reformers conducted visits and surveys of the city's slums, wrote and spoke publicly about what they observed, and proposed a series of actions – from the introduction of a building code to the construction of model tenements – that promised to improve slum-residing individuals through the improvement of their housing conditions. The effects of these efforts on people's lives were considerable. Some residents saw their housing renovated or new sanitary facilities installed, while others saw their lodgings condemned and were thrown into the street. More than just a series of actions, however, the reformers' efforts helped to constitute a new logic of public action, a new form of urban planning that sought to reshape and improve human life from beneath. The reformers' attribution of individual pathologies to the material environment, in effect, transformed how the development and regulation of material conditions – the traditional task of urban planning – could be conceived and pursued. Planning, in a broad sense, would now be encouraged to take its bearings from the perceived condition of human beings and to organize material conditions in such a way that human lives were protected and improved.

The reformers' vision of collective life was ultimately a very limited and subjugating one. The normal or optimal state of life, for the reformers, was one that effectively mirrored the characteristics of white, middle-class life. The conditions that the reformers observed in the Halifax slums registered, for them, as a series of departures from white, middle-class norms; the improvement that they envisioned was inevitably one of social and spatial normalization. There is no question that housing conditions in the slums differed, in general, from those in middle-class neighbourhoods, or that wider access to certain middle-class comforts (e.g., sanitary facilities, insulation, heating) could be beneficial to the city's poor and working-class residents. The same housing conditions, however, could be diagnosed in many different ways, and it is far from clear that the perspectives developed by middle-class outsiders were the most adequate to the task of improving them. Certainly, Mrs Orton saw her situation rather differently than the reformers. The best evidence, moreover, suggests that poor and working-class residents were opposed to the reform era's creeping interventions in their lives and might have proposed a very different program of housing reform, had they been allowed to speak. There is thus a certain silence at the centre of the nascent planning regime. At the very moment when planning began to take "life" as its object, a great number of Halifax residents were cast outside the category of normal life and thereby denied any role in devising the planning initiatives that would reshape their surroundings.

Limited in many ways, the most evident merit of the reformers' analysis was to underwrite their own privilege and power. Its benefit was to constitute the reformers themselves as authoritative knowers in the public sphere and to obscure the social relations that produced, at the same time, their own privilege and slum residents' deprivation. The capacity of the reformers to speak intelligibly and authoritatively about the city was dependent upon the social and spatial norms that simultaneously rendered the slum describable and its residents speechless – too morally wayward and physically depleted, that is, to have anything important to say about their own lives and living conditions. The reformers' attribution of individual pathologies to the material environment, in turn, occluded attention to the potential social and historical causes of this environment itself. An analysis like Engels's or DuBois's, which would ultimately call into question the privileges of the reformers' themselves, had no way to appear within an environmentalist perspective. In the end, the reformers' efforts succeeded in bringing public attention to problematic housing conditions and rallying public support for their remediation, but did so in a way that gave over the lives and living conditions of poor / working-class residents to the machinations and objectives of others. Modern planning gained its foothold here: in spaces whose pathologized inhabitants were constituted not as political subjects but as the objects in someone else's project of improvement.

It might come as a surprise that, in a city widely known for the destruction of an impoverished Black community, the first plan to demolish and redevelop an entire community targeted a largely white neighbourhood. It was the residents of the upper streets, and not Africville, that endured the most explicit pathologization in this period and that experienced the most intense surveillance and interventions of reformers. Properly understood, however, this initial emphasis on white lives and living conditions underscores rather than undermines arguments about the role of anti-blackness in the modern planning regime. The pathologies of white residents, in this context, tended to be seen as different and less profound than those attributed to Black residents. In some cases, this led to the provision of racially segregated reform efforts (such as those advocated or supported by the HCW). In other cases, it led to reform efforts exclusive to white residents. It is telling, in this respect, that nothing like a model tenements plan was ever proposed for Black-majority sections of the city. It indicates, for one thing, the apparent capacity for white residents to be normalized and the desire of reformers to bring them closer to normative whiteness. It also indicates the apparent durability of Black pathologies: their exteriority with respect to planning's normalizing orientation. In the end, planning's efforts to create a "higher" life in this period occurred on the frontiers of blackness, producing coercive and subjugating articulations of concern for white residents and little concern whatsoever for Black residents.

3 Planning the Town White: Comprehensive Planning, Scientific Racism, and the Destruction of Africville

As some Haligonians were seeking to remake the city's slums, a series of city mayors, councillors, and bureaucrats were developing a rather different approach to the problems and possibilities of the "reform era." This approach was expressed, most concretely, in a series of new spatial interventions introduced between 1890 and 1915. In this period, underground sewers and water mains, historically absent, were gradually implemented across much of the urban terrain. City streets and sidewalks, historically unadorned, were gradually paved and outfitted with electric street lighting. Private land use and development, minimally regulated in the past, was increasingly subjected to a regime of land-use zoning and (in some cases) state-directed redevelopment projects. These interventions, though their benefits would not reach all parts of the city, were generally described in ambitious and seemingly inclusive terms – as efforts, that is, to improve the lives of the "overall population" or the "city as a whole." The scope and character of these efforts received their clearest definition from Francis Doane, the city's chief engineer and de facto urban planner in this period. Appearing before city council in 1914, Doane explained that modern planning was not just about laying out street or providing "expensive boulevards and parks available only for the rich." Its purpose, instead, was to augment the health, happiness, and prosperity of the overall population. "The health of the people is [planning's] first care," he explained to council, "convenience next, with economy considered all through."[1]

The initiatives of Francis Doane and other city officials constituted a second and somewhat different trajectory through which modern planning gained a foothold in Halifax and other North Atlantic cities. Departing from the more narrow-focused initiatives of contemporary housing reformers, these efforts sought to understand and manage vast, city-wide processes of urban development and aimed to achieve a series of beneficial effects on the overall population. The emergence of planning on this more expansive scale, often dubbed "comprehensive planning," was enabled by new forms of knowledge that brought intelligibility to complex and broad-based urban processes, as well as new sources of institutional power that both allowed and depended upon the management of such processes.[2] These forms of knowledge and power converged, among other places, in the formation of a nascent urban planning profession and the gradual establishment of formal urban planning departments in cities across North America.[3] The result was an increasingly professionalized and comprehensive form of planning, a form of planning backed by technical expertise and driven to operate upon cities "as a whole." Embodied in municipal officials like Francis Doane, this new form of planning took hold of human life on an unprecedented scale. For the first time, the lives of city residents – not just "pathological" individuals, but the entire population – were bound up with the actions that urban planning took, and did not take, to produce and regulate their material surroundings.

Generally overlooked in the development of comprehensive planning is its particular entanglements with contemporary forms of scientific racism. While racism, in some form, had already existed for at least four centuries, the second half of the nineteenth century witnessed the establishment of a new raciology that both hardened and modestly reworked prevailing racial hierarchies.[4] Essential to this new perspective was the view that (ostensible) racial differences were biological or hereditary, rather than geographical, in their origin. Essential as well was the view that the condition of large-scale human aggregates like "nations" and "populations" was determined in part by their relative incorporation of superior and inferior racial characteristics – which is to say, superior and inferior "races." This new perspective, loosely rooted in eighteenth-century natural history, nourished widespread and less-than-scientific concerns about (white) racial purity and numerical dominance, as well as the seemingly vulnerable racial fundaments of national identity, progress, and geopolitical strength.[5] More concretely, it prompted the adoption of practices in a range of domains, from public health to immigration, which sought to uphold and improve population-wide vitality through distinctly racial means: through the proliferation of superior races, the diminution of inferior races, or both at the same time.[6] Practices like these, widely documented outside the field of urban planning, ought to raise questions about the possible imprint of scientific racism on the seemingly population-wide ambitions of early comprehensive planning, especially as these beneficial ambitions seem to have been suspended, if not fully inverted, when planning turned to racialized communities like Africville.

The initiatives of Francis Doane and other reform-era city officials laid the foundations for a more state-directed, professionalized, and comprehensive form of urban planning in Halifax. Emerging in a period of unprecedented urban expansion, these new initiatives included the construction of sewers and water mains, the paving of streets and sidewalks, and the rational zoning and periodic redevelopment of private land uses. Their ultimate aim was to improve the condition of the population or city "as a whole," to produce a form of aggregate life in the city that was more healthy, more convenient, and more prosperous than ever before. When it came to Africville, however, these efforts took a rather different form. Living conditions, rather than being improved, were generally ignored by contemporary planning and were often *worsened* through initiatives meant to produce benefits for the broader population. Effects like these, seemingly at odds with planning's ambitions, suggest the particular racial foundations upon which these ambitions were conceived. Consistent with ascendant scientific racism, planning equated the strength and progress of the population with its racial "whiteness" and configured its spatial interventions accordingly. Black lives, regarded as an impairment to the overall population, entered the field of planning's concerns only as an expendable population upon whose *land* projects of greater "population-wide" health, convenience, and prosperity could be envisioned and fulfilled. Displacing blackness, symbolically and physically, was thus integral to the formation of comprehensive planning and its city-wide interventions – not just in Africville, that is, but across the entire terrain that it was taking within its grasp.

Urban Development and Comprehensive Planning

The terrain that Francis Doane and other city officials sought to understand and manage was a rapidly changing one. Indeed, the corollary of the population growth and industrialization that I noted in the previous chapter was an unprecedented process of urban expansion that both extended and reorganized the physical setting of urban life in Halifax. Until 1850, the setting of the city had been confined largely to the compact quadrilateral staked out by Cornwallis and his associates a century earlier (the downtown), as well as a pair of adjoining "suburbs." The first suburb, generally known as the Old North End, extended northward from the edge of the downtown and the upper-streets slum towards North Street (see *figure 3.1*). Divided into two hundred home sites, this area attracted a relatively diverse set of residents. Brunswick Street, featuring relatively large plots of land and a clear view of the Bedford Basin, was initially home to the city's most prosperous residents, while Gottingen and Agricola Street (farther west) were populated by working-class English and German households. The second suburb, known as the Old South End, extended southward from the edge of downtown towards South Street. Also divided into two hundred home sites, the Old South End was originally more homogenously working class than its northern counterpart, especially in the eastern section known popularly as Irish Town. Beyond the downtown and the two suburbs, the rest of the Halifax peninsula remained at midcentury a bucolic patchwork of small farms, semirural homesteads, and winding dirt roads.[7]

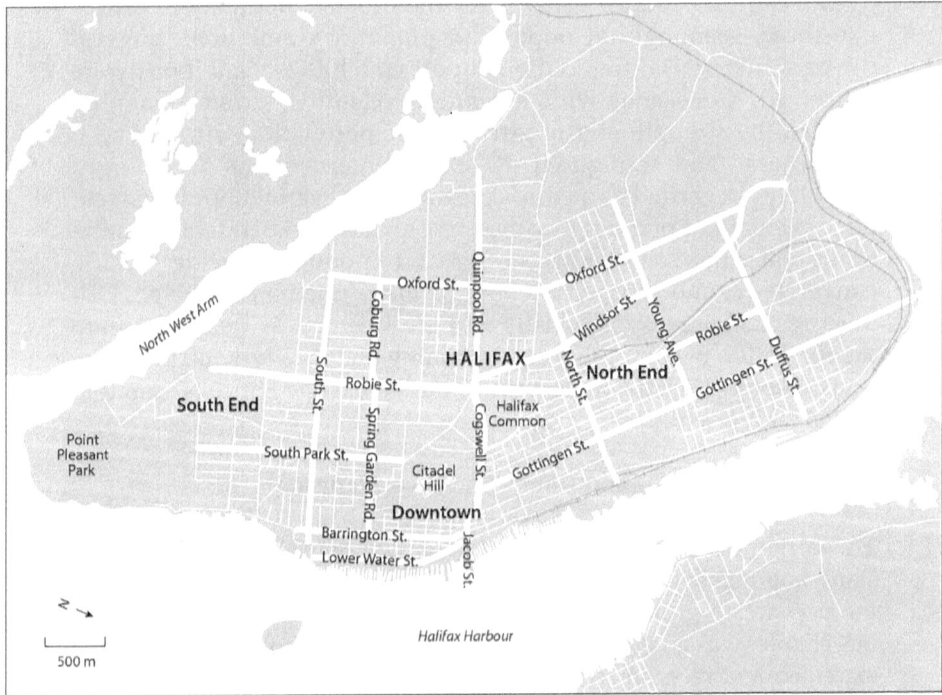

Figure 3.1 Map showing North End, South End, and downtown, 1878. Map created by Eric Leinberger.

One of the most dramatic changes to the physical terrain was the development of industrial operations in the northern section of the peninsula. Especially transformed by this development was an area known as Richmond. Spreading across an area north of the Old North End, Richmond was produced as an industrial district through the purchase and subdivision of several old farms and homesteads in the mid-nineteenth century, creating a large open space for new development. Already a favourable industrial location due to its proximity to the Halifax dockyards, the district's appeal was further enhanced by the arrival of the Intercolonial Railway in 1854.[8] Passing directly through Richmond, the new railway enabled the transportation of raw materials and finished goods between the industrial district and the rest of Canada, and was eventually attached to smaller spur lines that served particular industrial subdistricts. Tapping into this well-serviced geography was an expanding set of new industrial operations. The largest of these, the Halifax Sugar Refinery, was established in 1880 and eventually employed 120 workers in two rotations (day and night). Another important operation, the Nova Scotia Cotton Company, was established in 1882 and employed three hundred workers (mostly young women) in its best year of operation. Alongside these towering installations, a series of smaller-scale manufacturing and processing operations appeared in the last two decades of the nineteenth century, many of them located in tight-packed subdistricts along rail lines or along newly opened roads like Kept and Campbell.[9]

The development of industry in Richmond was accompanied by significant changes to the surrounding residential landscape. One of the most significant changes in this period was the migration of the city's economic elite from Brunswick Street to newly built Georgian mansions along streets like Young Avenue and Tower Road (south of the Old South End). Pleasantly removed from northern industrial expansion, the new South End residential district became, by the 1890s, the homogenously elite enclave that it has continued to be ever since.[10] The north of the city, meanwhile, densified and expanded in tandem with the growth of the city's working-class population. In the Old North End, the development of Maynard and Creighton Streets offered tight-packed saltbox homes to working-class homeowners, many of them Black migrants from the upper streets or peripheral Black communities, and spurred further commercial development along Gottingen Street. Farther north, the industrialization of the Richmond district was paralleled by the development of new residential streets and subdistricts. Though still oriented towards the working class, residential development in this area included several Georgian "estates" (generally smaller than the new South End mansions, but ornate and expensive), as well as hundreds of smaller homes that tended to offer more interior space than those in the Old North End. By the turn of the century, a residential district roughly the size of the Old North End had been established in Richmond, with a built form that signified its more prosperous working-class and sometimes middle-class inhabitants.[11]

All of these developments would have important implications for the region's Black population. The city itself, at midcentury, was home to around eight hundred Black residents, while another 1,700 lived in smaller settlements in the city's periphery.[12] Black people had, in fact, lived in Halifax since its founding in 1749. Among the first non-Indigenous arrivals to the city in that year were several enslaved Black people, the property of the city's more prosperous settlers.[13] Over the next fifty years, enslaved Black people were bought and sold at the Halifax docks, and Halifax-based merchants profited from the trading of slaves and slave-produced commodities between Nova Scotia and the British West Indies.[14] The most significant growth in the city's Black population occurred between 1783 and 1784, when Loyalist migration from the United States (following the Revolutionary War) brought to Nova Scotia roughly thirty-five thousand white Loyalists, 1,200 to 2,000 Black people enslaved by white Loyalists, and three thousand free Black Loyalists. The Black Loyalists were people who had escaped their enslavement to American rebels to fight on the British side of the Revolutionary War and were provided residence, land, and freedom in Nova Scotia by the vanquished British state. The freedom they found in Nova Scotia was always a relative one. It was constrained, among other things, by their residence in a society that still practised slavery and where the threat of the re-enslavement was ever present.[15]

Two further migrations between 1796 and 1834 augmented the Black population of the Halifax region. The first group of migrants, six hundred to nine hundred Jamaican Maroons, evaded British slavery in the Caribbean to settle in the Halifax region in 1796. Finding conditions unacceptable in their new home, most but not all of the Maroons moved on to Sierra Leone and the new city of Freetown four years after their arrival. The second group, roughly two thousand Black refugees, escaped their enslavement in the United States to fight on the British side of the War of 1812. Like the Black Loyalists, they were offered land and residence in Nova Scotia after the war, ultimately making the move in successive waves between 1812 and 1834. The arrival of these Black migrants, especially the Black Loyalists and the Black Refugees, transformed the region's demographic composition and created a social geography that is relatively to unique to Nova Scotia. Channelled largely towards uncleared rural land, these migrations resulted in a series of segregated Black communities across the province, most of them established on the periphery of existing white cities and towns. On the periphery of Halifax, the largest new Black communities were North Preston, East Preston, Hammonds Plains, and Beechville.[16]

One effect of mid-nineteenth-century urban expansion was to draw the Halifax region's outlying Black communities into the orbit of urban society. Rural subsistence had always been a challenge for these communities. The land given to them by the British state was generally rocky and ill suited to agriculture, and few Black households received anything close to the full one hundred acres that they had been promised.[17] In these circumstances, the opportunities presented by a growing Halifax economy and a more dependable network of road connections into the city would be hard to ignore. Accordingly, in the second half of the nineteenth century, Black men could increasingly be observed trekking to the city for intermittent work on the Halifax docks, in industries like shipbuilding and in a series of low-skilled trades like road building and construction. Black women, meanwhile, travelled to the city to work as washerwomen or domestic servants, or to sell a variety of fruits, vegetables, herbs, and handicrafts at the weekly Halifax market. In time, these new connections between peripheral Black communities and the urban economy compelled some residents to establish a permanent presence in the city. Among this group, roughly three hundred to four hundred settled in the Old North End along newly opened Creighton and Maynard Streets, the geographical hub of the Halifax-based Black community from the mid-nineteenth century onward. Another fifty or so settled at the northern edge of the peninsula along newly constructed Campbell Road.[18]

The Campbell Road settlement, known popularly as Africville, became the outlying Black community closest to the central city. Though the terrain on which Africville stood had likely been occupied by some Black residents as much as a century earlier, it was not until the 1840s and the opening of Campbell Road that the community became more firmly established.[19] It was in this decade that two Black men, William Brown and William Arnold, purchased fifteen acres of land at the northern tip of the peninsula from a white merchant and began to construct their homes. Other residents soon moved to the community from

Preston and Hammonds Plains, and established themselves on portions of Brown and Arnold's original fifteen acres. By 1851, Africville was home to eight Black families (54 residents), a small Baptist church, and a one-room school house. Still relatively peripheral, Africville's location allowed residents to maintain a series of rural practices like cultivating vegetable gardens; raising goats, chickens, and horses; and fishing, swimming, and conducting baptisms in abutting Bedford Basin. At the same time, the location provided easier access to waged labour in the city, and most adult residents worked intermittently in the various low-skill positions that were accessible to Black people in this period. In the latter half of the century, as industry expanded northward, opportunities for waged labour seem to have expanded modestly for Africville residents. The same process, however, tended to imperil the relatively independent and still-rural existence sought after by the community's early inhabitants.[20]

Africville was, to be sure, an economically poor community. Like Black people across the province, Africville residents lived on small tracts of relatively infertile land and could gain access only to the lowest-paid and most precarious forms of waged labour. Accordingly, the homes constructed in this period were modest in size and form, consisting mostly of narrow, two-storey saltbox homes erected with community-supplied (rather than paid) labour. And yet, the poverty and lack evinced in these details seem to have been exceeded and partially eclipsed by other aspects of life that Africville residents consistently affirmed and appreciated. One resident, referring to her youth in late nineteenth-century Africville, told an interviewer in the 1960s that she "didn't see no hard life all the time [she] was comin' up."[21] Other residents affirmed Africville's sense of community and mutual aid; the religious life of the Baptist Church; and the security and freedom made possible through homeownership, racial separation, and semirural living. "Living in Africville ... you were free to go as a kid: fishing, swimming, you name it," one resident recounted. "It was like a resort in the back of the yard."[22] Details like these, tragically, seem to have been entirely illegible to urban planners in this (and every other) period.

The city's first significant efforts to orient and improve broad-based processes of urban development began in the last two decades of the nineteenth century. The development of the city, until this point, had been a largely private affair. Its major products, new homes and businesses, appeared on privately owned land, and nearly all important decisions pertaining to this development were made by private builders and property owners. As new homes and businesses spread across the landscape, then, the city was little more than an observer of this process. It made little attempt to influence the forces that were rapidly remaking the city's industrial, commercial, and residential terrain. The city's financial and technical investments in new urban infrastructure, moreover, were largely confined to the design and construction of new roadways – an *enablement* to new development, but not a significant influence on its form or social effects. Broader infrastructural investments were absent: the city's streets and sidewalks at midcentury remained unpaved (and thus, a dusty or soupy mess, depending on the season); sewerage remained a distant dream; and potable water still needed to be retrieved by hand from area reservoirs.[23] The mid-nineteenth-century city, reminisced Halifax mayor James Hamilton in 1901, "could well afford to have provided itself with a sewerage system and all the modern features of ... utility and adornment" but was sadly "blind to its opportunities."[24] This situation would change rather dramatically over the next fifty years.

The first infrastructural "opportunity" to be seized by the city was the construction of underground sewers and water mains. A movement in this direction began, somewhat provisionally, in the 1880s, but the construction remained eminently slow throughout this decade. Though citizens had reportedly been "aroused as to the necessity of proper sanitation," the prevailing Sewerage Act required benefiting property owners to pay a portion of the installation costs up front, and few could afford do so.[25] This obstacle was attenuated in 1890, when the city finally convinced the provincial legislature to allow it to issue an unprecedented $400,000 in municipal bonds. With money to spare, the city could now afford to bill property owners for their portion of the installation costs over a ten-year period and proceeded, between 1890 and 1889, to install an unprecedented (for Halifax) 206 block-length sewers.[26] In 1901, the pace of sewer construction received a further boost when the municipal board of health was authorized to order the installation of sewer connections to any Halifax home when it was deemed to be "in the interest of public health." Henceforth, as Deputy Mayor Robert MacIlreith remarked (begrudgingly) that year, local residents would have the right to "have water and sewerage extended to their houses, in no matter how out-of-the-way place they may locate them."[27] The new board of health mandate and another $150,000 municipal-bond issue in 1903 enabled the construction of a further seventy-eight block-length sewers between 1901 and 1908.[28]

As the board of health's involvement suggests, the construction of sewers and water mains was viewed primarily as a public-health measure. It shared, in this sense, the basic aim of the planning initiatives that I discussed in the previous chapter. And yet, there are important differences between initiatives like the model tenements and the construction of infrastructure like sewers and water mains. The former, for one thing, is a targeted and thorough intervention; its aim is to thoroughly remake and ultimately normalize the lives and living conditions of particular individuals. The construction of sewers and water mains, in contrast, is a dispersed and partial intervention; its aim is to attenuate (rather than eliminate) health-related pathologies at the population-wide (rather than individual) level. These subtle differences are described by Foucault as the markers of two slightly different configurations of knowledge and power. The first, dubbed "disciplinary" power, focuses on the lives of discrete individuals and aims to achieve a thorough physical and behavioural normalization. The second, dubbed "biopolitical" power, focuses on the lives of broad-based aggregates like "populations" or "nations" and circulates through interventions that are more dispersed (in their application) and more modest (in the expected effects).[29] The construction of sewers and water mains, like the other interventions that I examine in this chapter, exhibited the broad-based outlook of biopolitics more than the narrow gaze of disciplinary power.

Providing orientation to these new interventions was the emergence of new forms of knowledge that rendered broad-based processes and characteristics intelligible for the first time. Problems of population-wide ill health and disease, invisible to the naked eye, were increasingly discernible in this period through relatively abstract, statistical forms of knowledge, like annual "death rate" statistics. Relying on such statistics, one city official described Halifax's public-health problem in 1906 as a specific deviation from the nation-wide "normal." The annual death rate, he told the public, was four hundred units "higher than it should be in this favoured locality."[30] The problem evoked here, it should be clear, was not the condition of particular individuals in relation to an individual norm, but the condition of the overall population in relation to a national average (taken to be the "norm"). The problem, moreover, was not that specific individuals had died or become unhealthy, but that an abnormal *rate* of ill health and death had appeared within a measurable city-wide aggregate. It was a problem of this kind that sewers and water mains were intended to solve. The aim of such infrastructure was not to normalize the lives of particular individuals but simply to *reduce* the prevalence of broadly experienced risks to the overall population. The aim, as one city official put it, was to take meaningful steps "toward safety" through the "removal of sources of danger to the community."[31] Similar forms of knowledge and similar ambitions would underpin each of the planning initiatives that I discuss in this chapter.

Alongside the installation of sewers and water mains, the city's efforts to shape urban development in this period eventually included more aesthetic measures, like the paving of streets and sidewalks and the installation of electric street lighting. The city's efforts in this regard began in the late 1890s, when it ramped up investments in paving materials and equipment. By 1905, these efforts made it possible to announce that the city's "more important business streets" and "most travelled sidewalks" were fully paved.[32] The city's investments in electric street lighting expanded roughly in tandem, greatly transforming the experience of city streets that had previously been either dimly illuminated (by gas lamps) or not illuminated at all. The purpose of surface paving and street lighting was described in various ways but most often centred on their contribution to "public convenience." A concept that has since fallen out of usage, "convenience" referred in this context to spatial conditions that were believed to promote positive experiences among the population, experiences that city officials variously described in terms of "agreeableness," "contentedness," or simply "happiness." At its most basic level, a positive experience could arise from simply being able to walk from one place to another without sinking into the mud or kicking up dust. But the sought-after experience was related, as well, to the intangible aesthetic or visual impression created by a network of well-maintained and well-lit streets.[33]

The promotion of a happy or contented form of life had appeared among the priorities of modern states since the seventeenth century, and there were few issues as important to the early planning profession in North America and Western Europe.[34] In Halifax, it gained attention, initially, as a potential response to intensifying political discontent in the late 1890s. As Mayor Hamilton observed in 1899, several years of increased municipal spending, borrowing, and taxation had sowed dissatisfaction among many local residents. These residents questioned, he explained, not just whether particular politicians ought to be re-elected, but also whether municipal government itself was perhaps "too expensive an institution."[35] The creation of increased "convenience" through investments in surface paving and electric street lighting were (somewhat ironically, given the cost) one of the most significant steps that the city took to repair the shattered confidence of the citizenry. City streets, Mayor Adam Crosby explained in 1902, were "constantly under the public eye," and if the city could simply provide "good streets [and] good sidewalks," then the citizens "would not have much reason to complain [about city government]."[36]

A few years later, the city discovered that investments in public convenience could do more than just please existing residents: they could also help to attract new ones. For Robert MacIlreith, mayor of Halifax from 1906 to 1908, the "growth of the city" was the foremost objective. The achievement of this objective, he reasoned, depended on making the city "an agreeable place to live in and do business in," and this required, more than anything, the creation of more pleasant and convenient streets.[37] Drawing a clear connection between convenient public spaces and a growing population, MacIlreith pushed through a $100,000 program of surface paving and street-light installation during his first year as mayor. Leaving office in 1908, he was able to report that great "progress [had] been made" in these respects.[38]

The ultimate effect of the city's new planning initiatives, from the installation of sewers to the paving of streets, was to constitute a new relationship between the municipal state and local residents. These interventions brought the state closer to the lives of the population; they made the state a factor in these lives, both public and private. Henceforth, the question of whether a person remained healthy or fell ill, or whether a person's life was agreeable or disagreeable, was partly a function of the state and the urban planning practices it deployed. The interventions of the board of health discussed in the previous chapter certainly created such a connection for particular individuals (especially the residents of the city's slums). The new infrastructure investments, in contrast, established such a connection on a much broader scale. State power would now be connected to the lives of the overall population (rather than just particular individuals) and would capitalize upon this connection through the management of an expansive urban terrain (rather than just particular homes). Integral to this new form of power, the power of comprehensive planning itself, was the recognition that the condition of the population was bound up with the condition of urban space. Planning, consequently, could be seen not only as a *potential* effect on people's lives but also as a necessary effect on these lives. From now on, planning interventions undertaken or not undertaken could be recognized as having life-altering – either life-improving or life-harming – consequences.[39]

While the city's attention to the quality of people's lives certainly expanded in this period, it was also subject to certain limits. The construction of sewers and water mains, for example, slowed in the first decade of the twentieth century, and not because all areas had received these services. On the surface, the slowdown was the result of straightforward financial calculations. Citizens, as I noted, expressed their displeasure with increasing municipal spending, borrowing, and taxation in the 1890s, and the merits of further infrastructure investments were constantly debated from this point forward. But the very conception of these interventions also seems to have validated a potential slowdown in their provision. To the extent that the infrastructure was meant to address aggregate-level public-health metrics – especially metrics like the annual death rate – the required amount of this infrastructure would tend to remain, at best, an open question. Concretely, it would likely be possible to eliminate "excess death," to attenuate the overall rate of death, without providing sewers and water mains to every residential dwelling in the city.

The paving of streets and sidewalks and the installation of electric street lighting were subject to similar limitations. Mayor MacIlreith's passion for these additions to "public convenience," for example, seems to have waned towards the northern end of the Halifax peninsula, where his rival Adam Crosby, returned to the mayorship in 1908, remarked that it was "frequently very difficult to get from one house to another without going ankle-deep in the soft mud on the sidewalks."[40] Once again, these limitations were related not just to financial calculations but also to the conception of the interventions themselves. Notably, the "public" in the conception of "public convenience" clearly referred to something less than the full population of the city. Indeed, the "public" or "public interest" was consistently invoked in this period in relation to a second element within the population, a "particular" or "proprietary" interest that, in contrast to the public interest, needed to be left unheeded. As Mayor Alexander Stephen explained in 1897, the interests of the "public" needed to be carefully distinguished from those of "particular class[es] or bod[ies]," and it was only by isolating and dismissing the latter that "the true interests of the city" could be served.[41] This public-proprietary binary, common to public discussions in reform-era North American cities, marked a clear division within the population. Improving "public convenience," consequently, did not mean improving the lives of all residents. It required, in fact, that a boundary be drawn and that some residents' lives be purposely left unserved, inconvenient, and less than agreeable.

The limitations of these planning interventions were particularly evident in the community of Africville. Located within city limits, Africville was situated somewhere outside the stated aims of the nascent comprehensive planning regime. The sewage system that the city significantly expanded between 1890 and 1910, for example, never reached the homes of Africville – in this period or ever. The board of health's mandate to order sewer construction when it was "in the interest of the public health" was consistently ignored when it came to this community. Running water, which citizens of Halifax were able to expect in their homes, "no matter how out-of-the-way ... they may locate them," was similarly absent in Africville.[42] Rather than running water, the city's efforts in Africville were limited to modest assistance with the construction of shallow well in 1852 (an action taken in response to petitions from the residents), as well as assistance with the repairing of this ill-functioning water source later on.[43] Surface pavement and street lighting were consistently withheld in Africville as well. Indeed, the community eventually came to be known precisely by its absence of pavement and associated conveniences: "Where the road ends," it was often said, "there's Africville."[44]

While the basics of sanitation and convenience were withheld from Africville, this is not to say that planning was *absent* from the area. In tandem with its evident failure to *improve* living conditions in Africville, planning was simultaneously taking actions that would make conditions worse. This negative effect was brought about, principally, through the regulation of land use. From the 1850s onward, the most undesirable and noxious facilities in the city had a tendency to be sited on Africville's doorstep. In the 1850s, a prison and a "night soil" deposit pit were constructed in the area by the city. In the 1870s, a whole series of new industries were added to the surrounding landscape (an oil-plant-storage facility, a bone mill, a cotton factory, two slaughterhouses, a tar factory, a coal-handling facility, and a foundry). In the same decade, the city constructed an infectious diseases hospital at the edge of Africville, and in 1903, the city added a trachoma hospital on a plateau overlooking the community. As might be expected, these facilities fouled the air, contaminated the water table, and nourished an expanding horde of rodents. At least some of these land-use decisions were made, importantly, at a time when the city believed that planning should seek to improve people's conditions of life. In a seeming paradox that I examine below, this is precisely the objective that some of these decisions were meant to achieve.[45]

The effects of planning in Africville could certainly be observed in the condition of the material environment. They could be observed in sanitation facilities not provided or in the stream of human waste passing from the trachoma hospital and straight through the community. They could also be discerned, however, in the lives that depended on this environment. Without sewers or running water, Africville residents were left to rely on outdoor toilets and shallow makeshift wells that habitually ran dry in the summer and that incorporated harmful contaminants from the ever-degrading water table. As a result, illnesses that were prudently kept at bay in the rest of Halifax remained a threat in Africville well into the twentieth century. In the 1960s, with sewers and running water still not installed, a city official speculated that only the tenacity of Africville residents' own immune systems had staved off major outbreaks of disease. Meanwhile, enduringly unpaved roads (along with infrequent snow ploughing) could make it exceptionally "inconvenient" to move around in Africville and, especially, to come and go from it. In the spring thaw, the "ankle-deep ... soft mud" that city officials had specifically identified as a problem in the North End certainly prevailed in Africville. Due to excess water, the road leading into the community would break apart, vehicular transportation (if not pedestrian) would become impossible, and many food supplies, health services, and other basics of life would become effectively unavailable.[46]

If the city was undisturbed by conditions in Africville, it was not due to a lack of knowledge. As early as 1852, representatives from Africville met with city officials to apprise them of problematic conditions in the community and demand municipal services that were already available to other city residents (see *figure* 3.2). The city refused these demands in all but two cases, agreeing to install a community well in 1852 and agreeing to repair the well in 1902. At least two of the land-use decisions that badly impacted life in Africville, moreover, were calculated precisely to avoid such impacts elsewhere. The new trachoma hospital, for example, was originally slated to be built in another location, several kilometres from Africville. However, residents near this location raised concerns about the effects of the hospital on their health and well-being. The city saw these concerns as reasonable – meaning, it agreed the hospital was dangerous – and switched the location to Africville.[47]

In these and other ways, planning in Africville entailed an inversion of its ambitions elsewhere in the city, an inversion that often allowed its broader ambitions to be achieved. To protect public health, planning devastated Africville's health. To maximize public convenience, planning maintained and worsened Africville's inconveniences. The health threats and inconveniences imposed upon Africville were thus integral to early comprehensive planning. No mere oversight, they were largely a calculated means to a greater end: the promotion of a healthier, happier life for a "city" or "population" within which the lives of Africville residents figured nowhere.

Taxation, Town Planning, and "Economic" Land Use

As the construction of sewers, water mains, and other infrastructure began to stall in the early 1900s, a second set of planning interventions, more economic in their objectives, began to occupy the attention of certain city officials and civil-society organizations. Calls for this type of intervention were first expressed in Halifax at a relatively mundane forum on municipal taxation in 1901. The forum was convened by City Hall at the prodding of the Halifax Board of Trade, which had been campaigning for significant changes to municipal taxation since the early 1890s. In the course of the three-day forum, several board of trade members advanced the argument that certain elements of the prevailing system of taxation were unjust to local businesses, as well as detrimental to the growth and prosperity of the city. The taxing of "personal property" (e.g., stock-in-trade and machinery) and "improvements" (e.g., buildings) was singled out as a problem. These forms of wealth, board members argued, were the product of individual initiative (and thus, unjustly taxed), as well as fundamental to the economic competitiveness and overall prosperity of the city. The taxing of land, in contrast, was seen as legitimate. This form of wealth, board members argued, was an *effect* of others' initiative and wealth-creating activities (and thus, justly recuperated through taxation), as well as an impediment to economic competitiveness and city-wide prosperity. On the basis of this analysis, the board members introduced and supported a rather novel tax reform: the replacement of all existing municipal taxes with a "single tax" on land values.[48]

The board's analysis in the 1901 public forum relied on a particular perspective on urban land that was new to public discussions in Halifax but relatively well established in political-economic theory. The perspective is attributable, first and foremost, to the English political

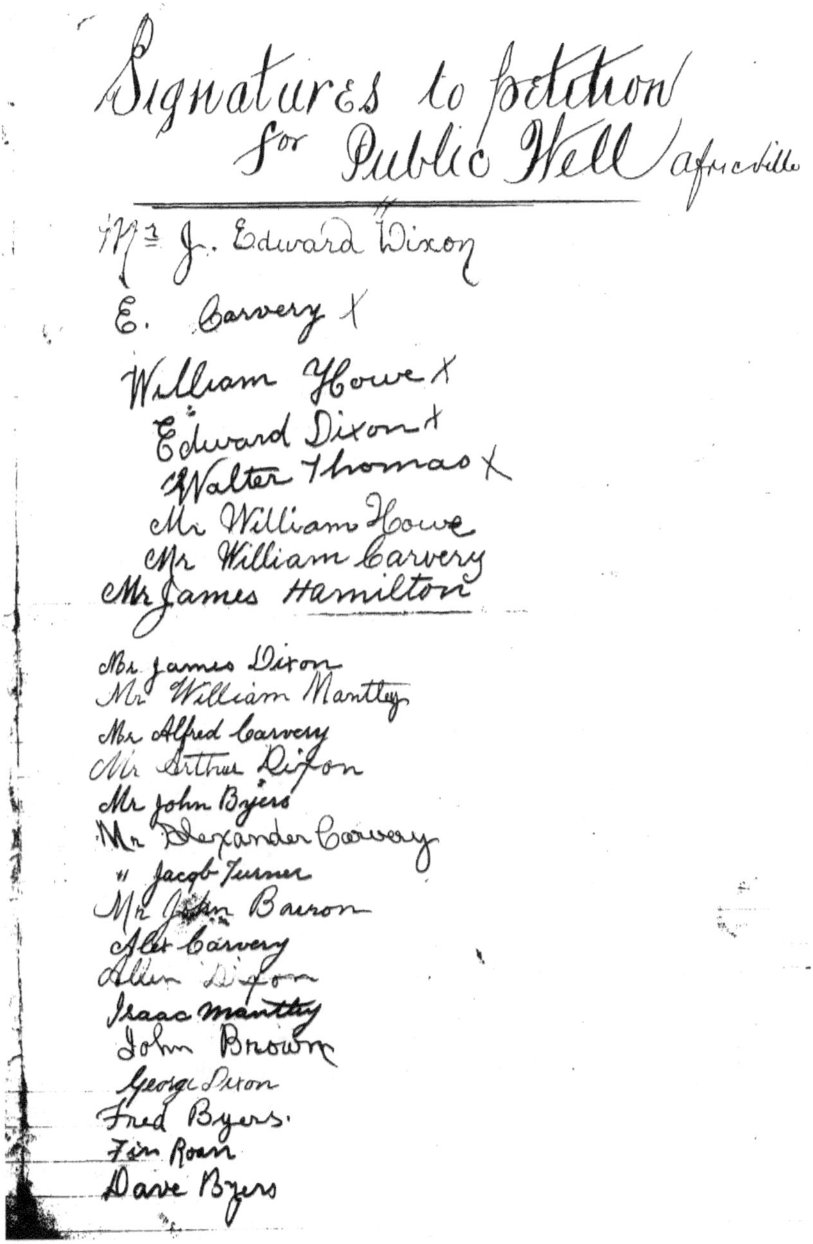

Signatures to petition
for Public Well Africville

Mr J. Edward Dixon
E. Carvery X
William Howe X
Edward Dixon X
Walter Thomas X
Mr William Howe
Mr William Carvery
Mr James Hamilton

Mr James Dixon
Mr William Mantley
Mr Alfred Carvery
Mr Arthur Dixon
Mr John Byers
Mr Alexander Carvery
" Jacob Turner
Mr John Barron
Alex Carvery
Allen Dixon
Isaac Mantley
John Brown
George Dixon
Fred Byers.
Tim Roan
Dave Byers

Figure 3.2 Africville petition for community well, 1909. Halifax, City Council submissions, HRMA, RG 25-102-1B, 1901–23, 363. Image courtesy of HRMA.

economist David Ricardo. Ricardo's seminal 1817 *On the Principles of Political Economy and Taxation* is perhaps best known for its development of the "labour theory of value," but its arguments about land demand attention as well. Departing from previous thinkers, Ricardo defined "land" in purely static, unalterable terms. Land, for him, referred to nothing more than "the original and indestructible powers of the soil."[49] Any changes in these "powers," any alteration in the land's fertility or productivity, needed to be categorized as an "improvement" rather than a change to the land itself. Combined with Ricardo's labour theory of value, this static definition of the land effectively eliminated its potential role in the creation of economic value, a role that earlier thinkers had sometimes minimized but never fully abolished. Payments for the use of land were thus to be considered, strictly and entirely, a form of "rent" rather than value-linked "profit." Any increase in rent, moreover, needed to be seen as a by-product of other, more productive activities (i.e., labour), as well as a potential *impediment* to these activities. Higher land rents, in other words, could create disincentives or obstacles to the development of optimal improvements and the pursuit of value-creating activities more generally.[50]

Ricardo's perspective on land most often entered political discussions in North American cities through the derivative work of the American political economist and reformer Henry George. George's seminal 1879 work, *Progress and Poverty*, explicitly acknowledges its debt to Ricardo and seeks to develop policy reforms appropriate to the problems that the older theorist outlined.[51] Like Ricardo, George describes land as inert and non-value creating, and singles out land speculation as an especially pernicious and parasitic activity. Indeed, George's political project and political career (he ran for mayor of New York City in 1886 and 1897) was largely founded on the premise that land speculation and landlordism were the primary ills of capitalist society, and that both capitalists and workers would benefit from their elimination. The solution to these ills, for George, was straightforward. The introduction of a "single tax" on land values, he asserted, would tend to realign the incentive structure of the domestic economy to the benefit of "the community as a whole."[52] Pernicious activities like land speculation, heavily taxed, would instantly become more costly and would tend to be eliminated over time. Meanwhile, a whole range of collectively beneficial activities like the improvement of bare or underimproved land would become less costly, more viable, and ultimately more profligate. George's isolation of a single obstacle to community-wide progress, an enemy to capitalists and workers alike, gave his thinking widespread appeal, and Halifax became one of many North Atlantic cities to give his views a public hearing.[53]

The efforts of the Halifax Board of Trade during the 1901 forum on taxation had little effect in the short term. The city, judging the single tax a "purely academic" subject, refused to recognize the merits of this (or any other) tax reform and vowed instead to remain with the prevailing tax regime.[54] These efforts were significant, nevertheless, in introducing a new perspective on taxation to the Halifax public, and the ensuing years witnessed expanding support for the single-tax idea and a broadening conception of its potential benefits. A series of editorials in the *Evening Mail* between 1910 and 1912 advocated the single tax on the grounds that it would force landowners either to improve the land or to sell it to someone who would, and therefore "throw open" the multifaceted economic opportunities that "the earth offers to man."[55] Other supporters, like Nova Scotia Technical College president Frederick Sexton and the Local Council of Women, supported the single tax on the basis of its potential effects on slum housing and thus upon the health and morality of low-income tenants. Pointing to the failure of Armitage's model tenements plan to eradicate the city's slums, Sexton advocated the single tax in 1912 on the premise that it would "do away with many of them [the city's slums]" through rather different means.[56] For these supporters, evidently, the single tax was not simply a salutary means of collecting public funds but a socially beneficial intervention in local land use and development as well.

The city, at last, came to appreciate the logic, if not the precise form, of the single tax. After extensive deliberations, the city introduced several important reforms to its tax system between 1914 and 1916. The long-criticized tax on "personal property" (e.g., stock-in-trade and machinery) was finally discarded at this point. More importantly, the existing tax on "real property" was divided into two differently taxed elements: land and improvements. The tax on improvements, while not wholly eliminated, was scheduled to remain at a fixed rate over time, whereas the tax on land would be allowed to expand in proportion to the city's increasing expenses. The rationale for this reform, penned by the city's chief solicitor Frederick Bell, reflected the political-economic analysis of urban land that had gained traction in Halifax over the previous fifteen years. The weighting of taxation towards land values, Bell wrote in 1916, would tend to summon municipal revenues from the most justifiable of sources, a form of individually held wealth that "the

City itself" rather than individuals "ha[d] created." As an added bonus, this reform would tend to induce a continually better form of land use in the city and therefore "benefit the community." As taxes on land values increased, the cost of land would be "cheapen[ed]," the owners of land would be "pressur[ed]" to improve it or to sell it, and a widely beneficial process of building, renovating, and property development would be "promot[ed]."[57]

Conceived in these terms, the new land tax can be placed alongside earlier efforts to act upon the population through spatial means. The aim, in this case, was to augment the prosperity of the population through the promotion of better land uses – meaning, in effect, the penalization of underimproved land and the promotion of ever-greater improvement across the urban terrain. Woven through these efforts, importantly, was a particular and particularly consequential contradiction: the well-being of the population could, it seems, be secured through interventions that observably harmed certain members of this population (e.g., landowners). For the city, this contradiction was resolved rather straightforwardly. Being that community-wide activities (not the actions of individual landowners) produced the value of urban land, the city had the right to manage urban land in the interest of the entire community. "The city," suggested Frederick Bell in his explanation of the 1916 land tax, "may be regarded as a huge combination of a market and apartment house," in which a business or household "pays for the space occupied" through taxation.[58] Property owners, Bell's explanation suggests, had become mere tenants in an essentially city-owned edifice. The efficient management of this edifice, in the interest of the population as a whole, was now the city's official right and duty.

The most enduring effect of the 1914–16 tax reforms was perhaps the new forms of state knowledge that it called into being. In order to implement the new tax regime, the city's tax assessors needed to be able to prize apart the ostensibly separate values of land and improvements, two forms of personal wealth that had thus far been assessed as an undifferentiated whole ("real property"). To enable this kind of assessment, the city introduced a complex system of materials and practices between 1916 and 1918 that had been developed and implemented elsewhere in North America by the George-inspired property assessor William Somers. Implemented at a cost of $2,000 – three times the annual salary of a city assessor – the new system was valued primarily for the intelligibility that it brought to once-indiscernible phenomena: the hypothetical market values of two objects (land and improvements) that were seldom bought or sold on their own. This new knowledge, necessary for tax purposes, would soon provide a concrete and seemingly objective input to broader discussions of urban land use, both current and optimal. As I discuss below, these discussions tended to carry forward the particular conceptions of land and improvements that underwrote arguments for their separate taxation. Land was a source of worry. Improvements, and ever-further improvements, were an inherent good. The future of the city's poor and poorly improved areas, including Africville, would ultimately be shaped by this logic and the forms of state knowledge that rendered it actionable.[59]

The adoption of new taxes on urban land was paralleled by the emergence of other land-related initiatives that relied on roughly the same political-economic logic. These initiatives were linked, most immediately, to long-time city engineer Francis Doane. Hired into this position in 1892, Doane's responsibilities tended increasingly to exceed those of a contemporary civil engineer. In the absence of a formal urban planning department, Doane served as the city's de facto planner from his initial hiring until 1916, when this title was finally rendered official. Throughout this period, Doane was chiefly responsible for overseeing the distribution of streets, sewers, and water mains on the Official Plan. Other tasks included handling issues like the establishment of public parks, the proper storage of garbage, the upkeep of private lawns, the installation of ornamental street lighting, and the remaking of certain downtown streets into aesthetically pleasing boulevards. Absent from this work, notably, was any explicit attention to the economic characteristics of the urban terrain – its actual and potential contribution to value creation and city-wide prosperity. This changed in 1914, after Doane represented the city at the country's first National Town Planning Conference in Toronto and had the first of a series of influential encounters with the British-born urban planner Thomas Adams.[60]

The 1914 Town Planning Conference, attended by Doane and sixty other representatives of Canadian municipalities, was organized and funded by the federal Commission of Conservation. The latter was a relatively short-lived but influential public institution that aimed to bring about a more "efficient" form of resource use in Canada, as well as a more healthy, long-living, and productive national population. In the curious formulation of the commission, both natural resources and human beings (dubbed "human resources") could be grouped under the category of "life," and the commission's primary role was to ensure the efficient management of life in this expansive sense. Within this mandate, urban land assumed an important place. Seen as a natural resource that needed to be used efficiently, land was also seen as a major influence on the health, longevity, and productivity of urban populations. To improve the management of urban land, the commission eventually lured Thomas Adams to Canada to provide leadership to the nascent field of urban (or "town") planning. Adams's keynote lecture at the 1914 conference, one of his first tasks with the commission, provided a much-appreciated introduction to his thinking for many municipal representatives. Later, from 1915 to 1921, Adams served as the commission's Advisor on Town Planning, a position that saw him visiting and disbursing on-the-ground advice in many Canadian cities, including Halifax.[61]

Adams's foremost contribution to planning in Canadian cities was the attention he brought to the "economic" or "efficient" use of urban land. The notion of "economic" land use, for Adams, was rooted in the same political-economic theories that underpinned arguments for the single tax and may, in fact, have been borrowed directly from Henry George.[62] Like George, Adams saw bare and underimproved land as an impediment to the overall progress and prosperity of the city. Such a condition, Adams argued, tied up scarce capital in an unproductive investment, restricted the supply of housing and business premises, and generally increased the cost of living and doing business in a city. Improvements to land, in contrast, were a boon to "the community as a whole," and it was the presence of sufficient improvements that indicated, for Adams, that the most "economic" use of the land had been achieved.[63] Consistent with the aims of the commission, Adams was concerned less with the promotion of *perfectly* economic land use than with the eradication of the most grievous departures from this standard. Bare land and rundown or poorly built structures were the problem to be addressed; they constituted, as Adams put it, a "condition of property injurious to life."[64] As these descriptions suggest, there was more than just economic value and prosperity at stake for Adams in the use of urban land. It was the overall condition of human life, including "the health and contentment of citizens," that seemed to be impaired by uneconomic land uses, and it was in service of this broader end that Adams invited planners to look critically at prevailing land uses.[65]

Like George's argument for the single tax, Adams's conception of economic land use scripted privately owned land as a population-wide concern and a terrain, therefore, ripe for state intervention. One of the effects of this view was to broaden the legitimate scope of urban planning, which had thus far been constrained by the assumed sacredness and "privateness" of individual property rights. Planned alterations to privately owned land, in the prevailing view, would violate the rights that the state was pledged and often founded to protect.[66] The idea that the use of privately owned land could be "injurious to life" or an impairment to the overall "health and contentment" of the citizens could thus release planning from its previous bonds and carry its power across the entire urban terrain, public and private. Essential to this broader purview, importantly, was the articulation of a social aggregate – "life" or "the community" – whose well-being seemed to stand above or against that of particular individuals. Like the single tax, in other words, Adams's promotion of community-wide "health," "contentment," and "prosperity" seems to have been compatible with actions that foreseeably impaired the lives of particular community members. Concretely, in cases where certain individuals happened to own or live upon underimproved land, their prevailing health, contentment, or prosperity could be strategically disrupted, even sacrificed, in the pursuit of the more "economic" land use upon which the city's *overall* well-being seemed to depend.

Indeed, among the various measures that Adams outlined to promote the most economic use of land, some of them would clearly sacrifice the land's immediate impact upon people's lives to achieve favourable city-wide outcomes. Rather ominously, Adams recommended that infrastructure like sewers, running water, and surface paving be withheld from areas of underimproved land.[67] While he appears to have considered such measures a penalty to selfish landlords – a social class that Adams, like George, explicitly denigrated – they could just as easily apply to the impoverished owners of low-value housing, while the ultimate effects of the measures could easily spread to the *tenants* of underimproved premises. Like George's single tax, therefore, Adams's brand of urban planning seems to inscribe an epistemic division between the overall population (that planning is meant to serve) and particular individuals (whose interests, or lives, planning may need to impair in the service of the overall population). Precisely how this division would be drawn in practice remains an open and essential question, in Halifax and every other city that Adams advised in this period.

Adams's lecture at the National Town Planning Conference seems to have left an enduring impression on Halifax's Francis Doane. Upon his return to Halifax after the conference, Doane delivered a lengthy address to city council in which he set out the "higher ideals" that he had learned to associate with urban planning practices. More than just laying out streets or building "expensive boulevards and parks available only for the rich," Doane explained, planning assured the "economy" of urban processes – meaning, more than anything, the economic use of urban land. The latter, as Adams had taught him, was not the primary *end* of planning but rather the means through which its broader and multifaceted ends could be achieved. In describing these broader ends, Doane summarized both the message of the Town Planning Conference and the orientation of the planning interventions that Halifax had slowly introduced over the previous twenty-five years. "The health of the people," Doane announced, "is [planning's] first care, convenience next, with economy considered all·through."[68] In this statement, a whole series of planning objectives and concerns had finally come into unison. A comprehensive form of planning was now conceivable. Public health and convenience would remain important planning concerns, and it would sometimes be possible to address them individually (e.g., through the construction of sewers or sidewalks). Woven "all through" these concerns, however, would be the underlying issue of economic land use, the promotion of which was fundamental not just to population-wide prosperity but also to the city's overall health and contentment.

The combined effect of the 1914–16 tax reforms and Francis Doane's lecture to city council was to officialize a set of ideas about urban land that had gradually gained acceptance over the previous fifteen years. With the "improvement" or "economic use" of land now firmly hitched to the overall well-being of the community, new questions would need to be addressed in urban planning deliberations. Where had the land been improved? Where had it not been? What could be done to protect the improvements that had already been added to the landscape? What could be done to promote improvement in the future? What, most importantly, could be done in cases of unimproved or underimproved land? These questions found a partial answer in the 1914–16 tax reforms: bare and underimproved land existed throughout the city, and it would simply be penalized, its owners "pressured" to improve it or to sell it, through taxation. They found another answer in Doane's first two actions after the National Town Planning Conference. The first action was to establish the city's elite South End as an exclusively residential zone.[69] Through this action, an extension of the zoning protection provided to a single South End street in 1907, the city's highest-value residential properties would be protected from the encroachment of value- and health-impairing industrial and commercial land uses. Doane's second action was to craft the first official plan to seize and redevelop the entirety of Africville.

The plan to redevelop Africville, announced in 1915, was the culmination of a series of smaller actions that contravened the increasingly predominant view of urban land and its significance to the population. Oral histories, for example, recount that the city stopped granting building permits to Africville property owners sometime in the early twentieth century.[70] The promotion of improvement, a population-ameliorating priority elsewhere in the city, was evidently inverted when it came to the land and population of Africville. A similar contradiction structured the city's expanding efforts to protect the wealth and health of the population through land-use zoning. Residential-only zoning, a recognized priority in the South End, was never offered to the homes and residents of Africville, and it was treated as a de facto industrial zone from the late nineteenth century until 1947, when this status was rendered official.[71] Precluded from improving their land and increasingly surrounded by value-destroying industrial operations, Africville residents would see their land forcibly degraded by a planning regime that saw "improvement" as the basis of the population's health, convenience, and prosperity. The land tax, in this context, simply penalized a situation Africville residents had no power to change. No amount of financial "pressure" (as Solicitor Bell described it) could induce a process of improvement that the state had precluded Africville residents from taking.

One of the city's most ambitious efforts to improve the use of urban land was, in fact, the plan to redevelop Africville. The plan in question was submitted to city council in September 1915 by Francis Doane. The submission states: "The Africville portion of Campbell Road will always be an industrial district and it is desirable that industrial operations be assisted in any way that is not prejudicial to the interests of the public [i.e., in this case, Africville residents]; in fact, we may be obliged in the future to consider the interests of industry first."[72] The vision conjured in the plan, a vision of industry taking root in the place of Africville homes, was clearly compelling to city council. The latter accepted Doane's submission without debate and added that the plan's potential "advantages for the City" were sufficient enough to justify using the available municipal legislation to "expropriate part of the whole of the property known as Africville."[73] A year later, Doane reaffirmed the earlier proposal, writing: "In the near future, all property in this district [Africville] will be required for industrial purposes, and it will be abandoned as a residential district."[74] This submission, too, was accepted by city council without debate.

The 1915 plan, though its advice would remain unfulfilled in the short term, provides a relatively clear view of the constitutive underside of this period's consolidating planning imperatives. The plan, for one thing, advanced the first coherent, rational argument for the seizure and redevelopment of Africville in its entirety. This argument, importantly, would become increasingly familiar in the years following its initial formulation and would ultimately be reprised in the discussions that brought an end to Africville in the 1960s. Bits and pieces of Africville had, of course, been regarded as seizable before 1915. In 1853, the Nova Scotia Railway Company extended tracks across the edge of Africville and expropriated several properties in the process. This theft of land was effectively sanctioned by the city in its stubborn failure to intervene and in its refusal, years later, to hear the petitions of dispossessed residents.[75] Later, in 1907, a large section of Africville land was nearly expropriated by the city to provide a setting for an Imperial Oil refinery. It was only the company's decision to establish the refinery across the harbour in Dartmouth that thwarted the expropriation.[76] The 1915 plan, however, proposed something different. It called for the seizure of the entirety of Africville, and it called for the state (rather than private businesses) to initiate and carry through this wholesale erasure.

Another important and historically unprecedented aspect of the 1915 plan was its articulation of the benefits that could be derived from the seizure and redevelopment of Africville land. The plan, like Henry George's single tax and Thomas Adams's promotion of economic land use, was expected to provide "advantages for the City," even as it would entail significant disadvantages for particular residents. A forcible division was thus inscribed between the population or city "as a whole" (whose well-being planning aimed to enhance) and the various individuals whose well-being would be dramatically undermined – indeed, consciously "abandoned." This particular formulation of population-wide benefits and individually endured costs was new to the planning-related discussions of this period, and its entry into the sphere of articulability would significantly shape the short- and long-term situation of Africville residents. When an actually implemented 1962 plan advised that Africville be demolished to make way for "industry" and asserted that "the economic wellbeing of [the] community depend[ed]" on such an action, it essentially reiterated the deformed calculation of benefits and costs that first appeared in public discussions in the 1910s.[77]

And what, precisely, were these costs? The actual impacts of the 1915 plan on the residents of Africville clearly need to be assessed in relation to the (literally) vital importance that the city had come to ascribe to urban space. The city, as I suggested above, had come to regard urban space not just as an expression of state territoriality, individual property rights, or even property value, but as the fundamental and indispensable basis of a healthy, convenient, and prosperous life. Approached from this perspective, the 1915 plan – according to the city's own view of things – proposed not simply to expropriate land or disregard certain political interests but also to withdraw one of the major bases of human life, to revoke what it had come to see as *living conditions*. Concretely, the fulfilment of the plan would effectively sever Africville residents from the homes and surrounding material conditions that served to support and uphold their existence. The plan would do so, moreover, at a time when securing alternative living arrangements in the city was extremely unlikely (as both Francis Doane and city council would have known). A prevailing housing shortage in the city, already recognized as acute in 1909, had become considerably worse in 1914 with the onset of the Great War and the arrival in Halifax of military personnel far too numerous to house. Hundreds of soldiers, unable to secure accommodations in the city, were housed in tents on the Halifax Common, a few blocks from City Hall. It is hard to imagine displaced Africville residents faring any better.

Ultimately, the 1915 plan would have significant effects on the lives of Africville residents, even in the decades-long interval before its actual implementation in the 1960s. The very *slating* of Africville for redevelopment seems, in fact, to have introduced a new and compelling rationale against the undertaking of any positive planning interventions in the community. In the period between the 1915 plan and the actual destruction of Africville, the area was sealed off from any infrastructure improvements that the city might eventually have considered appropriate to provide and that were indeed provided to the semicircle of residential communities that were gradually constructed on Africville's perimeter. Once Africville's future had been decided, as Clairmont and Magill suggest, periodic proposals from the community and its allies to have sewers or running water installed were met with the argument that "the days of the settlement were numbered ... and it wasn't worth the cost of putting in water [or other services] for the time that they were to be there."[78] And so, as time and "progress" wore on, a gulf of ever-widening proportions came to separate life in Africville from life in the rest of the city. It was this gulf that an Africville resident described in 1962 in explicitly ontological terms: "We ain't *living*," he told an interviewer that year, "we're just *existing*."[79] The stated ambition of comprehensive planning – the creation of a more healthy, convenient, and prosperous form of collective life – could scarcely have been more fully contorted.

Comprehensive Planning and Scientific Racism

Understanding the contradictions of comprehensive planning requires attention to the establishment, in the second half of the nineteenth century, of a new and distinctly "scientific" form of racism in Halifax and around the world. Racism in some form had always existed in Halifax, of course. The city's founding in 1749, for example, was achieved through a brutal and often grotesque campaign to annihilate the supposedly "savage" Mi'kmaw people. A racist conception of African people, meanwhile, made it possible for the latter to be retained as slaves by British settlers from the city's very first year until the abolition of slavery across the British Empire in 1834.[80] There is no indication, moreover, that the abolition of slavery upended or even significantly altered the prevailing racist conception of African-descended people. A particular form of social domination was abolished. And yet, the anti-Black ontology that racial servitude produced and required spilled over into the period that Saidiya Hartman calls slavery's "afterlife," in the form of widespread beliefs about Black inferiority and their inherent unsuitability for anything but slavery.[81] What came into being in the second half of the nineteenth century, then, was not racism itself, but a new form of racism. This new form, a form that most scholars call "scientific racism," would have far-reaching consequences for Halifax's white and racialized populations, as well as for the regime of urban planning that increasingly oversaw and managed their living conditions.

The roots of scientific racism are located in eighteenth-century natural history, anatomy, and theology. Seeking, more than anything, to classify human and nonhuman phenomena, European scientists and theologians like Buffon, Merkel, and de Pauw ultimately constructed a more elaborate and implacable foundation for perceived intrahuman differences (including supposed "racial" differences). Essential to this foundation was the claim that group-level human characteristics were the product of biology rather than geography. These characteristics, in other words, were no longer to be seen as the product of human socio-physical development within relatively distinct regional or continental geographies (the dominant view for at least three centuries). Instead, these characteristics were believed to be lodged in the biology or "blood" of individuals and were viewed, therefore, as transmitted from parent to child through the generations.[82] This claim led, perhaps unwittingly, to the increasingly prevalent view that human aggregates like "populations," "nations," and "societies" contained an assortment of biologically differentiable elements, and that broad-based survival and progress was partly a matter of propagating "superior" elements, diminishing "inferior elements," or both at the same time.[83]

Distinctions between ostensibly superior and inferior elements, while not only drawn along racial lines, tended to promote a new and dangerous view of racially subordinate groups. These groups' supposed inferiority, once geographically based and potentially changeable in the long term, was now conceived as close to immutable. At the same time, the effects of this inferiority, once confined largely to the lives of the inferior themselves, were now registerable in the overall life of the population, whose survival and progress their continued existence was now believed to impair. The implications of these claims were significant. Though produced within particular scientific and theological discourses, these claims gradually entered into and reconfigured a range of public debates in Europe, North America, and around the world. A particularly popular version of these claims took the form of so-called social Darwinism, a banalized version of nineteenth-century biology. Here, a pop-science conception of the "survival of the fittest" provided an explanation for the present condition of human societies, as well as an image of the way social progress and improvement could be achieved over time. As these ideas entered societies already structured by racial hierarchies, their practical implications were as predictable as they were violent. The fittest racial group was deemed – by those with the power to decide – to be white people. An even fitter society, meanwhile, was believed to be achievable by aiding, improving, and proliferating its supposedly fittest elements. An ever-fitter society, the much-anticipated result of rational progress and improvement, was an ever-whiter society by definition.

The effects of scientific racism, however, were more complex than a simple rescripting of existing racial hierarchies, in part because the meaning and boundaries of certain racial categories were in the process of changing as the new racism took hold. The Irish, in particular, saw their relationship to the dominant racial category remade in the course of the nineteenth century. In Ireland itself, long-standing distinctions between Catholics and Protestants (understood as racial distinctions) began to wither in the later years of the eighteenth century. The rise of an Irish Catholic bourgeoisie and the changing imperial stance of England towards Ireland in this period helped to rescript a supposed racial difference as an ethnic division within the same race – a less significant difference, to be sure.[84] In North America, a similar transformation occurred a few decades later. Irish immigrants (and especially Irish Catholics) were often seen as a separate racial group in eighteenth- and early nineteenth-century North America, their racialization placing them perilously close to Black populations. It was only in the mid- to late nineteenth century that Irish racialization was finally altered in this context and they "became white." The whitening of the Irish, as Noel Ignatiev emphasizes, was a contingent achievement. It was the result, he writes, "of choices made, by the Irish and others, from among available alternatives."[85] Most importantly, the Irish chose inclusion in whiteness rather than its abolition as a category and an arbiter of social privilege and dominance.

The whitening of the Irish is clearly observable in nineteenth-century Halifax. The city's Irish population grew considerably in the 1830s and 1840s, due partly to immigration and partly to relatively high birth rates, such that Irish Catholics comprised over 40 per cent of the city's population by midcentury.[86] As in other cities, Irish migrants to Halifax tended to settle in the poorest sections of town, first neighbouring and then displacing the local Black population. The initially degraded social status of Irish Haligonians began to change in the 1850s, when provincial voting rights were extended from property owners (alone) to all adult males. This change made it more important for political parties to win the support of the Irish population, which had been significant in size for at least two decades but consisted primarily of tenants rather than property owners.[87] Federal immigration policies, meanwhile, began to merge the once-distinct English and Irish categories of migrants into a single category. Beginning in the mid-nineteenth century, migrants arriving at the Halifax Pier were classified as either "British" or "foreign" and were channelled into receiving quarters organized according to this British-foreign binary.[88] Symbolically, the dominance of Britishness (rather than Irish-excluding Englishness) came to be reflected and imposed through practices like the opening of the Public Gardens in

1841, a seventeen-acre park northwest of the downtown that expressed a specifically British tradition of horticulture and landscaping.[89]

The broadening of the dominant racial category did not fully prevent the pathologization or subjugation of Irish people. Differences in social class, as demonstrated in chapter 2, continued to shape the condition of people's lives, "white" or otherwise, and eventually abetted practices of pathologization that operated in and across all racial categories. Inclusion in whiteness, however, still provided clear advantages. It meant, most importantly, that any pathologies that might be attributed to the Irish or any other white people would tend to be conceived as contingent rather than immutable – something remediable through normalizing interventions like the model tenements project. Because they were subject to alleviation, white pathologies would seem to pose no fundamental (i.e., biological) obstruction to society-wide progress, fitness, or improvement. White people, even if pathologized, could conceivably enter the realm of "fitness." There was a future that included their continued existence.

The place of Indigenous people within the new racism was somewhat ambiguous. In some contexts, the rise of scientific racism caused Indigenous people to be seen as biologically retrograde – not just racially inferior but permanently so.[90] In other contexts, however, Indigenous people could be seen as racially inferior but still improvable. The latter was generally the view of the Canadian Department of Indian Affairs, the policies of which aimed, in various ways, to coerce and discipline Indigenous people into normative humanness. The institution's belief in the potential normalization of a racially distinct and inferior population could seem to contradict the tenets of the new racial logic that pervaded public discussions and usually guided state practices towards racialized groups in this period. It was consistent, however, with centuries-old practices of settler-colonial rule in North America. Sustained across various changes in racial logic over time, these practices consistently aimed to eliminate Indigenous claims to nationhood and sovereignty; this could occur through death or through the forced assimilation of Indigenous people into settler culture and political society. The continuation of these practices in a context marked by scientific conceptions of racial difference put Indigenous people in an ambiguous position. Their potential for improvement tended to position them closer to full humanness than some other racial groups. And yet this very proximity to humanness underpinned the grave and distinctly settler-colonial forms of violence visited upon them: the violence of elimination through forced assimilation.[91]

The position of Black people in the new racial logic was more straightforward. Long-standing conceptions of Black pathology were preserved. Only the ostensible cause and implications of this pathology were revised. A new perspective on the source of Black racial inferiority began to predominate on both sides of the North Atlantic in the middle of the nineteenth century.[92] In the United States, a long list of scientists made a name for themselves in this period by defining the precise, hierarchical relationship between the country's various racial groups. The Swiss-born naturalist Louis Agassiz provided a particularly influential account in his contribution to the 1854 compendium *Types of Mankind*. Having previously described Black Americans as the country's most "degraded and degenerate race," Agassiz now explained that different degrees of advancement/degeneracy were the markers of different species of the human being. The differences between the races, he explained, were akin to those between different species of "monkeys or other animals."[93] In Nova Scotia, pseudoscientific conceptions of Black inferiority began to appear in public discussions in the same period. An 1853 editorial in *Provincial Magazine*, for example, claimed that Black people had "progressed but little from their original condition" since arriving in the province.[94] A change in geography from Africa to North America seemed to have produced no improvement among African-descended people. Their supposed inferiority could thus be attributed to biology rather than to geography. Claims like these became more common in Nova Scotia and across Canada as the century progressed, making scientific racism the country's dominant expression of anti-blackness between roughly 1870 and 1930.[95]

This newly scientific form of anti-blackness circulated through a whole series of social and political practices from the mid-nineteenth century onward. The reform in provincial voting rights in the 1850s that aided the Irish population, for example, was framed explicitly in relation to immutable Black pathology. Noting that Black Nova Scotians were often property owners and thus allowed to vote, the Halifax daily *Sun* framed the resulting political injustice in bioracial terms. How, the *Sun* asked, could Black people, whose "intellectual capacity" barely exceeded that of "the inferior order of the animal creation," be allowed to vote, when "intelligent handicraftsmen and labourers" were presently shut out?[96] The resulting reform, as expected, elevated the political position of Irish people at the same time that it diminished the position of Black people. The attention of provincial political parties quickly turned towards the large, newly enfranchised Irish population, while abandoning the attempts they had once made to win the support of Black voters. A similar shift occurred in the Halifax labour market. By the mid-nineteenth century, the Irish constituted a new and substantial "white" working-class population that employers could rely upon instead of the Black population. The productivity of Irish workers, like their fitness for voting rights, was frequently defined in opposition to the wayward and undisciplinable work habits of their Black counterparts.[97]

In the 1850s, popular culture became another venue of scientific anti-blackness in Halifax. Travelling minstrel shows from the United States began to touch down in Halifax by ocean steamer in this period and presented the public with a comic and demeaning portrayal of the Black personality based on the stereotypes of the US South. During the same period, local newspapers published editorials in which white writers reflected on the future of the society and the question of whether Black people, now seen as tethered biologically to their inferiority, had any real place within it.[98] In a representative example, an editorial in the Halifax *Morning Post* described Black Nova Scotians as "an unproductive, destitute, and *begging* class," and suggested that "the Slavery of the Southern States was ... in *truth* and *practicality*, a more suitable life for the Negro."[99] The suggestion that Black people were fit only for slavery was nothing new, of course. What was new was the "problem" of Black existence in a context that had outlawed slavery and increasingly interpreted racial difference in biological or hereditary terms. Conceptions of Black pathology that once enabled slavery and thus white advancement now seemed to weigh upon the productivity and prosperity of the broader population. Black pathology now signified a kind of disease or impurity within the social body, a substance that impeded (as a biological element) rather than supported (as a source of free labour) the advancement of the white population.

Believed to be unproductive workers, Black residents also came to be described as morally depraved and prone to criminality. While similar claims, as discussed in chapter 2, were frequently made about poor white residents in this period, the perceived extent of Black immoral and criminal tendencies was unequalled. An editorial in the *Provincial Magazine* put the matter starkly. "We have no hesitation," the writer announced, "in pronouncing [Black Nova Scotians] far inferior in morality, intelligence, and cleanliness, to the very lowest among the white population."[100] By the early twentieth century, such perspectives had become sufficiently ingrained in Halifax that a person's "blackness" could be submitted in a court case as evidence of a person's culpability. Ironically, it could also be submitted in the defence of a Black accusee. Mirroring legal practices that were common in the Jim Crow South, a Halifax attorney sought to diminish the culpability of his Black client in the 1910s by emphasizing the latter's inferior mental capacities. Black people, the attorney explained, possessed "very strong passions and feelings ... without the mental qualities [to] offset them."[101] Such conceptions of Black immorality and criminality seem to have been especially pronounced with respect to Africville residents. Indeed, the name "Africville" functioned in this period as a synonym for criminality and vice, due partly to the illicit activities like gambling and sex work that were known to occur there. These activities, though they largely involved white outsiders, were accorded a stigma that tarnished the public image of Africville rather than its white visitors.[102]

The imprint of scientific racism, including scientific anti-blackness, is perhaps most apparent in state policies intended to shape the demographics of the national population. Canadian immigration policies, for example, were strategically altered in the late nineteenth century to favour European (and ideally British) immigrants, and special efforts were made to prohibit Chinese and African people from immigrating to Canada from the 1910s until well after World War II. Juridical controls over interracial "miscegenation," though never as widespread as in the United States, were instituted by the Canadian state in various ways, including the provisions of the 1876 Indian Act that nullified the status of Indigenous women who married non-Indigenous men. In the early twentieth century, eugenics programs aimed at preventing the reproduction of "feeble-minded" individuals – a biopolitical category that reflected prevailing racial anxieties, even if some white people were included within its boundaries – were implemented in many parts of Canada, including Halifax.[103] These and other state actions, intended to strengthen the national population, were structured by new forms of professional and popular science that rendered the strengths and weaknesses of the population intelligible in racial terms. To protect or improve the population in this context was to augment its white elements, diminish its non-white elements, or both at the same time. Comprehensive planning, importantly, was established in the same context and embodied the same population-shaping objectives as these more recognized expressions of scientific racism. Its connection to the latter, thus far ignored by scholars of state racism and urban planning, clearly needs to be examined.

One of the clearest connections between comprehensive planning and scientific racism in Canadian cities was the elimination of the last remaining urban Indigenous reserves between 1905 and 1925. This series of actions, concentrated in Western Canadian cities like Vancouver and Victoria, expressed a cunning medley of settler-colonial logics and urban planning ideals. In all cases, these actions sought to relocate Indigenous people to nonurban reserves in order to better oversee, discipline, and assimilate them into normative humanity. Depending on the case, they also sought to improve the city's public health, achieve a more "economic" use of urban land, or create a peopleless "natural" area.[104] In Halifax, historic and ongoing colonial practices since the city's founding had all but eliminated the urban Mi'kmaw population. Only one Mi'kmaw resident was listed for Halifax in the 1901 census, an almost imperceptible Indigenous presence that, as such, attracted no discernible attention from planners or other municipal authorities. In neighbouring (rural) Dartmouth and Halifax County, however, seven Mi'kmaw reserves and at least 130 Mi'kmaw residents existed at the beginning of the twentieth century, and a series of actions on the part of the state and civil society sought to eliminate them. These actions culminated in a Department of Indian Affairs project in 1919 that relocated all Dartmouth and Halifax County Mi'kmaw residents to the Millbrook Reserve outside Truro, Nova Scotia. The lands they once occupied, including three three-hundred-plus acre reserves at Sambro, Ingram River, and Ship Harbour, were seized and resold by Indian Affairs in a process riddled with illegalities.[105]

The elimination of the Dartmouth and Halifax County Mi'kmaw reserves in 1919 invites comparisons with the plan to redevelop Africville, announced four years earlier. Very broadly, it can be observed that both initiatives envisioned the state-initiated seizure and redevelopment of land belonging to racialized groups. And yet, the initiatives were also implemented by quite different state institutions (the federal Department of Indian Affairs in the first case and the Halifax municipal apparatus in the second) and embodied somewhat different racial imperatives. The dominant view of Indigenous people in this context, as I noted, saw them as pathological but improvable, and the elimination of urban and near-urban reserves aimed partly to achieve this proffered improvement: an enforced assimilation into Canadianness that would finally eliminate Indigenous claims to nationhood and sovereignty. This view, when applied to questions of land use, made it possible to justify the seizure and redevelopment of Indigenous land but also required that the dispossessed be provided alternative, ostensibly normalizing living conditions elsewhere. Thus, the 1919 seizure of Mi'kmaw land in Dartmouth and Halifax County was accompanied by a clear plan to rehouse the affected residents – against their will – at the Millbrook Reserve. The dominant view of Black people, I now want to show, contributed to a different kind of planning.

Scientific anti-blackness fundamentally shaped comprehensive planning in Halifax. The rise of scientific racism in the late nineteenth century helps to explain the core contradictory of early comprehensive planning: namely, its espousal of population-improving ambitions and its suspension of these ambitions when it came to Africville. The imperative to sustain or strengthen the population, in this context, was actually an imperative to distinguish between biologically superior and inferior elements. It was an imperative to nourish and proliferate superior elements, the supposed embodiment of strength and progress, and contain or diminish the inferior elements that weakened the overall population and slowed its overall progress. In a context shaped by racial slavery and enduring, postemancipation conceptions of Black pathology, this new perspective rescripted and "scientized" existing forms of anti-blackness. Thus, it was white life that incarnated characteristics like health, happiness, and productivity. It was white life, in its survival, improvement, and expansion, that could improve these characteristics at the population-wide level. Black life, in contrast, exhibited these characteristics in their most depraved form or not at all. Black people, believed to be inferior "to the very lowest among the white population," were cast entirely outside the population insofar as it concerned planners and other state officials. The apparent contradiction between the expansive ambitions of nascent comprehensive planning and its operation in Africville was thus no contradiction at all. The population or city "as a whole," insofar as it concerned comprehensive planning, included the residents of Africville only through their exclusion. Their lives, scarcely recognizable *as* lives, were simply not relevant.

At a finer scale, the displacement of blackness from the domain of aggregate humanity – the population or city "as a whole" – is evident in all of this period's major planning ambitions and interventions. Sewers and water mains, constructed in the interest in public health, needed to extend only as far as the homes of the white public. Africville residents, unhealthy in their blood, existed somewhere beyond the sphere of the "public" and its ever-vulnerable but still protectable health. Surface pavement and street lighting, intended to provide "convenience" and "agreeableness," were also irrelevant beyond the habitual terrain of the people whose agreeableness mattered: the people who, through the creation of a more agreeable city, were meant to be retained in the city or enticed to settle there. Land-use zoning, meant to improve the population's health and prosperity, required that white health and property values be shielded from various noxious facilities. Black health and property values, already a detriment to city-wide health and prosperity, could be left unprotected and consciously impaired through the siting of facilities like the Infectious Diseases Hospital that produced (intelligible) white health and (unintelligible) Black death in tandem. Targeted redevelopment, finally, could conceivably produce "advantages" for the population as a whole through the seizure of Africville land and its conversion to more "economic" uses. The redevelopment's foreseeable disadvantages for the land's inhabitants registered nowhere in this operation, as they figured nowhere in the conception of the population or city that was to be served.

The 1915 redevelopment plan for Africville is particularly evocative of the convergence of comprehensive planning and scientific racism. On the surface, the plan entailed a straightforward economic operation, the kind of operation that David Harvey and other Marxist critics of urban planning helpfully elucidate. The clearest aim of the plan was to seize and redevelop land that appeared "underimproved" and therefore less than "economic." This economic logic, I have suggested, entered reform-era planning partly through the efforts of the Board of Trade to shift municipal taxation from value-producing personal property and improvements to non-value-producing land. These efforts, more than just focusing public attention on the supposed evils of bare and underimproved land, also called on the municipal state to play a new role. The state, as the 1916 Tax Act explained, was now to regard the urban terrain as "a huge combination of a market and apartment house" and to see itself as this terrain's landlord. The same economic logic appeared in the teachings of Thomas Adams and the work of his Halifax-based pupil, Francis Doane. For Adams, like the Board of Trade, ensuring the "economic" use of land was an essential objective. It was the precondition, in fact, for the attainment of all other planning objectives. Encountering Adams's perspective at the National Town Planning Conference, Francis Doane promised upon his return to Halfiax to prioritize "economy" in all spheres of planning practice. He certainly saw the redevelopment of Africville as an opportunity to achieve this objective.

But "economy" was not the only logic expressed in the Africville plan. A second logic becomes discernible when one recognizes that comprehensive planning viewed the urban terrain less as an expanse of more or less economic land uses than as the material substrate of human life: the "living conditions" with which life was believed to be intertwined. This perceived relationship between life and living conditions was fundamental to all of the planning initiatives of this period, and it was treated as inviolable – something not to be damaged – even in the case of the much-pathologized district of the upper streets. The latter, like Africville, was targeted for redevelopment in this period. The plan for the upper streets, however, explicitly recognized the dependence of people's lives upon their homes and surroundings. The aim of the plan, in fact, was to improve people (not land use) through the improvement of their environment, and the plan was ultimately abandoned due to fears that its fulfilment would displace and render vulnerable the residents of the upper streets. The plan for Africville, in contrast, made no mention of improving the residents' lives (because they could not be improved) and expressed no concern about their displacement (because they were, in a sense, already displaced). Anti-blackness, this suggests, redendered acceptable a redevelopment plan that elsewhere in the city, focused on other people, would not have been. Anti-blackness severed Africville lives from their living conditions and opened up a space for the improvement of other lives: the only lives that could be improved.

The place of Black people within comprehensive planning is thus a kind of no-place. There appear to be no Black living conditions, to paraphrase the Dred Scott decision, that the state is bound to respect. The result is an activity, urban planning, that carries elements of racial slavery into a supposedly postemancipation context. Describing the spatiality of Black enslavement, African Nova Scotian poet and historian Sylvia Hamilton invokes an Africville-like form of enforced placelessness. In a poem written from the perspective of an enslaved woman, she writes: "Come in from the fields one day / to find out we been up and sold / we invented temporary."[106] The "temporary" spatiality invoked by Hamilton is also conveyed, in different ways, by many scholars of anti-blackness. Katherine McKittrick, notably, argues that the "enforced placelessness" of the slave plantation "normalized black dispossession" both before and after emancipation.[107] Tracing such continuities between slavery and its afterlife is essential to understanding comprehensive planning, as well as the broader form of power that it expresses. As I claimed, Foucault's theorization of biopolitics helpfully demonstrates how the management of living conditions serves the project of protecting and improving populations. And yet, racial slavery figures nowhere in his account of biopolitics or, indeed, of scientific racism. The work of Hartman, McKittrick, and other scholars of anti-blackness rectify this problem, showing how racial slavery constituted a relationship between the human and its less-than-human other that provided a foundation for scientific racism and the forms of state action (including, I would argue, comprehensive planning) that gave life to this form of racism.

Ultimately, situating Africville within the broader aims of comprehensive planning reveals much more than the suspension of these aims in the vicinity of a significant Black community. It reveals much more, that is, than the bodily or biopolitical violence committed against Africville residents through the withholding of infrastructure and improvements provided elsewhere and the conscious degradation of Africville land. It also locates anti-Black damage and violence, most observable in Africville, in less observable locations – indeed, in the very centre of comprehensive planning and its various positive achievements. Anti-Black violence is inscribed, I want to emphasize, in the very conception of nascent planning concerns like "public health," "convenience," and "economy," none of which applied to Black existence, and all of which were promoted, in part, through damage inflicted upon Black lives. While something *like* public health, convenience, and economy could certainly be conceived and promoted without anti-blackness, the early history of comprehensive planning did not provide or pursue such a possibility. Instead, it braided together white health and Black illness, white convenience and Black frustration, white economy and Black dispossession. It produced, in effect, an all-encompassing terrain of white vitality and Black vulnerability, a planning-specific result of the general social antagonism described by Nicholas Brady: "It is [through] the obliteration of our ontological status [as 'human'] that blackness opens up a terrain for white people and the greater society to live."[108] This, more than anything, is what needs to be discerned in the emergence of comprehensive planning.

Conclusion

Modern planning owes its existence, in part, to a series of new ambitions and spatial interventions that appeared in Halifax and other cities between 1890 and 1915. Like the initiatives of contemporary housing reformers – another point of emergence for modern planning – these initiatives took human life as their object and sought to improve the prevailing condition of life through spatial means. Departing from the more narrow-focused initiatives of housing reformers, however, these initiatives harboured much broader objectives. Spatially, these interventions sought to manage complex, city-wide processes of urban development and expansion. Socially, they sought to achieve positive effects on the multifaceted existence of the entire population. Enabling these interventions were new forms of knowledge, from public health to political economy, that brought intelligibility to broad-based urban processes, as well as new sources of institutional power. As in other North American cities, these forms of knowledge and power tended to converge in the actions of the municipal state (rather than well-intentioned reformers) and an expanding cadre of city-employed and technically trained professionals like Francis Doane. The major effect was to embed life-targeting knowledge and power within the full physical and social expanse of the city. It was to render the condition of human life itself, the life of any and all city residents, dependent upon the calculated actions of state-executed, professionalized, and comprehensive urban planning. The most far-reaching and ultimately destructive actions of twentieth-century planning can be traced, in large part, to these reform-era ambitions and interventions.

Despite their seemingly expansive ambitions, the planning interventions examined in this chapter were never distributed equally across the urban terrain. The community of Africville, in particular, was left untouched by these interventions' positive aspirations and forced to bear the costs of positive aspirations actually fulfilled elsewhere. These seemingly incongruous effects can be attributed, in part, to the economic calculations of various city officials but relate more fundamentally to the racial fissures constitutive of emerging conceptions of aggregate human life like the "population" and the "city as a whole." Consistent with contemporary forms of scientific racism, these conceptions were premised on hierarchical divisions between biologically "stronger" and "weaker" elements, and tended to route projects of society-wide survival and advancement through an almost ineluctable racial calculus – an evaluation, if nothing else, of different "races," varying degrees of advancement, and their varying effects on the advancement of the overall population. The ascent of scientific racism, it is widely noted, provided a new rationale and logic for the formulation of explicitly white-supremacist policies in a range of domains. Early comprehensive planning, I have argued, produced a spatialized version of the period's broader white supremacist and anti-Black preoccupations. For planning, improving the life of the population meant improving white life. Accordingly, the emergence of comprehensive planning effectively put the urban terrain in the service of white life and thereby produced a series of spatially derived improvements in white health, convenience, and prosperity alongside and through the creation of Black dispossession, vulnerability, and death.

Moving analytically between Africville and the broader city helps to make sense of planning's operation in these two domains. It helps to demonstrate, for one thing, that planning's destructive operation in Africville was the result less of the residents' impoverished class position in the urban economy than of their negated ontological position within an emerging conception of aggregate humanity. The living conditions of upper-streets residents, also poor, received at least some improvement-oriented attention in this period, and an ambitious plan that might have withdrawn these conditions (the model tenements plan) was firmly blocked. The very different fate of lives and living conditions in Africville underscores the racial specificities of their subjugation. A broader view also helps to discern how scientific anti-blackness shaped comprehensive planning across the entire city, not just in Africville. The promotion of improved public health, convenience, and economy across the urban terrain was deeply shaped by the suspension or contravention of these concerns in the vicinity of Africville. The effects of anti-blackness are inscribed, therefore, in roads paved and not paved. In streets brightly lit and those left dark. In noxious facilities sited far away (for some residents) and dangerously close (for others). In various "economies" and their differently experienced effects. Anti-blackness inheres, in short, in the many lives and spaces safeguarded in this period, as well as in the lives and spaces that were sacrificed and defiled for the benefits of others. The city and the new form of planning that came to preside over it would each be rather different without the fissuring effects of scientific anti-blackness.

Situating Africville within the broader concerns of nascent comprehensive planning helps, more than anything, to unsettle the conception of human flourishing that gained acceptance in this period. Africville residents, in contrast to city planners, never regarded their lives as subnormal or pathological, as a deficient version of some higher, normal life embodied by white people. They certainly wanted the infrastructure and services provided to white people, and they fought continuously, from the founding of the community until its eventual destruction in the 1960s, to receive these selectively provided benefits. Their aim here, however, was not to ascend to a normality defined by the white majority but rather to safeguard and improve a much-valued form of individual and collective life that they had maintained in the face of planning-induced impairment and violence. These efforts to honour and improve a form of life that was *different* without being *abnormal* undercut the supposed expertise and supposed comprehensiveness of contemporary planning. Outside the official conception of human life and official efforts to improve it lies a rather different form and practice of life, neither "normal" nor "pathological." It is on this basis, unrecognizable to official planning, that an altogether better form of planning might one day be constituted.

4 A Calibrated Rush for Progress: Urban Renewal, Anti-Blackness, and the Diverse Effects of a Totalizing Planning Project

The twenty-five-year period after World War II was the most transformative and destructive in the history of modern planning in Halifax. Under the direction of postwar planning, long-standing neighbourhoods across the city were aggressively razed to the ground, their residents scattered in all directions. Old commercial buildings that had once defined the visual character of the city were torn down and replaced with a new landscape of high-density office towers, shopping centres, and apartment buildings. Old roadways were widened, new cross-harbour bridges were constructed, and a network of high-volume expressways began to be imposed amid (and sometimes through) the city's homes and business premises. By the late 1960s, when the city was forced to reexamine some of its priorities, postwar planning had directly redeveloped at least thirty-five acres of urban land and displaced upwards of five thousand city residents. For planners and city officials whose projects had seldom gained traction in the past, it was the glorious realization of long-obstructed urban dreams. A "slum-free modernized Halifax," as the Halifax *Herald* put it, was emerging in the dust and debris of the centuries-old urban fabric.[1] For other residents, especially those caught in the crosshairs of postwar planning projects, the process was something else entirely: a nightmare of unprecedented destruction and a shocking expression of the power over local living conditions that planners had somehow amassed at their expense.

Postwar planning in Halifax was the local expression of a broader process of planned change in cities across North America, Europe, and much of the world. As in Halifax, this process often resonated with pre-existing local aspirations and planning proposals but depended for its fulfilment on the much vaster ambitions and capacities of the postwar federal state. Promoted by federal institutions in this period was an evolving package of policies, collectively termed "urban renewal," that imagined urban progress in the form of three broad objectives: the "best use" of urban land (achieved primarily through "slum clearance"); the normalization of aberrant populations (primarily through the construction of public housing); and the improvement of urban and interurban traffic circulation (primarily through the development of expressways). Together, these objectives formed an integrated and comprehensive planning program, a program that would ostensibly adapt centuries-old cities to the requirements and possibilities of an increasingly urbanized, industrialized, and mass-based society. An ambitious undertaking, this program was structured and enabled by the provision of unprecedented levels of federal funding; the prestige and technical capacities of professional planners, engineers, and architects; and the stability of a political process almost entirely shielded from citizen input and contestation. The result was twenty-five years of creative destruction that has often been described as the imposition of a foreign and totalizing new spatial order upon the lives and living conditions of everyday city residents.[2]

And yet, urban renewal was more than an aggressive assertion of technocratic power. A closer look at the major planning reports and debates of this period reveals a concurrent and seemingly countervailing concern with the condition of people's lives. Urban renewal entailed a concerted effort to document people's lives, to trace their evident imperfections, and to deliver the spatial prerequisites of a markedly better, more modern form of life. Even slum clearance, the foremost cause of displacement in this period, was driven partly by the belief that slum residents were ill affected by their present living conditions and could achieve a better form of life elsewhere (i.e., in state-provided public housing). These efforts, despite their sensitive, benevolent veneer, were inhabited by a profoundly destructive logic. The condition of people's lives was consistently gauged in relation to dominant norms, and the failure of individuals or populations to embody these norms signified a form of pathology and the possibility, if not the necessity, of a spatial intervention carried out by outside authorities. A better life was thus imposed more than offered. Its imposition, moreover, carried rather different consequences depending on the perceived distance of particular individuals or populations from dominant norms, a distance measured partly in racial terms. Those pathologized and displaced by planning in the postwar period included over five thousand poor and working-class residents, both white and Black. Black residents, though not planning's only targets, were nevertheless attributed a deeper form of pathology and were exposed to a subtly different and more devastating form of displacement.

Urban renewal in Halifax was the fulfilment of a long-standing vision in which the remaking of spatial conditions would serve to remake and improve the population. The details of this process were outlined in a series of technically proficient planning studies, while their fruition was enabled by the cost-sharing provisions of 1950s and 1960s federal policies like the evolving National Housing Act. Renewal began in earnest with the redevelopment of the downtown core and the displacement of its poorest residents. From here, it proceeded through the construction of public housing, the redevelopment of two further "slums," and the upgrading of the city's transportation network. Described as a "headlong rush for progress" by some of it opponents, urban renewal had its most damaging effects on city residents whose lives and living conditions seemed to fall below sought-after standards.[3] The imposed "improvement," while it affected pathologized white and Black residents alike, took the living conditions of white residents as its assumed starting point. It was these conditions, subtly different from those of Black residents, that renewal sought to improve. The improvement of Black living conditions, in contrast, was never seriously considered, and the imposition of an essentially white model upon their lives resulted in the wholesale destruction of the specific conditions that had allowed Black residents to survive in an anti-Black city. Urban renewal can thus be described as a totalizing project with subtly divergent effects – effects, indexed to class- and race-based pathologizations, that would prove difficult for anti-renewal activists in the late 1960s to bring into their analysis and contest.

Remaking the Downtown

Halifax entered the post-World War II period with modest hope and great trepidation. The war itself brought a certain respite to the economic and demographic stagnation that had plagued the city since the end of the previous world war. During the interwar period, manufacturing employment in Halifax declined by half (mostly *before* the Great Depression); retail and wholesale activity remained static; and population growth lagged substantially behind the cities of Central and

Western Canada. The onset of another war reversed all of these trends – at least for a time.

The city's population suddenly ballooned, as eighteen thousand Navy officers and six thousand Army and Air Force personnel made their way to the city (often with family members in tow).[4] Demand for goods and services increased in tandem with the population, greatly boosting the profits of local businesses (especially bars and theatres). Along the harbour, the footprint of the Navy base was enlarged significantly, and the civilian Halifax Dockyard (tasked with repairing an endless stream of war-ravaged vessels) hummed with activity twenty-four hours a day, providing employment for upwards of three thousand Halifax residents. During the same period, however, the war-related investments of the federal Department of Munitions and Supply overwhelmingly aided the industrial sectors of other regions (i.e., Ontario and Québec) instead of the Maritimes and presaged severe challenges to come for the recently revived Halifax economy. The underside of sudden population growth, moreover, was a series of social problems like insufficient and overpriced rental housing, a situation that was expected to persist after the war. Capitalizing on the possibilities of a militarized city while addressing its problems was one of the foremost tasks of urban planning in the 1940s and after.[5]

While attuned to local particularities, postwar planning in Halifax was also shaped by nascent national and international priorities. The shape of these priorities had already come partly into view during the war, with the federal state's passage of new labour-union rights and new social programs like unemployment insurance and family allowances. Moves like these helped to constitute the broad public-policy formation that, in Canada and other North Atlantic countries, has been called Fordism. Hegemonic during the three decades after World War II, Fordism aimed to augment and sustain economic expansion through supports to domestic industry (like protective tariffs) and a range of social programs that would help to create a productive workforce and a sizeable consumer market.[6] Fordism was, to a great extent, an urbancentric policy formation. Its prescriptions for nonurban locations, in fact, most often entailed the encouraged migration of their residents towards more populous, urban agglomerations.[7] Owing to this focus, urban planning had a significant role to play in the achievement of Fordist ideals. Especially important to Fordist urban planning in Canada was the passage of the revised National Housing Act (NHA) in 1944 and the creation, two years later, of the Central Mortgage and Housing Corporation (CMHC), an arms-length federal institution charged with implementing the new NHA. The NHA / CMHC duo would provide indispensable financial and technical support to postwar planning in Canada and served as the primary mechanism through which Fordist visions of society were woven into the restructured industrial, commercial, and residential landscape of the city.[8]

Planning for the postwar period in Halifax began amid the ongoing throes of war itself. In 1943, the city struck a twelve-person "civic planning commission" with the broad aim of ensuring that future property and infrastructure development achieved "the best use [that] may be made of the land available in the [c]ity."[9] The outcome of the commission's work, submitted to council in 1945, was the city's first-ever master plan, a 156-page document that gave concrete expression to the urban dreams that emerged, nascently, in early comprehensive planning. These dreams were most vividly expressed in a series of hand-drawn images distributed through the Master Plan. Featured here were images of wholly new commercial spaces, with a tailor, a cobbler, and a green grocer located together in a single complex (*figure 4.1*); images of city streets heading directly and efficiently from their starting point to

Figure 4.1 Plan for community shopping centre, 1945. Halifax, *Master Plan* (Halifax: City of Halifax, 1945), 39. Image courtesy of HRMA.

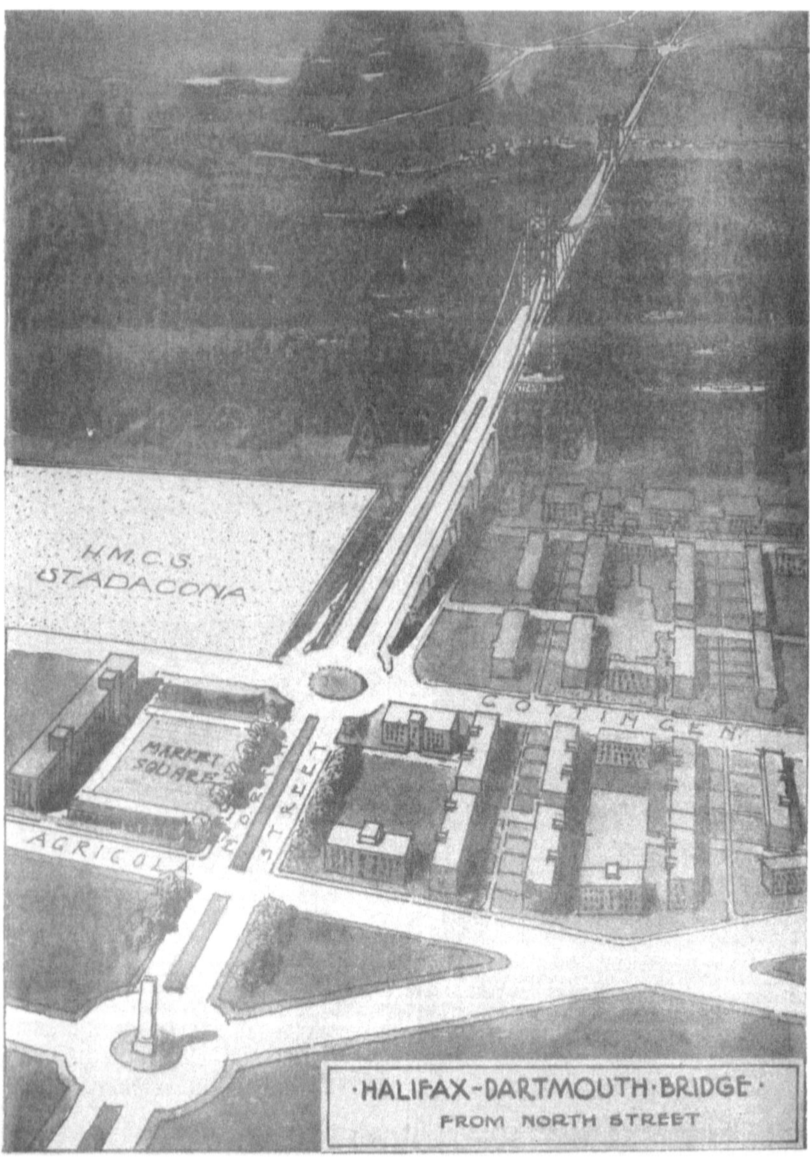

Figure 4.2 Plan for diagonal roadway, 1945. Halifax, *Master Plan* (Halifax: City of Halifax, 1945), 25. Image courtesy of HRMA.

their end point, with fewer interruptions along the way (*figure 4.2*); images of a city, above all, in which the lingering problems of the past had been transcended by the rational plotting of the city's needed public and private infrastructure. These aspirations, while expressed in physical form, were nevertheless biopolitical in their fundamental aims. Like early comprehensive planning, the physical transformations outlined in the Master Plan were meant primarily to act upon the city's population. They were meant to enable population growth, improve public health, correct social pathologies, and ultimately "safeguard and promote the general welfare of the community."[10]

Like other planning blueprints of the urban renewal period, the practical advice of the Master Plan centred on three elements: the elimination of the city's slums, the construction of public housing, and the improvement of the city's transportation system. The prospect of slum clearance was clearly the plan's greatest preoccupation, as well as the primary means through which its central aim (the "best use" of land) was to be achieved. Supporting the plan's advice on this issue was a form of analysis that had first appeared in the 1915 plan for Africville but would now be carried out more systematically. Gathering together a mass of property assessment data, the plan compared the average value of improvements in various areas of the city to the average value of the subtending land. The result of this comparison was an impeccably concise and calculative answer to the question of the landscape's best use: areas with a high ratio of improvement-value to land-value were deemed to be achieving the best use of land, while areas with a low ratio were not. This message was clearly delivered on a single page, midway through the report. Here, beneath a table of data in which the average value of land and improvements for various areas of the city were presented, the report advised that "the foregoing figures clearly indicate the necessity for a slum clearance and adequate [re]housing program" in areas of less-than-best land use. The areas specifically targeted in the plan included the old upper-streets slum, "the greater part" of the Old North End, the entirety of Africville, and a small section of the South End.[11]

In fact, the "necessity" of slum clearance could only partially be indicated through an analysis of land-use data. As the plan makes clear, the use of land would need to be evaluated alongside a consideration of the land's inhabitants: the people who would eventually be displaced in the pursuit of "better" land uses and a correspondingly higher level of "general welfare." Like the 1915 plan for Africville, accordingly, the assessment of land was closely accompanied in the plan by an assessment of the population in relation to particular norms. The number of inhabitants per room in low-income areas was compared to wealthy areas and labelled "overcrowded." The cost of social services provided to low-income areas was compared to wealthy areas and labelled "disproportionate." The (nonexistent) water and sanitary services available in low-income areas was compared to wealthy areas and found to degrade the poor residents "physically, mentally, and morally."[12] These and other assessments reworked the bifurcated terrain of earlier planning initiatives, reproducing a category of residents whose lives departed from prevailing norms and seemed to require spatialized (i.e., planning-provided) remediation.

Not surprisingly, the spatial distribution of social pathologies was shown roughly to overlap with that of the city's less-than-best land uses. A two-pronged rationale for slum clearance was thereby constituted that soon received the assent of city officials, city bureaucrats, and local organizations as diverse as the Halifax Board of Trade and the Halifax Welfare Council.[13] Pivotal to these actors' support, in many cases, was the belief that slum clearance would benefit the people whose lives it would disrupt and displace. That this belief was never tested against the wishes of the displacees themselves – and that it would be maintained in the face of displacee *opposition* – indicates the contradiction at the heart of postwar renewal in Halifax and elsewhere. The people most affected by renewal were silenced, their wishes never solicited, even as the renewal project was widely described as serving their "own good."[14] The pathologization of slum residents, their eviction from the status of political subject, was therefore essential to the constitution of postwar planning expertise. Physically and behaviourally abnormal, slum residents could scarcely be regarded as having anything to contribute to the formulation of population-improving planning initiatives, even when it was their homes and their lives that were most explicitly targeted for improvement.

The city's approval of the Master Plan in June 1946 was followed by a series of false starts. The first attempt at slum clearance targeted a three-block area of the Old North End, a section that happened to overlap with the long-time heart of the central-city Black community.[15] The plan was met with opposition from certain neighbourhood leaders, including Baptist preacher and Nova Scotia Association for the Advancement of Coloured People (NSAACP) president William Pearly Oliver. Pointing out that the Black residents of the targeted area were generally homeowners rather than tenants, Oliver challenged the city's plan on the grounds that people "who have had the spirit of citizenship and spunk" to purchase or build their own home should not be subject to displacement.[16] City council, for its part, seems to have been concerned less about potential displacees than about the potential financing of the project. At least half the cost of acquiring and demolishing the targeted properties could have been covered by the 1944 NHA provisions for the "clearance, replanning, rehabilitation, and modernization of slum areas." Access to this funding was conditional, however, upon a city's agreement to construct low-income public housing in the cleared location. Toronto had already tapped into these condition-bound NHA provisions to finance its massive sixty-nine-acre Regent Park redevelopment project in 1948, but it was the only Canadian city to do so. Halifax, like most cities, envisioned something other than low-income housing on the site of its erstwhile slums, and it ultimately abandoned the plan for the Old North End for want of suitable financing.[17]

More flexible federal financing arrived in 1956. NHA-provided slum-clearance funding, once tied to the construction of public housing in the same location, was now made available to projects that delivered areas of "blight" to their "highest and best use." These looser financing provisions had their intended effect, spurring NHA-financed slum-clearance projects in Vancouver, Montréal, Ottawa, Hamilton, and a host of smaller cities.[18] Halifax officials caught wind of the changes a few months before their introduction and began to prepare an NHA-eligible project. A University of Toronto planning professor, Gordon Stephenson, was contracted by the city to produce a comprehensive "urban renewal" study, a prerequisite for NHA slum-clearance funding and an item for which NHA funding was available. The professor, a former student of Le Corbusier's, outlined his vision for the city in a detailed, two-volume analysis known as the Stephenson Report. Regarded as the blueprint of urban renewal in Halifax, the report added a veneer of technical expertise and political legitimacy to a set of planning objectives that, rather than novel to the document, had gradually achieved acceptance among city officials over the preceding half century.[19]

At a high level, the report embodied the major priorities of postwar planning: the better use of high-value land, the normalization of pathological populations, and the improvement of traffic circulation. Its most concrete advice centred on the eradication of the city's slums. Central to this advice was a table of data that made it possible to compare the average value of land to the average value of improvements for all 119 blocks of the city. Areas with relatively low-value improvements were deemed to be falling short of the "best use" of the land and were therefore targeted for potential redevelopment.[20] Supplementing this analysis of property values, as in the Master Plan, was an array of social statistics – drawn, in this case, from every conceivable public institution. The pages of the report were thus a veritable atlas of normality and pathology, a detailed charting of what it meant to be human and less than human in the postwar context. Areas of good health were set apart from areas of poor health. Areas of high crime were set apart from areas of low crime. Through certain formulas, it was even possible to distinguish areas of "overcrowding" and "unwholesome sanitary conditions" from their norm-abiding counterparts. The major output of this analysis was the conception of nine advisable redevelopment schemes, the fulfilment of which would entail the displacement of up to seven thousand residents. Disruptive as these actions would be, their aim was an ostensibly humane one: the improvement of the city's "human welfare" through the rehabilitation of its most pathological spaces and people.

Receiving the completed report in September 1957, council voted almost immediately to proceed with "Scheme 9," the redevelopment of a fourteen-acre and 1,620-resident section of low-income housing north of City Hall. The area, roughly identical to the targeted terrain of the 1905 model tenements plan, was highlighted in the report as the location of "the worst tenements" in the city, as well as the potential site of a best-use-achieving office and commercial district.[21] The area came to be called the Central Redevelopment Area (CRA), and its long-desired demolition finally became feasible on 30 January 1958, when Prime Minister John Diefenbaker arrived in Halifax to put his signature on a $1.9 million slum-clearance package. Consistent with postwar slum-clearance schemes in other Canadian cities, the costs of the CRA redevelopment were to be shared between the CMHC (75 per cent), the province (12.5 per cent), and the municipality (12.5 per cent).[22] Financing, the major obstacle of the model tenements plan, would not impede postwar efforts to remake the same area. The state, at all three levels, would play the financial role that "philanthropic capitalists" briefly envisioned but ultimately shirked.

The redevelopment process was launched in February 1958, when the city began the process of buying up and demolishing CRA-located properties. At this point, letters were sent to the area's property owners, advising them that their property was needed by the city and outlining the amount of compensation they would receive. Owners who refused the city's initial offer, generally the assessed value of the property plus 5 per cent, were sometimes offered a higher amount but were most often subject to involuntary expropriation (in which case the amount of compensation was settled by the municipal court). In the case of rental properties, the buyout of a property owner left the city with a collection of tenants (now *its* tenants) who also needed to be dealt with. Upon taking ownership of a rental property, the city then sent a letter to the tenants informing them that their existing home was "no longer available to them" and that they were required to vacate the premises.[23] Though displaced tenants were generally offered no compensation, they sometimes qualified for the provision of "decent, safe, and sanitary" housing in another location (a stipulation of CMHC-provided slum-clearance funding).[24] The envisioned location of this "decent housing," however, was a public housing project (Mulgrave Park) that was not yet completed at the time of most tenants' eviction. Thus began an agonizing process in which tenants, in the best of cases, were ejected from their homes and transferred through a series of temporary dwellings – often city-owned properties elsewhere in the CRA that were themselves targeted for demolition.

The situation of the city's low-income tenants greatly worsened as time passed and planners' ambitions grew. In January 1958, just as the clearing-out of the CRA was beginning, the city passed a new bylaw (Ordinance 50) that required the demolition of any building in the city that was discovered to fall below minimum standards. The result, over the next three years, was the elimination of at least 250 housing units outside the CRA through the application of the ordinance and the elimination of at least another two hundred more units through demolitions undertaken by individual landlords in anticipation of the ordinance's application to their building.[25] Concerns about the expanding scope of enforced displacement were duly raised by some city officials early in the process. A report submitted to the Redevelopment Committee in April 1958 revealed that five hundred to six hundred people had already been evicted from their homes with nowhere else to live, and that upwards of one hundred people were "put on the streets" in a single evening to enable the demolition of a fifteen-building section of the CRA. Even more people would be rendered homeless, the report warned, if the city's redevelopment project was not immediately suspended.[26]

A few members of the Redevelopment Committee, including Mayor Leonard Kitz, expressed alarm at the report's findings and suggested that a slower, piecemeal approach to redevelopment could be adopted. "The houses being torn down," the mayor suggested, "[are] certainly not fit for accommodation, but at least they [are] shelters for some people."[27] Most participants, however, agreed with the argument of Gordon Stephenson (the planning professor and now paid consultant to the city) that "a frontal attack is the only approach at the present time."[28] The only amendment to the original plan adopted by the committee at this point was its enlargement: the addition, that is, of three new phases. The first new phase, approved in May 1958, involved the elimination of thirty-nine low-income housing units on Maitland Street (just north of the CRA) to make way for a parking lot. The second, approved in the same month, involved the destruction of at least fifty-three housing units on Clyde Street to provide a parking lot for the Spring Garden Road commercial district. The third, approved in May 1959, involved the elimination of several commercial and military buildings on Upper Water Street (just east of the CRA) to enable the eastward extension of Cogswell Street and the construction of a new ferry terminal on the waterfront. These new phases, along with Ordinance 50, contributed to an ever-broadening slum-clearance and redevelopment program that the city eventually termed "blight removal."[29]

Opposition to the city's actions was frequently manifested by those targeted for displacement, including business owners in the CRA. Located within the CRA were a handful of small businesses, from Kay's lunch counter to Atlantic Auto Repair, each of which catered to the neighbourhood-based clientele.[30] For these displacees, the redevelopment process generally disrupted, and often extinguished, the basis of their business model: their connections to a surrounding customer base. The Citadel Tavern, once located on the corner of Duke and Argyle Streets, provides a case in point. First contacted by municipal officials in December 1958, the tavern's owner refused the city's initial offer of $21,735 (the assessed value of the building plus 5 per cent) on the grounds it omitted any compensation for the potential "extinguishment of [the] business" carried out in that location.[31]

Seeking to relocate the business elsewhere, the tavern owner soon found all of his efforts impeded by the same municipal apparatus that was compelling him to move. The Redevelopment Committee flatly refused to consider the possibility of re-establishing the tavern in the same area (once redeveloped), while the owner's requests for liquor licences in a series of locations outside the CRA were rejected by the Tavern Licensing Committee. By the summer of 1961, the Citadel Tavern was engulfed by the dust and debris of dozens of bulldozed CRA buildings and was increasingly emptied of customers. Finally shutting its doors in October of the same year, the tavern's owner demanded $120,000 in compensation for the city's having "deliberately put [him] out of business and at the same time stubbornly refus[ing] to allow him to relocate his business elsewhere." The city, deeming the requested amount "fantastic," pushed the case to the expropriation court, where the owner was eventually awarded $50,500 and finally compelled to leave his old tavern to the bulldozers.[32]

Tenants, too, sometimes resisted the redevelopment project. Rejecting the view that their lives would be better elsewhere, some residents informed the city that they "just want[ed] to be downtown, having lived [there] ... for most of their lives."[33] Other residents refused the city's order to relocate, compelling city council to pass new legislation in March 1960 that allowed it to dispatch the bailiff to deal with rebellious tenants.[34] Some residents, finally, simply refused to pay rent to the new owner of their dwelling (the city). Exemplary of the latter response was the Fleet family, a nine-member tenant household on Brunswick Street. When the city acquired their building in September 1959, the Fleets evidently stopped paying rent. A year later, the building was demolished, and the family was relocated to a city-owned apartment building on Starr Street, where they also refused to pay rent. Soon enough, this building too was tapped for demolition, and the family was relocated to the emergency-housing facilities at Wellington Court, where they refused, once again, to pay rent. Addressing the case in November 1961, the Redevelopment Committee was informed that "Mr. Fleet has consistently refused to cooperate with either the City Welfare Department or with City Staff ... [and] gives the impression that he feels the City owes him accommodation." There was "reason to believe," the report continued, "that he may be influencing other tenants in the area." In response to the report, the committee resolved to evict the Fleets from the emergency-housing complex and have Children's Aid "take control of the children" if the family did not soon find another home. The latter move, though costly to the city, was touted as "establish[ing] a valuable precedent."[35]

The clearing-out of the CRA, largely completed by the end of 1961, left an indelible mark on the city's physical and social landscape. As the destruction proceeded, a terrain of densely packed wooden homes and small businesses was transformed into a vast hollow crater that Haligonians, with fresh memories of war, often compared to the bombed-out cities of post-World War II Europe (see *figure 4.3*).[36] Combined with the broader "blight-removal" project, the clearing of the CRA expelled nearly four thousand people from their homes between 1958 and 1961, with fewer than 1,500 ultimately relocated to newly constructed public housing.[37] For those who qualified, relocating to the Mulgrave Park project involved a waiting period as long as three-and-a-half years. In the meantime, it also meant accepting whatever alternative accommodations were offered to them by the city, potentially moving a second or third time (as their temporary accommodations were demolished), and keeping up with rental payments. Refusing to relocate or falling behind on rental payments resulted in an eviction order and the termination of the city's responsibility for the residents' rehousing. Those who successfully moved into Mulgrave Park, finally, were required to pay a monthly rent that often exceeded the amount they had paid in the CRA, as well as a series of up-front relocation fees that totaled roughly one month's rent. Many Mulgrave tenants, as I discuss below, found themselves evicted a short time after moving in, due either to rental arrears or to their failure to exhibit appropriate domestic behaviours.

Figure 4.3 Central Redevelopment Area (CRA), 1967. Halifax, Regional Police Department records, HRMA, RG 102-16N-0068.6. Image courtesy of HRMA.

The possibility of rehousing, however, was not available to all displacees. Tenancy in Mulgrave Park, for one thing, was restricted explicitly to families. Single people, couples without children, boarders, and senior citizens were excluded from any city-provided housing and were compelled to make do within a private housing market that was widely acknowledged to be inadequate and that city-ordered demolitions were rendering even less adequate.[38] The problem of dishousing, when it was acknowledged, was generally blamed on the federal state. Referring to the estimated 440 nonfamily residents of the CRA targeted for displacement, a 1957 city report concluded that "there is no reason why they should not fend for themselves, particularly since there is no financial assistance available under the NHA for this purpose."[39] Indeed, CMHC/NHA provisions drew a clear line through the country's poor neighbourhoods, funding the clearance of entire areas and the rehousing strictly of these area's families. In Halifax, at least one thousand nonfamily residents were dishoused by these demographically selective provisions by the end of 1961, their subsequent whereabouts unknown and unexplored.[40]

Many families were ultimately disqualified from city-provided housing as well. Some families were perceived to lack the "moral character" required of public housing and were barred from demonstrating otherwise.[41] Other families failed to respond quickly enough to the city's offer of relocation and were never added to the Mulgrave Park waiting list, while still other families were added to the waiting list but were never actually offered a housing unit, either because not enough units were constructed or because their income was too low.[42] In addition to the one thousand displaced nonfamily residents, then, at least 1,600 family members were also dishoused by the CRA redevelopment and blight-removal project without being offered new accommodation. None of this, however, tarnished the city's appraisal of these projects or their outcome. In a continuation of the pathologizing logic of the early twentieth century, the city's major report on blight removal in 1961 concluded that displaced tenants had simply "misunderst[oo]d" the city's offer of assistance or else had "resist[ed] persuasion and pressure to improve." Tenants who were offered no assistance in the first place were thus rendered invisible, while those who viewed a forced relocation as something other than "assistance" or "improvement" were pathologized and discounted. These dispensations, similar to those of early twentieth-century planning initiatives, grounded the report's conclusion that the city had "no need to apologize for any phase of its blight removal project" and that the latter, in fact, ought to be established as a permanent feature of the city's operations.[43]

In 1962, with the CRA finally cleared of its residents and buildings, part of the city's attention turned to the rebuilding process: the creation of a new and better downtown core. Planners' visions for the CRA site had evolved noticeably over the previous five years. The Stephenson Report, the original blueprint for the area, outlined a new commercial development that would include a three-level parking garage, new government offices, corporate and professional offices, wholesale establishments, and a major hotel.[44] The establishment of these functions, a major change in land use, was to occur through a development process that nevertheless mimicked the existing scale of the downtown and that retained the existing framework of downtown streets. A rather different vision was eventually outlined by Robert Grant, who was hired as the city's first director of development in 1961. A former military officer and CMHC official, Grant's ambitions for the city were sweeping, and his autocratic management style gave him considerable influence over planning processes throughout the 1960s. For Grant, the downtown core was in "grave danger."[45] The size of its commercial spaces was too small, he felt, to retain the department stores and other metropolitan-scale commercial facilities that were already migrating to new shopping malls in the west end of the city. Grant's proposal, eventually accepted by the city, was to upscale the downtown, to develop a set of high-rise buildings on the CRA site that was purposefully at odds with the scale of the existing downtown – until the entire downtown was upscaled as well.

The fulfilment of this vision took several years to occur. The slow pace was due, in part, to its reliance on the initiative of private property developers, a form of enterprise that scarcely existed in Canada at the time and that federal urban renewal policies were meant, in part, to create.[46] The only respondent to the city's 1962 call for development proposals was a British company, the Woking Group, that was granted the project in 1963 but soon announced that it was unable to bring together the capital required to move forward. The CRA, as a result, remained a purposeless empty crater, as well as an increasing source of embarrassment for city officials. In 1965, Navy Major-General K.C. Appleyard publicly chided Mayor Charles Vaughn about the lack of progress on the CRA development. The mayor, in turn, challenged Appleyard to prove that he could achieve anything better. The outcome was a now-famous visit by Appleyard to the bourgeois Halifax Club, where he encouraged the club's wealthiest members to create a property development company that could carry out the rebuilding of the CRA. Responding to Appleyard's proposal were ten of the province's wealthiest merchants and industrialists, who each agreed to contribute $20,000 to the capitalization of a company that would be called Halifax Developments Incorporated (HDI) and that would quickly enter into negotiations with the city over the redevelopment project.[47]

HDI's proposal for the CRA, dubbed "Scotia Square," was one of three received by the city in 1965. The proposal, ultimately selected, won the favour of decision makers primarily on the basis of its relatively high proportion of high-value office space and, thus, its relatively good use (quantitatively defined) of the cleared terrain.[48] After winning the contest, HDI hired Boston-based architect Carl Koch to translate the rough Scotia Square proposal into a realizable development.

Figure 4.4 Scotia Square and Cogswell Interchange, 1970. Halifax, Development and Planning Department photographs, HRMA, RG 35-102-105-1-35. Image courtesy of Calnen Photography.

A long-time associate of Bauhaus cofounder Walter Gropius, Koch's modernist credentials concurred with the HDI's ambitions but had thus far been demonstrated primarily through the design of suburban homes and subdivisions.[49] Outstripping these earlier ventures, Koch's design for Scotia Square would saturate the CRA site with a series of angular, interconnected towers: three fourteen-storey office buildings, a ten-storey hotel, three twelve-storey apartment buildings, and a giant shopping mall (see *figure 4.4*). Ignoring the existing street grid, the development would fully eliminate two east-west streets, as well as sever three major north-south arteries (creating a major barrier between the North End and the downtown). After a round of consultations and small revisions to the design, construction was launched in 1967, with the new towers appearing on the Halifax skyline, one by one, between 1969 and 1973. Piece by piece, a new downtown was beginning to take shape, a methodical march towards progress that would ostensibly achieve the land's "best use," re-establish the downtown as the heart of the city, and catalyse a city-wide process of growth and development.[50]

Just as Robert Grant and other planners had hoped, the CRA redevelopment helped to launch a broader upscaling of the downtown in which private actors (rather than the state) took on the task of buying and levelling older buildings. Between 1964 and 1966, five significant downtown sites were cleared for development, each of which had previously contained eight or more older buildings. Upon these sites, a phalanx of concrete towers gradually appeared on the skyline alongside Scotia Square: the twelve-storey Centennial Building, the thirteen-storey Citadel Inn, the thirteen-storey Royal Bank building, and the seventeen-storey Bank of Montréal building. None of these towers were high-rises by the standards of larger cities. New office towers in Toronto and Montréal were often three times taller, and Ottawa-based developer and CMHC head Robert Campeau lambasted Halifax for putting up "uneconomically" minuscule, low-density structures.[51] Taken together, however, the development of these towers dramatically reconstituted the form, style, and value of the downtown. In contrast to the new towers, the area's older buildings could now seem tangibly less efficient in their use of land, the airspace above their roofs providing a marker of the property value they had yet to achieve. From a very different perspective, the older buildings could now seem temporally and aesthetically "historic," their form and height a marker of the city's unique and disappearing "heritage." This second perspective, a clear conflict with the first, would eventually motivate the first significant political challenge to postwar planning in Halifax.

Remaking the Population

As new office towers began to dot the Halifax skyline, the attention of some planners had already shifted to other locations and priorities. Between 1960 and 1968, much of planners' attention was devoted to the city's North End and the development of a series of public housing projects geared towards low-income residents (especially slum-clearance displacees). Efforts to better house poor and working-class Haligonians, as I have shown, date back to the turn of the twentieth century, and the public housing projects of the 1960s bore the traces of these earlier efforts. Like the 1905 model tenements plan, these projects clearly aimed to act upon and improve (i.e., normalize) the affected populations through spatial means. They were an expression, in Foucault's terms, of disciplinary power. At the same time, these projects fit within and enabled the broader urban renewal project of this period. The effects of public housing, therefore, were to be gauged not just in terms of the individual lives they normalized but also in the population-wide, biopolitical terms of urban renewal writ large. Most concretely, public housing served as a receptacle for (some of) the residents displaced in the pursuit of "better" downtown land uses and tempered, therefore, the potential social objections to these pursuits. The interdependence of best-use-achieving redevelopment and public housing construction was evident not only in the federal NHA's requirement that slum-clearance displacees be provided "decent, safe, and sanitary accommodation" in another location but also in similarly worded provisions in the 1945 Master Plan and 1957 Stephenson Report.[52]

The rehousing of pathologized urbanites in postwar Canada was paralleled by similar interventions in nonurban locations. At the same moment that Halifax planners were envisioning the relocation of the city's poor and working-class residents, a combination of federal and provincial officials in Newfoundland were preparing similar plans for the province's scattered outport (fishery-based) communities. These efforts culminated in the joint federal-provincial Resettlement Act of 1965, the effect of which was to eliminate 119 outport communities and relocate to more populous centres over sixteen thousand Newfoundlanders.[53] At the same moment too, federal Department of Indian Affairs officials were devising a plan to centralize the rural Mi'kmaw population of Nova Scotia. Announced in 1942, the plan called for the relocation of over 1,700 Mi'kmaw people (roughly 83 per cent of the total Nova Scotia Mi'kmaw population) from seventeen smaller reserves to a pair of larger reserves in Eskasoni and Indian Brook. The latter, from this point forward, would be the only recognized home of a people that once inhabited the entire province (and more). The plan was opposed by most Mi'kmaw people and never fully achieved its ambitious aims. In 1949, when the plan was abandoned, only half of the targeted residents had been relocated to Eskasoni and Indian Brook. A greater number, it seems, responded to the state's latest disruption of their lives by departing the province for locations in Central Canada and the United States.[54]

The forced centralization the Mi'kmaq and postwar urban renewal, though implemented by different state institutions and driven by different socio-racial imperatives, evince some clear similarities. The centralization, like slum clearance, assumed that the land inhabited by the displaced could be better used and that the pathological "vice, immorality, and poverty" of the displaced required them to be relocated and rehoused elsewhere.[55] Indeed, an important 1945 Indian Affairs report on the ongoing centralization project explicitly analogized the situation of the Mi'kmaq and poor (non-Indigenous) urbanites. "The Indian is sick," the report observed, because he or she is "undernourished, ill clad, and forced to live under conditions only found in the lowest of slums." Actions like the centralization project, the report concluded, would help to cure "the Indian" by enabling better state "supervision" and "rais[ing] the standard of living of these people."[56] The link between centralization and urban renewal, however, lies in more than just their similarities. Colonial policies like the centralization plan, in controlling the location of Indigenous inhabitance, ensured that very few Indigenous people lived in urban areas like Halifax in this period. If urban renewal displaced relatively few Indigenous people, then, it was largely because other state actions – similar in form to urban renewal – were functioning to preserve cities as relatively Indigenous-free spaces.

In urban areas, the construction of public housing embodied the political ambiguities of Fordist policy in general. There is no question that proponents of public housing in Canada were often deeply concerned about the substandard living conditions of the urban poor, and their proposals were at least partly framed in terms of social justice: the alleviation of housing inadequacies that were systemic in nature. There is something historically unique and almost radical in the relatively widespread conviction among postwar planners and policy makers that capitalism was systemically unable to provide for the housing needs of poor and working-class residents. Filtered through these views, however, was a distinctly normative conception of proper living conditions and proper citizenhood. While explicitly eugenicist concerns about "race degeneration" were seldom invoked in the postwar period, discussions of public housing were nevertheless premised upon a middle-class and white conception of the ideal national population and generally viewed public housing as a means of bringing tenants' lives into harmony with this class- and race-specific ideal. This particular perspective on public housing helps to explain the focus of CMHC-funded projects on low-income *families*. The aim of public housing, as Sean Purdy notes, was to create spaces in which a normative population could be birthed and reared. The child-raising nuclear family was thus the consistent target population of public housing, and housing units were explicitly designed to aid and uphold the traditional mother's work of homemaking and child rearing (the activities that it was assumed would give shape to the next generation).[57]

Like other elements of urban renewal, the construction of public housing was pursued with minimal input from the most affected populations. The design, layout, and furnishing of public housing was generally entrusted to CMHC architects (though they sometimes worked in collaboration with local firms), and the ultimate approval of the designs was the purview of bureaucrats and elected officials. The centralized character of public housing decision making was clearly spelled out in a January 1958 meeting of the Halifax Redevelopment Committee. Referring to the Stephenson Report's promise of "satisfactory" housing to people displaced by slum clearance, one councillor asked: "To whom must the housing be 'satisfactory' – the city or those who occupy it?" Robert Grant, the presiding CMHC official and eventual Halifax director of development, replied sincerely: "The Prime Minister."[58] The same top-down character tended to extend from the construction of public housing to its eventual management. Despite occasional nods to citizen participation, tenant selection criteria were established in closed-door meetings; tenants' lives were closely monitored and regulated by housing officials who worked, but did not live, on site; and tenants' efforts to modify their own living conditions (e.g., through the hanging of clothes lines) were often interrupted by the authorities. The shielding of decision making from tenant input was consistent with the overall effects that public housing was meant to achieve: the inculcation of physical and behavioural norms among a population singled out precisely for its nonexhibition, and thus nonknowledge, of such norms. A space of normativity would be created top-down or not at all.[59]

In Halifax, efforts to build public housing in the city began to move forward in the 1950s. The construction of a small, 161-unit housing project on Bayers Road in 1949 was the period's first achievement, but much larger possibilities emerged with the completion of the Stephenson Report and the potential federal funding that came with it.[60] The report called for the construction of roughly 1,100 new public housing units over the proceeding twenty-five years, beginning with a 348-unit project on a site called Mulgrave Park. Located at the northern end of the peninsula, Mulgrave Park was an eleven-acre former farmstead that had come under federal ownership and had been dotted with temporary housing during World War II. After the war, the site was transferred from federal to municipal ownership on the condition that it be used for low-income housing. The construction of public housing on the Mulgrave site became an official city objective in December 1957, when the project received council approval as a repository for (some of) the residents that would be displaced from the CRA. The costs of the project, expected to top $4.3 million, were borne primarily by the CMHC, which was authorized to cover 75 per cent of the construction and operating costs of Canadian public housing in this period. The city's contribution, 12.5 per cent of the total, was certainly significant, but so too was the expected payoff. The construction of Mulgrave Park, explained Mayor Kitz in 1958, was "an investment in the future" that would "rais[e] the standards of living of the people and improv[e] family living." Effects like these, he concluded, could scarcely be measured.[61]

These effects were to be achieved, in part, through the architecture and outfitting of the housing project itself. Consistent with other CMHC-funded projects in this period, Mulgrave Park included a mix of low-rise and high-rise housing units. Two eight-storey apartment towers were built at the southern end of the site, while the remaining area was outfitted with three-storey, townhouse-style units. The project's overall density, at thirty units per acre, was no lower than that of the "overcrowded" downtown slum and produced a packed-together landscape, with narrow laneways between most of the buildings and no significant open space. With overcrowding understood in terms of inhabitants per *room*, however, the project could be considered a major achievement.[62] Over two-thirds of the units contained at least three bedrooms, enough to fulfil the middle-class norm of partitioned sleeping quarters for parents, boys, and girls. The units also provided separate kitchens large enough "that cooking and eating [could] be done in them with enough space" for both activities and were outfitted with unit-specific household appliances, including fridges, electric stoves, and washing machines. The provision of unit-specific appliances, though questioned by some city counsellors, was considered integral to the overall housing initiative. A CMHC architect, faced with questions about the appliances' cost and potential misuse at an October 1958 city council meeting, conceded that some misuse could be expected at first but proceeded to underline the long-term stakes: "If proper housing is not made available to the present generation," he asked, "when are we going to raise the standards?"[63]

In addition to their new domestic environment, tenants' lives were acted upon through more direct, managerial techniques. The composition of the Mulgrave Park population, for one thing, was the subject of continual discussion and regulation. As I noted above, nonfamily members were explicitly excluded from public housing, as were families who failed to maintain their rental payments while stationed in temporary accommodations after their displacement. Extremely poor households, meanwhile, were admitted to the project in very limited numbers, both to avoid unduly low rental payments to the municipal Housing Authority (which were set at one-quarter of tenants' monthly income) and to address concerns that Mulgrave Park would become another homogenously poor "slum." Once admitted to the project, tenants' lives were continuously overseen and evaluated by Housing Authority officials stationed in one of the buildings. Tenants who exhibited poor "moral character or personal habits," though tolerated initially in order to avoid the appearance of mistreating the people that the city had promised to rehouse, were eventually forced to leave. Six months into Mulgrave Park's operation, the city decided to take aggressive action against misbehaving tenants, and evictions were soon carried out at a rate of two per day, "supplemented by [the] action of the police as required."[64]

Adding to Mulgrave Park's habit-reforming environmental and managerial techniques was a set of more positive, pedagogical measures. New tenants, for example, were instructed in the proper use and care of household appliances, while a partnership between the Housing Authority and local nonprofit organizations enabled the provision of physical recreation programs and study groups for the project's population. The latter initiatives, a city councillor explained in 1962, would do more than simply occupy the tenants' spare time. The tenants, having been inserted into "clean and decent accommodations for the first time," would be instructed through the pedagogical initiatives "to improve themselves and become better citizens."[65] It was thus through a whole series of actions – environmental, managerial, and pedagogical – that Mulgrave Park would fulfil the long-deferred dream of modern housing reformers: the creation of a "higher form of living" among people whose prevailing (unimproved) living conditions seemed to make this impossible.

Mulgrave Park, intended to absorb CRA residents as soon as they were displaced, was completed in a series of stages between November 1961 and June 1962. The causes of the thirty-three- to forty-month delay were manifold and interlocking. The negotiation of a financing agreement between the city, the province, and the CMHC proved to be rather complicated, and the details were still being ironed out two months *after* the dishousing of the first CRA residents whom the project was meant to accommodate. The design of the new housing took another ten months, as the CMHC's architects struggled to please their employer and Halifax officials alike, while the selection of a suitable construction firm occupied an additional eight months. The construction process, finally begun twenty months after the first units were originally scheduled to be completed, entailed its own series of setbacks and cost overruns. Expected to cost $4.3 million, the final bill for the project exceeded $5 million.[66]

The opening of Mulgrave Park in June 1962 was nevertheless greeted with considerable fanfare. Mayor John Lloyd, flanked by dozens of men in suits, appeared before an outdoor podium and dozens of media microphones to celebrate the completion of the city's first major public housing project (see *figure 4.5*). Long-time CMHC brain trust Humphrey Carver was also present and would later praise the aesthetics of the project in his 1975 memoir. "I have always thought that Mulgrave Park ... is a masterpiece in its handling of a very difficult hillside site," he wrote. "The place has a vigorous harbourside character and its walls and steps are full of sculptural surprises."[67] In the background of the opening ceremony, 348 low-income families, a small subset of those displaced by "blight removal" in the preceding three-and-a-half years, were finally allowed to settle into the new homes and the new lives that people like John Lloyd and the well-dressed men at his sides had long ago promised to provide them.

The completion of Mulgrave Park, tied to the CRA redevelopment, quickly bled into a broader rehousing project. A broader project was the official aim since city council's acceptance of the Stephenson Report and its vision of roughly 1,100 new public housing units. The

Figure 4.5 Opening of Mulgrave Park, 1961. Halifax, John E. Lloyd fonds, CR 9B.15.1, credit Maurice Crosby Photography. Image courtesy of HRMA.

Redevelopment Committee, moreover, seems to have viewed every step in the direction of this aim as a positive one. As early as 1957, when no Mulgrave housing units had yet been completed, the committee concluded that "housing has been good business for the city" and began to explore new and larger rehousing initiatives outside the CRA and Mulgrave Park.[68] A pair of further rehousing initiatives were ultimately pursued. The first initiative centred on the old School for the Deaf property on Gottingen Street. With its three-storey building and sprawling six-acre grounds, the Gottingen Street property was identified as a potential redevelopment project in 1959, when the province announced that it would soon be moving the school's operations to the town of Amherst and would be willing to transfer ownership of the property to the city. The city's initial vision for property was relatively modest. The aim was simply to convert the old school building itself into some form of low-income housing. In April 1960, however, it was decided that the project should be enlarged and that the conversion of the area *surrounding* the school property be considered for development as well. Testament to the city's unshakeable confidence at the time, it was soon decided that a fifteen-block section of the Old North End be marked for potential redevelopment and that a study of the area be undertaken to gauge its applicability for federal slum-clearance funding.[69]

The city's decision was followed by a pair of official studies that illuminate as much about the logic of postwar planning as they do about the area studied. The city-commissioned study, carried out in the summer of 1961, involved a building-by-building survey of the fifteen-block area and the classification of each building according to its attainment or potential attainment of the city's minimum building standards. The eventual findings of the survey would be disappointing to a government that had already earmarked the entire area for demolition. At least 75 per cent of housing units, the survey revealed, either attained minimum standards or *could* attain these standards with a

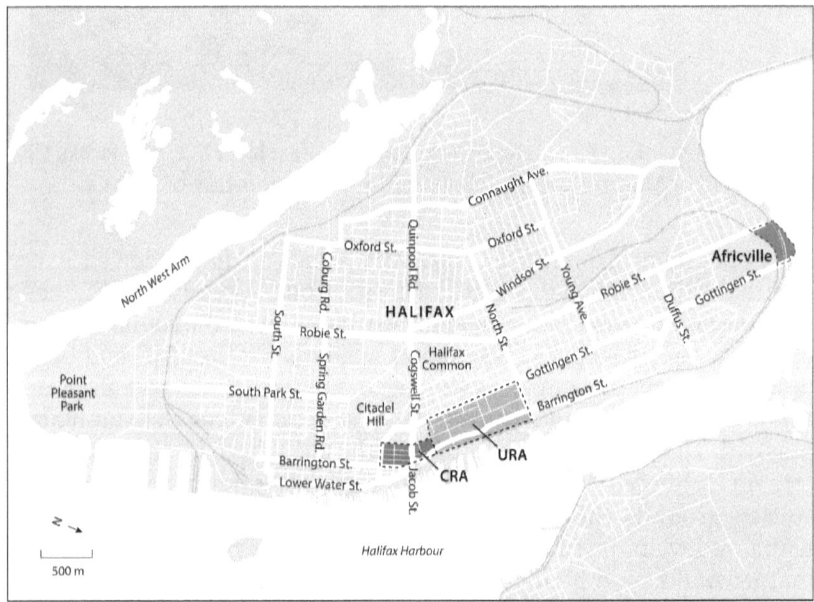

Figure 4.6 Map showing three redevelopment areas. From left to right, these are the Central Redevelopment Area (CRA), the Uniacke Redevelopment Area (URA), and Africville. Map created by Eric Leinberger.

reasonable investment in rehabilitation. These findings were consistent with the reservations expressed earlier in the process by two members of the Redevelopment Committee, one of whom argued that there were "some very nice places" in the targeted area.[70] None of this, however, disrupted the city's belief in the area's "blighted" status. After reviewing various options at a June 1962 meeting, council voted unanimously to pursue the redevelopment of the entire area, now labelled the Uniacke Redevelopment Area (URA), and to open up negotiations with the CMHC about project financing.[71]

The second study of the area, carried out by CMHC officials, outlined what the redeveloped URA would look like. Immediately written off in the study were nearly all of the area's residential structures. Although it was conceded that most housing units were either decent or restorable, the aim of improving the city's housing conditions was considered best achievable through the razing of all existing homes, with the exception of a handful judged to possess "historic" interest. Into the open space thus created the study plotted a series of new land uses. Around 49 per cent of the area would be devoted to new housing units, while 25 per cent of the area (a section bordering on the naval base that contained around 320 "improperly" sited homes) would be reserved for industrial or defence purposes. The remaining area would be devoted to future road-widening projects (17 per cent) and the creation of new "open spaces" (11 per cent). The overall project, divided into six successive phases, would entail the destruction of at least 980 existing housing units and the construction of around 1,100 new ones. While these figures suggest the absence of permanent displacement, the study expected at least half of the new units to be occupied by families displaced from areas outside the URA and entailed no provisions whatsoever for nonfamily displacees (in the URA or elsewhere). The fulfilment of the project would therefore permanently displace roughly two thousand residents – more than half of the URA's current population and four hundred more than the number permanently displaced by previous blight-removal actions.[72]

Not surprisingly, the city's plans for the URA were met with vigorous opposition from many of the area's residents. Some residents pointed out what should have been obvious: many of the area's homes were far from "blighted," and at least $200,000 worth of renovations had been undertaken in recent years to bring certain homes up to Ordinance 50 standards. Others emphasized that many residents were elderly people, who would be "unable to obtain mortgages on new properties." They would therefore "be forced to live in apartments and their small savings would soon be dissipated."[73] Eventually, a petition condemning the redevelopment project was circulated in the neighbourhood, and the signatures of 151 residents were collected. Responses like these, however, did little to divert the city from its established course of action. In a major report in April 1963, the issue of citizen opposition was taken up and very efficiently brushed aside. Noting that some URA families felt attached to their homes "for emotional or financial reasons" and would "inevitably be upset" if their homes were taken away from them, the report quickly transported the issue onto more confident, technical terrain. Living conditions in the area, the report suggested, were often "substandard and unsatisfactory," and the redevelopment would therefore tend to provide "the greatest benefit for the greatest number of people." Opponents of the plan were clearly not the "greatest number." The petition may have amassed 151 signatures, the report concluded, but the targeted area contained upwards of four thousand improvement-needing people.[74]

Having written off the project's opponents, the city launched the URA redevelopment in 1964. Over the next three years, a landscape of old saltbox homes and simple tenements was ripped through by bulldozers and rebuilt as a 184-unit housing project called Uniacke Square. Like Mulgrave Park, the housing units of Uniacke Square were outfitted with a private bathroom, a separate kitchen, and a set of modern appliances. Nearly all of the units contained at least two bedrooms, while over half contained four bedrooms. The density of the overall project was slightly lower than Mulgrave Park (at twenty-eight units per acre) but nevertheless produced a packed-together residential landscape. The near entirety of the project consisted of long rows of two- to three-storey townhouse-style buildings, the sole exception being a six-storey apartment tower on the southwest corner of the site. Beyond these buildings lay an open field on the terrain of the former School for the Deaf edifice, as well as a smaller park on the southeast corner of the project.

The completion of the URA project's first and second phases in 1967 provided new homes for roughly one thousand residents and received praise in the local media for delivering "modern living" to once-deprived people.[75] That the redevelopment project had dishoused at least one thousand people, half of them permanently, was never mentioned in these accounts. This logic, the peculiar algebra of urban renewal, would continue into the project's next two phases. In the end, all but one of the project's six phases were put into motion.

Thus, an additional seven hundred housing units in the URA were either destroyed or repurposed, and nearly three thousand more people were displaced: the scarcely tallied costs of an overall redevelopment project that created 1,100 new housing units.

The final slum-clearance project of the postwar period concerned the long-pathologized community of Africville. The identification of Africville as a slum predated the urban renewal period by at least a half century, and official renewal studies relied greatly on these pre-existing perspectives of the community. The Master Plan, while it demonstrated the slumliness of other parts of the city through detailed calculations, relegated Africville to slum status in a swift, dataless sentence. Africville residents needed to be removed, the plan concluded, "as soon as reasonably possible."[76] Similarly, the Stephenson Report's otherwise meticulously data-backed analysis of urban conditions was momentarily suspended when it came to Africville. About the community, the report concluded, "there are only two things to be said." The first was that "the families [would] have to be rehoused in the near future"; the second was that "the land which they now occupy will be required for the further development of the City."[77] Demonstrating the pathological status of a Black community evidently required little effort in this (or any other) period. The assumed displaceability of Africville residents, moreover, allowed planners to project into the area a whole array of other land uses, from a "most desirable" residential district to an employment-boosting industrial zone, which would ostensibly benefit the overall population.[78] Africville residents, of course, had never been part of planners' imagined "overall population" or "city as a whole." It would be difficult, in this case, to imagine a land use that would not benefit "the city" more than the homes of Africville residents.

Conditions in Africville had improved little, if at all, since the early twentieth century. Africville homes, though sometimes relatively sizeable and well maintained, were most often small, weather-beaten, and rundown. City services like street paving and running water continued to be absent in Africville, and new industrial facilities, including an extension of the city dump, continued to be established along the community's perimeter. As might be expected, these conditions had real consequences for the lives of Africville residents, including heightened rates of water-borne disease (due to contaminated well water); more deadly incidents of fire (more difficult to extinguish due to absent water services); and various accidents and fatalities linked to surrounding industrial facilities. Africville residents, however, tended to see these conditions very differently than urban planners and other city officials. For one thing, they were more likely to link observable conditions to their more distant historical and institutional causes. Africville residents could often trace the sequence of events and political decisions that had produced the problems in their surroundings, and they understood that white racism, rather than Black pathology, was their fundamental cause. As one resident remarked in 1962: "The city didn't do anything to improve Africville ... because we were coloured. If they had been white people down there, the city would have been in there assisting them to build new homes, putting in water and sewers and building the place up."[79]

More importantly, Africville residents tended to recognize and affirm the forms of community vitality, mutual aid, and subsistence that they had managed to sustain amid oppressive, externally imposed circumstances. Their lives, though certainly impaired by urban planning, were not defined by this impairment. The community had gained renown, for example, for the success of Africville-raised athletes like world boxing champion George Dixon, as well as various Africville-based sports teams and musical ensembles. Africville Baptist Church, meanwhile, remained an important hub of religious and cultural life, and Black Nova Scotians from across the region could be expected to descend upon the community every Easter for weekend celebrations and shallow-water baptisms in Bedford Basin. Economically, Africville residents maintained vital practices of subsistence tied to the land (small-scale vegetable cultivation and animal husbandry), to the water (fishing), and to the surrounding area ("scavenging" in the nearby dump). In most cases, finally, Africville households owned their own homes, and families often used the potential subdivision of Africville-owned land and the mobilization of community-supplied construction labour to extend the benefits of homeownership to successive generations. All of these practices helped to shield Africville residents from the worst effects of anti-Black racism and to create forms of individual and social life that people greatly valued. Indeed, a 1962 survey by the Dalhousie Institute of Public Affairs found that roughly two-thirds of the residents liked living in Africville and had no interest in leaving.[80]

These perspectives ultimately mattered very little to the city, even as improving the lives of Africville residents came to be touted as one of the central reasons for the redevelopment project. This new rationale, absent from the city's 1915 plan for Africville, was cited in all of the major planning reports of the period and came to the forefront of redevelopment discussions in the 1960s. At this point, the national media had begun to publish dramatic stories about Africville, shaming the city for allowing problematic conditions to persist, and University of Toronto sociologist Albert Rose had delivered his expert assessment of the community in a 1962 report commissioned by the city. Professor Rose, like the national media, described the impoverishment and racial segregation that he observed in Africville as a grave social injustice and concluded that "the only solution to this problem was to get the people out of there and into something that more approximated a normal way of life."[81] Rose's conclusion was echoed throughout the rest of the 1960s by prominent Halifax planners, politicians, social workers, and journalists. Thus, whether the aim was to create a "better" use of urban land or to help Africville residents adopt "a normal way of life," the elimination of the community was part of the solution – whether Africville residents agreed or not. It would take "courage," a local journalist wrote in 1964, for the city "to move persons who do not want to be moved ... even as it will surely be for their own good."[82]

The redevelopment of Africville was approved by city council in 1962 and officially launched two years later. The terms of relocation offered to Africville residents varied widely. Homeowners (with clear, legal title to their property) were offered an average of $7,847, while other residents received as little as $500. Once an agreement was reached, the city moved rapidly to have the residents' belongings removed and either bulldoze or burn down the residents' home. One morning, residents awoke to find that the Baptist Church had been bulldozed in the dead of night. Later, two boys were nearly crushed when the city's bulldozers arrived unannounced and began to plough through a shed in which they were playing. When, as sometimes occurred, residents refused to relocate, the city began an expropriation process, and (illegally) presented the latter as something that residents had no rights or mechanisms to contest. By 1969, all but one Africville resident, Aaron "Pa" Carvery, had been removed from the community, and the construction of a new cross-harbour bridge that required Carvery's land was in full swing. Anxious to avoid costly construction delays, the city threatened Carvery with expropriation. When this failed to move him, the city offered him a suitcase containing $14,000 in cash, which Carvery found insulting and refused. Finally, in October 1969, Carvery agreed to compensation of $14,398, paid by cheque, and reluctantly prepared to leave his long-time home. On November 23, his home was brought to the ground, and Africville was no more than a memory.[83]

Africville residents, once they departed their old home, soon found the city's promises of a better life contorted, disavowed, or both. Some residents were offered a place in public housing, where the taps delivered safe drinking water and sanitation was much improved, but where other conditions of living were noticeably absent. Restrictions on living arrangements in public housing often broke up extended families that had once lived in the same house. Land-based economic subsistence, creatively forged in Africville, was no longer tenable in public housing, and Africville residents who were previously homeowners were forced to pay a monthly rent for the first time in their lives. Other residents, deemed "unsuitable" by public housing authorities, had to find a new home in a tight, racist, private housing market. Some residents endured racist attacks in predominantly white neighbourhoods, while others were compelled to leave the region entirely. Other promises to improve Africville lives were similarly scaled back or abandoned. An adult-education program promised to Africville relocatees was cancelled after the first year. A city-promised employment program, meanwhile, provided paid work to between thirteen and fifteen displacees but was suddenly disbanded in 1965. Welfare benefits that the city had included in relocation agreements were disbursed to some displacees, but only until 1967, when the social worker in charge of disbursement left his position and the individual taking over the file refused to recognize the residents' special status.[84] "The gaping wound we opened," writes African Nova Scotian poet David Woods about Africville, "Not understanding ... The new evil unleashed across those steel tracks."[85]

The fate of Africville residents was not altogether unusual in this period. Their removal from the land was, of course, one part of a much broader project in which thousands of poor and working-class residents, the majority of them white, were forcibly displaced from areas like the CRA and URA. Planners' disregard for Africville residents' own desires was similarly commonplace, affecting everyone from the owner of the Citadel Tavern to the renewal-fighting residents of the URA. Cross-race commonalities like these have led many scholars of urban renewal, in Halifax and elsewhere, to argue that renewal was a classist rather than also a racist project.[86] A closer look, however, renders such conclusions untenable. While poor residents, white and Black, were similarly pathologized by renewal planning, the alleviation of these pathologies was premised on features of impoverished life that were, in fact, unique to white residents. Planners assumed, in particular, that poor residents rented rather than owned their present homes, and that their lives would be improved to the extent that they were allowed to rent *better* homes. That Black residents, in Africville and elsewhere, tended to own their homes and depended on land- and community-based forms of subsistence was *known* by city planners, but it figured nowhere in the model of improvement they devised: a model that, in the best of cases, provided better *rental* housing for renewal displacees.[87] Black residents, to the extent their lives concerned urban planning, were thrust into a project of improvement designed for others and noticeably at odds with their own situation.

Despite noticeable differences, then, urban renewal mirrored early comprehensive planning in the place it offered to Black people – a place that was really no place at all. Like early comprehensive planning, urban renewal could envision improvement and progress only within the parameters of whiteness, a process of change channelled between a white present and a white future. Like early comprehensive planning, it follows, urban renewal can only be partially understood through Foucauldian work on the conception and management of human life. This work, though attentive to the role of norms in the management of individuals and populations, overlooks the position of blackness in relation to normality and pathology. As Joy James suggests, the multicontinental enslavement of Black people entailed their eviction from the category of the human in the period in which Foucault locates the emergence of modern, life-managing power. Blackness, consequently, lies outside the conceptions of normality and pathology that Foucault examines, and there is no program of normalization (as Foucault theorizes it) proper to Black life.[88] The point is not, it seems to me, that programs of normalization are never applied to Black lives, but that such programs, when they do exist, take hold of Black lives as if they were white. In the urban renewal era, this meant seeing poor Black residents as tenants when they were not and when, in fact, multiple city-produced reports recognized that they were not. It meant displacing from the mind the possibility of progress that *began* with the real conditions of Black life and *ended* somewhere other than normative whiteness.

To highlight the racial specificities of postwar renewal is not to excuse or ignore the thousands of white lives that were disrupted, displaced, and undermined by renewal policies, especially those who, lacking "family" status, were never offered entry to the period's life-improving public housing projects. It is, rather, to show how race entered into the formulation of a planning project whose targets were not *only* racialized and that produced, for this reason, subtly different consequences for targeted white and Black residents. These differences, however subtle, were indeed important. White residents targeted by urban renewal received, in the best of cases, a form of improvement that forcibly disrupted their lives, disregarded their agency, and encased them in a paternalistic and subjugating form of "higher living" (i.e., public housing). Black residents targeted by urban renewal received, in the best of cases, a form of improvement that conceptually effaced and practically destroyed their existing modes of survival, from homeownership (which reduced their need for money) to land- and community-based forms of subsistence – everything that allowed them to endure and make a life in an anti-Black city. The result was a decimation of life across the Black experience of urban renewal, even those fortunate enough to gain entry to public housing. Urban renewal, for Black displacees, was not just paternalistic and subjugating but quasi-genocidal.

Improving Traffic Circulation

The destruction of Africville was the last major initiative of the urban renewal period, though it was not intended to be. A whole series of further planning projects were on the drafting board at the time of Aaron Carvery's expulsion, and planners' backs were bent to the task of moving them forward. Many of these projects, ultimately left unfinished, were meant to improve the so-called circulatory system of the city: the network of roads and bridges that carried car traffic across the city's expanding landscape. The circulatory system was believed to be improvable, to some extent, through relatively modest changes. The 1945 Master Plan concluded that traffic congestion in the city was often the result of entirely "unnecessary interference" on important streets. Accordingly, the plan proposed a series of interference-removing solutions that included the elimination of curbside parking, the sequestering of delivery making to the back (or side) of commercial buildings, and the shifting of pedestrian traffic on commercial streets like Gottingen, Agricola, and Quinpool to dedicated shopping complexes with off-street parking lots.[89] Alongside measures like these, however, planners also devised more elaborate and socially disruptive interventions, from the stitching of a new "diagonal" roadway through the fabric of an Old North End neighbourhood to the imposition of a whole new network of high-volume expressways and water-spanning bridges upon the existing urban landscape.

The improvement of traffic circulation was an integral part of postwar renewal in cities across North America. In the United States, the postwar period gave birth to thousands of new expressway projects designed to carry traffic both between cities and within them. Within cities, expressway projects were meant primarily to facilitate the functional separation of land uses and suburban expansion that other planning policies were seeking to produce, rendering it feasible for people to travel efficiently between increasingly distant places of residence, work, and leisure. In many cases, the new expressways cut through already developed areas, and the destruction produced in the process was sometimes seen as an added benefit of these projects. New York City's Robert Moses, one of the most ambitious transportation planners of this period, described the construction of expressways through already-built sections of the city as a process of "hack[ing] your way with a meat axe." The route of the Cross-Bronx Expressway, a seven-mile project completed under Moses's oversight between 1965 and 1973, "hacked" northward at one point for no other conceivable reason than to plough through a set of old tenements home to over five thousand Jewish, African American, and Puerto Rican residents.[90] In Baltimore, city leaders eagerly blasted the I-170 expressway through the Black neighbourhood of Harlem Park before even *planning* the roadway sections that would connect the expressway to the broader transportation network – sections that were never ultimately constructed. Dubbed "the highway to nowhere," the I-170 directly displaced at least one thousand Black families and catalysed a disastrous neighbourhood decline, while contributing almost nothing to the city's traffic circulation.[91]

North of the border, major expressway projects were devised and partially carried through in all major Canadian cities, as well as in a host of smaller centres like Saint John and London. As in the United States, the construction of expressways was integral to the new urban landscape that postwar renewal aimed to produce, and images of more efficient circulatory systems appeared in many of the CMHC-financed urban renewal studies of the 1950s and 1960s. For Montréal mayor Jean Drapeau, Canada's closest replica of the power-hoarding Robert Moses, traffic was the "blood" of the urban organism, and roadways were its blood-carrying "arteries." The growth of the city, Drapeau explained in a 1955 National Film Board documentary, put pressure on the prevailing circulatory system; unblocking the system, reducing "arterial" congestion, was thus a vital planning priority. The costs of city-wide survival, not surprisingly, were borne disproportionately by working-class and racialized neighbourhoods like the Saint Antoine district, the geographical heart of Montréal's Black community. Already harmed by a slum-clearance program in 1965, Saint Antoine was further wounded by the 1966–7 Ville-Marie expressway, which was re-routed from its original plan to blast through an additional section of the long-pathologized neighbourhood. In Montréal, as elsewhere in Canada, expressway construction hitched new sources of funding (especially the federal financing made available by the 1956 and 1964 NHAs) to longer-standing conceptions of population improvement. Through expressways, the population "as a whole" would experience the manifold benefits of improved traffic circulation, while nonnormative populations would bear the untabulated costs.[92]

High-volume expressways were part of urban renewal planning in Halifax from the beginning, and their conception embodied the major aims of the overall renewal project. Efficiency, an aim central to slum clearance, provided a rationale for expressway construction as well. The latter was believed to promote efficiency in at least two senses: the efficient movement of traffic through the circulatory system (something that expressways were believed to promote) and the efficient use of urban land (something that was pursued through *other* planning strategies, like the separation of residential and commercial land uses, that seemed to necessitate the construction of expressways). As in New York City, these two senses of efficiency were sometimes palpably fused in Halifax. The Master Plan's proposed diagonal roadway, for example, was devised to cut straight through the low-income Old North End on its way to the downtown ferry terminal (see figure 4.2 above). According to the plan, this configuration would not only "facilitate [efficient] movement to and from the main business district," but also dispense with considerable low-value housing and therefore "add to the value of the properties through which [the road would] pass."[93] The passage of the 1956 Housing Act amendments provided new incentives for this kind of two-pronged improvement. To the extent that a new expressway could be linked to a best-use-achieving redevelopment project, the CMHC would cover up to 75 per cent of the cost of acquiring intervening properties.

The centrepiece of this period's proposed circulatory improvements was undoubtedly the high-volume expressway that came to be called Harbour Drive. First suggested (albeit vaguely) in the Stephenson Report, Harbour Drive acquired greater concreteness in a set of engineering studies commissioned by the city in the mid-1960s. In these reports, the massive ambitions and technocratic visions of renewal-era expressway planning come to the foreground. Designed to carry six lanes of relatively uninterrupted car traffic, the expressway would rim the eastern edge of the Halifax peninsula from the base of a new harbour-spanning bridge in the north to the new shipping-container terminal in the south (see *figure 4.7*). Along the way, the road would rip through a series of existing structures, including a set of historic buildings at the northern end of the downtown, the homes of eighty to one hundred low-income families just north of the downtown, and a much-used children's playground still farther north. These by-products of circulatory improvement were either ignored in the engineering studies or else weighed against the ostensible benefits of an efficiently aligned roadway. The destruction of historic buildings, a 1965 study explained, was necessary in order to keep the expressway's road curvatures below the traffic-slowing threshold of four degrees. If desired, the report suggested, these buildings could always be "dismantle[d] and reconstructe[d]" in some other location.[94]

Guided by the engineering studies, the construction of Harbour Drive was meant to proceed in three phases. The first phase, the erection of the so-called Cogswell Interchange at the northern end of Scotia Square, proceeded roughly in tandem with the latter development. An adjoining expressway had always been promised to Scotia Square's developers; its fruition, the developers hoped, would carry suburban workers and consumers to its location and fill its cavernous garage with parked cars. Linked physically and ideologically to the renewal of CRA, the Cogswell Interchange qualified for CMHC funding (covering 75 per cent of land-acquisition costs) and was thus the easiest phase to move forward. In 1963, the city began to acquire and demolish an intervening set of residential, commercial, and military properties – some of them later deemed great expressions of the city's architectural heritage – and began construction of the interchange in 1967. The second phase of the expressway, a section extending south from the Cogswell Interchange to the container terminal, was meant to enter construction shortly thereafter. By 1966, detailed plans for Harbour Drive South (as the section was often called) had been drafted, and significant intervening properties along the east side of Upper Water Street had been acquired. These efforts would soon be challenged, as I discuss below, by the emergence of an unexpectedly determined network of activists opposed to the proposed expressway. The third phase, discussed in chapter 5, was meant to extend northward from the Cosgwell Interchange to

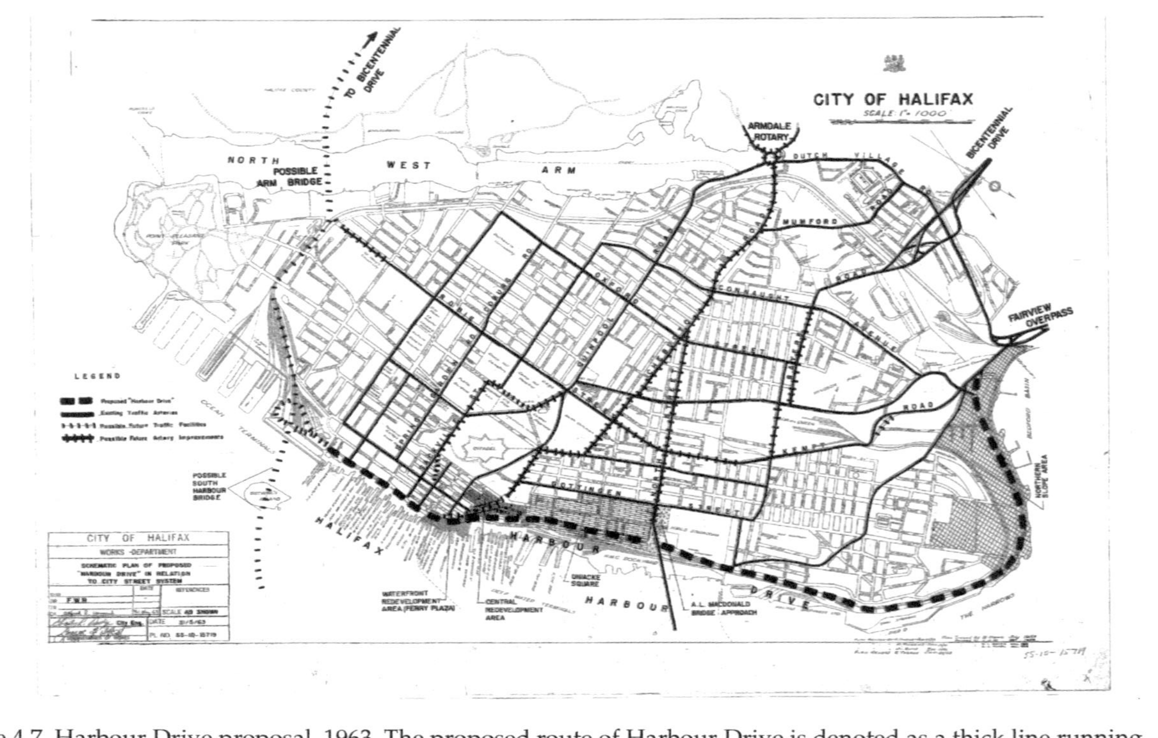

Figure 4.7 Harbour Drive proposal, 1963. The proposed route of Harbour Drive is denoted as a thick line running along the harbour at the bottom of the map. Halifax, Engineering and Works Department plans, HRMA, RG 35-102-39P, plan no. SS-10-15719. Image courtesy of HRMA.

the McKay Bridge at the tip of the peninsula. This phase, too, encountered strong and ultimately successful activist opposition.[95]

Opposition to the expressway's second phase (Harbour Drive South) emerged amid the flowering of urban-focused activism in North American cities. In the United States, the first signs of full-scale "expressway revolt" appeared in San Francisco, where the opposition of neighbourhood associations, environmental groups, and engaged journalists to the massive waterfront-rimming Embarcadero Freeway resulted in a majority city council vote against the project in 1959. Similar opposition movements gradually took shape in New Orleans, Boston, New York, and dozens of other US cities. In Canada, activists in Vancouver registered the postwar period's first victory, achieving the annulment in 1966 of a planned East-West expressway that would have ploughed straight through the city's Chinatown. Similar high-profile expressway battles soon emerged in major cities like Toronto, Montréal, and Edmonton, as well as cities as small as Kenora, Sarnia, and Brantford.[96]

Embodied in these campaigns, in many cases, was a relatively wide range of constituencies, objectives, and political orientations. One important constituency was the North American New Left. Like the New Left in general, members of this faction of the expressway revolt were most often well educated, employed in the liberal professions (or else studying to be), and proponents of what Luc Boltanski and Eve Chiapello call an "artistic critique" of contemporary society: a critique that focused upon the ostensibly deadening and conformist character of capitalism, culture, and the state. Expressway projects, from this perspective, were seen as a threat to cities' "aesethetic sensibilities" – a threat, among other things, to cities' prevailing architectural heritage, environmental qualities, and neighbourhood cohesiveness.[97] Alongside the New Left, the expressway revolts attracted a set of quite different constituencies, including a wide range of Old Left, anti-poverty, and Black liberation activists. Expressways, from this perspective, were viewed as a material threat to the working-class and racialized communities through which they were most often constructed – a threat that could impact residents whether they were physically displaced or allowed to remain in a negatively affected neighbourhood. The union of diverse constituencies and objectives, though not always equitably managed, boosted the political force of emerging anti-expressway movements and contributed significantly to the victories and policy shifts that they were able to achieve.[98]

While a broad-based urban movement would eventually emerge in Halifax, the first serious blow to postwar renewal in the city mobilized a relatively narrow group of residents, organizations, and state officials concerned with the preservation of the city's architectural heritage. At a moment when poor and racialized Haligonians were continuing to be thrown into the street by slum-clearance projects, these actors recognized the destruction caused by urban renewal in a very specific form: the potential destruction of centuries-old and largely empty commercial buildings. An opposition movement of this kind gained a political footing when, in 1963, the local Maritime Museum Board identified the old Privateers' Warehouse on the Halifax waterfront as a potential site for a new museum and approached the federal Historic Sites and Monuments Board about acquiring and retrofitting the structure. The museum board's inquiry led the federal institution to commission an architectural study of Privateers' Wharf and six surrounding buildings. Based on the study, the institution chose to designate the entire seven-building complex a "national historic site." The designation, though it did nothing to prevent the buildings from being demolished, attested to the enduring value of a section of the city that had come to be regarded as derelict and disposable, and it motivated discussions between the city and the federal Department of Indian Affairs and Northern Development (IAND), in which the latter pledged in 1964 to cover 50 per cent of the capital costs of any locally rooted effort to preserve and restore the designated buildings. The buildings, importantly, stood in the path of the Harbour Drive South project that the city was beginning to pursue with increased intensity in this period.[99]

Around the same time, the Halifax-based Heritage Trust of Nova Scotia (HTNS) began to expand its nascent heritage-preservation efforts in the city. Formed in 1959, HTNS focused initially on the preservation of particularly distinctive Halifax homes (usually South End mansions). By the mid-1960s, however, it began to challenge a series of privately initiated high-rise developments and state-directed urban renewal projects on the basis of these projects' detrimental effects on the city's particular historical character. Expressing an "artistic critique" of contemporary planning, HTNS viewed high-rise development and urban renewal as symptomatic of a "headlong rush for progress," a warlike attack on the city's "individuality" and historically constituted "sense of place."[100] "Big is better," the group claimed, had become the misguided maxim of postwar planning. The "gems of our architectural heritage" – especially the centuries-old commercial buildings in the urban core – were its foremost victims.[101] Among the group's most important concerns in the mid-1960s was the potential demolition of the heritage-designated waterfront buildings. Seeking to defend the buildings, the group submitted a series of submissions to city council between 1964 and 1968, in which the buildings were described as an invaluable and irreplaceable "reflection of [the city's] maritime heritage." Preserved and properly restored, moreover, these buildings were described as a potential anchor for a downtown core that productively fused the "atmosphere of the past" with the land-use needs of the present. In an elaborate 1968 submission, HTNS outlined a new vision for the old buildings and their surroundings, including the establishment of a public marina, yachting supply stores, new restaurants and boutiques, a travel agency, and a bank branch.[102]

Efforts to preserve the heritage-designated buildings achieved a significant advance in 1966, when long-time city councillor Allan O'Brien was elected mayor. O'Brien was known to be favourable to heritage concerns as a councillor.[103] True to form, one of his first moves as mayor was to appoint outspoken Heritage Trust member Lou Collins to the chair's position of the recently created Civic Advisory Committee on the Preservation of Historic Buildings. Collins, individually and through Heritage Trust, had been pressuring the city to preserve the heritage-designated waterfront buildings since at least 1964, when he provided city council with an elaborate restoration proposal modelled on Boston's Faneuil Hall Market, Baltimore's Harborplace, and New York's South Street Seaport. Given these earlier efforts, Collins's appointment to the advisory committee would establish a beachhead for heritage interests within an institution originally devoted to balancing heritage preservation with the fulfilment of "development proposals including traffic improvements."[104] At this point, in effect, the municipality was advancing in two opposite directions at once. Some municipal officials, including development director Robert Grant and chief engineer Charles Dodge, were taking significant steps towards the construction of Harbour Drive South. The city, having already completed the necessary engineering studies and acquired some intervening buildings, then notified the owners of the remaining intervening buildings in January 1968 that their properties "would be required by the city" by August of that year.[105] At the same time, Mayor O'Brien, Lou Collins, and a few other municipal officials were taking actions to preserve the very same buildings and therefore obstruct the planned expressway – at least in its proposed form.

The fate of Harbour Drive South was ultimately determined in a complex and contentious series of city council meetings between March 1968 and July 1969. In March 1968, council was asked to evaluate a pair of expressway development scenarios. The first scenario entailed a pair of one-way arteries along existing (but reconfigured) downtown streets. In the short term, this scenario would require the partial demolition of three heritage-designated waterfront buildings to provide a sufficiently wide artery along Upper Water Street. In the long term, it would also require the demolition of a set of historic buildings to the west of Upper Water Street, as the one-way arteries were expanded into a single, six-lane expressway through the downtown. The second scenario also entailed a pair of one-way arteries; the easternmost artery, however, was shifted slightly to the west. While this shift would allow the waterfront buildings to be retained, it would also require the immediate destruction of several historic buildings to the west of Upper Water Street and would embroil the city in a whole new set of financial obligations: the waterfront buildings, no longer needed for the expressway, would be left in the city's possession; the CMHC's promised support for their acquisition would most likely be withdrawn; and an entirely different set of buildings (those to the west of Upper Water) would suddenly need to be purchased. City council, ignoring the pleas of Lou Collins and HTNS to choose the second scenario, ultimately voted 11–2 in favour of the first option, preserving the urban renewal status quo.[106]

Seemingly well established at this point, political support for Harbour Drive South slowly unravelled over the next fifteen months. Following the March 1968 meeting, Mayor O'Brien and Collins travelled to Ottawa to seek federal funding to preserve the four heritage-designated waterfront building not threatened by the expressway. The result of their inquiries, in June 1969, was a commitment from the IAND to cover 50 per cent of the buildings' exterior restoration, but only if all seven heritage-designated buildings were included in the preservation project. The effect of the IAND's proposal was to strengthen the argument for re-routing the expressway and preserving the waterfront buildings. The buildings, once seen as burden to the city if they were not demolished, could now be devoted to a feasible and federally supported restoration project. The IAND proposal, while stoking a new round of public debate, failed to excite city council. Reviewing the proposal at a June 1969 meeting, council voted 5–2 to affirm the approved route of Harbour Drive South (an implicit rejection of the IAND-proposed restoration).[107]

This decision, however, was badly received by the Halifax public. Halifax residents, suddenly incensed, bombarded city councillors with angry phone calls, letters, and in-person confrontations in City Hall corridors. Over a two-week period, over five hundred residents voiced their discontent to City Hall, a level of formal communication that Mayor O'Brien considered unprecedented in the city's history. The local media, generally a strong supporter of urban renewal, suddenly adopted a more critical perspective on this specific renewal project. The Halifax *Mail-Star* published a particularly stinging set of articles in the weeks following council's decision and printed mail-in "coupons" that readers could sign and send to City Hall to convey their disapproval of the heritage-destroying expressway route.[108] This was an unprecedented stance for the *Mail-Star*. Neither the prior destruction caused by slum clearance nor the looming destruction of "Pa" Carvery's home in Africville motivated this kind of action by the newspaper. As criticism of council's decision intensified, Mayor O'Brien arranged to tour Margison and Associates' engineer W.A. Stewart through the waterfront buildings that the expressway would destroy. This, O'Brien hoped, would help to persuade the engineer to develop the best possible case for a re-routed expressway at a future meeting. Meanwhile, rumours began to circulate that certain local developers – eventually identified as John Fiske and Ben McCrea – were interested in restoring and repurposing the waterfront buildings.[109]

In the face of unprecedented backlash, city council opted to reconsider the expressway route one more time. Added to the discussion at this point was a new development scenario, prepared on relatively short notice by W.A. Stewart. This new scenario would shift the easternmost one-way artery slightly to the west, as well as narrow its width to just two lanes (see figure 4.8). These changes would spare not only the waterfront buildings but also the historic buildings to the west of Upper Water Street – buildings that even HTNS had been willing to see destroyed in March 1968, but that had attracted increasing attention from residents, state officials, and local entrepreneurs in the period since then. The new scenario, advantageous from a heritage-preservation perspective, would undoubtedly produce an "inferior" roadway, with nonoptimal roadway curvatures, lower average speeds, and lower traffic volumes. W.A. Stewart, present for council's discussion of the scenario, was noticeably unwilling to stand behind his own compromise-ridden design, highlighting its 20 per cent reduction in traffic-volume capacity and the "bottlenecks" that would be produced at the entry to the Cogswell Interchange. "During a rush hour period," he commented, "traffic could be backed up on Water Street down to the Hotel Nova Scotian [south of downtown]."[110]

The choice was thus eminently clear. To vote for the original scenario was to affirm the principles and priorities that had guided urban planning for more than twenty years. The logic of efficiency, in particular, would continue to triumph over the preservation of existing buildings, citizen objections, and various less "rational" planning alternatives. To vote for the new scenario, in contrast, was to underscore possibilities that had previously been absent from contemporary planning discussions. The city's architectural heritage and prevailing "sense of place" would be accorded significance, and new actors – including the advisory committee, HTNS, the IAND, and various heritage-concerned business owners, professionals, and developers – would capture a place in the city's planning regime. Council, at its July 1969 meeting, officially reversed its earlier stance, voting 6–4 in favour of the new heritage-preserving expressway route. Two of the affirmative votes came from councillors who had been absent from the June 1969 vote, while another vote, clearly pivotal, came from the long-time city councillor, real estate agent, and (former) expressway supporter Cyril Abbott. Harbour Drive South, in its high-volume expressway form, was officially dead in the water.[111]

The annulment of the expressway was a significant blow to urban renewal and a modest move towards something different. Its most immediate effect was to spare a set of historic buildings that, in the coming years, would become the basis of an ambitious and landscape-defining rehabilitation project. This project, begun in 1972, received financial support from all three levels of government and was carried out by a new heritage-oriented development company, Historic Developments Incorporated, established by John Fiske and Ben McCrea. Included in the project, in the end, were the seven heritage-designated buildings, as well as over twenty other historic buildings at the northern edge of the downtown. This collection of buildings, carefully reconstructed and repurposed, have become one of the city's signature commercial, cultural, and tourist districts: a vast expanse that includes, as HTNS once advised, high-end boutiques and restaurants, as well as the seventy-thousand-square-foot campus of the Nova Scotia College of Art and Design. More broadly, the annulment of Harbour Drive South signalled a potential shift in planning orthodoxy. Once committed to increased efficiency, planning was forced to attend to concerns about

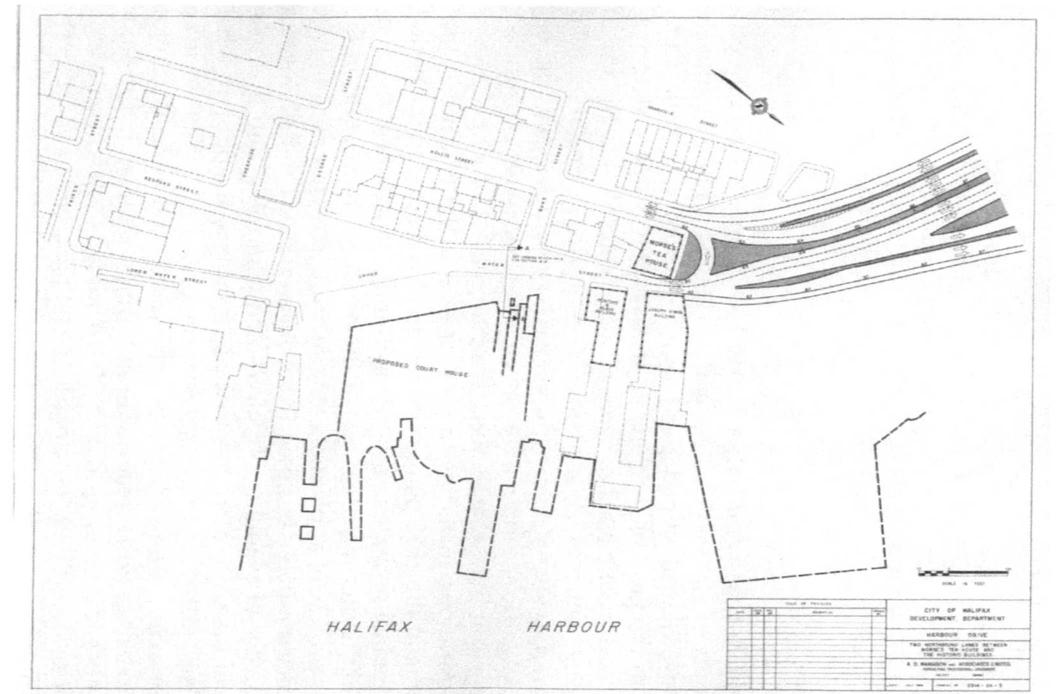

Figure 4.8 Proposed re-routing of the expressway, 1969. A.M. Margison and Associates, Evaluation of Alternate Proposals for the Connection of Upper Water Street to the Cogswell Street Interchange, HRMA, RG 625.725E-2314-SK-5. Image courtesy of HRMA.

heritage, architectural character, and place identity. Once guided by technical expertise and rational calculations, planning was now forced to deal with the ideas and interests of everyday citizens. Or at least *certain* ideas and interests. The disastrous effects of urban renewal on poor and racialized Haligonians had yet to motivate opposition outside the affected communities themselves. Clearly, these effects figured nowhere in the heritage-focused opposition of Mayor O'Brien, Lou Collins, or HTNS. This very limited form of opposition, however, would soon expand into a broader challenge to urban renewal, in which more residents and more concerns would find a place.[112]

Conclusion

The twenty-five-year period after World War II entailed an unprecedented process of planned change, both social and spatial. Multiblock urban "slums" were identified, purchased or expropriated by the state, and razed to the ground. A phalanx of new office towers, shopping complexes, and public housing projects were stitched into the urban fabric, offering "better" land uses, as well as "better" forms of life. Old roadways were widened, new bridges were constructed, and the beginnings of an efficient intracity expressway system were constituted. These changes, in many cases, were the culmination of long-standing planning aspirations, including those expressed in the 1905 model tenements plan and the 1915 plan for Africville. Obstructed in the period of their formulation, these and other aspirations found their means of fulfilment in the funding programs of the postwar federal state; in the expertise of professional planners, engineers, and architects; and in a political process reliably buffeted from citizen input. The result was a massive transfer of planning objectives and principles onto the lives and spaces of the city – a process that city residents, swept up in what Heritage Trust called a "headlong rush for progress," could do little to amend or avert. Alongside the new buildings and infrastructure it brought into being, urban renewal is enduringly signified in the older spatial forms that it brought to an end, including old neighbourhoods like the upper streets and the Uniacke street area, which are scarcely remembered today, as well as the traditional "maritime" sense of place that was partially superseded by placeless property developments and that was almost buried beneath an expressway.

Urban renewal, however, was more than a careless expression of technical expertise and quasi-totalitarian state prerogatives. Indeed, technical expertise and state power found their point of anchorage in other, more benevolent aspirations. Consistent with earlier planning initiatives, urban renewal found its primary vocation in the improvement of human life through spatial means. From the redevelopment of the CRA to the construction of Harbour Drive South, postwar planning sought to provide the spatial requisites of broad-based human flourishing – the continual improvement, as the Master Plan put it, of the city's "general welfare." The destructive power of urban renewal, rather than a departure from this objective, was ultimately rooted in a peculiar conception of its fulfilment. The improvement of life, for postwar planning, was everywhere framed in relation to norms that not all residents were perceived to exhibit. The nonexhibition of these norms by particular individuals or subpopulations, a condition widely attributed to the slums, signified a social pathology, as well as an opportunity for improvement. In some cases, the "pathological" were discounted and displaced in the pursuit of planning objectives (like the "best use" of land) that would ostensibly improve the "general welfare." In other cases, their lives became the very material of improvement. Their normalization, through initiatives like public housing, would ostensibly improve their own lives, as well as the "general welfare" – whether they agreed with this diagnosis or not. Technical expertise and state power found a purpose and justification in coercive, life-aiding ventures like these.

While the improvement of life tended to be understood in singular, normative terms, its practical effects were much more diverse. Heritage Trust's criticism of urban renewal as a "headlong rush for progress," consistent with many scholarly analyses of renewal, masks the ways that different populations were actually situated in relation to this "progress." The people most severely affected by urban renewal were the period's five thousand poor and working-class "slum" displacees, people who could achieve progress only through the forcible actions of outside authorities. Within this broad category, however, important distinctions need to be recognized. Impoverished white residents, though pathologized, could at least be imagined as progressing. There was an imaginable trajectory from their current condition to a norm-abiding, modern life. Impoverished Black residents, in contrast, were never imagined as progressing from their *actual* conditions. Planning never considered, that is, what progress might mean for people who were generally homeowners (rather than tenants) and generally practitioners of land- and community-based forms of subsistence (rather than fully reliant on the labour market or social assistance). The only progress available to Black residents was thus to be thrown into a white program of improvement that destroyed the basic conditions that had sustained their lives for decades in a difficult but still viable form. Postwar planning, unable to imagine progress from a Black starting point, could only eliminate the self-created conditions of life that distinguished them. For African Nova Scotians, as George Elliott Clarke suggests, modern "progress" began with the planning-induced disintegration of Black community *as* Black.[113]

The official vision of the city and its future, of course, was always subject to contestation. While affected residents' opposition to the redevelopment of the CRA, the URA, and Africville was effectively sidelined, a small group of heritage-supporting activists and city officials were able to halt the construction of an expressway that would have, in the eyes of planners, created a better life for the city as a whole. The campaign against Harbour Drive South annulled certain aspects of postwar renewal – a significant political victory – but it left other aspects uncontested and fully intact. Indeed, it is discomforting to note that the form of planning-induced destruction that was most widely recognized *as* destruction in this period pertained to a collection of (largely empty) historic buildings. The destruction of Africville, still in process at the time of the Harbour Drive struggle, was either ignored by heritage supporters or else (as in the case of Mayor O'Brien) actively pursued by them. Without dismissing the validity of heritage preservation, it is important to notice how *modest* was the shift entailed by this new planning objective: the symbols of a white, bourgeois, and colonial past were granted protection, while the material, present lives of poor and racialized Haligonians were left vulnerable. The postwar rush towards progress was evidently more or less "headlong," depending on the distance of its targets from dominant norms. Distinctions like these, the traceable cracks in a seemingly totalizing project, need to be recognized and their role in producing differently livable lives abolished.

5 "A Place to Enjoy Oneself": Anti-Renewal Activism, Citizen Involvement, and the Limits of Urban Amenity

The outlines of a relatively new form of urban planning in Halifax began to appear in the final phases of an expanding struggle over postwar urban renewal. A struggle that began in the mid-1960s as a relatively isolated contest over the fate of certain historic buildings gradually widened and intensified in the late 1960s and early 1970s, as new activist organizations, newly elected politicians, and newly formed state institutions entered the fray. Collectively, these opponents of urban renewal represented a diverse and sometimes conflicting series of constituencies, objectives, and ideologies. And yet, the extensive and multifaceted consequences of renewal policies in Halifax provided these groups with a common political target and a generally shared commitment to the creation of a new, postrenewal future. Among the various planning ideas that gained support in this context, the most consequential pertained to the aesthetics and experience of the downtown core. As one activist group explained in 1972, Halifax residents had begun to yearn for a new style of urban living, and they demanded a correspondingly new approach to urban planning. "We have [now] radically changed our ideas of what a city is all about," the group announced. The downtown, seen by postwar planning as a mere "commercial and financial centre," now needed to be seen as a terrain of varied and pleasurable urban experiences: "a place to live, work, and enjoy ourselves on a 24-hour basis."[1]

The demand that planning create "places to enjoy oneself" was a relatively common refrain in the anti-renewal movements of the late 1960s and early 1970s. At its core, the demand brings attention to the particular spatial conditions and subjective effects that urban planners have understood through the concept of "amenity."[2] A concept with a long history, amenity typically refers to spaces that are developed and used in such a way that they create positive feelings among proximate populations. Some of the spatial conditions that have frequently been thought to constitute amenity have included distinctive architecture, pleasant streetscapes, and the absence of "nuisances" like excessive noise and pollution. Some of the positive feelings that have been thought to emanate from amenity, meanwhile, have included "satisfaction," "happiness," and especially "enjoyment." While the concept of amenity appeared in European and North American planning discussions as early as the mid-nineteenth century, it tended to be subordinated to other concepts and priorities in mainstream planning practices until the emergence of broad-based anti-renewal and countercultural movements in the 1960s.[3] For many 1960s activists, amenity represented everything that was ignored and damaged by urban renewal policies, and their efforts to revive the concept helped to inaugurate an important shift in planning orthodoxy. When Halifax activists demanded a downtown in which to "live, work, and enjoy oneself," they were participating in this revival of amenity and the eventual shift in planning practices that it would bring about.

Significant in many respects, the new practices and priorities nevertheless preserved one of the most fundamental elements of the modern planning regime. Now, as before, planning's efforts to produce a better form of life would be indexed to a singular, normative conception of the human being. A normative human subject is observable, first of all, in the concept of amenity itself, a concept that attributes positive feelings to specific *spatial* conditions and therefore substitutes a particular experience of these conditions for the inevitably varied experiences of different urban populations. A normative subject is also apparent in the political processes through which many activists and state officials hoped to confront and supplant the prevailing urban renewal regime. As in other North American cities, opponents of urban renewal in Halifax frequently called for increased "citizen involvement" in planning processes as a potential counterweight to the enduring authority of renewal-supporting politicians, planners, and businesses.[4] Though potentially more democratic, calls for citizen involvement ultimately entailed a restrictive image of the involved citizen: an individual whose politics stemmed from individual "interests" that were widely shared and that tended not to conflict with the "interests" of others. In complex ways, this model of citizen involvement tended to normalize the activities of already-privileged groups and structured the new political processes to their benefit. Indeed, the emergence of a simplistic concept of amenity – a downtown that was presumed to allow *everyone* to "live, work, and enjoy themselves" – owed much to the normatively structured process through which new planning practices were demanded.

The political struggles of the late 1960s and early 1970s brought important changes to urban planning in Halifax. More than just bringing an end to urban renewal, these struggles brought new planning practices and priorities into the public domain and helped to constitute a significantly new period in planning history. Support for new forms of planning was nourished by the creation of new activist groups, the election of new politicians, and the formation of new state institutions. This support found expression and political power in the course of high-profile public forums on urban issues, the creation of a broad-based activist alliance, and a hard-fought battle over a planned expressway project called Harbour Drive North. As much as these struggles changed urban planning, however, they also protected important aspects of the status quo. Now-familiar distinctions between normal and pathological filtered into the political processes through which new planning ideas emerged and sharply delimited the terrain of human life that postrenewal planning would seek to nurture. The promotion of amenity, a key activist demand in this period, ultimately centred on a space – the downtown core – that had recently been cleared of poor and working-class residents and that remained distinctly off-limits to the local Black population. For these residents, the aims of the new planning practices were nothing new: the promotion of a better life that was never theirs to live and the creation of better places that were no place at all.

The Expansion of the Anti-Renewal Struggle

An expanding struggle over urban renewal in Halifax took shape amid the proliferation of political struggles in the city and around the world. Globally, the late 1960s were marked by the escalation of decolonization and anti-imperialist movements in the Third World, the formation of anticolonialist and anti-imperialist solidarity movements in the First World, and the development of political formations like Black Power and Red Power that sought to overthrow the "internal" and "settler" colonialism of First World countries. These movements emerged alongside various New Left and countercultural movements in the First World, whose political sensibilities and aspirations tended to be more "artistic" (focused on questions of aesthetics and alienation) than "social" (focused on questions of inequality, violence, and exploitation). North American cities, a vibrant site of social-movement formation, also became an important *target* of the same movements. Black Power activists' pursuit of intercommunal revolution at the global scale frequently involved local confrontations with urban renewal projects, as well as efforts to develop and implement more emancipatory planning alternatives. Countercultural movements, meanwhile, often mounted more artistic challenges to planning policies, including challenges to the "disappearance" of neighbourhood-based cultural practices and city-specific architectural identities that activists across the globe attributed to the creative destruction of postwar renewal. These and other strands of political contestation, though not always resonant, contributed to an increasingly vibrant and multifaceted challenge to policies and proponents of urban renewal.[5]

In Halifax, the late 1960s was a moment of unprecedented political vitality. In the span of a few years, at least forty new activist groups appeared on the political scene, many of them concerned to some extent with urban issues. The still-vital Ecology Action Centre, formed by student activists at Dalhousie University, dates to this period. Its promotion of efficient public transportation, among other things, helped to reframe planning discussions that had long centred on the development of efficient automobile circulation. New Black organizations like the Africville Action Committee, Blacks United for More Money, and the Black United Front (BUF) were other products of this period. The devastating effects of postwar renewal on Halifax-area Black communities drew these groups into urban planning debates, while their connections to flourishing civil rights and Black Power activism elsewhere nourished the effectiveness of their organizing and the insistence of their political demands. New tenants' associations and neighbourhood organizations, finally, provided a forum for local deliberations around planning issues and a vehicle for mobilization around specific planning projects. Particularly significant were the newly formed tenants' associations at Uniacke Square and Mulgrave Park, while important neighbourhood organizations included the Upper Hammonds Plains Community Development Association and the North End Neighbourhood Centre. The latter, led by a pair of (white) American expatriates with experience in the civil-rights struggle, eventually collaborated with BUF on a high-profile and successful campaign against slum housing (discussed in chapter 6).[6]

One of the most prominent groups to put forward a new, postrenewal vision of urban planning in Halifax was Heritage Trust of Nova Scotia (HTNS). By the late 1960s, HTNS had already achieved important victories in terms of heritage protection and the annulment of the proposed Harbour Drive South expressway project (discussed in chapter 4). Alongside these efforts, the group campaigned for an array of further changes in planning policy and vision during this period, including (most importantly) a set of height restrictions on new downtown property developments, which were finally instituted in 1974.[7] Labelled "view planes," these restrictions were meant to preserve certain views of Halifax Harbour from atop Citadel Hill, while allowing high-rise development to continue in certain locations. An important impediment to the prodevelopment thrust of urban renewal, the view planes also expressed a relatively new vision of urban planning. This vision emphasized the elements of city life that, while generally ignored and depleted by urban renewal, were considered important by many residents – elements described by HTNS as the city's "visual qualities," "individuality," and "amenities."[8] More than just spatial qualities, these elements were consistently described in HTNS's activities as the prerequisites of a particular set of experiences that urban life was meant to provide. A properly preserved heritage building, for HTNS, was a structure that provided "visual enjoyment," while the prevailing view of Halifax Harbour was a source of "environmental joy."[9] The idea that urban planning ought to produce enjoyable experiences was a relatively new one in Halifax, but it would soon find a broad range of supporters.

HTNS's vision of urban planning resonated with the objectives of other local groups. The Halifax Downtown Business Association (HDBA), revived and reconstituted in 1968, supported similar planning policies on the basis of their potential contribution to the downtown economy.[10] The economic characteristics of the downtown, of course, had been supported in certain respects by urban renewal policies. Most notably, slum clearance and the promotion of high-rise property development had increased the area's concentration of business management and administrative activities. Other aspects of the downtown economy, however, were harmed by these same policies. The opening of new indoor shopping spaces like Scotia Square, for example, had lured significant retail activity away from the downtown's older shopping streets. Meanwhile, the development of new residential suburbs – promoted by urban renewal – was generally accompanied by the construction of new retail spaces, including suburban shopping malls, which pulled retail activity away from the downtown entirely. The weakened position of downtown retailers was visible by the mid-1960s in boarded up storefronts along Barrington Street, and especially in the symbolically significant migration of the Eaton's department store from the downtown to the suburban Halifax Shopping Centre in 1964.[11] For the HDBA, supporting downtown retailers was an essential task, and it collaborated frequently with HTNS in this period on planning initiatives that promised to make the downtown a more attractive and distinctive place for Haligonians to spend their money.

Within the confines of City Hall, advocates of postrenewal planning policies found their strongest supporter in Allan O'Brien, an elected city councillor from 1956 to 1966 and the city's mayor from 1966 to 1971. O'Brien, as noted in chapter 4, was not a critic of renewal per se. He strongly supported the city's policies of "slum clearance" and the displacement of thousands of residents during his time as city councillor, and his reign as mayor is most vividly associated with the destruction of Africville, the most oppressive steps of which were taken during his mayoralty. At the same time, O'Brien vocally criticized the destruction of local heritage buildings and the damaging effects of renewal policies on the downtown retail environment. Expressing his concern about the departure of the Eaton's store from the downtown in 1964, O'Brien called for a reappraisal of the renewal program that was quickly transforming the central city. A downtown that was "primarily office [space]," he explained to council in 1964, would likely be "[in]sufficiently alive to support the amount of retail [activity] that is there now."[12] To sustain downtown retail activity, O'Brien suggested the exploration of several new planning policies, from the creation of a more attractive waterfront to the improvement of the city's public transit system.

One of O'Brien's most significant moves as mayor was to create an ad hoc "downtown committee," with HTNS and HDBA as founding members. Tasked with devising new planning objectives and policies for the downtown core, the committee organized a series of workshops and public forums; commissioned background studies on downtown land uses, pedestrian circulation, and physical design; and produced, in 1972, a completely new plan for the downtown entitled, "What Kind of Downtown Do We Want?"[13] Like the independent initiatives of HTNS, the Downtown Plan centred on the sensible qualities of urban space – the spatial conditions, that is, of a distinctly enjoyable urban experience. Concretely, the plan advocated the redesign of downtown streets to promote pedestrian circulation, the preservation of heritage buildings, and the encouragement of a mix of land uses (residential, commercial, and cultural). These and other policies, the plan suggested, would provide the underpinnings of a more pleasurable form of urban life. The downtown would become "highly concentrated" and spatially "varied," a stimulating environment through which "people [could] walk freely and pleasantly."[14] The downtown would remain a place to "work" – the development high-rise office buildings would still be promoted – but it would also provide the spatial conditions in which people could "live and enjoy themselves."[15]

These new planning initiatives, from the view planes to the 1972 Downtown Plan, gave public expression to long-standing but historically sidelined socio-spatial priorities. In a general sense, the initiatives' focus on "enjoyment" can be situated within a current of biopolitical power discussed by Foucault and a few other scholars.[16] The promotion of enjoyment, Foucault suggests, appeared in state practices in Europe as early as the seventeenth century, though it was not until much later that it became a significant state priority. In the mid-twentieth century, notably, the promotion of enjoyment became important to a new form of biopolitics that Foucault labels "vitalpolitics." The latter is most closely associated with the German political economist Alexander Rüstow, who coined and developed the concept in a series of mid-twentieth-century essays. Rüstow famously critiqued the "mania of [material] progress" in modern society and positioned "vitalpolitics" as a preferable alternative. In place of modernity's fixation on material progress, vitalpolitics would prioritize the immaterial "well-being and contentment" of the population.[17] In place of modernity's fixation on technical knowledge and centralized decision making, vitalpolitics would also redistribute decision-making power to the smallest feasible unit (most often, small-scale communities). As Foucault points out, Rüstow's combined emphasis on contentment and decentralized decision making would become commonplace in the 1960s, especially among New Left movements in Europe and North America.[18] In these and other contexts, sensible experiences of enjoyment or contentment became an important part of what it meant to be human and an important part of what it meant for the state to manage human beings as an aggregate.

The new planning initiatives in Halifax are also connected to a particular concept in urban planning. This concept, generally termed "amenity," points towards the sensible experiences that particular spatial conditions are thought to produce.[19] Though often associated with the post-1960s period, this concept has a much longer history in modern planning. In the late nineteenth century, for example, the renowned landscape architect Frederick Law Olmsted emphasized the "therapeutic" qualities of well-designed parks and argued that the creation of better (and larger) parks could help to counteract the "depression" and "irritability" that were otherwise inherent to urban living.[20] The spatial qualities of public parks, qualities Olmsted sometimes called "amenity," were described as essential to a well-adjusted and con tented urban life. A half century later, Boston civic leader Robert Wood argued that "the comfort and pleasure of [urban] inhabitants" ought to be emphasized not just in public parks but throughout the city, while Chicago planner Daniel Burnham prominently argued that the "nervous strain of city life" needed to be counteracted through well-devised planning practices that rendered people more "content."[21] In Halifax, Mayor Robert MacIlreith's 1908 contention that the city needed to be made a more "agreeable" place in which to live can be seen as another early call for the promotion of amenity.[22] In all of these examples, importantly, the creation of amenity was meant to act upon the population, producing the kinds of sensible experiences that Foucault and Rüstow associate with vitalpolitics. Though amenity is discussed by neither theorist, it clearly functioned as a planning-specific means of creating feelings of well-being, contentment, and enjoyment.

While generally concerned with the sensible qualities of urban life, the significance and specific meanings of amenity have tended to vary over time. Its significance, to begin with, tended to be minimized from the mid-nineteenth century until the end of the urban renewal period, due largely to the much greater significance attached to other planning priorities. Some planners, in this context, sought to promote amenity strictly in specific areas like public parks, while others sought to integrate amenity into a framework of (ultimately more significant) planning priorities.[23] The meaning of amenity, meanwhile, has been tied to an evolving series of general and roughly synonymous human feelings that it has been thought to produce, including "pleasure," "happiness," and "satisfaction."[24] More specific feelings, like "agreeableness" and "enjoyment," have entered discussions of amenity in particular periods and then fallen out of use. A similar evolution is evident in the spatial conditions that have been thought to underlie amenity. In general, these conditions have included beautiful architecture and urban design, convenient pedestrian routes and street furniture, and the minimization of nuisances like traffic and pollution.[25] In the 1960s, new activist and countercultural movements added other spatial conditions to the meaning of amenity, like "livability" and "cachet," while Richard Florida's early 2000s creative-class theory (discussed in chapter 7) brought attention to the amenity-linked qualities of "excitement," "authenticity," and "buzz."[26] All of these definitions invoke a lively, more-than-material conception of the human – a conception of human flourishing, upheld by urban planning, that exceeds more basic considerations like health, longevity, and welfare.

As HTNS and Downtown Committee pursued their work, similar planning proposals were being formulated by particular state institutions. By the mid-1960s, federal support for urban renewal had begun to unravel. The dominant thinking within the Central Mortgage and Housing Corporation (CMHC) began to shift from the promotion of large-scale renewal projects to the development of smaller-scale and community-driven alternatives, while Pierre Trudeau's Liberal government, elected in 1968, announced a two-year moratorium on urban renewal in November of the same year (a moratorium that was never lifted).[27] Around the same time, federal economic-development agencies began to see new forms of urban planning as a potential development-inducing catalyst in the country's "lagging" regions.[28] Particularly significant to the Halifax context were the planning policies of an economic-development agency called the Nova Scotia Planning Secretariat (NSPS). Formed in 1968, the NSPS was a unique and ultimately short-lived institution. One of its main tasks was to bring coherence to the various development programs of the federal and Nova Scotia governments, and its unconventional institutional structure reflected this mediating role. Funded by the federal Fund for Rural Economic Development and directed by federal-level bureaucrats, the agency was concerned primarily with provincial development projects and was expected to work closely with the Nova Scotia premier. Like other development agencies at the time, the NSPS took a strong interest in urban planning, especially in Halifax, and it ultimately played a key role in the annulment of urban renewal and the transition towards something different.[29]

The NSPS regarded the adoption of new urban planning policies in Halifax as the key to an economic turnaround in the city and across the province. Essential to this view was the assumption that Nova Scotia's rural areas were in the midst of an irreversible decline. The natural resource-based and semi-industrial sectors on which these areas depended had been stagnant for decades, the NSPS observed, and they would be increasingly unable to support these areas at their existing population levels in the future. The situation of urban areas – meaning, effectively, the Halifax area – seemed more promising. As the Atlantic region's largest city, Halifax was regarded as having the best chance of developing the high-end "service" or "knowledge" industries that the NSPS and other development agencies believed to be the future of First World economies. The city's chances here would be enhanced, the NSPS reasoned, to the extent that Halifax could become a much larger city, augmenting its population from 120,000 inhabitants in the late 1960s to around 500,000 by 1991. At the heart of the NSPS's plans for the province, therefore, was a massive shift in population over a two-decade period: a 400,000-person exodus from the region's moribund small towns and villages towards soon-to-be *metropolitan* Halifax. Urban planning, necessary for the accommodation of this larger population, would also be essential to its attraction. The promotion of amenity entered into the NSPS's vision as a kind of population "magnet" – the creation of a set of spatial conditions and associated feelings that could help to draw 400,000 new residents to the city.[30]

The promotion of amenity appeared frequently in discussions of economic development and the promises of the "knowledge economy," even in the 1960s. In 1966, the majority of the US economy became service based for the first time, and the significance of this transition gave rise to wide-ranging interpretations and speculations. In 1967, Daniel Bell's two-part article in *The Public Interest* provided an especially vivid and influential contribution to this discussion.[31] In the emerging "post-industrial" economy, Bell argued, the leading sectors would depend on the talents and training of elite scientists, mathematicians, computer engineers, and various professionals. The increasing significance of this professional class, in turn, would induce a whole series of changes in organizational structures, political priorities, and forms of urban living. On the latter issue, Bell predicted that the particular "social ethos" of technical and professional workers would soon become predominant. In a now-familiar proposition, Bell argued that these workers' demands for "more amenities, for a more urbane quality of life in our cities, for a more differentiated and better educational system, and an improvement in the character of our culture" would need to be taken seriously by any politician or policy maker who hoped to seize the opportunities available within a changing economic system.[32] Bell's depiction of a new, postindustrial ethos resonated with similar analyses at the time, including Rüstow's vitalpolitics (first available in English in 1961) and the cultural politics of the New Left.[33] His work would also give life and direction to many late-1960s discussions of urban planning and economic development in the United States, Canada, and elsewhere.[34]

North of the border, Canadian regional economist and planning theorist Benjamin Higgins had been developing a similar analysis since the late 1940s. An important public intellectual and trusted advisor to the Canadian state, Higgins had long espoused a relatively broad-minded approach to development and planning issues. As early as 1949, just as urban renewal was getting underway, he advanced the unorthodox argument that the "satisfaction" of the population was the proper objective of planning policies, and he urged professional planners to seek a "maximization [of] amenity" within "each bit of land" in the city.[35] In the 1960s, Higgins enfolded his earlier emphasis on amenity into his theorizations of the emerging knowledge-based economy and the advice that he provided to specific development projects in the Canadian cities of Kitchener-Waterloo, Moncton, and Montréal. The creation of amenity, he now argued, was fundamental not just to the "satisfaction" of the population but also to the attraction and development of the "new, scientifically oriented" businesses upon which First World economies would increasingly depend.[36]

The NSPS's analysis clearly paralleled that of Daniel Bell and other theorists of the new society that was beginning to emerge. Essential to this new society, for the NSPS, was not simply the predominance of knowledge industries and workers but also the distinctive interests that these workers possessed.[37] Knowledge workers, the NSPS argued, possessed a unique set of tastes and desires, and these would need to be recognized in the workplace and well beyond it. Work, for this population, was not regarded as a chore but an "experience." Work was meant to be creative, fulfilling, and propelled by workers' own subjective desires and "development needs." "In the future," an NSPS-funded report explained in 1971, "work becomes fun and, [along] with leisure activities, a component of a full, pleasurable existence."[38] Outside the workplace, this population would tend to express similar interests. Other workers might finish the working day in a commercial or industrial district and commute to their home in the suburbs; this new population, in contrast, was more likely to live in the city centre and transition relatively seamlessly "from work to theatres and from shopping to simply strolling" in the same general milieu. The city, for this population, was a place of enjoyment, a "place of contrasts ... where a wide variety of enjoyable experiences" provided the basis of self-chosen and self-actualizing "ways of life."[39]

It was on the basis of these speculations about the interests of knowledge workers that the NSPS ultimately proposed that a new form of urban planning was essential to the future of Halifax. Less fixated on imperatives like "efficiency," this new form of planning would need to recognize and enhance the aspects of urban life that tended to please the world's knowledge workers and that would tend therefore to increase the preponderance of this population segment within the city. Hence, the "algebraic models" and "technocratic" doctrines of the past would need to be left behind, and new attention would need to be devoted to certain qualitative characteristics: the look and feel of the city, its liveliness and vibrancy, and its overall package of differentiated and uniquely enjoyable experiences. In a word, urban planning would need to focus its attention on "amenity." Concretely, this would entail a collection of planning projects, including the preservation of heritage buildings, the creation of "aesthetically pleasing" streetscapes, and the "complete intermingl[ing]" of downtown offices and residences with "stores, theatres, galleries, lounges, restaurants, and so on."[40]

While a similar vision had been expressed in documents like the Downtown Plan, the NSPS linked this vision to a rather different rationale. More than providing "visual pleasure" or strengthening downtown businesses, the promotion of amenity in Halifax was regarded by the NSPS as the linchpin to an ambitious, region-wide transformation. It was through amenity, first of all, that the agency hoped to please elite knowledge workers, to recognize and satisfy their distinctive social ethos. The purpose of amenity, here, was consistent with other formulations. Its purpose was to produce sensible experiences within a population through spatial means. The pleasing of knowledge workers, however, was just the entry point to larger concerns. Its ultimate purpose was to catalyse a whole series of economic and demographic changes that the NSPS believed to be necessary. Through amenity, the NSPS reasoned, knowledge workers and businesses would be attracted to the city; the urban economy, in turn, would grow and thrive; and the excess inhabitants of the rural periphery (some of them future knowledge workers, some of them not) would be sucked up and siphoned into a more fruitful location. For the NSPS, in short, the promotion of amenity would help to make certain lives happier and more fulfilling. From there a whole set of economic and biopolitical objectives could be achieved. Amenity, for the NSPS, was the vital medium through which the economy and the population could be remade at once.

Encounter on the Urban Environment

The proposals of the Downtown Committee and the NSPS would not be implemented as easily as the two groups might have liked. Their ideas, for one thing, needed to be reconciled with the still-unfinished project of urban renewal in Halifax and the continuing support for renewal policies within the local political establishment. The NSPS, an agency funded by the federal government and allied to provincial representatives, was perhaps especially cognizant of the challenges that its proposed changes were likely to face among municipal decision makers. Any new ideas, moreover, would have to vie for attention amid the proliferation of planning-related proposals and demands emerging from the city's burgeoning activist movements. With new activist groups regularly appearing on the political scene in the late 1960s, urban planning in Halifax was criticized, challenged, and reimagined in many different ways, not all of them compatible with the visions of the Downtown Committee and the NSPS. As in other North American cities in this period, therefore, new planning priorities in Halifax would need to win over (or overcome) a relatively broad and heterogeneous set of political interests and actors. This process, the attempted channelling of a new form of planning through a network of local actors, would be deeply shaped by the new forms of "citizen involvement" that were beginning to gain traction among activists and certain state officials in this period.

Demands for increased citizen involvement were increasingly common in the late 1960s. In the United States, the "community control" movement was perhaps the most significant effort to ground government decision making around issues like public health, education, and planning in the communities most affected by these issues. In neighbourhoods across North America, moreover, 1960s activists formed a range of new (nonstate) institutions that were both controlled and run by community members, aiming, in some cases, to democratize not just public services but the economy as well.[41] At the same time, citizen involvement was gaining support among state officials and institutions in many parts of North America, though not necessarily for the same reasons or through the same mechanisms envisioned by activists.[42] Among Halifax-based activists, groups as diverse as HTNS and BUF advocated new forms of citizen involvement as a remedy to forms of decision making that they judged to be unaccountable to everyday people and aspirations. Met with reluctance among most municipal officials, these demands found support among sectors of the federal state, including the Department of Manpower and Immigration and the newly formed NSPS. For the NSPS, indeed, organized citizen involvement was seen as both conducive and necessary to the broad changes that it hoped to introduce in Nova Scotia, and much of its efforts and financial resources were ultimately devoted to the development of a more engaged and well-organized citizenry in Halifax.

The NSPS's support for citizen involvement emerged from its critical assessment of the existing political structure in the Halifax metropolitan region. The existing political structure, for one thing, was divided into three separate jurisdictions: the municipalities of Halifax, Dartmouth, and Halifax County. Planning at a wider metropolitan scale, a necessity if the area was to develop coherently into a 500,000-person metropolis, was believed to be impeded by this fragmented political structure and the recurring intermunicipal rivalries over resources and development that it fomented. The existing structure, the NSPS believed, was also mired in political conservatism and vested interests. Political forces in Halifax and the neighbouring municipalities could be expected to cling to the planning status quo rather than reconfigure planning practices to emphasize urban amenity, attract elite knowledge workers, and shift towards a knowledge-based economy. For these and other reasons, then, the existing political structure seemed to require a shake-up, and the promotion of increased citizen involvement across the metropolitan region was one of the ways that the NSPS hoped to achieve this.[43]

The NSPS's first effort to transform decision making in the Halifax region involved the creation of a new metropolitan-level institution called the Metropolitan Area Planning Commission (MAPC). Formed in 1969 and funded by the NSPS, MAPC was overseen by a pair of elected officials (each) from Halifax and the two neighbouring municipalities, and was tasked with carrying out planning and policymaking at this wider scale.[44] When, in 1970, the federal Department of Regional Economic Expansion (DREE) earmarked $200 million for infrastructure projects in the Halifax area, it was MAPC that was expected to channel this money into the appropriate locations.[45] With MAPC in place, the NSPS's next move was to nurture forms of citizen involvement that would both orient and bring legitimacy to the new metropolitan body. The aim, in practice, was to connect the area's citizens to relevant community organizations (both new and existing) and to enable these organizations to formulate planning-related demands, communicate these demands to MAPC, and generally provide "a strong, permanent

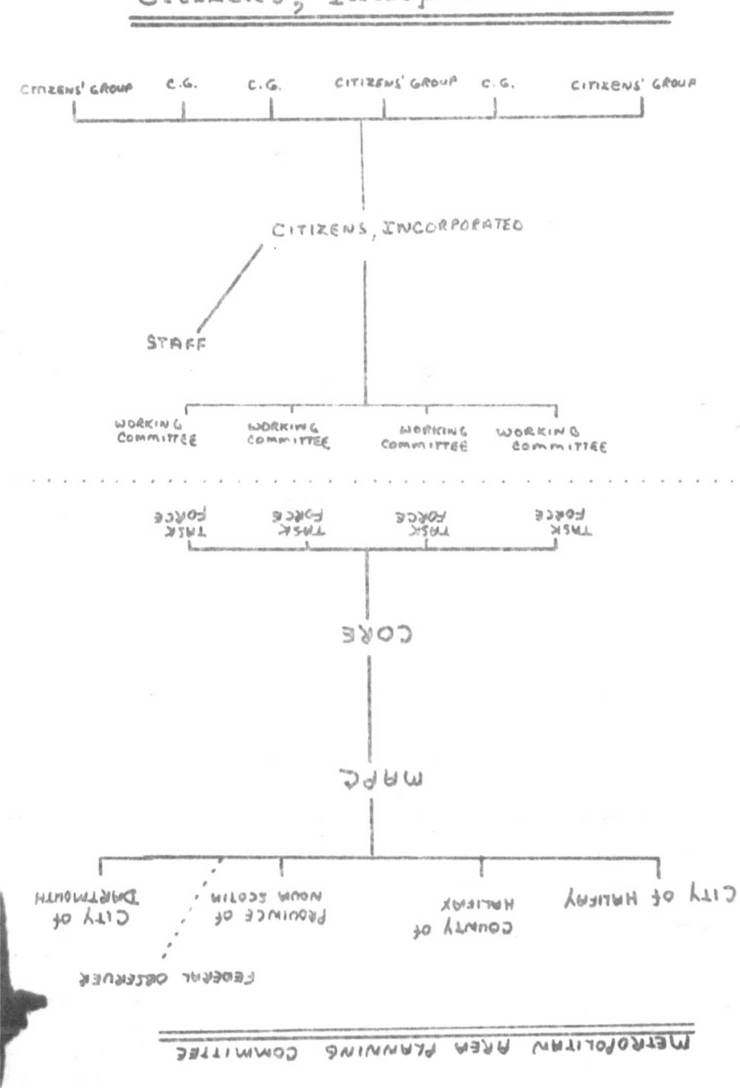

Figure 5.1 NSPS model of public participation, 1971. MAPC is on top, while a citizens' organization is at the bottom. "The 4th Estate," 4 March 1971, NSARM, Brenda Large fonds, MG 1, vol. 1436, no. 4. Image courtesy of NSARM and Brenda Large.

feed-in to the planning process."[46] As the secretariat-produced diagram in *figure 5.1* indicates, the two parts of the new decision-making structure were meant to fit together neatly and synergistically: the community would make its interests known from "the bottom," while MAPC would devise appropriate planning and policy solutions at "the top." This two-part structure, the NSPS hoped, would make it possible to introduce the planning policies that the region ostensibly needed and that the existing political structure was too fragmented and moribund to implement on its own.

The NSPS's efforts to promote citizen involvement in Halifax drew much of their practical inspiration from the work of the contemporary Chicago-based community organizer Saul Alinsky. Outlined in books like *Reveille for Radicals*, Alinsky's now-famous model of community organizing is distinguished, first and foremost, by the importance that it ascribes to individual "self-interest."[47] The latter, for Alinsky, is the inherent possession of every individual and "the prime moving force in [people's] behaviour."[48] The objective of community organizing, it follows, is to harness people's self-interests to concrete social and political outcomes. The aim, more specifically, is to produce the conditions in which groups of people can recognize the self-interests that they share – individual-transcending interests that he calls "community interests"[49] – and work together to further them. Formulated in this way, Alinsky's model could be used in a range of situations in which a diversity of concerns or objectives would need to be whittled down to just one (or a few). Activist-driven "community organization" was one such situation; state-facilitated "citizen involvement" was another. The appeal of Alinsky's model to state institutions was not as surprising as it might seem. While billed as a framework for "radicals," the model owed much more to the liberal theories Alinsky encountered as a student at the University of Chicago than to any radical tradition, and it fit perfectly with the liberal pluralist doctrines that some state institutions were adopting to manage citizen discontent.[50]

Borrowed from Alinsky, the NSPS's vision of citizen involvement informed one of the most important political events of the period: a week-long public forum in January 1970 called Encounter on the Urban Environment. The event, organized by the NSPS, centred on a group of twelve urban "experts," each of them selected (by the NSPS) for their expertise on particular urban issues. Among the dozen, the most significant were Ed Logue (a planner with experience in Boston and New York City), Lucius Walker (the director of the New York-based

Interreligious Foundation for Community Organization), and Benjamin Higgins (a professor of economics at University of Montréal).[51] The experts, though they came with experiences and knowledge to share, were also expected to listen to Halifax residents and tailor whatever advice they provided to the concerns and objectives that they heard local residents express. To enable this kind of dynamic, the experts would spend each day of the week-long event touring the city and meeting with thirty-five issue-specific citizens' groups (some of which were organized specifically for the event). At the end of the day, the experts would present their reflections and receive public feedback at an open-invitation public forum. The nightly forums, the most dramatic element of Encounter Week, brought urban issues into the public domain as never before. Attended in person by hundreds of local residents, the forums were also broadcast live on television, discussed each day in the local print media, and eventually commemorated in a two-hour National Film Board documentary.[52]

Among the recurring themes of the event was the future of the Halifax economy. Reiterating the NSPS's own conviction, many of the invited experts highlighted the postindustrial transition that was taking shape among First World urban economies and implored Halifax to move in this direction as swiftly as possible. As Benjamin Higgins explained, the Maritime region had only two real choices. The first was to encourage outmigration "and see the entire Maritime economy shrink to some 500,000 people or so, who could be supported comfortably, though not luxuriously, through a natural resource-based pattern of development." The second option was "to follow the New England example, and above all, the Boston area example," and pursue the development of Halifax as a thriving economy centred on "human resource" or "knowledge-based" activities.[53] Pursuing the second option would involve an economic and biopolitical transition similar to the one favoured by the NSPS. It would mean attracting and nurturing a highly skilled population in the region's largest city (Halifax), and it would mean using amenity-focused urban planning to do so. Essential to the future of province, Higgins told the public, was the retooling of Halifax's urban planning regime to prioritize the preservation of the city's architectural heritage and physical beauty, and to enable the creation of a downtown core that would be "strong," "dense," and loaded with opportunities to live, work, and play.[54]

Another recurring theme of the event was the proper structure of political decision making. Consistent (once again) with the NSPS's convictions, many experts argued that a profound shake-up of the existing political structure in the Halifax metropolitan region was required. As Atlanta-based expert on "governmental structure" Frank Steggart explained, better decision making would tend to require a twofold "reorganization of the public." He explained: "The reorganization of the public and other systems today really revolve around the dilemma, the dilemma of trying to concurrently *centralize* certain kinds of functions in authority and *decentralize* others ... You are likely to have more planning, programming, advisory bodies at the sublocal community or neighbourhood levels, [and] at the same time ... you are moving towards various forms of centralization within the governmental structure."[55] The first part of the described reorganization had, at this point, already been achieved through the creation of MAPC in 1969. The second element, the "community or neighbourhood level" element, remained to be fully introduced. It was Alinsky-style community organization – promoted, in part, through Encounter Week itself – that was expected to bring this element into being.

Alinsky's model shaped Encounter Week in several ways. In the lead-up to the event, for one thing, the NSPS urged local residents to organize themselves into groups on the basis of their individual-but-overlapping "self-interests." It was these groups, forty-three in total, that met with the invited experts in the course of the event. The idea that people ought to organize around their own interests (rather than, say, the interests of more marginalized groups) was new to many activists, and their organization into interest-based groups would certainly affect the kinds of concerns they were able to express during the event. Participants at the nightly forums, however, did not always follow the model's basic tenets and needed to be corrected or brought to order by the invited experts. One violation of the model singled out by the experts was the expression of an unduly *narrow* interest, an interest that pertained to a relatively small group of people and could not, therefore, become a widely shared "community" interest. As Ed Logue explained:

> We've heard this evening a French concern, we've heard a black concern, we've heard an artist concern. We've heard an Indian complaint about the interesting and medieval prohibition laws you have here. It seems to me clear that if you go on the way you are functioning, with *each at his own concern and without aligning yourselves with other people* who wish to change the system, you are not going to change anything. *Until you do get together*

> *with one another over common objectives, I don't think you are going to change this society very much,* whether you are French, female, black, or Indian.[56]

Logue's criticism was consistent with advice provided by Alinsky both orally and in writing, and it helps to illuminate some of the limitations of the espoused organizing model. The interest-possessing individual at the core of Alinsky's model, like so many modern conceptions of the human being, ultimately functions as a regulatory norm. It posits, that is, a singular, normative conception of the "human" that not all individuals are able to emulate. In practice, the concept of the interest-possessing individual functions, in the first instance, to divide the population into a series of fragments. Individuals, identified by their interests, become distinguishable from one another. Their relationships to other individuals, in turn, become legible strictly in the form of their shared interests, their commonality as, for example, "French, female, black, or Indian." Once identified, finally, the various interest-sharing fragments can be compared and evaluated on the basis of the perceived broadness or narrowness of their shared interests and disciplined where necessary (as Logue's critique makes clear).

The consequences of this operation are readily apparent. A relatively broad interest is treated as normal, fully acceptable. A relatively narrow interest, in contrast, is regarded as pathological, as well as a potential obstruction to a necessary population-level process (i.e., citizen involvement). The line between normal and pathological, importantly, is not drawn on the basis of an abstract, pre-established standard of broadness or narrowness. Neither Alinsky nor Logue defines the specific number of people or the proportion of the population that must be included in a proper "community interest." Rather, as Foucault's remarks on biopolitical norms suggest, the practical assessment of the population during an event like Encounter Week enables differential normalities and pathologies to be identified within it.[57] It was the practical formation of interest groups and their participation during Encounter Week, in other words, that allowed the relative broadness of group-level interests to be measured and a standard, normative broadness to be identified. The broadest, "most normal" interest, of course, implicitly pertained to those participants who required no correction from the invited experts: an unmentioned and uncorrected group of white, male anglophones.

In addition to unduly narrow political interests, the experts sought to correct participants who expressed conflictory interests. As Logue explained, social advancement was fundamentally about "improv[ing] the lot of those who do not have enough while not penalizing those who are comfortable with the system as it exists." The problem, Logue claimed, was that certain groups were failing to acknowledge this reality; they were expressing conflictory, "revolutionary" interests, rather than "pragmatic" ones.[58] For other experts, like University of London professor Martin Regin, the expression of conflictory interests was an example of "indignation without strategy," a pointless and naive evasion of the consensus-seeking processes through which real "change takes place."[59] The targets of such corrections went unnamed, but they could have applied to many participants at Encounter Week. The event was, at times, a relatively boisterous and disorderly affair, with participants sometimes criticizing not just elected officials, planners, and developers but also the invited experts themselves. Muriel Duckworth, the city's most well-known feminist activist and cofounder of the Nova Scotia Voice of Women for Peace, famously labelled the invited experts the "twelve apostles" and rebuked the event's organizers for inviting twelve *men* to direct the city towards a better future. Evidently unsettled, Northwestern University sociologist Scott Greer described Duckworth's intervention as "a brief, sort of powder puff assault by the Women's Liberation Front."[60]

More than anyone, the experts' criticism of conflictory interests applied to the participating members of BUF. A visible presence at Encounter Week, BUF was formed in 1968 after a pair of visits to the city by American Black Power activists (including Stokely Carmichael and two Black Panthers) and had become the primary political vehicle for the province's eighteen-thousand-strong Black population.[61] A bricoleur of political ideologies, BUF's overall objective was the attainment of Black self-determination across Nova Scotia: the vesting of decision-making power in the hands of Black people. That Black self-determination could be a conflictory interest was made clear at the event by Rocky Jones, a founding member of BUF and minister of information for the Afro-Canadian Liberation Movement. For Jones, real social change emerged from the self-activity of oppressed people, and he rejected the idea that change could be achieved through alliances with the "white bourgeoisie" or through the advice of the white "intelligentsia."[62] More broadly, BUF's pursuit of Black self-determination (explored in detail in chapter 6) clearly involved a challenge to white supremacy and, thus, to the Alinksky-defined interests of white people. This conflictory interest, the pursuit of Black self-determination, violated the basic terms of Alinsky's model and would call out for correction as a result

Together, the two pathologies identified by the invited experts helped to mark the boundaries of an extremely narrow terrain of political involvement – narrow, at least, for marginalized groups. On the one hand, marginalized groups could be criticized if they expressed too narrow an interest or if they failed to involve themselves in the political process. On the other hand, to involve themselves in the political process would mean accepting, even defending, the privileges that other groups had acquired at their expense. As critics would later point out, Alinsky's model of community organization provides very little room for intercommunity divisions, such as racial, gender, or even class hierarchies, to be recognized or addressed.[63] The impetus of the model is to identify points of overlap within a set of interests, rather than points of conflict. A situation of oppression can be challenged, therefore, only to the extent that dominant-group interests are somehow (implausibly) preserved in the process. The practical effect of these strictures is to inscribe a mechanism of subjugation within a political model that professes to be concerned with radical social change. Greater citizen involvement in Halifax, while described by the invited experts as a bottom-up "revolt" or "grass-roots outcry,"[64] would in fact be compelled to adopt a rigid, constraining form that pathologized and silenced any movement towards radical, structural change.

The pathologizing structure of Alinsky's model would ultimately affect much more than the proceedings of Encounter Week. The new amenity-focused planning practices advocated by groups like HTNS, the Downtown Committee, and the NSPS would be deeply marked by the forms of political expression that were and were not considered to be normative. The silencing of BUF activists during Encounter Week is particularly significant in this respect. BUF, more than any other local group, had struggled to illuminate and contest the new social geography that postwar renewal and spatial practices had brought into being. As BUF pointed out, postwar renewal had dishoused thousands of poor and racialized Halifax residents, including over 1,600 one-time residents of the downtown – precisely the space that HTNS, the Downtown Committee, and the NSPS envisioned as the site of a uniquely "enjoyable" urban experience. Abetting the dishousing of downtown residents, moreover, were various practices of racist spatial regulation that the proposed form of urban planning could have sought to eliminate but did not. "As in Alabama," BUF activist Buddy Daye told the media in 1969, "colour lines are drawn in Halifax."[65] Black residents, BUF pointed out, were routinely discriminated against by local landlords, employers, and retailers, and these practices seem to have been especially common in the downtown core. Of the racial discrimination cases handled by BUF and the Nova Scotia Human Rights Commission between 1968 and 1975, over two-thirds pertained to downtown locations.[66]

As BUF's actions make apparent, it was a space uniquely cleansed of poor and (especially) Black residents that groups like HTNS, the Downtown Committee, and the NSPS had come to see as a uniquely enjoyable space. The policies advanced by these groups, moreover, neither recognized nor sought to amend these historic and ongoing practices of expulsion. Their proposals, in keeping with established conceptions of amenity, sought to produce greater "enjoyment" through physical rather than (also) social measures. *Space* would be rendered more enjoyable, an increase in enjoyment would therefore be produced, and yet the practical barriers to this space would remain unmentioned and fully intact. The significance of the new planning practices was thus a matter of perspective. For those who could actually "live, work, and enjoy" themselves in the downtown, the turn to amenity was a real change. Their lives might indeed be rendered more enjoyable. For Black residents, in contrast, the new planning practices were hardly "new" at all. Now, as before, planning would be harnessed to a conception of the human from which they were expelled. Planning's new practices of citizen involvement would offer recognition to political interests that were not their interests, while its promotion of amenity, guided by the interests of normative citizens, would produce enjoyment precisely where they were not. Displacing blackness, politically and spatially, would be just as integral to the new planning practices as it was to those of the urban renewal period.

MOVE and Harbour Drive North

Another phase of the struggle over urban renewal in Halifax began shortly after Encounter Week. Many Halifax activists were energized by Encounter Week and felt more devoted than ever to ending urban renewal and introducing something different. The NSPS, meanwhile, explicitly saw the week-long event as a first step among many, an initial spark that would alight more sustained and powerful forms of citizen involvement in the city. The aims of local activists and the NSPS found common expression in February 1971, when a three-day activist retreat was convened in rural Kentville, Nova Scotia. The retreat was funded by the Nova Scotia government and overseen by an NSPS-selected community organizer. Attended by thirty

Halifax-based activists, the event was intended to enable the formation of new forms of solidarity and collaboration. Retreat participants represented a variety of organizations, from the HDBA to Halifax Welfare Rights, and they did not necessarily share the same political analysis or objectives. After a major "blow up" on the first day, however, participants were able to find a certain common ground and reach at least one important agreement.[67] While continuing to pursue their own political work, the majority of the participants agreed to contribute to the development of a significant multiorganization alliance on urban issues. The alliance, eventually Movement for Citizens' Voice and Action (or MOVE), was the most important product of the retreat, and it would soon become a major force in urban politics in Halifax.

Returning to Halifax after the retreat, MOVE activists quickly got down to work. With a small start-up budget, the activists rented an office in the downtown, purchased office supplies and equipment (including a much-used reproduction machine), and sketched out an organizational structure. The direction of the alliance was delegated to a thirteen-person volunteer board, with Halifax architect Allan Duffus as the organization's first chairperson, and a series of permanent committees were soon formed to deal with issues like housing, education, and the environment. MOVE's member groups, twenty-three at this point, were eligible to contribute representatives to the board and to the issue-specific committees, and were automatically provided access to MOVE's meeting room, equipment, and other resources. Soon, member groups also began to receive the monthly *MOVE Bulletin*, a lively and informative newsletter that featured provocative cartoons as well as detailed information about the actions and concerns of MOVE members (see *figure* 5.2). From these small beginnings, MOVE's operations expanded steadily over the next two years. In December 1971, it received a six-month, $65,000 grant from the federal Local Involvement Program (LIP), which allowed the alliance to hire six full-time staff members and support its member groups in hiring fourteen full-time staff. Some of the MOVE staffers were formed into an in-house research team, which was tasked with studying important planning initiatives and sharing their findings with MOVE members. Over the next year and a half, MOVE's LIP grant was extended to May 1973 (for a total grant of $207,000), and its membership increased to around forty local organizations.[68]

From the outset, MOVE was premised on the concept of communities making decisions for themselves and forcing politicians and bureaucrats

Figure 5.2 *MOVE Bulletin* cartoon, 1973. *MOVE Bulletin*, DUA, MOVE Collection, MS 11-1, box 9.[69]

to respect these decisions. As an early manifesto explained: "MOVE is an [alliance] of groups deeply concerned with rumored developments in the Metro Area which would vitally affect the [local] quality of life ... and many of us, the 80% of the population, [want] a say in the decision making, traditionally done by 20% of the area's citizens ... Whatever [planners] are doing or not doing, they are doing it to our community: affecting our future; influencing how much money we will make; and what kind of environment we will live in ... We should not have our future set out for us in newspaper headlines."[70]

Seeking to bring together such a vast constituency was both ambitious and politically complex. It meant, for example, that the leadership of the Halifax Downtown Business Association was expected to sit at the same table as the representatives of two public housing tenant associations, while HTNS's concerns about architectural heritage were expected to be discussed alongside the concerns of Blacks United for More Money, Welfare Rights, and the Africville Action Committee. Efforts to build diverse and complex social movements, however, were far from unusual in this period. In cities across North America, solidarities were constituted across vast differences in ideologies and social position in order to combat particular urban projects and (sometimes) to define alternative futures. More broadly, the civil rights and Third World decolonization movements relied significantly on the involvement of activists whose social position protected them from the problems (i.e., racism and colonialism) they sought to combat.[71]

The civil-rights movement was sometimes described as a point of reference for MOVE, and at least a few of its white members had some experience either supporting civil-rights groups or combating racial discrimination by other means. Notably, the alliance's chairperson from October 1971 to October 1974 was the white feminist activist Muriel Duckworth, then in the early stages of her now-celebrated activist career. Prior to joining MOVE, Duckworth had been involved with the Nova Scotia Association for the Advancement of Coloured People (NSAACP). Her primary political project, Nova Scotia Voice of Women for Peace, also maintained a committee devoted partly to combating racial discrimination. The committee, active between 1962 and 1963, involved three Black women and six white women. Its primary activity was to investigate and publicize practices of racial discrimination among Halifax-area employers, including the giant Simpson's department store. Its members also met to discuss Gordon Allport's recent book, *The Nature of Prejudice*, and collectively brainstormed potential ways of "freeing ourselves and our children from prejudice."[72] Combating discrimination and prejudice, though necessary, is a much smaller task than unmaking anti-blackness as a set of relations, discourses, and practices that situate Black lives outside the human.[73] These modest actions suggest, nevertheless, the willingness of Duckworth and the white members of the committee to learn about and challenge forms of oppression that they did not themselves experience.

Despite some activists' valuable prior experience, holding together a broad-based alliance like MOVE often proved difficult. One early conflict encountered by MOVE centred on the relationship between the alliance and the NSPS. While the NSPS described its involvement with MOVE as a genuine effort to support grass-roots citizen involvement, some activists had other impressions. Don Grady, a MOVE member and young sociology professor at Dalhousie University, argued that politicians and bureaucrats sought only to "cool out" grass-roots activism and that the NSPS's involvement with MOVE would only result in something that "looks like a citizen organization," but that actually works to "subvert the process of [citizens] getting involved."[74] Grady's proposed name for the activist alliance, Movement to Organize Everything Existing, reflected his vision of a more autonomous and radical urban movement, as did his efforts to expel Fred Lennarson, an NSPS employee who was seconded to MOVE to provide activist training. The conflict between Grady and Lennarson eventually devolved into a fist fight on a Dalhousie sidewalk, an event that forced the alliance to discuss and clarify its relationship to the NSPS but whose expression of masculinist bravado also disgusted some MOVE activists.

Another early conflict concerned the accountability of MOVE board members and paid staff to the alliance's various member organizations. While election to the board of directors was officially open to representatives from all member groups, the composition of the board was dominated in the early years by representatives from more privileged groups and was reportedly distrusted by groups composed of poor or working-class members. Meetings of the board, in addition, were initially held behind closed doors, restricted to the thirteen board members alone. Even staff members, when they had something to contribute to a meeting, were forced to wait outside the boardroom until their specific moment to speak and were quickly ushered out after having spoken. Paid staff, meanwhile, had little contact with MOVE member groups in the early years. Isolated from the membership and much more involved in day-to-day MOVE activities than anyone else, paid staff were able to shape the alliance's operation to an unjustifiable extent and were eventually accused of working on their own pet political projects at least some of the time. Small reforms introduced in the fall of 1971 and the spring of 1972 resulted in a (modestly) more diverse board of directors, as well as open-door board meetings. In contrast, the issue of accountability to MOVE member groups was never fully resolved, leading to simmering tensions within the alliance and contributing to its eventual downfall.[75]

Though it encountered certain conflicts, the alliance was able to remain relatively cohesive in the early years. In large part, this was because member groups needed to agree on so little. While it was assumed that alliance members would, on occasion, adopt a common position on particular urban issues, MOVE's primary purpose was simply to support the efforts of existing organizations and encourage the creation of new organizations.[76] Support provided to MOVE member organizations in the early years included access to resources like meeting space and equipment, the monthly *MOVE Bulletin*, and eventually MOVE-prepared research briefings. The alliance also provided various forms of activist training, including instruction in Alinsky-style community organizing.

Alinsky's work was a major influence on MOVE activists, and it deeply shaped the alliance's organizing and training activities. From February to September 1971, the main MOVE trainer was the Alinsky-trained (and originally NSPS-employed) organizer Fred Lennarson.[77] Several MOVE activists and member groups also received training directly from Alinsky during a weekend workshop at the Maritime School of Social Work in Halifax in 1971. Training resources made available at MOVE headquarters, finally, included Alinsky's *Rules for Radicals*, a two-part National Film Board documentary called *Encounter with Alinsky*, and MOVE-authored booklets that were modelled on his approach. In accordance with Alinsky's model, MOVE trainers encouraged Halifax residents to join or create activist organizations on the basis of their self-interests and taught existing organizations how to sustain the kinds of inclusive, democratic processes that would allow genuinely shared interests and political positions to be articulated. This form of training was meant to enlarge and strengthen the Halifax activist scene, without requiring its diverse member groups to adopt the same viewpoint, objective, or ideology.[78] The aim, as an internal document noted, was to bring Halifax-based organizations together like a school of fish. The fish, though still distinct from one another, would create a form of collective power great enough to outmatch the "big fish" of the Halifax establishment.[79]

The alliance's first and only attempt to forge a collective political campaign began in the fall of 1972, when it elected to challenge the city's plans to construct a major six-lane expressway dubbed Harbour Drive North. This expressway was, in fact, the third phase of a larger project whose first phase (the Cogswell Interchange) had already been completed and whose second phase (Harbour Drive South) had been abandoned in the face of political opposition in 1969. The abandonment of the expressway's second phase (discussed in chapter 4) was a major setback, but it did nothing to preclude the pursuit of the northerly third phase, a section that would rim the Halifax harbourfront from the edge of the downtown to the northern tip of the peninsula. Indeed, the city still possessed many of the properties along this section's proposed path that it had purchased in 1965. It also had an outstanding promise to the developer of Scotia Square (Halifax Developments Inc.) that it would construct a high-volume expressway to carry customers, workers, and cars into the now-completed megadevelopment and four-storey parking garage.[80] In the summer of 1972, MOVE activists began to hear rumours that the city was seeking to secure DREE funding to move forward with the expressway's third phase, and they decided to take action against it.

The decision to oppose Harbour Drive North, though it was made at a routine meeting of MOVE's thirteen-person board in September 1972, was assumed to advance the interests of its many and diverse member groups. It is not hard, in the end, to see how this assumption was reached. MOVE's criticism of the expressway, revealed most vividly in a self-published magazine from the fall of 1972, evoked a lengthy and diverse trail of destructive consequences and harmed political interests. The proposed expressway, the magazine explained, would clog the downtown with additional automobile traffic and parking lots, and destroy a set of historic buildings at the northern edge of the downtown. It would also displace between eighty and one hundred families from a low-income neighbourhood north of the downtown and bury a much-loved children's playground still farther north. The projected effects of the expressway on the Halifax downtown were evoked in the magazine with special intensity. In the alliance's most vivid critique, the expressway was consigned to the logic of an outdated planning paradigm and judged inimical to the kind of downtown that the city and its residents now required. MOVE explained: "In the past, the [downtown] was conceived of as only a commercial and financial centre, [while] the residential areas of the city were removed to the suburbs. However, in the 1970s we have radically changed our ideas of what a city is all about. The downtown area is now thought of as a place to live, work and enjoy ourselves on a 24-hour basis."[81]

The effects of the expressway, of course, would tend to matter differently to different MOVE member groups. Some groups, for example, might take issue with the effects of Harbour Drive North on low-income families, while others might take issue with its effects on the aesthetics and experience of the downtown. The description of the downtown as a "place to live, work, and enjoy ourselves," in particular, was a clear invocation of the amenity-centred vision that certain groups (i.e., HTNS and HDBA) had been promoting in their own work and that would tend not to inspire the same enthusiasm among other groups. Members of BUF, for one, faced bigger problems in the downtown than a proposed expressway. Prevalent practices of racial discrimination in the area meant that neither living nor working nor enjoying oneself was a practical possibility for Black people in the downtown. Many members of the two public housing tenants associations, meanwhile, had been displaced from the downtown in the city's late 1950s "slum-clearance" program and could scarcely afford to rent the housing that now existed there. That this vision belonged to some groups and not others, however, was not a problem. The imperative, as Alinsky's model suggests, was that concerns about downtown amenity be placed alongside other concerns and that a combined, alliance-wide position be constructed on this basis. It was the *sum* of the different effects of the proposed expressway that mattered; it was the magnitude of this sum that made stopping the expressway an alliance-wide interest.

MOVE's opposition to Harbour Drive North began immediately after the September 1972 meeting. The alliance was then at its peak in terms of staff levels and public profile, and it quickly established a committee to deal specifically with Harbour Drive and assigned one of its staff members to work on the issue full time. In the next five months, MOVE activists organized potentially affected neighbourhoods, held meetings and public events, prepared and circulated anti-expressway propaganda (see *figure 5.3*), lobbied higher levels of government, and pressured the city to engage the public in a meaningful dialogue before proceeding any further with its plan. Seeking to understand and undermine the city's rationale for the expressway, three MOVE activists showed up at City Hall one day and demanded to see all council minutes and city reports relating to the project. The relevant material turned out to be substantial. The activists spent the next month within the walls of their opponents' headquarters, reading through reports, making notes, and gradually pulling apart the city's loosely formulated plan. The results of this work were evident in MOVE's later campaign materials and written submissions to the city. Plans for Harbour Drive, MOVE would assert, overstated the expressway's effects on circulation between several areas of the city, underestimated the amount of land that would be required for infrastructure like on-ramps, and failed to consider various alternatives (e.g., a ferry crossing from Dartmouth). Claims like these helped to weaken the supposed technical expertise that underpinned the proposed expressway and the broader urban renewal regime.[82]

As these actions suggest, the battle over Harbour Drive North was a crucial moment in the struggle over urban renewal in Halifax. The expressway had been a central component of the city's planning agenda since at least 1957, and it was explicitly supported by the near entirety of the local political establishment: the city's mayor, its director of development, the city's largest property developer, its two most influential business associations, and much of the local print media. It was roughly this configuration of actors that the NSPS believed would cling to the established planning agenda and obstruct the introduction of new planning practices. Ironically, however, the NSPS also supported the Harbour Drive project. For the NSPS, the proposed expressway was essential to the circulation of the 500,000 residents that would eventually populate the Halifax region, and it would play this role, apparently, without detracting from the "enjoyment" and "amenity" of the new downtown. At stake in the battle over Harbour Drive, therefore, was not simply the continuation or interruption of urban renewal but also the particular form that an alternative, postrenewal future might assume. MOVE, while it accepted much of the NSPS's vision for the city, saw the proposed expressway as an obstacle to the realization of this vision – including the creation of an amenity-rich downtown. The specific meaning of amenity and the specific form of postrenewal planning would be worked out, in part, in a tense struggle over a differently understood expressway.

An important moment in the Harbour Drive struggle occurred in November 1972, when the city convened a routine public forum to discuss its drafted municipal development strategy. The fifteen-page draft contained few concrete details but included, on its final page, a diagram

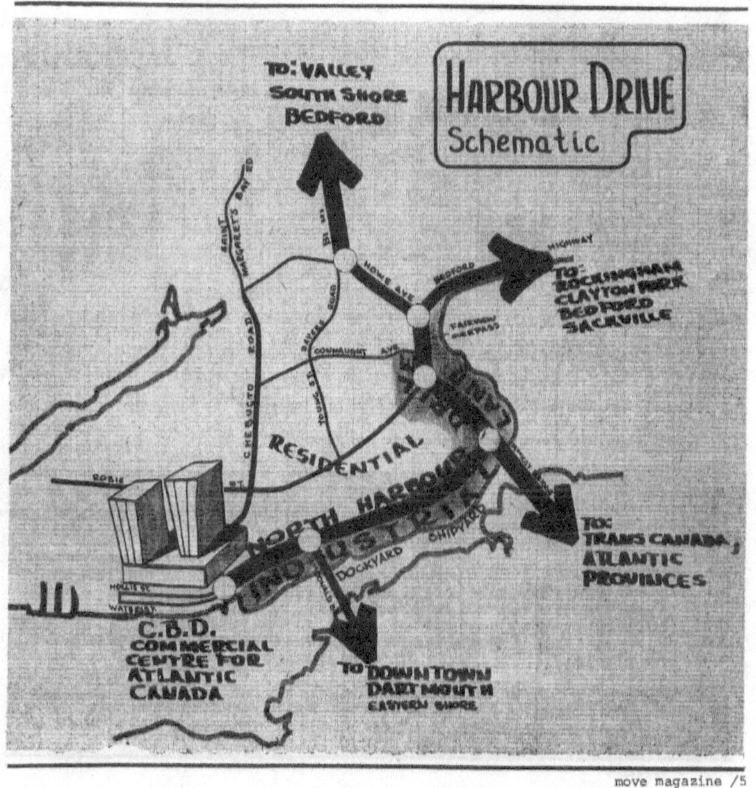

Figure 5.3 MOVE satirical image of Harbour Drive, 1972. *MOVE Magazine* 1, no. 1 (1972), 5. DUA, MOVE Collection, MS 11-1, box 9.

that seemed to indicate the city's intention to move forward with the Harbour Drive North expressway.[83] MOVE activists, having read the draft, were among the roughly four hundred residents who attended the November public forum, and they called on city officials to explain whether and why a new expressway was in the works. The city was evidently surprised by MOVE's intervention. As the city's head planner later remarked, the aim of the drafted plan was merely to provide "a basic policy document dealing with those factors affecting the city on a wide scale," and it had only been presented to the public because recent amendments to the Nova Scotia Planning Act required it.[84] It was not, in other words, a plan of action, and it provided few details on specific projects because few had been rigorously worked out. Finding city officials unable to discuss or defend the expressway at the public forum, MOVE pressured the city to hold a second forum, during which Harbour Drive North would be an explicit and central topic of discussion.

The second public forum, held in January 1973, proved to be the defining moment in the struggle over the proposed expressway. Attended by roughly five hundred residents, the forum saw city officials visibly chastened by the opposition that their policies had encountered and much less certain of their ability to see these policies implemented without significant citizen buy-in. Prior to the event, in fact, city council had discussed how it might regain the support of the public. The answer, for one councillor, was to relinquish the physically ascendant position of past public forums; rather than sitting on a raised podium as usual, he suggested that councillors and other city officials sit "down with the people," ideally on a set of chairs laid out "in a semi-circular arrangement."[85] MOVE, in contrast, planned to assert itself. In the lead-up to the forum, MOVE activists had compiled a list of forty-five major questions that city officials had failed to answer in previous meetings and mailed the list of questions to various higher-level government officials. Among the recipients of the list were representatives of DREE, the federal agency that the city was reportedly talking with about funding the proposed expressway.[86]

MOVE's input to the January public forum centred on the same forty-five questions. The questions ranged widely and were meant to undermine the potential rationale for the Harbour Drive expressway, bit by bit. "For whom is Harbour Drive being built?" "Has Council considered that the public favours public transit?" "What compensation [is] Council making to those persons displaced for the Harbour Drive roadway?" "Where have these persons been placed?" "Has [City] staff ever presented other alternatives to Council?" More broadly, MOVE's questions interrogated the planning doctrines within which a high-volume expressway made sense, doctrines that it relegated to a now-distant and transcended past. Reprising its view of the downtown as "a place to live, work, and enjoy ourselves," MOVE asked whether "the dumper expressway idea, which has remained basically unchanged over 27 years, still has any relevance to the kind of city we now want to live in."[87] The city, as expected, was taken aback by the questions and had no credible answers to provide. Unable to defend the planned expressway at the public forum, the city first deferred the questions to a later date (promising to respond in writing) and then scrapped the project instead.[88] Although no public announcement was ever made, the city ceased all discussion of the project after the January public forum, and it would never again include the project in a major planning document.

The defeat of Harbour Drive North was an important victory for MOVE and a major turning point in urban planning in Halifax. The overseers of post-World War II urban planning had lost their once-unchallenged grip on the city; new political actors and new, postrenewal planning ideas had gained recognition. The importance of organized citizen involvement in planning decisions, one of the new planning ideas, was explicitly accepted by the city in a report later in 1973 and became a familiar practice in the years thereafter.[89] The other new idea, the creation of amenity-rich spaces, was clearly reflected in the city's eventual municipal development plan (published in 1980), which expressed a commitment to making the downtown a better place to "live, work, and enjoy oneself."[90] As I discuss in chapter 7, these two planning ideas remained central to urban planning in Halifax more than thirty years later. The city, in the course of its most recent planning initiative, could seem to be channelling the ghost of MOVE activists in its depiction of the downtown as a "vibrant, 24-hour" space and in city planners' repeated assertion that citizens, not experts, would need to shape the future of this particularly important area. The promotion of citizen involvement and the production of amenity, two ideas promoted by activists and renegade bureaucrats in the 1960s, have become part of the new planning orthodoxy in the period since then.

For MOVE, the defeat of Harbour Drive North was also a point of rupture – the beginning of the end, in fact, for the short-lived activist alliance. Its decline was caused, in part, by financial difficulties that began more than two years earlier. In October 1970, just as MOVE was being formed, the Conservative provincial government headed by Ike Smith fell to Gerry Regan's Liberals. Regan, it turned out, had no interest in the "reorganized public" that had begun to be put in place, and he succeeded in pressuring the federal government to disband the NSPS and its alternative planning activities by the beginning of 1971. This action deprived MOVE of its most promising source of ongoing, reliable funding.[91] Alternative funding in the amount of $207,000 was eventually secured through an LIP grant, but countervailing political forces, this time stemming from the municipal government, eventually brought this funding to an end. Angered by MOVE's opposition to Harbour Drive, Mayor Walter Fitzgerald (elected in 1971) pressured the federal government to rescind all future LIP funding to MOVE and its various member groups. Fitzgerald is also alleged to have met with the low-income members of MOVE and ordered them to drop out of the alliance or risk having their municipal funding terminated. The mayor's intervention was effective. Federal funding to MOVE ceased in May 1973, and the low-income groups were compelled to consider, more earnestly, whether their interests were really served by working with activists and organizations whose viability was less precarious and less tied to state funding than their own.[92]

But the Harbour Drive campaign did more than anger certain government officials and curtail its funding possibilities. The defeat of the expressway was also followed by the sudden departure of four MOVE member groups, including the two public housing tenants associations and BUF. The departure of these groups may have been partly caused by Mayor Fitzgerald's threats, but it was linked by some MOVE activists to problems internal to the alliance.[93] The most common criticism of MOVE in the spring of 1973 was that it continued to be controlled by middle-class board members and paid staff and that its political activities, including its opposition to Harbour Drive, reflected essentially middle-class concerns.[94] The latter claim is hard to accept fully. The expressway campaign, though devised and waged primarily by middle-class activists, clearly sought to address a relatively diverse range of concerns, including those of low-income residents in the neighbourhood that the expressway would have ripped through. After several decades of pathologizing slumology, moreover, MOVE's defence of the latter neighbourhood provided a more positive, even affirming perspective. The neighbourhood, MOVE argued in its campaign materials, contained an irreplacable network of social ties, as well as important "social amenities" like churches, public spaces, drop-in centres, and shopping facilities "responsive to [area residents'] income levels."[95] The neighbourhood, in other words, functioned and served its residents quite well. These aspects of the campaign need to be remembered. MOVE was controlled largely by middle-class activists, but its political concerns were not so monolithic.

A more persuasive critique, outlined in an internal MOVE report, focused on problems inherent to the political model that the alliance relied upon. Noting that the departed member groups represented some of the most marginalized populations in the city, the report criticized the prevailing assumption that the interests of MOVE member groups could simply be added up and addressed in tandem. As the report explained, problems like racism, inadequate housing, and unemployment were generally not experienced by the more privileged members of the alliance and could only be alleviated by *challenging* the interests of the city's better off (including those of some MOVE members). Consistent with my discussion of Encounter Week above, the report problematized the basic tenets of MOVE's Alinsky-style organizing model, underscoring the ways that the model normalized the interests of already-privileged groups. A normal interest, according to the model, was broad and nonconflictory. A pathological interest, in contrast, was narrow and conflictory – precisely the kind of interests possessed by marginalized groups. The issue is not that the interests of marginalized groups could never be recognized; the Harbour Drive campaign showed that they could be. The issue is the *kind* of interests that could be recognized. The departed groups, the report concluded, had seen their most fundamental interests (i.e., those that conflicted with the interests of privileged groups) taken off the table. For this reason, it had been "very difficult" for the groups to achieve anything significant through the alliance, and they had become "non-participants" long before their formal departure.[96]

Understood in this way, the effect of MOVE's organizing model was not just to normalize privileged political interests but also to normalize and sanctify a privileged vision of the postrenewal city. MOVE's vision of the downtown, as I noted, located enjoyment in an especially exclusive space, a space recently cleared of poor and working-class residents and uniquely inhospitable to Black residents. In so doing, it codified an exclusive experience of enjoyment as enjoyment itself (barring other potential definitions of enjoyment) and valorized socio-spatial conditions that were predicated on historic and ongoing practices of displacement. This, in the end, is the conception of enjoyment that was allowed to enter MOVE's Harbour Drive campaign and that became an urban planning ideal in this period partly because of the campaign's success: the enjoyment experienced by people who do not face displacement or racial discrimination in spaces where other people *do* face these problems. None of this, of course, is unique to Halifax. In cities across North America and around the world, the spaces that have been identified as amenity-rich and enjoyable in the post-1960s period have often been those most acutely transformed by recent and ongoing practices of displacement. In some cases, the displacement of certain populations (e.g., homeless people) is explicitly advocated in planning discussions in order to promote amenity and enjoyment. In other cases, displacement occurs for other (non-planning-related) reasons, and the end result – an ostensibly amenity-rich space – is experienced as enjoyable by people who do not need to know how it was produced.

Such limits to the conception and production of enjoyment are seldom, if ever, recognized in the critical urban planning literature. Nor, indeed, are they recognized in Foucauldian analyses of late twentieth-century forms of biopolitics. Foucault's analysis of vitalpolitics helpfully traces the rise of new biopolitical priorities, including the creation of contentment and the decentralization of decision-making processes. These priorities, I argued, were essential to the transformation of urban planning that began in the late 1960s. And yet, Foucault's inattention to the role of anti-blackness in constituting modern conceptions of the human leaves him unable to register the racial limits of these priorities. In contrast, scholars of anti-blackness have often examined how experiences of white enjoyment are predicated on dehumanizing forms of anti-Black violence, subjugation, and displacement.[97] Particularly relevant to urban planning is Lewis Gordon's analysis of the experiential correlates of anti-Black ontologies – the lived experience, that is, of a world in which the normative human is constituted in opposition to blackness. At the level of experience, Gordon argues, anti-blackness confines dominant feelings of vitality, feelings of really living, to spaces of whiteness. It also expunges these feelings from spaces that are even partly Black. "There is 'something' absent," he argues, "whenever Blacks are present."[98] As Gordon's analysis suggests, dominant experiences of vitality and enjoyment are actually nothing more than that: the experiences of people who are dominant, people who are recognized as fully human. These lively experiences, moreover, seem to depend on the nonpresence, the displacement, of less-than-dominant people – people viewed as less than human.

These limits *need* not exist. They can always be undone, at least in small ways. It is always possible, in particular, to question dominant conceptions of enjoyment and the spatial conditions that underpin it. The prevailing limits to the enjoyment of the Halifax downtown were indeed known. They were known by MOVE's working-class and Black member-activists. They were also known, to some extent, by more privileged MOVE members like Muriel Duckworth, who had been involved in struggles against racial prejudice and discrimination (and thus knew something of their prevalence). It was always possible, then, for these limits to be challenged and undone, and for an altogether different experience of enjoyment – an experience that privileged white people might have needed to struggle to recognize and experience as enjoyment – to be articulated and produced. What obstructed such actions was not necessarily racial prejudice or any other *individual* disposition but rather a conception of space (i.e., amenity) and a model of citizen involvement that militated against such actions. At a time when the civil rights and Third World decolonization movements were enlisting privileged people to fight against their narrow self-interests in the name of something considerably better, activists in Halifax were instructed to turn inward, to fight for their own interests, and to support others on the condition that others supported them. For this reason more than any other, a great opportunity to reimagine and remake the city, not simply to annul urban renewal but also to recentre city making on the lives of the most subjugated, was never seized.

Conclusion

The late 1960s and early 1970s were the most vibrant and imaginative period in Halifax planning history. Two decades after the publication of the 1945 Master Plan, the effects of urban renewal were omnipresent and multifaceted, and new political forces began to place themselves in renewal's path. The growing strength of these forces, from activists to certain state officials, was expressed in events like Encounter on the Urban Environment, and it coalesced (for a time) in the formation of MOVE and its renewal-ending campaign against Harbour Drive North. These same events and initiatives, however, were structured by a constraining model of citizen involvement that ostensibly supported the collaboration of different activist groups but actually privileged a form of activism that only certain groups were able to embody. Normalized in this model was the expression of a widely shared and nonconflictory political interest; pathologized in the model was the expression of a narrow and conflictory interest. In practice, the effects of this model were to sanctify the privileges of dominant populations (i.e., white, middle-class residents), enshrine the status quo as a neutral baseline, and disqualify any political project that traced oppression or subjugation to its beneficiaries. Strictures like these suffocated within an expansion of "citizen involvement" the forms of contestation that held the greatest promise to excise subjugation from urban planning and the broader society. It also allowed a simplistic and restrictive vision of amenity to become the pivot around which a shift in planning practices was achieved.

Whether the new planning practices and priorities represented a significant change is ultimately a matter of perspective. For many Haligonians, the opportunity to participate in planning decisions was highly prized, and it provided them with some sense of control over the previously distant, alienating, and quasi-authoritarian processes of urban planning and development. For many residents, the new emphasis on downtown amenity was also a significant change. Historic buildings, once highly vulnerable to destruction, were now treated with respect. A mix of land uses, including places to live, cultural venues, and restaurants, was now a recognized planning ideal rather than a problem to be overcome. And the everyday *experience* of the downtown, people's feelings in and about the area, now held as much weight in planning discussions as the abstract calculations of City Hall bureaucrats and out-of-town experts. These changes, consistent with those introduced through anti-renewal activism in other cities, took urban planning in a relatively new direction, and their effect in the period since the 1960s has been to create a downtown that looks and feels very different than the one imagined in renewal-era documents like the Master Plan. For the thousands of Halifax residents who can be found walking along a downtown sidewalk on a summer evening – people on their way to a show, a bar, or a restaurant, or without any clear destination in mind – the area is undoubtedly a better place than uninterrupted "renewal" would have created.

For other Haligonians, in contrast, the new planning practices were less significant. The opportunity to participate in planning decisions was ultimately conditional and constrained. Excluded from decision-making processes were the kinds of political expression that might have altered, or at least recognized, the hierarchical racial and class relations that structured contemporary society and planning practices. The significance of amenity was also a matter of perspective. For working-class

Haligonians, the promotion of amenity would simply revalorize and refurnish a space from which many had been displaced in the preceding decade and in which the cost of the remaining housing was prohibitive. For those with a long memory, moreover, the sudden valorization of the area's public life might seem a strange and insulting reversal of the decades-long repression of poor and working-class public life in the vicinity of the old upper streets. For Black residents, some of whom were among the thousands physically displaced from the downtown, the turn to amenity could be even less significant. In the face of prevalent anti-Black discrimination from landlords, business owners, and retailers, the downtown was clearly not a place for Black people to live, work, or enjoy themselves, and the new planning practices promised no alteration to this situation. Indeed, the idea that enjoyment is the result of particular spatial conditions tends to efface the various *social* practices, like racial discrimination, that actually exclude Black people from these conditions and tends to naturalize this exclusion through the claim that *these* conditions – these effectively *white* conditions – are the epitome of enjoyment itself.

Given the limitations of the "new" planning priorities, it is worth asking how enjoyment became a planning priority in this specific time and space, a space uniquely emptied of working-class and (especially) Black populations. In a general sense, it has frequently been argued that white enjoyment is, or can be, a product of Black subjugation. There is a form of white pleasure, it has been argued, that emanates from scenes of anti-Black violence (like lynching) or from exhibitions of white mastery over the Black body.[99] Though white enjoyment of this kind was no doubt experienced to some extent in 1960s Halifax, the events that I have described in this chapter point in a somewhat different direction. White residents, whether they enjoyed *acts* of Black subjugation or not, seem to have enjoyed its *effect*: a downtown produced through historic and ongoing acts of anti-Black discrimination and displacement. Displacing blackness, regardless of whether or not white residents directly participated in it or sanctioned it, shaped the spatial experience that came to be valorized and labelled "enjoyment" in this period. It is partly for this reason, perhaps, that the Halifax downtown devolves semiregularly into "race riots," events catalysed inevitably by the appearance of Black people where they were not expected to be – places of enjoyment that blackness seems to interrupt.[100] A different, nonracist form of enjoyment is surely possible, but it is unlikely to be imagined or produced so long as the limitations to the present conception remain unrecognized and politically unspeakable.

6 Planning by Other Means: The Black United Front and the Struggle for Self-Determination

One of most significant challenges to anti-Black racism in Halifax history began at an exceptional meeting at the North End library in November 1968. The meeting, attended by five hundred Black Haligonians, took place amid the ongoing ravages of urban renewal and the dramatic escalation of Black struggle around the world. In a room closed off to the media, politicians, and the entire white population, Black residents gave voice to their collective frustration with the anti-Black status quo and debated potential political responses. Although people's perspectives and political positions varied widely, the discussion evinced a new combativeness on the part of the Black community.[1] White-controlled institutions, many agreed, needed to be confronted and challenged rather than supplicated, and new Black-controlled institutions needed to be created. At the end of the meeting, participants agreed to develop a new political organization, a Black "united front" that would combat anti-blackness with new intensity and produce a greater degree of Black self-affirmation and empowerment.[2] Expressing the more confident direction of Black activism in Halifax, the eventual director of the Black United Front (BUF), Jules Oliver, announced that Black people would "no longer adhere to [a] system" that was averse to racial justice. Either that system would be transformed, or Black people would create their own system. "Your [white] system can function as you wish," he told the local media. "Black people will function as we wish."[3]

Rooting itself in Black communities across Nova Scotia, BUF provided an impressive demonstration of Black people "functioning as [they] wish" within a range of domains, including urban planning. Within all of these domains, BUF's central objective was the cultivation of "self-determination" among Black people – an increasingly common objective of Black struggle in this period in North America, Africa, and the diaspora. The principle of self-determination, for BUF and other Black organizations, refers to the ability of an oppressed group to participate in the decisions that affect their lives. It was the logic or means through which, as BUF often put it, oppressed people could define "their own destiny."[4] Defined in this way, the principle offered an orientation and end goal to a range of political projects, from the criticism of institutions that denied people their self-determination to the development of new structures that recognized and enhanced people's sense of agency. The increasingly widespread adoption of the principle by Black activists in North America contributed, in the late 1960s and early 1970s, to vivid confrontations with contemporary urban renewal policies and the invention of new forms of urban planning that took Black lives as their starting point and foremost priority. For Black people to "function as [they] wish," urban planning needed to be transformed. Wedded to this pursuit, the principle of self-determination provided a useful framework through which planning could be critiqued, confronted, and reinvented.[5]

More than simply altering planning policies, the pursuit of Black self-determination put in question the normative core of modern planning. To prioritize Black lives was necessarily to reject the white norms that defined the limits of the "human" and structured planning practices accordingly.[6] It was to reject dubious claims about Black particularities and to see actual particularities as something other than a pathological deviation from a white-defined "universal" standard – something to normalize, exclude, or destroy. It was, in sum, to see Black lives as a specific and valid "genre" of human being and (potential) human flourishing. The meaning of the "self" in self-determination, however, could be interpreted in different ways and could uphold contrasting kinds of politics. While it could be taken to refer to individual Black "selves," all of whom needed to be allowed to determine their own destinies, it could also invoke a collective "self" whose common destiny needed to be achieved. The latter interpretation, adopted by at least some Black activist groups in this period, has been criticized for substituting a singular definition of blackness for the inevitably diverse experiences of Black people (including their different experiences of class, gender, and sexual oppression).[7] This version of self-determination, though it sidesteps white normativity, conjures a normative Black subject in its place and risks sidelining or subjugating any Black lives that exceed its boundaries. BUF's interpretation of self-determination varied over time, from the antinormative to the normative, and it is essential to track these variations and their consequences.

BUF's engagements with urban planning in Halifax provide an unparalleled demonstration of planning by other means, planning that centres and prioritizes the lives of people pathologized by the modern planning regime. Carrying forward a long history of Black struggle in Nova Scotia, BUF consolidated a diversity of Black communities, perspectives, and strategies into a potent challenge to prevailing anti-blackness. Its criticism of dominant planning practices in Halifax exposed the white norms and privileges that structured city making to the detriment of Black communities. Its self-developed planning initiatives, in turn, demonstrated what planning can look like when oppressed people are allowed to create their own conditions of living. Unfortunately, these experiments in planning by other means were relatively short-lived. BUF received state support at the outset in the form of a substantial five-year federal grant. Its expansive vision of self-determination, however, quickly met with hostility from state officials at the municipal, provincial, and federal levels. For the state, BUF's expression of Black concerns and demands could be tolerated, but the claiming of power by Black people could not. By 1974, BUF's initial grant had expired, and state efforts to contain, reorient, and repurpose the organization had achieved their desired effects. Though BUF would endure (in name) until 1996, its once-expansive vision of self-determination was forcibly narrowed to the representational and normative, and its once-liberatory purpose was reduced to the operational: the self-administration of enduring Black poverty.

The Black Struggle in Nova Scotia

As a vehicle of Black resistance, BUF carried forward a long and impressive history of Black struggle in Nova Scotia. The region's first Black residents, enslaved Africans, were known to evade their captivity. These fugitive acts, a reclaiming of one's own life from the grip of enslavement, prompted slave-owning white Nova Scotians to develop new forms of legislation and policing that would (never quite successfully) fix enslaved people in place. Early non-enslaved Black residents, meanwhile, practised similar forms of resistance. The three largest groups of migrants – the Black Loyalists (1783–92), the Maroons (1796), and the Black Refugees (1813–34) – had each escaped slavery elsewhere in the

Americas before being shipped by the British to Nova Scotia. It was their self-liberation, as Halifax poet El Jones describes it, that allowed them to migrate and remake their lives in a new land. Once settled in Nova Scotia, the struggle continued in new forms. Throughout the nineteenth century, Black Nova Scotians fought to receive the land they had been promised; resisted attempts by the state and white citizenry to steal the land they acquired; and petitioned the state for essential services and infrastructure like schools, churches, water wells, and functioning roads. Many residents also fought to maintain their freedom in the face of white attempts to re-enslave them and / or their family, and fought for wider freedom by campaigning for the abolition of slavery in the British Empire (until 1833) and the United States (until 1865).[8]

As the above suggests, these forms of struggle only sometimes involved recognizable organizations and overtly political actions. Only sometimes, moreover, did they achieve recognizable victories. And yet, as a host of Black scholars have argued, Black resistance cannot be viewed or evaluated simply in terms of its overtly political content, its victories, or its concrete contributions to racial equality and justice. For one thing, the force of anti-blackness in the world is colossal, and even modest Black challenges to it have often been met with a disproportionate and physically violent response from the state, the white citizenry, or both.[9] A focus on recognizable victories, moreover, tends to occlude the many other effects that Black struggle produces. One important effect, as Sylvia Hamilton points out, is simple survival. Black existence in Nova Scotia, she argues, was under threat from the beginning. It had to endure on poor-quality soils, in the absence of state support, and in the face of racist attacks, and it only did endure because Black people found ways to keep each other alive.[10] These actions, in producing survival, also point towards other ways of being, other "genres" of the human that exceed the frame of white normativity. A collective conception of well-being, for example, has often been asserted by Black Nova Scotians in the face of government offers of assistance premised on a more individualistic conception (e.g., offers of land that would require people to leave their home community). These and other effects of Black struggle, effects that exceed the remit of political victories, need to be recognized. Black struggle, as Sarah Haley argues, is not just about great triumphs but also about "the practice of life, living, disruption, rupture, and imagined futures."[11]

Black struggle in Nova Scotia, when it occurred through more organized and visible forms, adopted many of the same structures and strategies that nourished Black resistance in the United States and elsewhere in the diaspora. A. Philip Randolph's labourist strategy, for example, found expression in the Halifax chapter of the Brotherhood of Sleeping Car Porters. Booker T. Washington's "accommodationist" strategy of Black self-help and education provided the framework for the Dartmouth-based Nova Scotia Home for Coloured Children. Small chapters of Marcus Garvey's separatist Universal Negro Improvement Association were also established in Halifax, Dartmouth, and Preston, and Garvey himself gave a stirring speech at Halifax's Cornwallis Street Church in 1937.[12] The most persistent form of organized Black struggle, however, centred on the Black Baptist Church. Present in every major Black Nova Scotian community, the Baptist Church provided a locus for community building and discussion, a vehicle for political advocacy, and an essential "training ground" for several generations of Black leaders, teachers, and other professionals. The formation of the province-wide African United Baptist Association in 1854, moreover, provided formal links between otherwise relatively isolated Black communities across Nova Scotia and (eventually) across North America. These organizational links strengthened existing church-centred political struggle and enabled the creation of several province-wide political organizations. The Nova Scotia Association for the Advancement of Coloured People (NSAACP), the most significant Black organization prior to BUF, was created under the leadership of an exceptional Baptist preacher, William Pearly (W.P.) Oliver, and relied on the social links and circuits of political ideas that Black religious life in Nova Scotia made available.[13]

As in other parts of the diaspora, Black resistance in Nova Scotia exhibited a complex relationship to white social and cultural norms, an ever-present "strife," as Fred Moten describes it, "between normativity and the deconstruction of norms."[14] Normativity, the attempted demonstration of Black adherence to dominant norms, was most clearly expressed in the "respectability" politics of the late nineteenth and early twentieth centuries. The aim of respectability politics, in Halifax and elsewhere, was to gain white recognition of Black morality, industry, thrift, and sobriety. Essential to this demonstration of moral normativity, of course, was an act of differentiation from other (ostensibly less moral) groups, and Black performances of morality were no less dependent than those of white moralizers on the pathologization of less privileged groups, including less privileged Black people. In 1883, for example, Black petitioners challenged the relegation of Black children to segregated and under-resourced North End schools. These children merited better, they argued, than to be confined to schools "little better that those heretofore kept up by charity for vagrants and outcasts" and located squarely in the "most degraded quarter of the city."[15] Similarly, Africville residents' 1919 petition for additional police services was premised on the recent arrival in the community of "many persons … living openly in a state of debauchery, which must corrupt the minds of the youth, for we are more or less subject to our environment."[16] In both cases, the demand for improved services is premised on (certain) Black people's moral respectability and, thus, their distinction from other groups: vagrants, outcasts, and the debauched.

A half century later, the same strategy was expressed in W.P. Oliver's intervention at a 1954 public hearing on urban renewal. The hearing was called to discuss a recent proposal to demolish and "renew" a five-block area of the Old North End, an area that overlapped with the long-standing heart of the Black community in central Halifax. Oliver was one of Black Nova Scotia's foremost leaders at the time, having served as the minister of Cornwallis Street Baptist Church since 1937 and an influential member of the NSAACP since 1945. Appearing at the hearing, Oliver took a strong position against the renewal plan: "I am opposed to taking people out of their homes and compelling them to live in apartments. God gave us the privilege of living as families. Men and women who have had the spirit of citizenship and spunk to save and build a home should be allowed to live as first class citizens."[17] Echoing the respectability politics of an earlier period, Oliver's statement pitches the injustice of the city's plan on the terrain of Black residents' assimilation to dominant behaviours and norms. Having established families and purchased homes, he suggests, Black residents had exhibited the requisite behaviours of the "first-class citizen" and deserved to be treated as such. The city's plan, in contrast, would treat them as something different, or less, than their behaviours warranted.

While this strategy could be politically effective at times, its limitations should be clear enough. In effect, the assertion of normativity (potentially) removes the taint of pathology and inferiority from a certain population, while leaving unchallenged the existence and validity of a normal/pathological distinction. In Oliver's case, the strategy places the Black residents of the Old North End within the bounds of normativity and first-class citizenship, while exposing other residents – tenants and unmarried individuals, in particular – to potential pathologization and displacement. The latter, of course, is precisely what soon unfolded a few blocks to the south, when urban renewal was visited upon the predominantly tenant and often unmarried residents of the "downtown slum." These residents, many of whom were Black, would be left stranded by political arguments and tactics that sought the inclusion of particular groups within the boundaries of pre-established normative categories rather than a dissolution of such categories. Africville residents would be similarly stranded. The selective inclusion obtained through arguments like Oliver's was not always or necessarily a political miscalculation. There existed important differences and divisions *within* the Black population, and at least a few political projects in nineteenth- and twentieth-century Halifax seem to have aimed explicitly to further the interests of the Black elite. An affirmation of prevailing norms could be politically useful in these cases, reassuring the white population that prevailing social hierarchies would simply be adjusted, not dismantled altogether.[18]

A different strategy, the attempted "deconstruction" of prevailing norms, achieved its widest adherence in the late 1960s with the emergence of a broad-based Black Power movement in the United States, parts of Canada, and elsewhere. Connected symbolically and often politically to the decolonization movements of the Third World, Black Power applied an anticolonial lens to the subjugation of Black populations in First World cities and regions. Central to Black Power, accordingly, was the identification of dominant institutional and normative formations as fundamentally white supremacist or colonialist, formations to be be demolished or radically transformed rather than included within. Dominant institutions, from the nation-state to white-led civil-rights organizations, were regarded with suspicion, if not hostility, and the creation of independent, Black-controlled institutions was seen as indispensable to Black advancement. Prevailing norms, meanwhile, were judged to be unrealizable, undesirable, or both. In various ways, Black Power challenged the authority of dominant norms to circumscribe the potential meanings of the human. It did so, in part, by insisting that Black life as it presently existed was a viable, nonpathological "genre" of the human among many others. In most cases, activists also sought to cultivate new genres of social, cultural, and political life, most often by affirming present or past Black traditions in Africa, North America, or elsewhere in the diaspora. Together, the development of new institutions and new norms provided the clearest means of establishing, in Black communities in the First World, the forms of advancement and self-determination that were being pursued by the colonized nations of the Third World.[19]

The arrival of a Black Power perspective in Halifax was closely connected to the work of younger Black activists, especially Burnley "Rocky" Jones. Born to a socially engaged family in the outskirts of Truro, Nova Scotia, Rocky Jones witnessed the effects of racial segregation and oppression as a matter of course in his youth, and he developed a critical perspective on the world early on. In his early twenties, having left Truro for Toronto, Jones came into contact with the Canadian branch of the US civil-rights movement, which had begun to organize protests and other events in solidarity with US-based struggles. As one of the only Black people at these events, Jones quickly attracted the attention of the news media and other activists, but he won attention on the basis of his political analysis as well. Jones was critical of white activists for presuming to speak for subjugated Black people, and he challenged the solidarity movements' focus on US racism to the exclusion of its homegrown, Canadian variant. Speaking to a largely white audience of civil-rights supporters in Toronto, Jones brought concerns about racial injustice back home: "You're a symbol of what has happened to me – every cop I ever came across, every teacher I ever had, was white."[20]

Returning to the Maritimes in 1965, Jones carried forward this initial critique of Canadian racism and his belief in Black agency. His first major project in Halifax, a youth centre called Kwacha House cofounded by Jones and his wife Joan Jones, was intended to provide a venue for young people to discuss their problems, develop an analysis, and organize for social change on their own terms. "The kids are willing ... and able to look at the issues," Jones said at the time. "If you can show the kids that the system out there that they're living in is a basically racist system ... if they realize that, then you can do things."[21] An analysis of systemic racism emerged at Kwacha House, not through dogma but through a collective discussion of Black people's experiences in domains like education, housing, and employment. The destruction of Africville, then still in progress, provided a recurring and poignant topic of collective discussion. The pain and hardship experienced by Africville "relocatees," Jones would point out, demonstrated that "nothing should be done without the compliance and active involvement of the people to be affected by the action."[22]

In 1968, Jones attended the Congress of Black Writers in Montréal, an event that brought together some of the leading thinkers and organizers of the worldwide Black liberation movement. As the only Canadian presenter at the event, Jones was asked to fill the opening slot of a speaking roster that also included figures like C.L.R. James, Stokely

Carmichael, Walter Rodney, James Forman, Rosie Douglas, and members of the Black Panther Party. His presentation wowed the audience, providing a radical perspective on Canadian racism and the emerging possibilities for mass-based, revolutionary struggle. Black Canadians, he argued, needed to build alliances with Indigenous people and working-class Québeçois; only this would constitute a large enough base to fundamentally change society.[23] By the end of the event, Jones had developed a strong rapport with Carmichael, Douglas, and members of the Black Panther Party. On Jones's invitation, Carmichael and the South African musician Miriam Makeba (also Carmichael's wife) travelled to Halifax at the conclusion of the congress for two days' of relative rest and relaxation. A month later, Rosie Douglas and two Black Panthers (T.D. Pawley and George Sams) came to Halifax for more explicitly political reasons.[24]

These visits to Halifax proved to be significant. Carmichael's visit, though not intended to be "political," ignited a firestorm of controversy. Carmichael, already a veteran civil-rights activist at twenty-seven years old, had recently become one of the world's best-known proponents of Black Power, a doctrine that he defined in different ways in different contexts. Described as a program of Black self-reliance and political unity in certain contexts, Black Power was increasingly described by Carmichael as entailing Black armed self-defence, retributive violence, and worldwide revolution "by any means necessary."[25] Carmichael's arrival at the Halifax airport was attended by the local police, who ultimately kept him under surveillance for the entirety of his stay. Meanwhile, Halifax residents and the local news media insisted on knowing what had brought Carmichael to the city and what he expected to achieve. Granting an interview to the *Chronicle-Herald*, the activist confirmed many residents' preconceptions. "We are internationalizing black power," he announced. "We recognize all the problems that black people of Halifax have and we wanted to begin some coordination so that we can move against racism and capitalism."[26]

In town for just eighteen hours, Carmichael's most public action in Halifax was an impromptu visit to the Arrows Club, where he discussed Black resistance informally with interested clubgoers, including eventual BUF director Jules Oliver and young Africville activist Eddie Carvery, and where Makeba was ultimately convinced to take the stage alongside local Black artists. The Arrows, a Black-owned and racially integrated social club, was fully encircled by police officers before Carmichael, Makeba, and Jones ever arrived. Police snipers, according to at least one memoir, were also positioned on nearby rooftops.[27]

A month later, the arrival of Douglas and the two Black Panthers provided further evidence that an "internationalizing" effort was indeed underway, and helped to cement the linkage in the public mind between Black Power and the threat of violence. On 23 November, George Sams was pulled over by the Halifax police and submitted to a search that uncovered three unregistered rifles and (eventually) a revolver inside the car. Sams was arrested immediately, and officers were dispatched to bring in Rocky Jones. Jones was the registered owner of the car, and he admitted to police that he owned the three rifles – for hunting purposes – but not the revolver. Soon released from police custody, Jones fanned the flames of escalating white fears by distributing, on the campus of Dalhousie University, leaflets that called for Sams's release. The text of the leaflets was intentionally provocative: "If there is no justice for Black people in the system then we must prepare to destroy it, and replace it with another system – our system. For the White man and his justice the party is just about over."[28] As sensationalized reports filled the local media, these incidents provoked fears of impending political violence but also suggested the vast extent of the city's racial problems. While nearly all public figures, white and Black, spoke against the use of political violence, some expressed a careful sympathy with the pent-up anger that might lead a Black person in a violent direction.[29]

In the midst of heightening tensions, a "Black family meeting" was called for 30 November at the North End library. The idea of a family meeting – closed off to the white community, the media, and all political representatives – came from the two Panther members. The Panthers had attended the meetings of groups like the NSAACP during their visit and had been taken aback by the dominant roles played by white people in group discussions and, thus, in the articulation and leadership of Black political struggle. Attended by around five hundred people, the meeting was the largest event ever in which Black Nova Scotians would be able to discuss the problems of the present and chart pathways to a better future on their own terms. These terms, of course, were not easily agreed upon, and the perspectives expressed during the meeting were understandably wide-ranging. Whatever political action might emerge from the meeting would need somehow to recognize a range of perspectives: those of older leaders like W.P. Oliver, for whom Black exclusion from "the system" was the problem to be addressed, and those of young radicals like Rocky Jones, for whom "the system" itself was the problem. It was on the Panthers' suggestion that a "united front" strategy was given consideration. Such a strategy had recently been implemented in Washington, DC, the Panthers explained, and it had provided an effective mechanism for stitching together a diversity of Black perspectives, organizations, and communities into a potent political force.[30]

By the end of the meeting, the idea of a "Black united front" had gained widespread approval among participants, and an initial plan of action had been established. Carrying forward the idea would be a nine-person interim leadership committee, whose members included young radicals like Rocky Jones and Denny Grant; older, more conciliatory leaders like W.P. Oliver and Gus Wedderburn; and Edith Gray, the sole woman on the committee. As these names suggest, the composition of the committee was as diverse as the project of a "united front" might imply, its nominal "unity" a not-yet-achieved reconciliation of competing strategies and ideologies. The clearest imprint of Black Power ideas, at this stage, was simply the organization's all-Black leadership and membership, a major departure from racially integrated organizations like the NSAACP. For the first time, Black Nova Scotians would have a political organization of their own, an organization composed entirely by them and accountable strictly to them. Inscribed in the very formation of the organization was thus a new belief in the capacity of Black people to define and bring about a better future on their own initiative. The formation of BUF was thus the first expression of the politics of Black self-determination that the organization would devote itself to implementing in Halifax and across Nova Scotia.

Black Self-Determination and Political Confrontation

The transition from an appealing idea and newly formed leadership committee to a full-fledged organization occurred in less than a year. In January 1969, members of the interim leadership committee travelled to Ottawa and undertook a series of discussions with federal officials that led, in August of that year, to the provision of a substantial government grant. The grant, funded under the first year of a new federal anti-poverty program, provided up to $100,000 per year over a five-year period, a sum that reflected the particular socio-political conditions of the time. On the one hand, the rise of sovereigntist movements in Québec in the 1960s had unsettled the prevailing Anglo-Saxon conception of Canadian nationhood. The federal response, following the 1963 Royal Commission on Bilingualism and Biculturalism, was to recognize and support not just French Canadians as a second "founding nation" but also a host of other ethnic groups as cultural minorities within the now-multicultural nation.[31] On the other hand, the escalation of radical Black activism in the late 1960s (mostly, but not only, in the United States) had spawned new anxieties in Ottawa. The Royal Canadian Mounted Police (RCMP), it turns out, had pushed the federal government to fund BUF as a means of quieting more radical formations in Nova Scotia, while the federal cabinet committee that ultimately evaluated BUF's application recommended that it be fully funded on the grounds that "absence of support might enable black militants to take over from the moderates [within the interim leadership committee]."[32]

The acceptance of federal funding, as I discuss later on, proved to be a controversial move among Black Nova Scotians, and it would shape the new organization and its aims in ways that would become more apparent as time passed. Its major short-term effect, however, was to enable the creation of a significant and powerful Black institution almost overnight. In the four months following the announcement of federal funding in August 1969, a province-wide BUF governing council and a board of directors were put in place, a team of five full-time employees was hired, and office space and materials were procured. Overseeing the day-to-day work of the organization would be Jules Oliver, the son of W.P. Oliver and BUF's first executive director. Appointed to the position by the board of directors in October, Oliver would work primarily from BUF's newly established head office in the Halifax North End, with the aid of two administrative assistants. A presence outside of the Halifax area, meanwhile, would be provided by four field organizers, who would be stationed across the province and would be responsible for liaising with specific Black communities.[33]

The scope of BUF's activities was remarkably vast. Its core concerns were usually described as education, employment, and housing, and most of BUF's activities could indeed be slotted under one of these three headings. As the province's most high-profile and well-funded Black organization, however, BUF was continually called upon to address new concerns, from individual cases of racial discrimination and police brutality to the absence of Black-serving programs in domains like foster parenting and entrepreneurship. Some of these concerns BUF simply could not address. Others it took on wholeheartedly, introducing new campaigns, new programs, and even new spin-off organizations as time passed. Fundamental to BUF's work, no matter the specific campaign or program, was an overarching and unerring commitment to the achievement of Black self-determination. Described as BUF's "most pressing" purpose, the achievement of self-determination was taken to mean the development of "ways and means for Black people to affect their own destiny."[34] In practice, this could mean criticizing and confronting dominant institutions that precluded meaningful Black participation in the decisions that affected their lives, but it could also mean developing alternative programs that affirmed Black capacities and responded directly to Black-defined needs. It was this two-pronged approach to self-determination, an approach stressing both political confrontation and the development of new programs, that most clearly shaped BUF's activities in the early years.

In framing its objectives in terms of self-determination, BUF was relying upon a long-standing principle of Black resistance in Africa, North America, and elsewhere in the diaspora. First expressed in the religious practices of enslaved Black communities in the antebellum US South, the principle of self-determination came to wider attention through the work of early twentieth-century Black organizers like Marcus Garvey, Cyril Briggs, and Harry Haywood. For these later figures, the subjugation of Black Americans was seen as analogous to that of formally colonized Black people in Africa. The achievement of self-determination was thus understood in explicitly national terms (i.e., as the liberation of subjugated nation, whether in Africa or North America) and was believed to be best pursued through the coming together of Black people beneath the sovereignty of a separate, Black nation-state. In the 1960s, visions of Black self-determination animated many sections of the Black liberation movement, especially the more militant Black Power wing. For North American Black Power activists, the principle offered a promising alternative to the politics of "civil rights" (which were judged too accommodationist, slow moving, and dependent on the support of white elites), as well as a symbolic linkage to the ongoing anticolonial and anti-imperial struggles of the Third World. In the speeches and actions of Black Power activists, self-determination was something that white supremacy had denied the oppressed people of the world – in the Third World and the First – and that could be seized by the oppressed only through world-spanning solidarity and unified revolutionary struggle.[35]

For its 1960s adherents, Black self-determination continued to be understood primarily in national terms but did not necessarily require the creation of separate nation-states. More fundamental to the principle in this context was the development of independent Black organizations, the mobilization of militant confrontations with unaccountable (white-controlled) institutions, and the introduction of alternative programs that would address and affirm the specificities of Black lives. For the Black Panther Party, the pursuit of self-determination began with the creation of an all-Black organization (the Party) and the development of Black-specific "self-help" programs, but would be fully achieved only after a revolutionary transformation in which society was reorganized on the basis of decentralized, self-governing institutions and communities. For more mainstream activist groups, in contrast, the pursuit of self-determination entailed a significant reconfiguration but not *dismantling* of the existing capitalist and nation-state structure. The US-based Congress for Racial Equality (CORE), for example, adopted a politics of self-determination in 1966 that emphasized committed, bottom-up organizing and institution building around everyday Black concerns like housing, employment, and access to public institutions. While eschewing revolutionary objectives, CORE nevertheless placed more faith in the capacities of poor Black people and espoused a more combative, confrontational form of politics – targeting problematic landlords, employers, and state institutions – than many other civil-rights organizations. BUF, despite the circumstances of its founding and the often-radical rhetoric of Jules Oliver, pursued a politics of self-determination that looked much more like CORE's version than that of the Black Panthers.[36]

As a framework of confrontation with existing institutions, the principle of self-determination could be an incisive and potent instrument. For BUF, the principle helped to illuminate the fundamental causes of Black subjugation and articulate appropriately transformative political demands. The problem of Black poverty and unemployment, for example, could now be viewed as the product of precluded self-determining capacities: the centuries-long white monopolization of the dominant means of production and overseeing state institutions. In light of this, the welfare payments disbursed to Black households were best understood as a tiny compensation for long-standing injustices rather than a form of benevolent aid that recipients may or may not deserve. "We dismiss once and for all the myth that people are responsible for the conditions of poverty and alienation which they are forced to [endure]," announced a BUF-created welfare-rights group called Blacks United for More Money in 1971. In a context of profound racial and class domination, welfare payments need to be considered "a right, as inalienable ... as the human dignity which our society now steals from the majority of people."[37] In a similar vein, BUF pressed the federal and provincial governments in 1971 to channel $300 million towards a long-term fund for Black-controlled social programs. This massive sum was described by the organization as a relatively paltry form of "reparations" for the Black-endured injustices of slavery, economic exploitation, and state domination.[38]

Formed amid the ongoing project of urban renewal, BUF was drawn almost inexorably into a series of confrontations over the prevailing urban planning regime. As noted in chapter 5, BUF quickly established itself as the city's most high-profile exponent of a race- and class-based analysis of postwar renewal. In doing so, it joined its voice to those of Black organizations across North America, who were forced to combat very similar planning projects. Five years after James Baldwin famously declared that urban renewal in US cities was a project of "Negro removal," BUF described the displacement of Black and working-class residents as the basic prerequisite of postwar planning and its totalizing objectives. "In brief, the center of Halifax and the old northern suburb [are being] saved for the developer," a BUF report explained.[39] The ostensible benefits of public housing, meanwhile, were analysed, picked apart, and dismissed. Projects like Mulgrave Park and Uniacke Square, BUF argued, were largely an instrument of social control and top-down supervision; they were "concentration camps" that kept "the Blacks and the poor Whites ... contained and supervised ... as prevention against [them] moving into surrounding suburbs."[40] Some form of subsidized housing was indeed needed in Halifax, BUF maintained, but it would need to be designed on the basis of explicit, Black-defined specifications. Existing housing projects, like urban planning in general, had been conceived and managed in the total absence of Black self-determination, and this was an essential problem that needed to be addressed.

From this general critique of urban planning, BUF developed a range of concrete actions. One of its first actions was to contest the city's decision to promote a white urban planner to the position of planning director over a more qualified Black candidate, who was also a well-known Black activist and BUF board member. The Black candidate, Carlyle Warner, had been employed as the city's chief long-range planner and had exceeded all the advertised qualifications for the higher-ranking position. Alleging that racism had informed the city's hiring decision, Warner issued a complaint to the Nova Scotia Human Rights Commission in January 1970. The commission, for the first time in its history, was unable to resolve a complaint through mediation and was forced to launch an official inquiry. In the meantime, Warner was demoted to a lower-ranking position at City Hall and was subjected to harassment from his coworkers. Though Warner had originally pursued the case on his own, BUF eventually stepped in with support as the situation worsened. In the end, the city was forced to pay $10,000 in damages to Warner but was allowed to maintain its white-directed planning department.[41]

A few months after Warner's complaint to the Human Rights Commission, BUF became involved with a second personnel decision at City Hall. In May 1970, the city offered its top executive position to a city manager from Oklahoma City named Robert Oldland. The latter, BUF soon learned, had not hired a single Black person during his tenure as city manager (though 20 per cent of the city's population was Black) and had spent much of the previous year attempting to crush a legal strike by the city's sanitation workers (95 per cent of whom were Black). Moving quickly, BUF worked with other anti-racist and labour activists in the city to challenge the Oldland job offer. In one action, over three hundred activists poured into city council chambers and refused to leave unless a committee was struck to examine the details of Oldland's tenure in Oklahoma City. Participating in the protest, Rocky Jones outlined the widespread opposition to Oldland among US civil-rights organizations and announced that Coretta Scott King was prepared to come to Halifax and provide her criticisms of the city manager in person. The city was ultimately unmoved by the protests, claiming that its own examination of Oldland's tenure had unearthed no reason for concern. A week after the protest, however, Oldland announced that he had reassessed his own career trajectory. He would in fact be rescinding his earlier acceptance of the Halifax job offer.[42]

In addition to contesting the personnel decisions that continually re-established white control of prevailing planning-related institutions, BUF interrogated the seemingly technical norms and standards that structured the most important planning programs of this period. In a detailed 1973 housing survey, BUF charted the profoundly racialized landscape that dominant planning practices had helped to produce in Nova Scotia. The survey, conducted by members of Black communities themselves, was meant to put "workable data" behind the widespread conclusion among Black residents (but not among white planners) that "housing [was] a crucial and dire need."[43] In Black communities, the survey found, 69 per cent of homes lacked running water and indoor plumbing, 50 per cent lacked central heating, and the vast majority required major repairs of some kind. Also observed in Black communities was a marked absence of recreation facilities, generally nonexistent public transportation and garbage collection, and public streets that almost universally lacked surface paving and remained unploughed in the winter.

These abysmal spatial conditions, the survey suggested, were the product of planning protocols that could seem technical in nature but whose effects were continually and profoundly anti-Black. Water and sewer services, for example, were provided only to settlements of a minimum population density. Omitted from service provision, as a result, were nearly all Black Nova Scotian communities, which tended to be isolated and relatively dispersed for very specific (i.e., racist) reasons. Central Mortgage and Housing Corporation (CMHC)-insured mortgages, meanwhile, were provided only to the owners of "serviced" properties, ensuring that Black communities already deprived of water and sewer services would also be denied an important means of financing home ownership, renovations, and capital accumulation. A whole range of housing subsidies, finally, were provided only to poor households earning at least $3,500 per year, a protocol that excluded the roughly 50 per cent of Black households who earned less than this amount and were consequently too poor to be classified as "poor." Sifting through these findings, it could hardly be more clear that the supposedly technical and race-neutral protocols that structured state programs in this period possessed a profoundly racial character, isolating and disqualifying the near entirety of the Black population from programs that might otherwise have been used to improve their material conditions. Improving the conditions of the Black population thus required a struggle against the accepted parameters of planning-related policies, a struggle that refused the norms inherent in these policies in order to recentre planning programs on the lived realities of Black Nova Scotians.

For BUF, the 1973 housing survey confirmed and strengthened its existing analysis of state programs, and its major effect was to bolster the militant actions that it had already begun to take. At a meeting in 1971, the organization blasted the CMHC for developing programs that lacked "any relevance for the majority of Blacks," and demanded that the institution channel funding towards a set of BUF-developed pilot projects.[44] In a brief submitted to the 1971 Royal Commission on Provincial-Municipal Affairs, BUF criticized prevailing municipal-level building codes, zoning regulations, and other planning policies for continually "disregarding the Black community's existence."[45] When a pair of state-commissioned planners convened a "consultation" in the Halifax-area Black community of Cherry Brook-Lake Loon, BUF stood with community members in their opposition to the consultant's narrowly framed proposals and top-down method of planning. While the consultants continually disqualified community members' questions and demands on the grounds that they were "political in nature and beyond … the scope of planning," Black activists insisted that planning was *necessarily* political and that its scope needed to be adjusted accordingly.[46] In letters and face-to-face meetings throughout the 1970s, finally, BUF repeatedly called on state agencies to address the absence of recreational facilities and other municipal infrastructure that had come to constitute Black communities in Nova Scotia as a categorically different, lesser kind of place.

While much of BUF's activism was directed towards the state, it also targeted a broader set of institutions and individuals whose actions significantly affected the living conditions of Black people. In the early years, BUF's head office in Halifax attracted a constant stream of Black Haligonians describing acts of racial discrimination and urging the organization to take action. The most frequent cases pertained to landlords who refused to rent to Black tenants, employers who refused to hire Black applicants, and businesses who either refused to serve Black customers or followed them like criminals through the aisles of their premises. Collectively, these cases illuminate the confining racial geography that prevailed in a city (and a country) supposedly exempted from Jim Crow-style racial segregation. "As in Alabama," BUF activist Buddy Daye told the national media in 1969, "colour lines are drawn in Halifax." The difference, he explained, was that "these lines are *quietly* enforced."[47] Learning to interpret and navigate this racial geography was evidently necessary for all Black residents, regardless of their social class. BUF director Jules Oliver, a graduate of Acadia University, often used his own experiences to highlight the class-transcending character of racial discrimination. "I can walk down a street in Halifax and I'm educated, and I know that I can go to various places that are advertising rooms for rent and I can be discriminated against," Oliver told the media in 1969. "It's a problem of attitudes. [And] they've been that way throughout history."[48]

As I suggested in chapter 5, there were clear patterns to these racial barriers. The "colour lines" invoked by BUF activist Buddy Daye seem to have been drawn with particular force around the city's downtown.

Over two-thirds of the racial discrimination cases handled by BUF and the Nova Scotia Human Rights Commission between 1968 and 1975 pertained to downtown locations. The centre of the city, the locus of so much planning attention and expenditure, was essentially nonexistent to the city's Black population. The city ended, in effect, at the perimeter of the North End.[49] Amending this situation, creating a better downtown for Black *and* white residents, would require an approach to city making that recognized the particular experiences, desires, and concerns that prevailing anti-blackness had created for Black residents, including concerns related to social practices like racial discrimination that uniquely structured their experience of urban space. BUF, always understaffed, was able to address only a handful of the racial discrimination cases that it received each year. One of its most important actions was simply to demand better results from the Nova Scotia Human Rights Commission, which BUF claimed was handling white complaints more quickly than Black ones and seemed overly "concerned with the rights of the respondent (the accused) ... rather than the real concern that an act [of human rights legislation] had been broken and someone had suffered for it."[50]

One of BUF's most effective attempts to improve Black living conditions through actions against nonstate institutions was its 1971 "campaign against slum housing" (CASH). The campaign was organized in collaboration with the North End Neighbourhood House, one of the city's most important anti-poverty organizations. Together, the two organizations canvassed the city's poorest rental units, inspected and documented housing conditions, and worked with tenants to take action against egregious landlords. In one strip of rental housing on Maitland Street, tenants were found to be living in especially poor conditions. The wiring in the building posed a fire hazard, rats were considered "part of the family," and children were known to drink from the toilet bowl when the plumbing failed.[51] After speaking with the tenants of these buildings, BUF and Neighbourhood House activists met with the buildings' landlord and ordered him to undertake a series of repairs within one month's time. When, a month later, the repairs had not even begun, campaigners set up pickets outside the landlord's other Halifax businesses and apartment buildings, and handed out flyers to passersby, which documented the conditions that prevailed in the Maitland Street buildings. As a result of this action, the targeted landlord finally began (and finished) the mandated repairs. Continued actions by BUF and Neighbourhood House, moreover, gradually compelled other slum landlords to upgrade their buildings (often to pre-empt an action against them) and contributed to a broader social movement that pressured the Nova Scotia government in 1972 to adopt the province's first-ever tenants' rights act.[52]

BUF's early confrontations in the domain of urban planning were significant and instructive. More than any other political organization in this period, BUF activists traced the life-degrading limits of post-World War II planning and called for fundamental, structural changes in its mode of operation. Postwar planning, BUF demonstrated, had been configured and implemented in such a way that its promises of a better life were consistently withheld from the Black population and were often achieved at the latter's expense. At fault, in some sense, was planning's myopic attention to lives and living conditions that were not Black people's, planning's fixation on a normative conception of the human that was implicitly white. BUF contested this conception of the human, throwing open the meaning of the human to include Black lives as they presently existed. But the problem, for BUF, was not just conceptual. Indeed, planning's conceptual limitations were themselves the product of a history in which meaningful Black input, decision making, and self-determination were precluded. As this suggests, the principle of Black self-determination provided a useful framework of critique and confrontation, a political lens through which BUF could identify the fundamental problems with planning discourses and practices. Black self-determination, in this case, was what the practices of dominant institutions reiteratively foreclosed and what, in its *absence*, provided planning practices with their damaging, racist character. Critiquing and confronting dominant planning institutions was essential to the achievement of Black self-determination in the long term.

Black Self-Determination and Alternative Social Programs

In addition to combating prevailing institutions and practices, BUF devoted significant attention to the development of alternative social programs. As Jules Oliver emphasized in 1970, "BUF plays two specific roles: the activist role and the programmatic role."[53] It was in the "programmatic" domain that BUF's endeavours most concretely expressed a different form of urban planning, a form of planning that not only recentred the lived realities of the Black population but also sought to cultivate Black self-determination at every stage in the process. The main goal of BUF's programmatic interventions, in other words, was not so much to resolve the problems of the Black population but rather to put Black people in the position of identifying and solving problems on their own initiative. BUF's planning interventions, consequently, focused as much on Black living conditions as they did on Black people's sense of self, their level of empowerment, and their ability to work collectively towards independently devised planning objectives. It was precisely the affirmation of Black individuals and their capacity to understand and resolve their own planning-related problems that made BUF's programmatic pursuits so different from the dominant planning regime and so unacceptable to existing structures of power.

BUF's efforts to enact Black self-determination through the development of alternative programs experienced rather mixed results. To some extent, the difficulties that it encountered were the result of certain irresolvable tensions within the espoused principle itself. Black self-determination, for many proponents, was seen as a more sensible and plausible political pursuit than the more mainstream, liberal pursuit of individual rights for all people. As the African American radical Harold Cruse explained in 1967: "America, which idealizes the rights of the individual above everything else is, in reality, a nation dominated by the social power of groups, classes, in-groups, and cliques – both ethnic and religious. The individual in America has few rights that are not backed up by the political, economic, and social power of one group or another."[54] The pursuit of individual rights, this view suggests, is naive at best. In reality, individual rights are never "given" but claimed, and the claiming of rights on the part of oppressed *individuals* ultimately depends on the concerted action of oppressed *groups*. A collective pursuit like Black self-determination is thus essential to the improvement of individual lives and the claiming of any individual rights that might be considered desirable.

Emphasizing the Black "collective," however, could entail certain risks. A Black collective, for example, would need to be conceived and organized, and it is highly likely – and perhaps unavoidable – that this operation would efface some of the important differences in Black people's lived experiences and political perspectives. A universal Black subject would tend to be constituted, a Black substitute for the universal white subject assumed in mainstream social practices. Achieving the "destiny" of *this* imagined subject, this ultimately partial subject, would become the emphasis of political struggle. In practice, moreover, the definition and representation of the Black collective could easily become the monopoly of the most privileged Black individuals and the most well-funded Black organizations. This process, to the extent it was allowed to occur, would tend to reinscribe the marginality of Black people whose oppression was not defined by race alone (i.e., people who also experience class, gender, or sexual oppression).

It should be clear that not all proponents of Black self-determination sought to *represent* the Black community in a political or epistemic sense. The creation of Black studies and Black arts programs are perhaps the best examples of initiatives in which the irresolvable tension between individual and collective self-determination was clearly acknowledged and kept firmly in view. While these initiatives required some definition of Black identity in order to distinguish themselves from mainstream (i.e., white) education and arts programs, their fundamental aim was to affirm and empower their individual participants to pursue their own means and ends. It was on the basis of individual empowerment spread across the Black community, in other words, that both individual and collective self-determination were expected to be achieved.[55]

In the early years, BUF's pursuit of self-determination clearly sought to nurture individual empowerment across the Black community rather than represent an ostensibly unified Black collectivity. Its confrontations with dominant institutions were meant to create space for Black individuals to make decisions for themselves, while its alternative social programs were meant to affirm and expand individuals' decision-making capacities. BUF's attention to individual empowerment stemmed from its analysis of anti-blackness in Nova Scotia as both an institutional and a psychological phenomenon. Centuries of racial slavery, BUF argued, were certainly reflected in the enduring configuration of dominant institutions, but they were also present as "an indelible imprint in the ... social-consciousness of Nova Scotians."[56] Centuries-old racial codes, in other words, had been (partially) accepted and internalized by Black individuals, resulting in a long-term "psychological genocide" that limited people's belief in themselves and their present capacities to make decisions for themselves.[57] The point, for BUF, was not to downplay the importance of institutional or structural changes – the need, that is, to confront and dissolve anti-Black institutions and social practices. The point was simply that anti-blackness existed both institutionally and psychologically, and that it was necessary to combat both manifestations at once. Indeed, a successful struggle against dominant institutions would seem to require an overcoming of the psychological effects of anti-blackness within the many individuals that would comprise such a struggle.

BUF's efforts to empower individuals passed through a range of programs that aimed to communicate and cultivate a more positive Black consciousness. A monthly newspaper called *GRASP*, introduced in 1970, provided a regular survey of Black Nova Scotian accomplishments, as well as a critical Black perspective on current events. A television series, first aired in 1972, produced and transmitted a retelling of the major events of Black history to a popular audience, Black and white.[58] BUF educational initiatives, meanwhile, aimed to incorporate Black history into educational curricula at various levels of schooling, as well as unseat the white norms that often paraded as the universal signs of educational achievement. The organization's engagements at the university level could be particularly forceful in these regards. Arguing that coerced "assimilation [to white norms] negates identity and the value of racial uniqueness," Jules Oliver challenged Dalhousie University to reorient teaching methods and materials towards the capacities of Black learners rather than seek to remould the latter in the image of their white peers.[59] In this case, as in many others, the empowerment of individuals and the transformation of institutions overlapped. Changing Dalhousie as an institution would help to empower Black individuals. More empowered individuals, in turn, would enter into and move forward the struggle for institutional change at Dalhousie and beyond.

The connection between individual empowerment and institutional transformation was particularly evident in the case of BUF's "cultural awakening program." Introduced in 1970, the program was designed to carry participants through twelve hours of transformative learning and group-based activities. The overall program was divided into three interlinked elements: cultural awakening, political action, and community organization. As this series of elements suggests, the aim of the program was to provide individuals with a new form of consciousness (an "awakening") as a precursor to engaged, collective action. The cultivation of Black "pride and knowledge" in the first part of the program, BUF assumed, would "enable [participants] to become a little more politically self aware." The teaching of concrete organizing and leadership skills in the later parts of the program would then allow individuals to put their new self-awareness to political use. By the end of the program, BUF hoped, participants would be sufficiently empowered, skilled, and motivated to return to their communities and organize around community-level problems "as they see them."[60]

While individual empowerment was approached head-on in programs like the cultural awakening program, it was an important consideration in nearly all BUF programs. Seeking to address the lack of recreational facilities in Black communities, for example, BUF encouraged the formation of community-specific committees that would identify and address their own recreation needs. On BUF's urging, recreation committees were soon established in at least ten Black communities in Nova Scotia, and hundreds of individuals were thereby drawn into the development of community-level recreation plans. Having left decision making to communities themselves, BUF's primary role in this initiative was to provide guidance and training in activities like the drafting of fundraising applications. Through this model, over $100,000 was raised for Black recreation facilities in 1970–1 alone, and a recreational landscape long abandoned by urban planning began to change. Playgrounds and sports venues were constructed, sports equipment was procured, and community centres were either developed or renovated. In addition to these concrete results, the self-determining capacities of Black individuals were clearly augmented through their involvement in these initiatives. As Jules Oliver noted in 1970, the recreation committees provided "fine examples of self-determination" in action.[61]

Housing programs provided another opportunity to nourish individual capacities. BUF's 1973 housing survey, for example, was designed to be carried out by members of the surveyed communities themselves. As BUF recognized, Black communities had long been "survey[ed] to death" by outsiders, while the capacities of Black individuals were left to languish.[62] Entrusted to community members, the housing survey became a vehicle of data collection, capacity building, and community organizing at once. The assessment of community needs, in this approach, was explicitly bound up with the process of organizing around these same needs and seeing them (potentially) addressed. The entire process, moreover, was tied to community-defined problems and desires, a whole program of socio-spatial change that took Black lives as its starting point and Black-defined futures as its end goal. Here as elsewhere, BUF's programs enabled new conceptions of the human. Their effect was not just to broaden the boundaries of dominant conceptions to include Black lives but also to put Black people at the centre of a process in which new forms of living would be created. BUF's programs, in sum, helped to constitute Black people as agents capable of remaking their lives and spaces in the company of others.

On BUF's urging, several important community-devised housing programs were conceived and implemented in the early 1970s, with features that sometimes departed significantly from the programs provided by state institutions. A 1974 affordable-housing program was targeted specifically to single-parent households, a domestic arrangement that was found to be common in Black communities and extremely ill addressed by existing state programs. Particularities among Black people, this program suggests, were duly recognized. Rather than treated as a pathology, a departure from a more privileged and normative form of Black life, they were affirmed and supported. Other community-devised programs were distinguished by their reliance on community-supplied and often voluntary construction labour, a traditional mainstay of home-building and home-renovation practices in Black communities. Hence, a 1971 "model community" program pioneered in Beechville and later promoted elsewhere used community-supplied labour to construct a series of cooperatively owned housing units. A 1975 "winter warmth" program, meanwhile, harnessed CMHC financial resources to community-supplied labour in order to reduce the per-unit cost of retrofitting Black homes and therefore spread the available funding across a larger number of units and households. As these examples suggest, BUF's emphasis on community involvement in the development and implementation of housing solutions not only helped to enhance individual capacities and self-determination but also resulted (at times) in program offerings that came closer to the particular problems and strengths of the province's Black communities.[63]

On questions of housing and many others, BUF's preferred approach in the early years was to support the self-organizing capacities of Black individuals and communities rather than position itself as the representative of an imagined Black collectivity. There were certainly exceptions to this approach, as I discuss below, and some BUF leaders seem to have had more confidence in the potential of self-directed and self-organized Black activism than others. However, the organization's approach remained univocal in its early reports and policy documents, and pervaded the majority of the organization's early practices. As its 1971 Master Plan emphasized: "It is not our role to do *for* the community, but rather ... [to] develop the kinds of avenues through which the community can satisfy [its] own needs."[64]

BUF's preference for bottom-up, self-directed political action was a major departure from the approach of earlier Black organizations in Nova Scotia, and it seems to have required some adjustment on the part of some Black residents and communities. As a BUF field organizer remarked in 1970, the concept of self-organization "is one that people find it difficult to adjust to; they prefer the organization to overcome obstacles for them."[65] And yet, people seem to have adjusted to the concept rather quickly. In early 1971, Jules Oliver observed that Black communities were "breaking away from traditional processes that do not often bring rewards" and showing "increased awareness with regard to the concept of self-determination." "[The] alienated in many of our communities are no longer remaining silent," he concluded. "They want to become involved."[66] Oliver's observations were later mirrored by Howard University professor Peter Paris, who undertook an independent assessment of the organization in 1972. BUF's efforts, he concluded, had given Black people "a new sense of worth and power ... in fighting social injustice."[67]

Whatever its appeal in Black communities, the principle of bottom-up social change nevertheless encountered some persistent challenges. One of the most formidable challenges was the enduring refusal of the provincial state to grant BUF any authority or purview in the domain of social programming. Relations between BUF and the province were hostile from the beginning, with BUF regarding the province's social welfare department as an inherently paternalistic enterprise that aimed to keep the Black population in a state of "dependence ... on governmental programs."[68] In a heated exchange in 1971, BUF informed provincial representatives that their top-down mode of operation was a continuation of the centuries-old paternalism and arrogance that had fuelled "land exploitation, economic exploitation, as well as [the] exploitation of human dignity."[69] The only admissible role for the social welfare department, in BUF's view, was to provide funding for programs that Black communities designed and implemented on their own. "Money should be released, no strings attached," BUF argued in 1971, "for people to develop [welfare] programs based on self determination."[70]

Ironically, the social welfare department had recently adopted the language of self-determination to describe its own approach, and it refused to cede any ground to its new competitor. As this power struggle continued through the early 1970s, provincial officials were sometimes accused of stoking divisions within Black communities or attempting to turn community members against BUF field organizers.[71] Challenges like these forced BUF to defend its standing in Black communities and distinguish its version of self-determination from the one employed by state institutions. Self-determination, BUF explained in

1970, necessarily involved "conflict and confrontation" with oppressive institutions and could not be promoted, therefore, by individuals whose "vested interest [was] tied up with the government."[72] The state, in other words, might talk about self-determination, and it might even encourage the participation of Black communities in its programs, at times. It could not, however, promote the kind of systemic or institutional confrontation that the self-determination of oppressed people truly required. This, for BUF, was a key difference, and one that showed why the state's version of self-determination was meaningless, if not hypocritical.

More challenging to BUF's programmatic pursuits than the obstinacy of the social welfare department was the state's more general control over usable financial resources. Nearly all of BUF's programs, after all, were premised on the availability of some form of funding, and its original five-year grant was never quite sufficient in this respect. BUF's hope, in the early years, was that the state could be convinced to channel some of the money that it was spending on its own social programs towards related but better-designed BUF programs.[73] Consistent with its emphasis on bottom-up program development, BUF's general approach in this period was to carry community-devised programs to the relevant state institution and request an appropriate level of funding. In very few cases did this approach bring positive results. More often, BUF was forced to fit its requests within the parameters of already-existing state programs, a dynamic that greatly diminished the innovativeness of its alternative programs and impaired the fulfilment of genuine self-determination. Most of BUF's housing programs, for example, were funded by the CMHC and needed, therefore, to fulfil the latter institution's funding criteria as much as (or more than) community-defined objectives. BUF was sometimes creative in its implementation of these programs, and it is likely that Black communities were able to access these programs and funding to a much greater extent as a result of BUF's efforts. The promotion and delivery of state-devised programs, however, was clearly not the role that BUF aspired to play.

Ultimately, securing state funding for alternative social programs seemed to require a stronger exhibition of collective strength, a stronger confrontation with state institutions. It was in this pursuit more than any other that BUF sought to position itself as the political representative of a unified Black constituency. Particularly expressive of this pursuit were the BUF-convened "tri-function conventions" that occurred four times between 1971 and 1974.[74] The conventions, nominally an organized encounter between Black communities and the provincial and federal levels of government, actually required Black Nova Scotians to express their concerns and demands to BUF. The latter, in turn, would represent their concerns and make collective demands upon state officials, face to face, at the conventions. At these events, BUF would regularly blast state officials for believing that a series of white-controlled programs could respond to Black needs and would demand that autonomous Black programs receive appropriate funding.[75] The effectiveness of tri-function conventions in pressuring state officials to support Black demands was ultimately rather limited. Vague government commitments were often made but were seldom carried through, and the interest of state officials in attending the events clearly waned over time.[76] The pursuit of greater state funding was nevertheless kept up. Private meetings between BUF leaders and state officials became more frequent and more important (to BUF) as time passed. In these private meetings, BUF was inevitably cast as the representative of the Black collectivity, even if its major objective was to win funding for individual-empowering social programs.[77]

BUF's promotion of alternative programs was a continual struggle within narrow, externally imposed boundaries. At their best, these programs tapped into the creative energies and grounded knowledge of Black individuals, producing innovative programs in tandem with enhanced individual capacities and empowerment. They envisioned a process in which Black people worked together to remake their lives – socially, politically, and spatially. BUF, in these cases, adopted the role of facilitator, rather than director; it pictured itself as "a catalyzing and activating agent, both within the community and ... against the external community."[78] Playing this role, however, seemed to require the claiming of some of the power and financial resources of state institutions. This was not an easily won achievement. It was largely to create possibilities for bottom-up planning and program development that BUF assumed the role of political representative, providing a "voice" to an ostensibly unified Black collectivity in the course of fraught negotiations with an oppressive, anti-Black state. While the adoption of this role might have been justified under the circumstances, it came with all of the risks associated with more constrained versions of self-determination: the positing of a normative Black subject, the creation of community-representing "race leaders," and so on. Over time, moreover, the adoption of this role would also open the organization to a range of criticisms from Black Nova Scotians, criticism that would tend not to apply in its more grounded, participatory pursuits. Such criticisms would ultimately be implicated in BUF's dissolution.

"The Slow Death of a Great Experiment"

While BUF endured as an organization until 1996, signs of its possible dissolution arrived relatively early. After a BUF board meeting in early 1971, New Glasgow representative Carrie Best described a gap that seemed to have opened up between BUF decision makers and the Black community, and she wrote, in a letter addressed to Chairman Carlyle Warner, that she might be witnessing "the slow death of a great experiment."[79] These early signs of trouble would be magnified significantly in the years to come, as criticisms of the organization and its imperfect accountability to the Black community proliferated and intensified. To some extent, the gradual dissolution of BUF was the outcome of processes internal to the organization itself: personal grudges and disagreements, recurring financial mismanagement, and strategic moves that seem plainly wrongheaded (at least in hindsight). These internal processes unrolled, however, upon an extremely difficult political terrain. With a few exceptions, prevailing state institutions seem to have resented BUF's existence from the very beginning, and their actions allowed the organization very little room in which to operate. A discussion of BUF's dissolution, then, needs to match internal processes to the external constraints and pressures that conditioned them.

In many ways, the rise and fall of BUF parallels the experience of other Black organizations in the 1960s and early 1970s. Across North America and the global diaspora, the resurgence of Black activism and autonomous community development in this period was met with overwhelming and often violent state practices of containment. Distrustful of Black activism throughout its history, the US state ramped up its surveillance and repressive activities in the 1960s through the establishment of several Black-targeting counterintelligence programs (COINTELPROs). Implemented by the Federal Bureau of Investigation (FBI), these programs targeted nearly every significant Black organization in the country. While the FBI famously labelled the Black Panther Party "the greatest threat to [the] internal security of country" in 1969, the agency also imputed violent and security-threatening objectives to Martin Luther King Jr and the Southern Christian Leadership Conference; Stokely Carmichael, H. Rap Brown, and the Student Nonviolent Coordinating Committee; the National Association for the

Advancement of Colored People; the Congress for Racial Equality; and dozens of campus-based Black student unions. Seeking to contain or eliminate these organizations, the FBI spied on prominent Black activists; promoted hostility and violence between Black organizations and among their members; infiltrated Black organizations and promoted illegal activities; arrested and imprisoned Black activists on false charges and fabricated evidence; and directly or indirectly assassinated important Black individuals. By 1971, when COINTELPROs were officially suspended, the FBI was responsible for the killing of dozens of Black activists, the imprisonment of hundreds of others, and the creation of a climate of fear and distrust that effectively decimated the most effective Black activist groups.[80]

North of the border, the Canadian state was less aggressive in its response to Black radicalism, perhaps because the latter never achieved the same mass-based adherence or posed the same level of political threat that it did in the United States. Still, important Black-targeting programs of surveillance and infiltration were indeed introduced by Canadian security agencies, either on their own or in collaboration with their US counterparts. George Sams, the Black Panther who visited Halifax in 1968, served as an FBI informant for over ten years and frequently encouraged acts of violence and aggression among Black radicals in order to justify their surveillance, assassination, or imprisonment by the state.[81] Whether his arrival in Halifax – with illegal arms in tow – was orchestrated by the FBI or the RCMP is not known, but it was certainly anticipated by various security agencies. Declassified RCMP documents reveal the agency's concern in 1968 that, in its words, "US Black Panther members have been actively engaged in attempts to gain control of the civil-rights leadership in the Halifax and area Negro community."[82] The Halifax police, meanwhile, were curiously well positioned at the local airport and venues like the Arrows Club before the arrival of Sams, Carmichael, and other Black activist visitors to the city. A tip-off or direct order from the RCMP must be assumed. Sams's visit also fits within a larger pattern in which his actions in a particular city helped to create an (imagined) association between Black activism and violence, and nourished public fears and backlash as a consequence.[83]

The RCMP, in addition to its possible work with George Sams, is known to have spied on Rocky Jones throughout the 1960s, 1970s, and beyond. It was so common for an unmarked police car to be parked outside Jones's Halifax home in the late 1960s that he would sometimes bring coffee to the officers or ask them for a ride. The officers would have to follow him anyway, Jones recalls.[84] RCMP surveillance files eventually obtained by Jones through access-to-information requests were substantial enough to fill dozens of boxes and documented the state's continued surveillance of Jones even as he shifted towards more mainstream activist pursuits.[85] The state's profound aversion to Black activism, radical or otherwise, is perhaps best exemplified in routine police actions, like the 1970 ticketing of BUF activist Buddy Daye for jaywalking and having a dog "at large." The jaywalking charge was reportedly the first that Halifax police had ever laid, and it came just one month after Daye had been publicly involved in contesting the city's decision to hire Oklahoma City's Robert Oldland as its top executive. As research on the surveillance and repression of Black activism in other settings demonstrates, these state practices have little to do with the threat of violence or other illegal activities. Rather, they constitute a response to Black visibility, agency, and self-assertion – veritable threats not to people's physical security but to the continuation of white supremacy and its associated privileges.[86]

The Canadian state's distrust of Black activism was clearly mirrored to a considerable extent within the broader society. The federal Ministry of Health and Welfare, in the period following the announcement of its $470,000 grant to BUF, received hundreds of letters from Canadian citizens, all of them critical of the grant. According to one letter: "This organization (BUF) is itself racist, revolutionary, and under the manipulation of communists. Apparently, 'Rocky Jones,' who publicly advocates violence against our society, is the leader of the organization." Another letter called BUF a group of "agitators" and suggested that the ministry's funding of the organization was equivalent to the Roman Empire's provision of bread and circuses to "mollify the multiple throngs of savages and barbarians."[87] Responses like these suggest the tiny boundaries within which Black activists were expected to operate in Canada, boundaries that would have major effects on BUF's political trajectory. The selection of Jules Oliver over Rocky Jones as the organization's first executive director was intended at least partly to allay mounting white fears and avoid a more significant, potentially violent form of white backlash. Within BUF's leadership, meanwhile, older activists like W.P. Oliver had several decades of experience with the white community behind them when, on several occasions, they recommended more conservative and conciliatory approaches to high-profile conflicts. In the midst of the Oldland controversy, for example, the elder Oliver conservatively advised that BUF representatives remain "behind the scenes" rather than involve themselves more publicly and risk retribution.[88]

While outright hostility was one debilitating response to Black activism in this period, selective accommodation was another. Halifax mayor Allan O'Brien, for example, welcomed BUF's arrival on the political scene and praised its potential to serve as a "communications vehicle" for the Black community. "By clearly identifying and describing their problems to the white community," he said, "the [organization] can open doors to useful discussions [about] possible solutions."[89] O'Brien's response to BUF, while positive in a certain sense, clearly missed something of the organization's political purpose, interpreting Black self-determination as the mere "communication" of a viewpoint without any meaningful change in prevailing relations of power. A similarly narrow perspective was expressed by the principal of Dalhousie University, who saw BUF as an effective representative of the Black community and therefore welcomed its involvement in the oversight of the recently established "transition year program" for Black and Indigenous students. The involvement that he imagined, however, was limited to the provision of occasional input, while all decision-making power was placed in the hands of "professional" educators. For BUF, of course, a program for Black students could not be overseen by a group of white professionals, and it rebuked Dalhousie's use of "token" participation as an example of "institutionalized racism" and the enduring "pretensions of white institutions."[90] For Dalhousie, as for Mayor O'Brien, Black activism was encouraged but tightly constrained. The expression of a perspective was warmly invited. The claiming of power was not.

At the federal level, the encouragement of a tightly constrained form of Black activism was most clearly expressed in decisions about funding. BUF's applications for federal funding in the early years were forthright in their intention to nurture Black self-determination in an expansive and empowering sense. The greatest need, BUF stated in its March 1969 funding application, was for Black people "to have a vital role in the making of decisions which affect *their daily lives and social status*."[91] Self-determination, in this moment, was clearly expected to be achieved in every domain that affected the lives of Black people. That the pursuit of this objective would sometimes require a confrontation with white-controlled institutions was downplayed in the text (for obvious reasons) but was implicit in the application's emphasis on the cultivation of Black solidarity, the creation of new Black citizens groups, and the promotion of new forms of collective action. Federal officials balked at the funding of self-determination in this expansive sense and instead channelled BUF's application towards a newly established program designed to improve the delivery of social-welfare programs. The grant provided to BUF in 1969 was therefore intended to involve Black people in the "identification and solution of problems" in the limited domain of social-welfare provision. Explicitly negating BUF's larger purpose, federal Minister of Health and Welfare John Munro announced that the grant was intended "not to fight a racial problem – but a poverty problem."[92]

The actual effects of federal funding on BUF's activities were difficult to foresee. While some BUF activists believed that the funding could be used for more radical projects, other activists were unconvinced. Indeed, the very decision to approach the state for funding in 1969 went against the wishes of many Black Nova Scotians, including certain members of BUF's interim leadership committee. The original funding application was delivered to Ottawa by W.P. Oliver and Gus Wedderburn without the consent of the full leadership committee, and the eventual acceptance of the grant eight months later occurred without obtaining the approval of the Black community at a second "Black family meeting" (as had been promised at the first meeting).[93] The pursuit and acceptance of state funding has consequently been described by some Black activists as an act of betrayal and a major shift in the new organization's trajectory. For Frank Boyd, a participant at the first Black family meeting, the pursuit of funding trapped BUF within the narrow parameters of the state-sanctioned "minority game" and wasted the more radical possibilities that existed in the late 1960s. Rocky Jones, meanwhile, took some distance from BUF at this point, redirecting his energies to the newly created Afro-Canadian Liberation Movement and the Dalhousie Black Students Union.[94] The federal grant, of course, came with little formal control over its actual use, and it is clear that BUF was able to use the funding in ways that its grantors never intended. More constraining, in the end, was the grant's nurturing of an organizational form that required continued state funding, and consequently continued state approval, in order to survive.

The constraints imposed by state funding became more tangible in the years to come. Always underfunded in relation to its program objectives, BUF regularly sought new sources of state funding in its early years. These efforts were almost always unsuccessful and tended, therefore, to deliver an important message: BUF could not confront the state and, at the same time, expect to be funded by the state. Faced with a choice between political confrontation and long-term (post-1974) state funding, BUF evidently chose the latter option. In 1973, with the expiry of its original five-year grant on the horizon, the organization adopted a significant change in direction. The ever-cantankerous Jules Oliver took his leave from BUF at this point, a move that he (and other activists) hoped would give the organization a new life. His replacement as executive director, Art Criss, was a relative outsider to the organization and therefore provided BUF with an opportunity to reinvent its relationship with the federal and (especially) provincial governments. Indeed, a year later, a top provincial bureaucrat reported that "our relations [with BUF] are good, and Mr. Chriss [*sic*] and his staff are working hand-in-hand with our Social Development Division."[95] A target of attack under Oliver's leadership, the province was now regarded as a kind of partner. So harmonious were Criss's engagements with the province, in fact, that provincial officials soon became a key advocate for BUF in its pursuit of long-term federal funding.[96]

Even with the province's support, securing long-term funding proved to be difficult for BUF. Requests for a ten-year extension to the original grant, a period of time that was meant to overlap with the official "decade to confront racial discrimination in Nova Scotia," was not simply refused but treated with condescension by federal officials.[97] A series of short-term extensions were eventually provided, securing BUF's survival until June 1975, but a long-term federal grant was bluntly ruled out. In the meantime, casual discussions about funding with municipal officials in Halifax resulted in a pre-emptive city council resolution stating that "no grant be given to the Black United Front."[98] Running out of options, BUF began to consider applying for a grant under the federal Canada Assistance Plan (CAP), a move that promised to bring in substantial long-term funding but that could also involve certain problems. For one thing, CAP grants were funded in equal measure by the federal and provincial governments. Receiving the grant would therefore bind the organization to the province for the first time and would tend to introduce constraints on province-level political confrontation that even Criss found worrisome.[99] More concerning still was the CAP stipulation that BUF register itself as a "provincially approved [welfare] agency" and establish a decision-making vehicle that would ensure a harmonious "co-ordination of services provided in Black Communities by the [provincial] Department of Social Services and the Black United Front."[100] Rather than facilitating the bottom-up development of social programs, BUF would now be tasked with delivering a set of programs that neither the organization nor Black communities had any role in devising.

With clear consequences for BUF's future, the implications of potential CAP funding led to protracted and wide-ranging debates within the organization. The creation of a new decision-making vehicle, a form of partnership between BUF and the province, was met with particular opposition. Vested with active decision-making power, such a vehicle would clearly move beyond the informal and powerless "steering committee" that had been mandated in BUF's original grant, and it could very well extinguish the remainder of BUF's political and programmatic independence. Evidently reluctant to give in, a few board members discussed the possibilities of pursuing "radical funding" from the Black Panthers or another Black Power group. Referring either to the violent repression that had effectively crushed the Panthers by this time or to the waning of a particularly radical moment in Black politics, it was concluded that "the social situation has changed drastically" since George Sams and T.D. Pawley had visited Halifax, and that "radical funding" was therefore unlikely to be obtained. With significant unease and regret in the air, it was ultimately decided that BUF would pursue CAP funding and accept the various "strings" attached to it.[101]

The acceptance of the CAP grant was a major turning point for the organization. From this point forward, BUF's major program offerings needed to be approved by the provincial state and therefore satisfy provincial objectives. Already an imposition in 1975, the province intensified its control over BUF programs in the years to come, gradually transforming the organization into little more than a Black delivery mechanism for state-devised programs. Meanwhile, the organization's engagements with state institutions were significantly reshaped. The confrontational style of meetings like the tri-function conventions was effectively retired. Encounters with state officials were now an opportunity for closed-door discussions of program offerings and possibilities, and an ever-increasing amount of BUF's energy and resources were devoted to shuttling its leaders from high-level meeting to high-level meeting.[102] Eventually, even the rhetoric of self-determination tended to fade away. In 1984, with a former military officer in the executive-director position, BUF described its purpose in the contrite language of consultation and information delivery: "find[ing] out what the black communities of Nova Scotia want, and then communicat[ing] these wants to the appropriate level of private or public interest."[103] The more liberatory of BUF's remaining social programs were those focused on cultural awakening and individual empowerment. Stripped of their original connection to collective action and institutional transformation, however, these programs lost much of their earlier significance and could easily be criticized for offering a mere palliative to the "psychological genocide" that BUF had once been determined to confront head-on.

One last attempt to restore BUF's transformative potential was made in 1988, when East Preston's Yvonne Atwell was elected to the position of executive director. Her vision was for BUF to become more "politically active and visible in the community," as well as more financially independent. "The more independent the better," she put it. "The more political the better."[104] In pursuit of this vision, she attempted to lure Rocky Jones back into the BUF milieu, offering him the position of research coordinator for a project that would examine structural racism in the criminal justice system. The move shocked the more conservative members of the BUF board of directors and prompted one member of the provincial government to threaten a withdrawal of state funding. Expressing the pliant position that BUF had come to occupy over the years, one board member publicly opposed Atwell's hiring decision on the basis that "the government would be afraid of Rocky." Another board member argued that Jones was too "politically active" and that BUF was not "ready for the political stage." In the end, the board voted 10–2 to rescind the job offered to Jones and soon proceeded to muscle Atwell out of the executive-director position.[105]

With Atwell and Jones expulsed, BUF could retake the position that it had occupied since the mid-1970s. The militancy of the early years was now long gone, as was the belief that Black self-determination needed to be built from the ground up – the belief that it required a confrontation with dominant institutions, a rejection of white norms, and a remaking of society on the basis of empowered, politically engaged individuals. Tethered to constraining and always-revokable state funding, BUF had become a mere political representative for the Black community and a dutiful conduit for state-devised poverty programs. These two remaining roles, a severe dilution of BUF's original mandate, were also extremely questionable ones. In the end, representing an unavoidably diverse and divided Black population proved to be as difficult in Nova Scotia as it was in other parts of North America, and it fuelled incessant criticism of the organization and its "representativeness" from the early 1980s onward. The delivery of social programs, meanwhile, could always be questioned on the grounds of efficiency and effectiveness, and this would tend to be especially true to the extent that BUF simply implemented programs that had been conceived by state functionaries.

It was ultimately this pair of vulnerabilities that underwrote BUF's demise. In the 1990s, state funding for ethnic minority groups (in general) was under fire from resentful white Canadians and the newly ascendant federal Reform Party. This funding, a small and mostly depoliticizing response to racial inequalities, was criticized for undermining national unity and kowtowing to "special interest" groups.[106] This political climate intensified the province's already imperious scrutiny of its financial disbursements to BUF. The province, having already accused BUF of inefficiency and financial mismanagement for several years, finally cut off funding to the organization in 1996 and established its own in-house Black organization, the Department of African Nova Scotian Affairs, two years later. Unimpressed by the representational and shadow-state functions that BUF had come to play over the years, the Black community received the province's decision with general equanimity. No protests were organized and no Black family meetings were called. As Rocky Jones recalls, BUF had ceased to be relevant and accountable to the Black community. "The programs that [BUF] offered were there because the government wanted them, not because of our needs or our definitions" he explained. Hence, "when the government finally pulled the plug, no one bothered to protest."[107] In late 1996, after a bumpy and often promise-filled twenty-seven years of existence, BUF disappeared quietly into the night.

Conclusion

For twenty-seven years, BUF was the most significant Black organization in Nova Scotia. Formed in the politically turbulent late 1960s, BUF carried forward a vibrant and centuries-old tradition of Black struggle in the province and managed to consolidate a diversity of Black concerns and strategies into a potent challenge to anti-blackness. BUF was most effective and inventive between 1969 and 1974, when its funding was secure and "without strings." In this early period, BUF confronted the subtle and not-so-subtle racism of prevailing state institutions, landlords, and employers, and devised alternative social programs that would positively transform Black communities from the ground up. Running through these confrontations and social programs was a consistent commitment to Black self-determination, a commitment that involved putting decision making in the hands of the people most affected by the decisions in question and making it possible for them to "determine their own destinies." Though the principle of self-determination *could* license the creation of "race leaders" – the spokespeople of an ostensibly unified Black community – BUF's early actions tended to regard Black people as their own representatives and sought to support their self-activity, self-affirmation, and self-representation. Incorporated into BUF's engagements with urban planning, this commitment to self-determination exposed the anti-Black foundations of dominant planning practices and informed the introduction of new planning practices that were better attuned to the lives and spaces of Black communities.

In some senses, BUF's approach to urban planning was nothing new. For BUF, as for professional urban planners, the overarching aim was to create a better form of life through the management of spatial conditions. Black lives, through urban planning, were meant to become healthier, happier, and more empowered – a form of life roughly consistent with the one envisioned by white urban planners in this period. And yet, BUF also tangled with established meanings and objectives, throwing open the potential meanings of the "human" in the present and the future. From the outset, BUF insisted in the viability of Black life as it presently existed. It challenged, therefore, prevailing conceptions of the human that placed blackness on their less-than-human outside. Where urban planning saw life-deforming pathologies among Black people, BUF saw mere particularities, and it envisioned and partially implemented a form of planning that took these particularities, including particularities *among* Black people, as their starting point. This insistence, a rejection of planning's assessment of life in the present, was ultimately coupled with a different conception of life's future. The better life that BUF envisioned in the early years was not defined simply in terms of improved material conditions or higher levels of personal income, bodily health, or individual well-being. It also involved the creation of Black people as agents, people capable of defining and achieving their own destinies in the company of others. Like other vehicles of Black liberation in this period, BUF envisioned a future in which Black people worked together, socially and politically, to define and achieve their destinies.

BUF's pursuit of these objectives departed from, and ultimately conflicted with, the prerogatives of prevailing state institutions and civil-society organizations. On the surface, BUF's pursuit of self-determination might seem to rhyme with the project of "citizen involvement" promoted by institutions like the Nova Scotia Planning Secretariat and implemented by activist groups like Movement for Citizens' Voice and Action (MOVE). A closer analysis, however, reveals important differences. BUF, rather than searching for the elusive collective interests that would ostensibly unite differently positioned social groups, committed to the achievement of the interests that meant most to Black people – even, and perhaps especially, when these interests conflicted with those of more privileged citizens. Rather than masking white privilege behind practices of citizen involvement devoted to abstract equality and inclusion, in other words, BUF sought to produce actual equality and inclusion through the intentional privileging of oppressed viewpoints and demands. This conception of politics necessarily and consciously put BUF in conflict with entrenched social and political power. The achievement of self-determination, for BUF, entailed a thorough wresting of power from other people and institutions. It involved Black individuals and communities gaining control over their own lives at the expense of external authorities, including BUF itself. Such a racialized redistribution of power, of course, proved to be intolerable to state officials at every level: municipal, provincial, and federal. The communication of Black concerns and demands was sometimes welcomed. The claiming of Black political power was not.

BUF's achievements require a careful assessment. The great possibilities that seemed to exist at the time of the Black Panthers' visit and the historic Black family meeting were never quite realized. The path to their realization was blocked, in part, by internal conflicts and (perhaps) poor strategic choices. But it was blocked, more forcefully, by the crushing weight of institutionalized anti-blackness, a structure of power constituted centuries earlier and constantly recreated in the state's response to Black survival and resistance. Black struggle, as Sarah Haley suggests, has always been dwarfed by the structure of power it confronts; it needs to be valued, consequently, for something other than the great triumphs it sometimes achieves.[108] BUF's achievements can be recognized in small victories and concrete changes, in homes constructed and material conditions improved, but also in the forms of life that it brought to mind and into the world. BUF worked the outsides of planning's race-limited conceptions and imperatives, insisting that Black life was something other than a pathological variant of white normality that, at best, could be rendered a little more normal, a little more white. It provided a vehicle through which other genres of the human could be collectively affirmed, sustained, and even improved. This work, though contorted and eventually extinguished by the state, would endure nevertheless in smaller, less visible acts of resistance in Halifax-area Black communities and in collectively preserved memories of what planning can look like when Black people claim the ability to "function as [they] wish."

7 Making Space for *Homo economicus*: Neoliberalism, Regional Planning, and the Boundaries of Economic Life

In the first decade of the twenty-first century, Halifax pursued a pair of new planning initiatives that were devised to carry the city into a different, better future. One of the initiatives, called HRM by Design, focused on the downtown core.[1] Mobilizing images and ideas common to early twenty-first century cities, the initiative involved a re-imagining of the downtown landscape. At stake in the process were the downtown's physical appearance, the feelings that it produced for city residents, its potential growth, and its role in connecting the city to the increasingly global flows of people and capital that would assure the city's future. The second initiative, the Regional Plan, focused on the broader terrain of the urban region, and its most peripheral (nonurban) spaces in particular. Though attentive to aesthetic issues, the regional planning process was more concerned with the location and distribution of future residential development. At stake in this process were the possibilities of home building and homeownership in particular locations, the future distribution of municipal services like sewerage, water, and public transportation, and the costs to taxpayers of a landscape that was more or less efficient for the municipality to service and maintain. The two initiatives, together, entailed seven years of work on the part of planners, elected officials, and thousands of participating residents. The result, by 2009, was a substantial renovation of the city's approach to planning and development, a revised approach expected to guide the city at least twenty-five years into the future.

The first major planning initiatives since the 1970s, HRM by Design and the Regional Plan bore the effects the far-reaching social, economic, and political changes of the previous three decades. Among the most important of these changes was the rise (in Halifax and around the world) of a new form of political thought and practice, often called "neoliberalism." This new logic, first codified by relatively obscure European economists in the 1930s and 1940s, acquired new significance in the period after the global economic crisis of 1973. This crisis, many have argued, shook the already unstable foundations of First World economies and nation-states, and accelerated an already-brewing economic and political transition. Economically, this transition entailed a shift from Fordist industrial production to more flexible and knowledge-oriented economic activities. Politically, it entailed a shift from Keynesian, welfare-state policies towards more neoliberal, market-oriented policies. At a high level, the rise of neoliberalism can be observed in actions like the privatization of once-public institutions, the cutting of taxes and state expenditures, and the adoption of policies like "free trade" that seek to facilitate the activities of global capital (no matter their social or ecological consequences). For urban planning, the shift towards neoliberalism is perhaps most evident in the declining importance of state-funded public housing. The latter, once considered essential to the populations ill served by the capitalist housing market, was fully deprived of federal funding by the early 1990s and found no place in early twenty-first century planning initiatives like HRM by Design and the Regional Plan.[2]

Neoliberal urban planning, a new development in certain respects, was consistent with earlier forms of planning in other respects. On the one hand, neoliberal planning was clearly more restrained and market focused in its objectives. After decades of efforts to nurture human life in a broad sense, planning would now seek to enliven little more than residents' economic lives: their ability to earn a living and buy a better life in the private market. On the other hand, planning's very attention to residents' economic lives, its efforts to nurture a specific image of life, placed it on familiar terrain. At the centre of HRM by Design and the Regional Plan was indeed a particular conception of the human being, a conception, often called *homo economicus*, that Foucault locates at the centre of neoliberal thought. As the name suggests, *homo economicus* is a figure of the human being stripped down to its barest, market-oriented forms of thought and action. *Homo economicus* is imagined to behave rationally and self-interestedly, constantly calculating the costs and benefits of potential actions in market and nonmarket spheres of life. Like the target of planning in earlier periods, importantly, *homo economicus* is also a normative conception of the human. It codifies, as normative, a set of market-oriented behaviours and objectives that reflect some people's lives much more than others. Tailoring planning practices to this figure, therefore, would tend to circumscribe the potential benefits of neoliberal planning within narrow boundaries, the boundaries of a normative life that, now as ever, would be established through the displacement of blackness.[3]

Planning in early twenty-first century Halifax adapted existing forms of thought and practice to a new context. The city, like others in North America, experienced a series of significant changes in the post-1960s period, including a marked shift towards service-based economic sectors; an increasingly regional pattern of residential and commercial development; and the imposed amalgamation of Halifax, Dartmouth, and two neighbouring municipalities. Responding to these changes, the city unveiled a pair of new planning initiatives that sought, in different ways, to produce the spatial conditions of a flourishing economic life. For HRM by Design, focused on the downtown core, the aim was to enable forms of residential and commercial development that would help to attract and retain relatively privileged city residents, a collection of "talented individuals" upon whom the city's future seemed to depend. For the Regional Plan, focused on the terrain of the newly amalgamated urban region, the aim was to produce a more cost-efficient form of peripheral residential development, a form of development that would benefit the region's households in economic terms (e.g., as homeowners and taxpayers). In both cases, a particular version of *homo economicus* provided a target for new planning practices: an outline of the form of economic life that planning would seek to support and (implicitly) not support. Expelled from this outline were various city residents and organizations, some of whom had wielded more influence in earlier periods. Most gravely affected, however, were the residents of the region's six major Black communities, residents who would now (as before) enable the creation of a better life for other people through the planning-induced worsening of their own.

Halifax in the Post-1960s Period

By the beginning of the twenty-first century, Halifax had been reshaped by over three decades of far-reaching economic, political, and geographical changes. Like other North American cities, Halifax endured a long and uncertain process of economic restructuring in the post-1960s period. Manufacturing sectors, never particularly strong in Halifax itself, remained enmeshed in a region-wide decline that had begun just after

World War II. Particularly significant losses in this period included the closure of Dartmouth's Volvo assembly plant in 1988 (resulting in two hundred job losses); the downsizing of Pratt and Whitney's Halifax-based jet engine plant in 1990 (210 job losses); and repeated job cuts in the region's shipbuilding, petroleum, and fish-processing industries.[4] Meanwhile, government cutbacks in the 1980s and 90s resulted in major job losses in the public sector, the traditional bedrock of the Halifax economy. These cutbacks, amounting to a $500 million disinvestment in the Halifax economy, were experienced in all major public sectors, including health care, education, and national defence operations.[5] As in other North American cities, these job losses were offset to some extent by the expansion of employment in various service-related, cultural, and tourism industries. Included in this expansion was the arrival of thousands of new, high-paying jobs in professional and administrative services. Also included, however, were more precarious and low-paying jobs in various "consumer service" sectors. As an otherwise optimistic 2008 city report observed, "Nova Scotia's three lowest paying industries ... have also been the fastest growing sectors of the economy in HRM (the Halifax region)."[6]

One of the most significant political developments of the post-1960s period was the 1996 amalgamation of Halifax, Dartmouth, and two outlying areas into a single entity called the Halifax Regional Municipality (HRM). The possibility of an amalgamation had been discussed as early as the 1970s, and a series of issue-specific efforts had also been made over the years to enable more coordinated decision making across the region. A formal amalgamation, however, was known to be unpopular among the region's residents and thus remained forever on the back burner. A new impetus for amalgamation arrived in 1992, when a provincial task force delivered a series of recommendations intended to achieve efficiencies and cut government spending at both the provincial and local levels. One of the recommendations, implemented in 1994, was a redistribution of responsibilities in which the province picked up the costs of certain municipally provided public-health and social-welfare programs, while the municipalities were delegated the costs of policing and road-maintenance activities that were then subsidized by the province in suburban and rural areas. The change, though it was billed as providing significant overall costs savings, would be extremely uneven in its effects. The province's two largest and most financially stable municipalities, Halifax and Dartmouth, would collectively save an estimated $11 million annually, while the smallest municipalities – many of which were already on the verge of insolvency – would collectively *incur* an additional $15 million each year. In this situation, the merger of larger municipalities with their cash-strapped satellites suddenly seemed to be a necessary measure.[7]

The prospect of an amalgamation in the Halifax region remained unpopular, and Liberal Premier John Savage called it a "crazy idea" in the 1993 election campaign that brought him and his party to power in the province. Once in power, however, Savage changed his mind, and his government ultimately imposed an amalgamation on the Halifax region in a 1995 act (that took effect in 1996). One reason for the move was the effects of the 1994 shift in government service costs, which saddled the Halifax region's two most peripheral and financially vulnerable municipalities with an additional $4.4 million in annual costs. Other reasons included the overall cost savings that an amalgamation was expected to achieve (savings estimated at $9.8M annually for the merged municipalities), as well as some potential improvements in region-wide planning and service delivery.[8] Five years after the amalgamation, the expected cost savings were nowhere to be found, but region-wide planning was indeed on better footing. In 1996, the once-competing economic-development activities of the four municipalities were merged into a pair of new region-wide agencies, the Greater Halifax Partnership (GHP) and the Regional Development Agency. Urban planning functions, meanwhile, were finally placed under the jurisdiction of an entity (the HRM) that could make coordinated region-wide decisions rather than just suggestions (as earlier regional planning agencies had been confined to doing). HRM by Design and the Regional Plan were the first major initiatives of the new HRM planning department, and they could not have had the same significance without the 1996 amalgamation.

The need for region-wide planning was certainly suggested by the prevailing form of post-1960s residential and commercial development in the region. Between 1971 and 2001, the population of the region grew by 37.4 per cent, from 261,423 to 359,111. The population of Halifax itself actually decreased by 2.3 per cent during this period, while Dartmouth experienced an increase of just 1.5 per cent. Post-1960s growth, then, was concentrated entirely outside of the urbanized Halifax-Dartmouth core, where the population expanded from 74,618 to 174,078 (or 133.3 per cent).[9] To a great extent, commercial development followed the suburban and exurban sprawl of the residential population, with new business parks and shopping malls appearing increasingly in the nonurban periphery. Following the early 1990s recession, nearly all new office space in the region was developed outside the urban core, where land costs were cheaper and suburban-living employees could enjoy a shorter commute to work.[10] While suburban sprawl was nothing new to the region – parts of Halifax and Dartmouth, after all, were once considered suburbs – it nevertheless presented new challenges in this period. For one thing, new suburban and exurban homes tended to be constructed on much larger tracts of land than in earlier periods, resulting in a much wider dispersal of the population and a correspondingly higher cost of municipal infrastructure and service provision. In contrast to earlier periods, moreover, new development occurred largely outside the jurisdiction of the region's two largest municipalities, leaving the regulation of development (until the completion of the Regional Plan) to an incohesive collection of smaller, under-resourced townships.[11]

More than just extending its physical footprint, post-1960s development substantially restructured the social geography of the Halifax region. The Halifax peninsula, historically home to broad spectrum of income levels, drifted gradually towards the middle and upper end of the spectrum between 1971 and 2001. At the beginning of this period, 25 per cent of the peninsula's census tracts were among the region's poorest and 19 per cent were among the region's richest. Thirty years later, a lower proportion (21 per cent) of its census tracts were among the region's poorest, while a higher proportion (26 per cent) were among its richest.[12] A similar trajectory can be seen in data on residential rents and renters. Between 1971 and 2001, the average rent on the peninsula increased 5.9 per cent per year, while the average rent elsewhere in the region increased at a (modestly) slower 5.4 per cent per year. As a result, rents on the peninsula, which were 5 per cent cheaper than those elsewhere in 1971, were 11.9 per cent more expensive in 2001. The distribution of renters in the region shifted accordingly. Whereas peninsula and off-peninsula locations had a similar number of renters in 1971, off-peninsula locations had almost double the number of renters in 2001. The peninsula, as these figures suggest, became more and more of a middle- and upper-income enclave in the post-1960s period, with relatively high incomes and high rents, while poverty was pushed increasingly to off-peninsula areas like North Dartmouth, suburban Albro Lake and Woodside, and once-rural Spryfield.[13]

On the Halifax peninsula, the signs of a restructured social geography were perhaps most evident in the historically working-class North End, where once rundown saltbox homes were progressively gutted and re-appointed for middle-class professionals. In the sector of the North End closest to the downtown, homes along Falkland and Bauer Streets that planners targeted for urban renewal in the 1950s came to be worth well more than the region-wide average. No longer pathologized, HRM planners announced in 2008 that this sector would "become one of the downtown's most desirable residential neighbourhoods with tremendous views of the Harbour and proximity to ... the services and shops of Gottingen Street."[14] The transformation of Gottingen Street, mentioned here as a selling point, began somewhat later than other parts of the North End but also occurred more rapidly. Described as Halifax's "most feared" area in the early 2000s, the street quickly became a favoured location for new cafés, green businesses, and professional-services firms. In 2008, work began on a new condominium building on the corner of Gottingen and Falkland. Located across the street from a homeless shelter and various poverty-serving agencies, units in the new development were marketed for as much as $320,000 (more than the median value of a single-family home in the Old North End).[15]

The rising fortunes of the Halifax peninsula were a boon to many homeowners, businesses, and investors, but they also created new challenges – even for property developers. Beginning in the early 1990s, the high cost of central city land (relative to the periphery) rendered it very difficult to develop profitable new residential or commercial properties. On the commercial side, it was estimated in 2008 that a newly developed office building in the downtown, to be profitable, would need to lease floor space for an average of $25 per square foot. The prevailing rents in the downtown, however, were at least $5 per square foot below this rate and had not increased over the twenty preceding years. Rents in suburban office parks, where land was cheaper, were at least $10 lower.[16] On the residential side, a few developers were able to overcome the prevailing challenge of high land costs by producing high-priced, elite condo developments (especially along the harbourfront), while other developers cut every material and aesthetic corner to produce condos that a broader middle-class population could afford.[17] Ultimately, the most significant challenge imposed by high land costs appeared in the realm of financing. Many Halifax developers continued to propose new central-city commercial and residential projects throughout the 1990s but failed to win over the banks with their optimism. As one developer explained: "We were ready to build and take the risk, but the banks wouldn't budge."[18]

In the early 2000s, the problem of development financing began to lessen, as major changes in worldwide financial markets began to have impacts on the city. The changes included a global flood of capital from high-tech industries to real estate sectors following the 2001 tech-stock collapse, as well as the development of new real estate investment vehicles like mortgage-backed securities. Channelling a global current of financial capital, the Halifax branches of major insurance companies, chartered banks, and investment houses each ramped up their financing of property development between 2001 and 2007. Local developers, consequently, were finally able to break through a decade-long impasse and submit (for municipal approval) nine new proposals for downtown developments in this period.[19] Nearly all of these proposals, however, were ultimately met with opposition by well-organized Halifax residents and organizations. In the most high-profile contest, Heritage Trust of Nova Scotia (HTNS) and three other organizations sought to block the development of a two-tower, twenty-seven-storey harbourfront project proposed by United Gulf Developments in 2004. Arguing that the project was "not compatible with the adjoining historic buildings," the four organizations fought the development at City Hall (where they lost) and then at the Nova Scotia Utility and Review Board (where they also lost).[20] Though the project was approved in 2007, the three-year political contest proved costly to United Gulf and caused the developer to abandon the project in its proposed form. More broadly, the contest showed that the challenges to downtown development included not just high land costs and difficult-to-obtain financing but also the potential opposition of groups like HTNS. Addressing this last challenge, as I discuss in the next section, would be central to the 2006–9 HRM by Design project.

Beyond the Halifax peninsula, post-1960s development processes occurred somewhat differently. The cost of peripheral land, for one thing, tended to be extremely low, while prevailing regulations allowed many development projects to proceed "as of right" (rather than through municipal application and approval). Seizing upon these development-friendly conditions was an expanding series of large-scale and often well-diversified residential development companies. The largest of these companies, Clayton Developments, began its operations in 1959 as a developer of middle-class homes in a subdivision named Clayton Park but eventually expanded into the market's higher end (suburban "estates") and lower end (townhouses and apartment buildings). Though some (later) companies chose to specialize in particular markets, the overall residential output of post-1960s peripheral development tended to mirror the evolving output of its largest actor: mostly middle-income homes, with an increasing proportion of higher-end and lower-end accommodations over time.[21]

Evidence of high-end suburban development, by 2001, was easily located. Nearly all of the Halifax region's wealthiest census tracts in 2001 were located in the suburbs and were developed in the post-1960s period (the sole exception being the Halifax South End).[22] In these elite areas, loose regulations allowed developers to build quiet, winding streets; occupy spaces like ridgetops and waterfronts that might otherwise have been seen as public "amenities"; and produce a landscape of dispersed homes whose market values were as disproportionately high as the municipality's costs of providing services and infrastructure to them. Among the various high-end developments of this period, two subdivisions in historically Black Upper Hammonds Plains (Kingswood and Glen Arbour) were repeatedly criticized during the 2001–6 regional planning process. Subject to minimal regulation, their development produced a sprawling, dispersed landscape that was exceptionally costly for the city to service and maintain.[23] Evidence of lower-end development was similarly locatable. Between 1971 and 2001, the share of the region's poorest census tracts that were located beyond the peninsula increased sixfold, from 3 per cent of the region's poorest tracts in 1971 to 18 per cent in 2001.[24] In these poorer settlements, also developed largely in the post-1960s period, loose regulations allowed developers to build long strips of nearly identical, three-storey apartment buildings, a relatively tight-packed residential landscape concentrated (most often) along existing peripheral roadways. This form of development, unlike dispersed middle- and high-end development, received little attention in the formulation of the Regional Plan.[25]

The appearance of an increasing number of low-income households in the Halifax suburbs is consistent with a broader process in North American cities, wherein the gentrification of central-city neighbourhoods is paralleled by the suburbanization of poverty.[26] There is no question that poverty suburbanized in the Halifax region in the post-1960s period. It needs to be recalled, nevertheless, that some of the areas that came to be called suburbs at this time were once relatively low-income rural communities, including various outlying fishing villages, agricultural subregions, and peripheral Black communities. Indeed, one of the most important impacts of post-1960s development was to radically transform the living conditions of the region's six major peripheral (nonurban) Black communities. These communities were the product of the specific patterns of Black migration to the region in

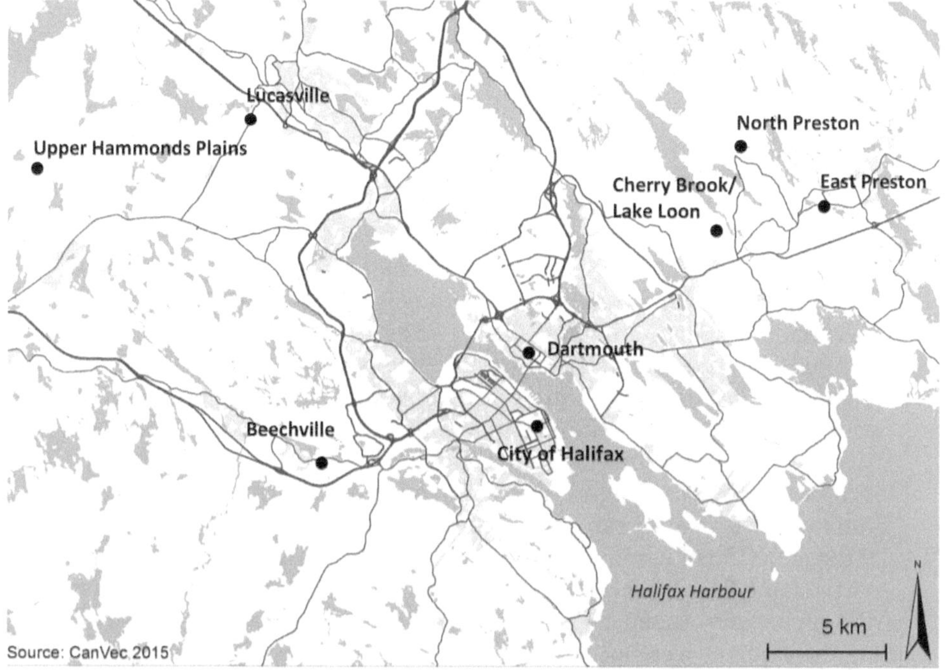

Figure 7.1 Map showing peripheral Black communities. Map created by Julia Gregory.

the early nineteenth century. Peripheral and segregated from the beginning, they largely retained these characteristics into the 1960s. Thereafter, in a process reminiscent of what occurred around Africville earlier in the century, each of these communities was increasingly engulfed by the expanding urban region and a newer, denser, and wealthier form of development. Particularly affected by these processes were the communities of Beechville and Upper Hammonds Plains (see *figure 7.1*). Still relatively isolated in the 1960s, these communities were fully engorged by new suburban homes and (in the case of Beechville) commercial properties by the early 2000s. While some of this new development was the work of individual homeowners, much of it was produced by large-scale suburban developers like Armco Capital and Fares and Company.

As elsewhere in the periphery, the new development surrounding the region's Black communities owed its profitability in large part to the low cost of land. Indeed, centuries of racial stigma tended to render this land especially low cost, its undesirability to white residents duly registered in its market value. As a 2002 report by the chair of the HRM regional planning oversight committee explained, "Both pride and prejudice play their parts in deterring development [in the vicinity of Black communities], along with real [*sic*] and perceived issues such as crime and quality of schooling."[27] The result was a particular kind of business opportunity: an opportunity to profit from the redevelopment of undervalued land – to the extent that the image of this land could be redeveloped at the same time.

A very basic way to change the image of the land was simply to change the name of the community in which it was located. Thus, a new subdivision in Upper Hammonds Plains was given the name White Hill's Run, while the residents of Beechville have seen (and fought against) repeated efforts to shrink the boundaries of their community in favour of neighbouring Lakeside. In a salient case in 1997, a set of newer homes and subdivisions located in (Black) East Preston were suddenly reclassified as belonging to (white) Lake Echo. The change, ostensibly initiated by Canada Post, was pushed forward by the white residents of the area (150 of whom signed a petition indicating they wanted to be part of Lake Echo), as well as by the HRM planning department (which had reportedly issued deeds to white residents years earlier indicating their homes were located in Lake Echo). At stake in the change, for white residents, was a major difference in property value. Homes built on undervalued Black-signified land would, in an instant, gain access to the higher market values typically associated with whiteness. For Black residents, the change meant losing a part of their community, created almost two centuries earlier, to newer white residents. The process struck some residents as a familiar one. Black East Preston resident and activist Doug Sparks called it "a Christopher Columbus scenario," in which white groups move into an area and ignore, if not actively negate, its heritage. Black protests of the name change were ignored by city officials, all of whom ultimately backed the change.[28]

Even without a name change, the very form of peripheral development tended to alter the image of Black-signified land. In Beechville, a 420-unit subdivision called Beechville Estates was developed in the historically Black community by Armco Capital in a series of phases between 1997 and 2004. The form of the subdivision was entirely typical for a suburban development. Every typical element, however, helped to distinguish the subdivision from the proximate Black community. The newly built homes conformed to a single, subdivision-wide style, with no visible relationship to the older homes of the Black community. The

Estates' road network branched off St Margaret's Bay Road (along which most Black homes were located) at two locations and forged an entirely separate world of newly built suburban crescents and cul-de-sacs. Adding to these distinguishing features was a simple marker at the entrance to the subdivision, a stone monument bearing a name (Beechville Estates) that was both typical for a suburban development and reminiscent of a slave plantation (the proprietors of which were among the first English-speakers to describe their homes as "estates"). Collectively, these elements of the new development helped to constitute a distinct (non-Black) image for the subdivision and made it possible for Armco to turn low-value land into significant profits. The developer's profits on the resale of the land (not the construction of homes) exceeded $1 million in the project. Evidently pleased with this result, Armco soon announced plans for a another residential "estate" in Beechville, a 306-unit project contested by many Beechville residents but quickly approved by city planners.[29]

In Beechville and other Black communities, post-1960s development had a series of damaging effects on people's lives and living conditions. Nearby lakes and woodlands historically used by Black residents were often rendered inaccessible. Traffic congestion on once-rural roads increased year after year. Community integrity, forged over the generations, was gradually diluted (as the areas' new residents made little effort to integrate). Black-owned land was sometimes stolen and sometimes expropriated. Urban planning, more than just enabling these processes through its loose regulations, also intervened at times to shape development to the detriment of Black communities. As peripheral development expanded in the 1970s, for example, new (white) home building in the vicinity of North Preston raised concerns about the quality of Dartmouth's water supply, a body of water called Lake Major that was located partly in North Preston. A by-law restricting building permits in the vicinity of Lake Major (a by-law in place since the 1950s but never enforced) was suddenly used to deny permits to North Preston residents. Residential development, relatively unregulated in general, would thus be strictly regulated in the case of Black residents. Encircled by new development and forced to bear its social costs, Black residents would be barred from undertaking and benefiting from new development. Well-organized resistance on the part of North Preston, East Preston, and Lake Loon residents eventually forced the city to adopt a land-use plan that apportioned development permits and restrictions more equally, treating "[Black] communities no different from others, regardless of race."[30]

A similar struggle over anti-Black planning practices occurred in Upper Hammonds Plains. In 1974, the City of Halifax (with the backing of the province) moved to protect its water supply by expropriating 365 acres of Black-owned land in the vicinity of Pockwock Lake, a body of water located in Upper Hammonds Plains. Black property owners, allegedly manipulated by state officials, were paid just $274 per acre of land.[31] Two decades later, Upper Hammonds Plains residents discovered that their own source of water, shallow-dug wells, had been dangerously contaminated by new development in the vicinity. The community, in response, asked the city to extend municipal water services to their homes. The city, having expropriated Black land to serve its own water needs, now refused a demand to supply water to Upper Hammonds Plains from a lake in their own community. Impressive, broad-based activism on the part of Black residents eventually had an effect, as the city finally agreed to their demand in 1998. In a move discovered by Black leaders a year later, however, the city inflated the cost of providing water to Upper Hammonds Plains by $600,000 in order to cover the costs of providing water to a nearby white community. Forced to fight again, Black residents carried the issue through a six-year legal battle, the resolution of which forced the city to return the money and finally allowed Black residents to enjoy clean water without subsidizing a process (suburban development) that had previously deprived them of it.[32]

The Halifax region, taken as a whole, changed considerably between the 1960s and the end of the century. The region's population grew and peripheralized, creating a much larger physical footprint weighted more heavily, in terms of population, towards suburban and exurban locations. The Halifax peninsula, though home to a smaller proportion of the region's population, became a wealthier and higher-rent terrain, a change most evident in the city's gentrifying North End. A boon to existing property owners, the peninsula's higher property values and rents created challenges for residential and commercial development in a context where relatively low-cost and unregulated land was available in the suburban and exurban periphery. Peripheral development, though shaped by an economic logic, worked upon and across a deeply racialized landscape. Its unfolding produced profits for developers and relatively affordable housing for families at the expense of Black land, living conditions, and community integrity. This regional context – its problems and its possibilities – was the object of the two major planning initiatives introduced at the beginning of the new century: HRM by Design (focused on the downtown) and the Regional Plan (focused on the city-region as a whole). A solution to certain development problems, these initiatives ignored entirely the problems experienced by peripheral Black communities encircled and rendered vulnerable by post-1960s development. Indeed, the initiatives' main impact on these communities was to create a set of new problems.

HRM by Design

Development on the Halifax peninsula, rather than the periphery, was the primary concern of the project called HRM by Design. Launched in 2006, the project's described aim was to provide a long-term "physical vision" for public and private development in the region's commercial core.[33] The project's scope, in its first year, encompassed a broad area labelled the "regional centre," an area that included downtown Halifax and Dartmouth, as well as the important (peninsular) commercial corridors of Spring Garden Road, Quinpool Road, and Gottingen Street. From 2007 onward, in contrast, the project focused exclusively on downtown Halifax, an area whose economic and aesthetic qualities were deemed to be essential to the success of the entire urban region. Accorded much more time and money than the plan for the regional centre, the creation of a physical vision for downtown Halifax included the establishment of new urban design and architectural guidelines, the definition of distinctive neighbourhood precincts, the design of pleasant streetscapes, and attention to a range of other "look and feel" issues that became central to urban planning in the post-1960s period.[34] With a focus on public input and participation, the downtown-focused phases of the project were advertised as an invaluable opportunity for residents to come together and design their ideal city, and residents indeed involved themselves in unprecedented numbers. At least two public events attracted over five hundred residents, while the overall project elicited the involvement of "literally thousands and thousands of residents" between its public launch in 2006 and the approval of the new plan in 2009.[35]

The overall project was divided into six distinct phases. Each phase was linked to a specific output and involved a significant public event at the beginning (to solicit public input) and at the end (to ratify the end result). Presiding over this process was an elaborate project team, including a staff-led steering committee, a team of outside consultants, and a resident-led urban-design task force. From the outset, the planning staff and (especially) the consultants encouraged the public to "dream big" and used images of successful cities and pithy quotations from world leaders to transport project participants beyond the boundaries of the existing city. Early public events, though poorly attended, mirrored the enthusiasm of their facilitators in the collectively developed vision that they established: a vision of distinctive, mixed-use neighbourhoods; exciting, vibrant spaces; protected heritage and a preserved sense of place; pedestrian-friendly streetscapes and enhanced sustainability; and beautiful, high-quality architecture. The results of the early phases were admittedly abstract and general. However, as the project proceeded and the output of each phase fed into the next phase, an increasingly concrete and practical program was expected to emerge.[36]

One of the most significant and well-attended events of the project took place at the Pier 21 Museum in September 2007, twenty-two months into the overall process. Heavily promoted beforehand, the event was attended by an estimated six hundred HRM residents, who seated themselves in long rows in front of a raised platform and a pair of large video screens. From the platform, the project team addressed the audience in words and images, providing an uplifting depiction of the great city that Halifax could one day become. On the video screens, photos and drawings gave concreteness to the vision that had been established in previous phases of the project. A bleak and alienating photo of downtown Carmichael Street was counterposed to a drawing of a redesigned and fully pedestrianized streetscape. A photo of a crumbling, empty parking lot on Upper Water Street was counterposed to a hypothetical mixed-use development, with an inviting café at street level. An overhead photo of the dystopian Cogswell Interchange (a relic of the never-completed Harbour Drive expressway) was placed alongside a sketched series of new buildings and public spaces, reminiscent of St Lawrence Market in Toronto (the home, incidentally, of the planning consultants). While the presentation sometimes had the air of a sales pitch, an appreciation of public participation came through as well. Time and time again, the project team stressed that the public needed to tell them what they wanted; they would simply help to make it happen.[37]

The repeated emphasis on public participation during the project would tend to sit rather uneasily with a second objective that was revealed at the Pier 21 event: that of clarifying and "streamlining" the prevailing development approval process. This second objective had its roots in the ongoing conflicts over proposed downtown property developments. As development after development was submitted for municipal approval and then subjected to a lengthy process of political contestation, the development industry began to criticize the overall length and ambiguity of the approval process and demanded that major changes be introduced. These efforts seem to have had their most direct effect upon HRM staff rather than on elected councillors. In February 2007, planning staff recommended that the scope of the design project be expanded to include a thorough overhaul of the existing approval process. Stressing the need for greater "clarity and predictability," staff explained that a revamped approval process would "provide an alternative to the current development climate, which is often contentious, and that often leads to appeals and counter-appeals of Council decisions."[38] With little debate, this recommendation and its associated financial cost (i.e., a doubling of the overall HRM by Design budget) were approved unanimously by the resident-led urban-design task force in early February and by city council at the end of the month.[39]

At the Pier 21 event, the commitment to revamping the approval process was revealed towards the end of the consultants' presentation, as well as in a large-scale poster on "development approvals and economic development" near the room's entrance. The presentation provided a graphic view of a new approval process, moving swiftly from application to confirmation without appearing to pass through a single public consultation or elected body. The poster, meanwhile, explained that a revamped process would improve the "clarity, predictability, and timeliness" of downtown development through the resolution of approval issues at a "strategic level."[40] In these still-vague indications, the problem of political conflict over property development seemed to be resolved through the elimination of any venue in which it could occur, the re-routing of development approvals through an efficient – because incontestable – set of procedures. To those who took notice, the proposed approval process might seem to introduce a certain tension into the overall design project. Public participation, in effect, was being solicited in order to eliminate all future public participation. City residents, through their participation, were asked to become the agents of their own long-term marginalization.

The resolution of this tension was ultimately routed through the increasingly well-known ideas of the urban theorist Richard Florida. Author of the 2002 book *The Rise of the Creative Class*, Florida emerged as a kind of urban guru in the early years of the twenty-first century, offering ideas and advice to First World cities that certain political actors were quite eager to receive. At the centre of Florida's theory is a collection of individuals whom he calls the "creative class." Included within this relatively heterogeneous group are a wide range of high-technology workers (e.g., scientists, engineers, and software developers); professional service providers (e.g., architects, graphic designers, and financiers); musicians and visual artists; and a whole collection of "eggheads, eccentrics, and ... non-white-bread types who are the source of new ideas."[41] Florida's essential argument is that this new class of individuals is essential to the vitality and viability of contemporary cities, propping up urban economies not simply through their labour but also through the hard-to-measure "creative ecosystem" that their existence in the city helps to produce. Essential to today's cities, in other words, are not just the actual employees of innovative businesses but also the social environment conducive to innovative thinking that even marginally employed creative individuals help to constitute. It is this environment, Florida argues, that stimulates creative output within a city and entices a large population of "creatives" to make a particular city their home.

Florida's argument is backed up by an array of colourful anecdotes and neat tables of data that (ostensibly) demonstrate a connection between a city's proportion of innovative businesses and certain indicators of latent creativity. Cities like San Francisco and Seattle, well known for their innovative economies, are shown to score very highly on Florida's "bohemian," "gay," and "foreign born" indexes. There is a causal connection indicated here, Florida argues. The source of innovation is not, he stresses, the presence of bohemians, gays, or immigrants themselves but the openness to new ideas and quirky lifestyles that are *indicated* by their presence in a city, an openness that, he argues, helps to make creative people feel at home. The categories formed in this analysis warrant attention. For one thing, categories like "gay" and "foreign born" participate in a broader post-1960s process in which social differences are symbolically reduced to their most aestheticized and apolitical form.[42] The difference between these groups and their opposite, the nongay or nonimmigrant population, is marked; the various differences internal to these groups, including differences in citizen status and social class, are not. Ironically, even *ethnic* differences are bracketed in a category, foreign born, that is used to signify ethnic diversity in Florida's analysis. The actual ethnic composition of the foreign-born population in a given city, which may or may not be diverse, is never examined. Thus, the "foreign born" becomes a homogenously ethnicized other, a marker of undifferentiated ethnic difference that signifies, above all else, the "openness" of the domestic-born population (implicitly ethnicized as white).

Perhaps more importantly, the category of foreign born, in constituting an undifferentiated ethnic other, places other signs of ethnic difference out of view. An equally simplistic category, nonwhite, could have signified ethnic difference just as well or indeed better than foreign born. The reason Florida does not use this category is clear enough. Centring nonwhiteness in US cities would mean centring a whole series of Black-majority cities like Detroit and New Orleans, which, for reasons that have nothing to do with these cities' lack of openness or creativity, possess relatively few "innovative" companies and relatively disastrous economic conditions in general. These cities become, in a sleight of hand, relatively undiverse, and their lack of diversity becomes the reason for their lack of innovation.[43] The main function of foreign born, then, is to signify an ethnic difference that is not Black, or at least not overwhelmingly so. The overt opposition between domestic and foreign born, already a problematic construction, occurs in an analytic space opened up surreptitiously by the displacement of blackness. One effect of this displacement is to allow Florida to identify a causal connection between innovation and ethnic diversity that otherwise (i.e., using other signifiers of diversity) would not exist. Another effect is to place blackness at the exterior of everything positive in Florida's theory, including diversity, openness, creativity, and economic success.

Other displacements emerge in Florida's analysis of the ostensible spatial determinants of creativity and innovation. The creative class, he argues, is drawn to particular kinds of spaces and activities. Especially attractive to this class are historic buildings, coffee shops, live-music venues, and neighourhoods whose authenticity and uniqueness create a feeling he calls "buzz."[44] To some extent, these claims simply rebrand a set of ideas that emerged several decades earlier in the struggle over urban renewal. The claim that a growth-sustaining creative class is attracted to "buzz" and "uniqueness" is not, at first glance, terribly different from the Nova Scotia Planning Secretariat's (NSPS) or the Movement for Citizens' Voice and Action's (MOVE) claim that "knowledge workers" would flock to a sufficiently "lively and vibrant" downtown. Both claims, decades apart, rely on a conception of space that planners have called amenity, a conception that locates population-pleasing effects in particular spatial conditions. Like the NSPS and MOVE, then, Florida's analysis severs experience from social position. He treats positive experiences like "buzz" as a universal response to particular spatial conditions, occluding the various social practices (including practices of displacement) that can differentially shape the experiences of non-normative populations. And yet, there is still a sense in the NSPS's and MOVE's vision that all city residents matter. The promotion of citizen involvement, albeit through a flawed model, at least *suggested* that everyone was entitled to a role in the creation of a better city. In Florida's thinking, in contrast, the concept of population-wide participation falls off the table. All that matters for Florida, in the end, are the lives of the creative class, and his only consistent political message is that these already-privileged lives have not been privileged *enough*.

In many ways, Florida's centring of an already-privileged population is consistent with post-1960s, neoliberal thinking in general. As Foucault explains, the rise of neoliberalism is marked by the centring of a conception of the human (*homo economicus*) once confined primarily to economic domains. This conception, from the 1970s onward, becomes the major target of biopolitical and disciplinary forms of power; it indicates the form of life that power seeks to produce and manage.[45] Consistent with Foucault's analysis of *homo economicus*, Florida's creative individual is largely an economic animal. The individual's primary feature is its "human capital," the between-the-ears substance that is assumed to propel "innovation, new firm formation, and ultimately economic growth."[46] An agent of economic growth, this individual also behaves like a pure economic actor, following a "simple economic rationality" in the workplace and every other sphere of life. Insisting that "we live by creativity," Florida argues that "we" (the creative ones) move around the world in search of the cities and spaces "that allow [creativity] to flourish."[47] The task for the state, it follows, is to augment the proportion of creative individuals in the population – logically, by creating the social and spatial conditions in which these individuals will "rationally" want to reside. The privileging of this narrow class of people, while it might seem to abandon the broader population, is described by Florida as the only means of creating the population-wide benefits of wealth, jobs, and tax revenues in a creativity-driven economy. Serve the creative class, in other words, and the benefits will trickle down to everyone else.

In Halifax, Florida's theory became increasingly well known in the years leading up to the HRM by Design project. In 2004, Florida was invited to the city by the Halifax Downtown Business Association and the GHP to deliver a widely publicized lecture on the city-wide benefits of creativity-nourishing urban development. Impressed by his ideas, the GHP soon commissioned Florida's disciples at the University of Toronto to analyse Halifax's creativity indicators. This study, and Florida's thinking in general, became the basis of the GHP's signature 2005–10 economic strategy for the urban region. Accordingly, the strategy identified as its primary goal the attraction and retention of "talented" individuals and the augmentation of the region's foreign-born population. Consistent with Florida's thinking, attracting immigrants was seen to boost the region's ethnic diversity and thereby stimulate creativity. The region's nonimmigrant Black residents appeared nowhere in this dynamic; their future, therefore, was not socially or economically important.[48] Following the release of its new economic strategy, the GHP moved to establish and fund a new organization that would ostensibly gather together the city's creative class and ensure its involvement in political debates. Taking the name Fusion Halifax, the new organization quickly acquired a wide membership among the city's young professionals and relied on Florida's theory to substantiate its own importance to the wider community.[49] "To attract and retain the best and the brightest of generations X and Y," the group announced in a 2007 newspaper editorial, "leaders must begin listening to what young residents have to say and must make tangible and sincere efforts to understand what we want for our future."[50]

For Fusion, as for the GHP, the key terms in Florida's urban theory were "talent" and "education" rather than "creativity" per se. Although the "creative class" was discussed by both groups, it was more common for them to highlight the city-wide importance of "young, smart people" or simply "young talent."[51] This slight shift in emphasis was certainly supportable by Florida's often vague pronouncements, and the GHP cited long passages from *The Rise of the Creative Class* that emphasized "highly educated people" (rather than "creatives") to reinforce its various talent-supporting proposals.[52] Politically, the major effect of these references to talent and education was to recentre Florida's unorthodox urban theory upon the very conventional constituencies that the two groups represented: young professionals (Fusion) and corporate employers (GHP), rather than artists and eccentrics. Interpreting Florida's theory to their advantage, Fusion and the GHP became the city's foremost advocates of talent-supporting urban policies and the primary agents through which a particular version of *homo economicus* – the "talented individual" – was pushed to the centre of public debates in Halifax.

During the HRM by Design project, the figure of the talented individual came to play an important role in the framing of planning proposals and political positions. At the Pier 21 event, the attraction and retention of a "talented workforce" was described as "critical" to the city's collective well-being and a fundamental consideration in the design of planning-related policies. "This emerging workforce," explained a poster at the event, "looks for quality of lifestyle when making location choices, and more and more that means a quality downtown." Emphasizing the qualities of "excitement" and "vibrancy," the poster explained that new development in the downtown would be needed to attract talented individuals and that the latter would require a revamping of the approval process, a revamping that would improve its "clarity" and "predictability."[53] Thus, a now-familiar conception of urban space, a conception that emphasizes the population-pleasing effects of particular spatial conditions

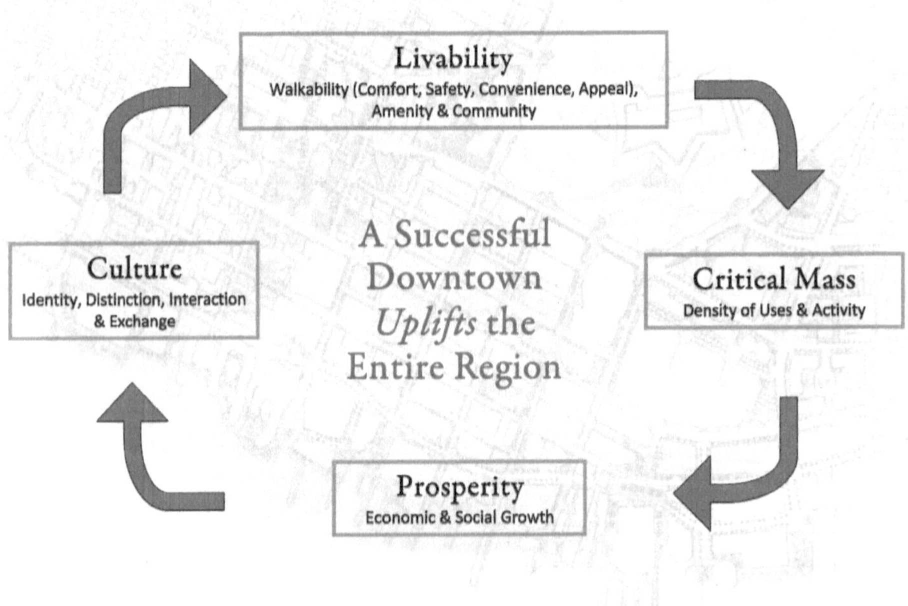

Figure 7.2 HRM by Design "upward spiral," 2008. HRM, *The Downtown Halifax Plan* (Halifax: HRM, 2008), 10. Presentation to open house, 16 April 2008. Image courtesy of HRM.

and ignores the historic and ongoing prevention of certain populations from enjoying these same conditions, was hitched to the project of regulatory change. The need to please certain individuals provided a new and more palatable rationale for a project that could have been harder to justify. The revamping of the approval process, which might otherwise have seemed a capitulation to the development industry, could now be seen as the catalyst of a complex "upward spiral" in which increased downtown development would attract footloose "talent" and the attraction of talent would benefit the city as a whole (see *figure 7.2*).

Vaguely introduced at the Pier 21 event, the proposed revamping of the approval process was soon explained in more detail. As described in an April 2008 discussion document, the new process would filter development applications through a pair of evaluation procedures, neither of which would involve direct input from the public at large or a vote on the part of city council. The first procedure would involve an assessment of proposed developments in relation to pre-established "form-based codes." The latter would set out, for every block of the downtown, the quantifiable criteria that developments would be required to meet (i.e., building heights, lot setbacks, and so on). The second procedure would assess the proposed development's qualitative or aesthetic characteristics. A detailed design manual would be produced and an unelected design committee would be composed from members of the local development community to assess the compatibility of proposed developments with the standards of the manual. The new, two-step process was described as delivering development approvals with the clarity and predictability required by the development industry. Downtown property owners, exclusively, would have an opportunity to contest decisions resulting from the process at a brief hearing (mandated by the city's charter), and property developers could always contest decisions unfavourable to them through the provincial review board. The broader public, in contrast, would be barred from all future participation in development decision making. It would, however, enjoy the city-wide rewards of the "upward spiral" inaugurated by the new approval process that excluded them.[54]

While the imagined upward spiral potentially widened the appeal of the proposed changes to the approval process, its supporting assumptions were frequently called into question during the design project. Indeed, planners' criticism of the approval process eventually required the suppression of a study that the city itself had commissioned as an input to the project. Prepared by Turner Drake and Partners, the study showed that the greatest obstacle to downtown development was not the length of the approval process but the high cost of developable land. Highlighting the gap between prevailing downtown office rents ($20 per square foot, at the high end) and the rents that a new downtown development would need to charge to make a profit ($25–$30 per square foot), the study concluded that a revamped approval process would do little to arrest the long-term shift of office activities towards less expensive, peripheral locations. Such a conclusion was disruptive to the argument that city planners were building, and it was dealt with accordingly. Delivered to the planning department by Turner Drake in November 2008, the study was withheld from city council and the broader public until March 2009, when it was branded with the label "under review" and quietly issued to council. Eventually discovered by local heritage activists, the study and its evident suppression would be used to discredit the arguments of planning staff in the final months of the design process.[55]

Also questioned by Halifax residents was the city's assumption that more development in the downtown would necessarily improve its aesthetic quality and attractiveness. HTNS, in particular, sought to highlight the attractiveness of the existing historic sections in the downtown, the splendour of the protected views from Citadel Hill, and the heritage-consistent development that had occurred (under strict controls) in cities like Québec City and Alexandria, Virginia. For HTNS, the existing development policies were not an obstacle to the city's attractiveness and prosperity but their conditions of possibility. The protection of heritage buildings and clear view planes from Citadel Hill, the group argued, were the foundation of the city's unique historic character and the major reasons that over eight hundred thousand people climbed Citadel Hill each year to admire the city from on high. In various submissions to the design project, the group highlighted the new building heights that would be allowed under the proposed regulatory changes and diagrammed their potential damage to the city's appearance. Images prepared by the group showed the new "view blockers" that could soon appear on the downtown skyline: tall, characterless boxes that would wall off the prevailing view of Halifax Habour (see *figure 7.3*). These images were disputed by planning staff, who prepared their own less horrific images of allowable downtown development, but they remained an important counterpoint to planners' argument that new development necessarily improved the city's aesthetic characteristics.[56]

Figure 7.3 Heritage Trust image of potential view blockers, 2009. Image courtesy of Save the View Coalition.

The conflict over the proposed regulatory changes endured until the final public event of the HRM by Design project, during which a final draft of the new downtown planning strategy (including a new approval process) was up for debate. Unfolding over two days in May 2009, the event was attended by hundreds of local residents, with eighty-eight people making short presentations and 126 submitting written documents. Among opponents of the planning strategy, a few criticized its lack of attention to public transportation, social housing, or democratic processes. The majority, however, focused on the look and feel of the existing downtown and the looming threat of less regulated property development. Expressing a common perspective, one resident pointed out that the city had originated as a seaport and military garrison, and argued that the new planning strategy would sever "the connection between these two threads in our history [and] destroy something that is unique and essentially Haligonian."[57] Another, calling the proposed regulations too "loose," argued that the city's irreplaceable history was at stake. "We cannot," she argued, "rebuild our history once it is gone, whether demolished, radically altered, or smothered."[58] HTNS, for its part, submitted a list of the ninety-five registered heritage properties that would be put at risk by the regulatory changes, as well as the "three dozen" heritage-supporting policies that the changes would revoke or restrict in the downtown core.[59]

To speak in favour of the city's historic character was not necessarily to oppose development itself. Many examples of heritage-consistent developments could certainly be pointed out, some of them located in Halifax's own downtown. It did, however, feed rather easily into a simply heritage versus development binary, with proponents of the latter characterized as wanting nothing more than to preserve the downtown as a kind of "museum."[60] At certain points in the public hearing, the criticism of heritage and museums seemed to drift into a denigration of museum lovers themselves. Heritage activists, it was sometimes suggested, were an essentially parasitic population that lived off the entrepreneurial energy of others, a cadre of university professors, nonprofit workers, and other types whose livelihoods were derived from the city's economic development, but who did not themselves contribute to it. Such a critique, mostly implied rather than stated outright, was inherent to new talent-centred planning strategy and supporting rationale. How else, except as a kind of parasite, could one describe residents whose vocations excluded them from the category of the "talented" and whose lives were generally incidental, if not disruptive, to the all-benefiting upward spiral?

Proponents of the planning strategy attended the public hearing in similar numbers and presented arguments that had become familiar in the course of the design project. The Urban Development Institute praised the clarity and predictability that would be achieved through the strategy, while the GHP emphasized the $2 billion in downtown development that had been deterred by the existing approval process (and that would presumably be unblocked upon its revamping).[61] The most significant presentations of the hearing were undoubtedly those of the youthful members of Fusion Halifax. Unanimously, Fusion members spoke in favour of the proposed changes and frequently underlined the city-wide importance of their particular perspective on the issue. As one Fusion member explained, the future of downtown development was simultaneously the future of the city's young and talented, and a failure to promote the former would eventually lead to the disappearance of the latter. "I've chosen to stay here," he told the forum. "If the [career] opportunities don't arrive, I might have to go somewhere else."[62] In supporting the new planning strategy, Fusion members were clearly doing more than just contributing their opinions to an arena comprised of equally important others. As the clearest representatives of the talented individuals upon whom the fate of the entire city seemed to depend, they were also providing the missing piece of an overall development model: a vision of the built form that would tend to please them, retain their presence in the city, and thereby enable the overall city to grow and prosper.

One month after the final public hearing, council approved the new planning strategy in a 20–1 vote. Hailing the outcome as a great "move forward," Mayor Peter Kelly explained that the "new streamlined approval process [would] stimulate economic growth and, ultimately, make our downtown a more vibrant place to live and work."[63] Despite Kelly's optimism, the actual effects of the regulatory changes would be difficult to predict. Without question, the changes eliminated the major regulatory obstacles to downtown development. And yet, the most significant barrier to development – the high cost of land – remained fully intact, and it was far from clear, at this point, whether the predictability and cost savings attributable to the regulatory changes would be enough to alter the unfavourable economics of development in the region's most expensive location. The clearest effect of the changes was to establish a new planning model. The principle of public participation, long considered essential to the creation of a better city, was now relegated to the past. It would survive only in the anaesthetized form of the new form-based codes and design manual that ostensibly incorporated public input, once and for all time. The relationship between planning and the population was also amended. Planning, rather than professing to serve a broad spectrum of the population, would now prioritize the lives of a particular class of people (the "talented") and serve the broader population indirectly: through the upward spiral constituted by the attraction and retention of innovation-spurring, talented individuals.

On the ground, this new planning model would tend to exacerbate urban processes that were already transforming the Halifax peninsula into a uniquely upper-income terrain. In the face of rising land costs, the city's response was not to attenuate this process but to clear this land of any countervailing political claims, the claims of any residents unable to afford the land at its present, ever-rising cost. To do so, it was argued, would not simply enable once-obstructed development but also enable a form of life – the life of a footloose, economy-growing *homo economicus* – upon which everyone's life now seemed to depend. In the short term, this meant reserving the downtown for the talented and the developers who would produce their places of work and residence. It meant making the downtown a space for *homo economicus*. In the long term, it would tend to mean approaching other spaces through the same lens, making space for the talented in any and all areas they might wish to claim. At some point, this could mean incorporating the rest of the Halifax peninsula into a project like HRM by Design and removing citizen input from development processes here as well (a project that the city ultimately began in 2011). In the meantime, it would mean allowing increasing rents and property values to do their work: displacing the peninsula's "untalented" Black and non-Black residents to the cheaper land of the periphery and making space, in their absence, for the population whose unique capacities would make everyone's lives better.

The Regional Plan

The Regional Plan was, in many ways, a different initiative than HRM by Design. Rather than focusing on the Halifax downtown, the Regional Plan sought to reconfigure planning and development processes across the vast 5,577 square-kilometre terrain constituted by the 1996 amalgamation of Halifax, Dartmouth, and two neighbouring municipalities. This terrain, as planners often stressed, had not been addressed by a significant planning process since the 1970s, and earlier processes lacked the coordinated region-wide decision-making capacities that were produced, for the first time, with the amalgamation. Rather than a coherent plan, then, regional development was regulated by a patchwork of eighteen small-scale and disjointed plans and political authorities. Vaster in scope than HRM by Design, the Regional Plan was also more abstract and policy focused. In place of street-level drawings and view-plane projections, the Regional Plan centred primarily on high-level images and analyses of different development scenarios: different distributions of future population growth across the region and different tabulations of these distributions' costs and benefits. Indeed, its aim was less to regulate the "look and feel" of future development than to identify where it could and could not occur. As one city councillor explained: "If we [decide] where and how growth occurs, we can do a better job of it, make more effective use of taxpayer money, and provide better and more effective services."[64]

The regional planning process officially began in 2001. Over the next two years, a regional planning manager was hired, a nine-person planning oversight committee (comprising elected officials, residents, and one high-level bureaucrat) was put in place, and an impressive eighteen technically oriented background studies were produced. The remaining process, lasting from 2003 to 2006, involved a complex and laborious process of public consultations and progressively amended regional planning drafts. A kick-off event, attended by 150 residents, was held in May 2004. Held at suburban Mount Saint Vincent University, the event was meant to stoke residents' interest in the planning process and receive input on a set of broad planning objectives devised by the oversight committee. Thereafter, public input was solicited through two years' of workshops, open houses, focus groups, surveys, private meetings with stakeholders, and public invitations to provide comments on a succession of planning drafts. Major drafts of the Regional Plan were issued to the public in May 2005, November 2005, and April 2006. After the release of each draft, Halifax residents were invited to contribute written feedback or speak at a public hearing. The final public hearing, held in May 2006, entailed nearly five hours of comments from fifty-eight different residents. All of these public events, the city reported, resulted in a planning process in which "all citizens had an opportunity to participate and to provide input."[65]

As in HRM by Design, public input to the regional planning process was forced to compete with other, more technical considerations. Especially important in this respect was planners' analysis of the costs of providing infrastructure and municipal services to differing forms of settlement: urban versus suburban, compact versus dispersed. This kind of analysis, often called a "service cost analysis," had become increasingly prevalent in regional planning processes in North America and around the world in the post-1960s period. Its origins lie partly in the work of neoclassical economists. This work, beginning in the 1960s, sought to illuminate the mismatch between the prices paid by residents for municipal services (via taxes) and the costs of providing these services to different forms of settlement. Viewing the state as little more than a service provider, this work showed that residents often paid similar prices for services that varied greatly in cost from compact/urban forms of settlement (relatively cheap) to dispersed/suburban forms (relatively expensive).[66] Around the same time, environmentalists began to tabulate the environmental costs of urban and regional development. Adding up costs like fossil fuel consumption and the destruction of natural areas, this work cast dispersed suburban forms of development, increasingly termed "sprawl," in a distinctly negative light. By the 1980s, these neoclassical and environmentalist perspectives tended to conjoin, with environmentalists (in particular) arguing against ongoing sprawl on both economic and ecological grounds. The Sierra Club expressed an increasingly common perspective when it argued, in a 1996 report, that unmanaged urban sprawl was costly to both tax payers and the environment.[67]

Neither of these perspectives, economic or environmental, has gone uncontested. Significant research in the 1990s, for example, found that more compact forms of settlement are not always more environmentally sustainable. The relationship between urban form and environmental costs, this work suggests, is ultimately more complex than a simple equation between compactness and sustainability.[68] The merger of economic and ecological perspectives on urban sprawl nevertheless provided a new framework of analysis with potentially broad-based appeal among policymakers, interest groups, and everyday residents. The response among urban planners was the development of various new planning approaches, from "growth management" to "smart growth," that aimed to achieve more compact, centrally located forms of urban and regional development. With few exceptions, these approaches eschew rigid development controls in favour of a system of market-based incentives and disincentives that promote (but do not mandate) the desired forms of development. Owing to their emphasis on market mechanisms, growth management and smart-growth approaches have been described as quintessentially neoliberal policies. Their effect, critics claim, is to confine the role of planning to the provision of efficient market conditions for property and infrastructure development, rather than also seeking to attain social objectives that may or may not be compatible with market efficiency.[69]

In Halifax, the regional planning process drew explicitly on the logic and tools of growth management. Its most significant input, accordingly, was the aforementioned service cost analysis, which estimated the annual costs of providing municipal services and infrastructure to various forms of residential development. Focusing on eight ideal forms, from "urban – high density" to "rural – low density," the study illuminated the substantial differences in municipal spending that were attributable to the different areas and households of the region. Whereas a household in a dense urban area would tend to require $1,416 in annual municipal expenditures, a low-density rural household would require more than three times this amount, $5,240 per year.[70] The high service costs in rural areas of the HRM, the report explained, were attributable partly to their peripheral location but also to the prevailing configuration of these areas' homes. Clearly intending to deliver a message, the study contrasted the costs of servicing a dispersed set of rural homes ($5,240 per home) to the costs of a hypothetical, denser grouping ($3,380). Having highlighted a similar relationship between residential density and service costs in suburban and urban areas as well, the implications of the study would be hard to miss. "As neighbourhoods become more dense," the study concluded, "service costs decrease."[71]

The result of the service costs analysis was a narrowly mathematical and one-dimensional conception of the regional terrain. In contrast to HRM by Design, which invited residents to reimagine the multifaceted qualitative experience of city spaces, the Regional Plan's most important input envisioned the present and future city as a landscape of varying service costs. This perspective, both simplistic and economistic, tended to overshadow the many other inputs to the planning process. In some cases, these other inputs were simply assimilated to the cost-focused perspective. Many of the other eighteen background studies, for example, went beyond the issue of service costs but ultimately bolstered the argument against dispersed forms of development by revealing the latter to be not just costly but also environmentally damaging, physically unhealthy, socially alienating, and so on. Inputs that were incompatible with the cost-focused perspective, meanwhile, tended to be ignored. An official analysis of the region's "cultural and heritage resources," for example, recognized the historical presence of the Mi'kmaq in the region but failed to consider how unextinguished Mi'kmaw claims to region or the growing Indigenous population within it might trouble the dominant conception of the region.[72] Another study, prepared by

Cantwell and Company, potentially troubled the cost-focused conception of the region in its mention of an unresolved Mi'kmaw land claim in northwest Dartmouth, a claim stemming from the illegal 1919 seizure of the remaining Halifax-area reserves.[73] The implications of the land claim, however, were never explored by HRM planners, and the claim itself went unmentioned in all subsequent planning documents.

That an analysis of service costs would favour more compact forms of development should have surprised no one. This finding was consistent, for one thing, with decades of similar analyses in other urban regions. The 1996 amalgamation, moreover, was premised on the idea that rural settlements cost more to service; bringing urban and rural areas together through the amalgamation was meant in large part to spread the costs of rural services and infrastructure, recently downloaded by the province, across the larger regional population. The release of the study, nevertheless, ignited forceful arguments about wasteful, costly forms of regional development that were frequently repeated during the planning process. Former Maritime Life CEO Bill Black seized upon the figures in 2004 to highlight the inequities of regional development and region-wide government. "Someone living in a bungalow on Novalea Drive [in Halifax]," he argued, "[is] subsidizing somebody who might be living in a half-million dollar house in [rural] Kingswood because of the relative cost of developing the services."[74] For many commentators, the disparities in service costs were symptomatic of a development process that lacked coherent direction and tended to occur at the whims of private developers. Pointing to their high cost of servicing, regional planning manager Anne Muecke argued that "large residential developments, such as Kingswood and Glen Arbour off Hammonds Plans Road ... should never have occurred."[75]

The prospect of density-promoting planning practices did not please the local development industry. Reciting a familiar neoliberal argument, the Nova Scotia Home Builders' Association warned in 2005 that such practices represented an "artificial involve[ment] ... in the system" that would harm the development process, increase the cost of owning a home, and force prospective homeowners to look outside the region for a place to live.[76] The other major development lobby group, the Urban Development Institute of Nova Scotia, described a similar connection between the regulation of development and the fate of everyday people. "This is an attempt to defer people's rights," argued the institute's president. "There's no way around it: people are going to be the losers."[77] Other business groups, however, saw the matter rather differently. Both the GHP and the Halifax Chamber of Commerce publicly supported the prospect of tighter development controls from the outset. Pointing to the excessive municipal spending and property taxes attributable to decades of "patchwork sprawl," the Chamber of Commerce argued that a comprehensive regional plan and a commitment to density-favouring "smart growth" were essential to the prosperity of the Halifax region.[78] Opposed by the development industry, therefore, the adoption of tighter development controls was supported by businesses whose connection to regional development was more indirect: businesses affected more by municipal spending and taxation than by the profits of peripheral property and infrastructure development.

In the end, the merits of new regional planning practices would be evaluated less in terms of their impacts on the municipality or local businesses than in terms of their effects on the economic lives of HRM residents. Elected officials, though perhaps concerned primarily with budgetary issues, generally described their concerns in resident-centred terms (e.g., in terms of tax implications), while business groups like the Urban Development Institute sought to demonstrate how a position that benefited their members was also in the best interest of "the people." Tracing the connection between potential planning practices and residents' economic lives was thus a recurring activity in the regional planning process and the essential aim of nearly all city-produced planning documents. Coursing through these activities, inevitably, were specific assumptions about residents' economic characteristics and objectives. Among the assumed characteristics of local residents were an aversion to municipal taxes, a desire to see tax revenues "efficiently" and "fairly" expended, and a positive orientation towards homeownership that emphasized its investment characteristics (and welcomed continually higher property values, therefore, as a form of financial gain). Residents were also assumed to be highly mobile and selective in their choice of homes, continually calculating the costs and benefits of alternative locations. Hence, new residents were assumed to be attracted to particular cities and neighbourhoods on the basis of their mix of social and physical qualities, and were expected to leave an area if its prevailing mix of social and physical qualities was suddenly or significantly altered.[79]

Taken together, these and other assumed characteristics provided an image of HRM residents as a collection of economically rational households, a periphery-dwelling version of *homo economicus*. For this imagined economic household, a full range of interests and desires were presumed to be fulfillable through rational actions in the regional housing-and-amenity marketplace. Economic gain was not this household's only desire. It was on the basis of economic factors, however, that its other desires could be fulfilled, and it was the essential responsibility of urban planning to ensure that these factors were well attended. This image of HRM residents, homogenizing and economistic, shaped the regional planning process in important ways. It tended to validate, for one thing, any planning practice that promised to sustain residents' economic lives, so conceived. Lower service costs (to the extent that they ultimately reduced taxation) were thus regarded positively. Conversely, a whole range of potential nonmarket planning concerns and initiatives were placed beyond consideration. It is notable, for example, that state-funded public housing was accorded no importance in the finalized Regional Plan. Perhaps more importantly, this image of HRM residents imposed limits on the range of people who could appear as legitimate participants in the planning process. Like the "talented individual" imagined in the HRM by Design process, the "economic household" operated as a restrictive norm in the regional planning process, effacing the participation and interests of people whose lives and living conditions departed from those of the assumed norm.

Particularly ill affected by the normative structure of the planning process were the region's peripheral Black communities, whose actual economic practices were sometimes the exact opposite of those of the economic household. Rather than mobile and selective in their choice of homes, for one thing, Black families often chose to remain in the same general area and even on the same plot of land for generations. To the extent that they wished to relocate, moreover, their options tended to be constrained by the low market value of Black homes and the low probability of finding an affordable home elsewhere. Altered social and physical conditions, assumed to cause HRM households to move, had certainly not prompted the residents of communities like Beechville or Upper Hammonds Plains to relocate in recent years (at least not by choice). Rather than treating their home as an individual- or household-specific investment, finally, residents of Black communities often passed down their home from generation to generation or subdivided their land to provide a setting for the communally constructed home of their children or parents. In this situation, the increasing property values that other HRM residents might treat as a positive development could be detrimental to the livelihoods of Black households. Indeed, the period between 2001 and 2013 saw residential property assessments in the historic sections of Beechville and Upper Hammonds Plains increase by an average of 11 per cent per year, leading to a series of tax-related property sales and foreclosures.[80] Processes that improved the economic lives of a normative household, in sum, could have quite different and potentially devastating effects on the lives of Black residents.

The implicit exclusion of Black communities from the field of planning's concerns had practical consequences throughout the five-year regional planning process. In 2004, for example, the city instituted a series of temporary restrictions on residential development across a large part of the region, including all six of the region's major Black communities. These restrictions, first adopted at a surprise meeting of city council in January 2004, were meant to freeze residential development until the new Regional Plan could be adopted. They were intended, in particular, to preclude property developers from subverting the planning process by submitting several years' worth of development applications before the new planning regulations could take effect. As the city explained: "Past experience in HRM has demonstrated that developers will undertake accelerated development approvals in order to avoid anticipated growth management regulations, significantly undermining the original intent of the plan."[81] The restrictions, in their original formulation, confined residential development to already-approved roadways and limited new residential building permits to a maximum of one per existing plot of land (even if an existing plot was, after the restrictions came into place, subdivided into multiple plots). Residential development would thus be temporarily confined to the region's estimated 3,800 existing undeveloped lots and estimated 1,550 approved (but not yet created) lots.[82]

As Black residents argued at the time, the temporary restrictions unfairly limited the small-scale home-building activities of Black communities in a clumsy attempt to rein in the large-scale development industry. Criticizing the application of a single policy to a wide range of circumstances, former Preston-area member of the provincial legislature Wayne Adams told a public hearing on the restrictions that "one size [did] not fit all" in this case.[83] East Preston resident Matthew Thomas, appearing at the same hearing, explained that the restrictions prevented residents of his community from "provid[ing] land for their families to use to build homes."[84] Small amendments adopted in May 2004 loosened the restrictions somewhat. Prohibited under the original restrictions, the creation of up to three "flag lots" (new lots created at the rear of a plot of land along a shared driveway) was now allowed on existing plots of land. The building of new public roads and the creation of up to eight new plots of land (on these new roads) was also permitted under particular conditions in an area of the periphery that included North Preston and East Preston.[85] Significant development restrictions, however, remained fully intact, especially for the region's four other Black communities and for residents who had already created the maximum of three flag lots. The adoption of the Regional Plan in 2006, moreover, offered no reprieve for affected Black residents. The centrepiece of the plan for peripheral areas was the establishment of eight development-friendly "growth centres" and the imposition of strict development restrictions everywhere else. Since none of the region's Black communities happened to be located in a growth centre, the approval of the plan effectively extended the temporary restrictions on their use of property into perpetuity.[86]

Aiming to bring order to the peripheral home-building market, the restrictions imposed during the regional planning process were never meaningfully adjusted to relieve their effects on the nonmarket home-building practices that sustained Black communities. This outcome can be traced, in part, to the aims of the process itself. From start to finish, the process focused on the well-being of a particular kind of household, an economic household whose interests and desires were fulfillable in a well-ordered housing-and-amenity marketplace. The imposed restrictions might indeed have created a better life for this kind of household. Their other effect, however, was to worsen the lives of residents whose engagements with peripheral land and housing occurred outside the market and beyond the boundaries of prevailing economic normativity.

In the end, the restrictions would fail to achieve even these limited objectives. As *figure 7.4* demonstrates, the area's largest residential developers clearly anticipated the looming restrictions and obtained their subdivision and development approvals early. With a surplus of approvals at their disposal, these companies were able to operate as if the restrictions had never been imposed, both during and long after the regional planning process. The effects of the restrictions, therefore, fell almost entirely on small-scale home builders. Black communities, severely ill affected by unregulated post-1960s development, would now see regulations introduced precisely where they were unhelpful and damaging: on their own activities and not on those that harmed them. Expressing a more widely held Black perspective on the Regional Plan, a resident of East Preston told planners that the process seemed to be an attempt "to take our land away from us like in the past."[87]

Figure 7.4 Subdivision applications, 1992–2010. Includes applications submitted within the HRM (minus Halifax and Dartmouth) by the area's ten largest developers. Data from Nova Scotia Property Online.

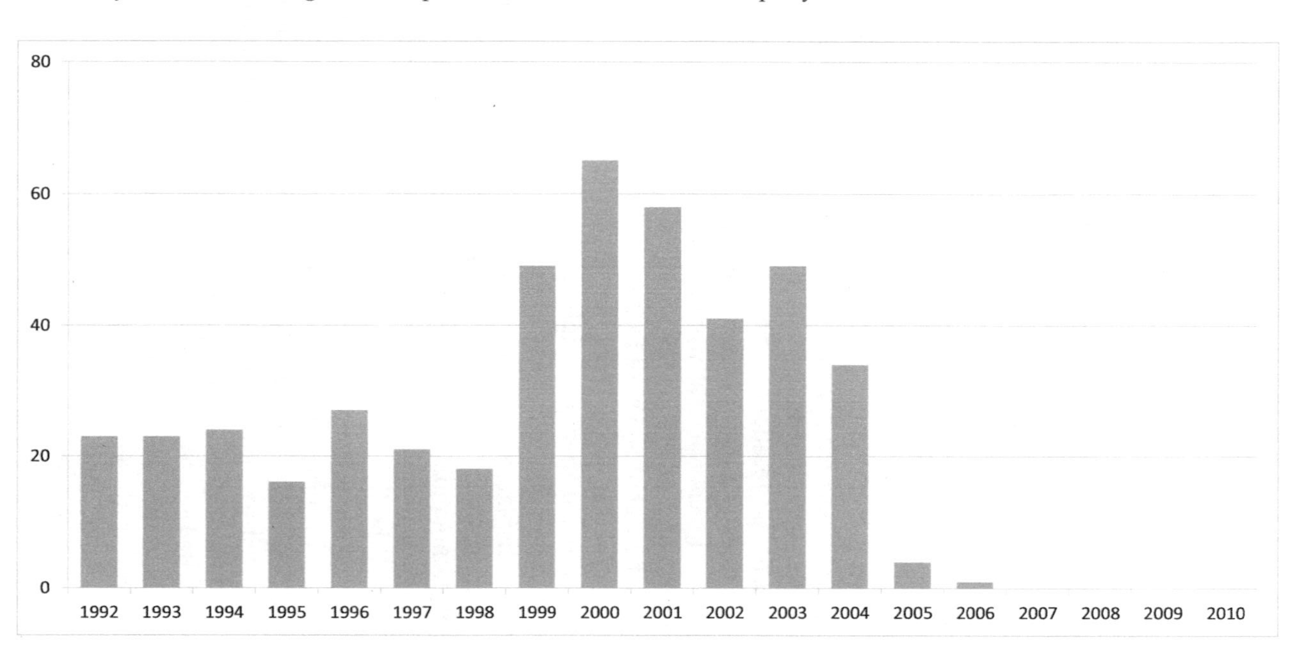

The negation of Black life was evident in more than just the plan's development restrictions, however. In addition to plotting the location of new homes, the planning process sought to determine the ideal distribution of future investments in municipal services and infrastructure. Addressing this issue, Black communities like East Preston expressed their interest in receiving both municipal water services and improved public transportation (which was limited in East Preston to a bihourly and weekday-only bus service). These requests were universally spurned by city planners. Water services, planners decided, were to be provided according to a new protocol that would favour densely settled and relatively central communities (i.e., the eight new growth centres established across the Halifax periphery). Improved public transportation, Black residents were informed, would also be provided on a basis that favoured growth centres.[88] Like the development restrictions, this approach to infrastructure and services was clearly tailored to the life of a normative economic household. Planning, in channelling new spending to particular locations, aimed to produce a denser, more efficient housing stock and thereby enable normative, market-interacting households to make choices that were more beneficial to themselves (as homeowners) and others (as taxpayers). Occluded in this vision, of course, were households whose forms of inhabitation were neither fully chosen nor market based: Black households whose ancestors had been *forced* to settle in dispersed, peripheral locations and who found it difficult, if not impossible, to live anywhere else.

This symbolic displacement of Black communities in these planning discussions is consistent with Katherine McKittrick's conception of "rational spatial domination." Uni-perspectival, rational representations of space, she argues, illuminate the world from a dominant perspective. Their effect, from the time of European conquest and enslavement to the present, is to normalize white spatial and self-possession, and conceal not just Black histories but also Black people's sometimes-different sense of place.[89] While this logic precedes the neoliberal era and can certainly be located in earlier planning initiatives in Halifax, the Regional Plan and its fixation on minimizing service costs took this logic to its extreme. The plan reduced both the regional terrain and its human inhabitants to their barest, rational elements – the elements that, without constituting the entirety of life and space, were assumed to provide the essential foundation for better lives and spaces. As McKittrick would anticipate, moreover, it assumed a rationality that reflected some people's lives more than others, and Black lives hardly at all.

Planning, unable to recognize the particular nonnormative and non-market histories of Black communities, could find no reason to support a form of settlement (peripheral and dispersed) that Black residents had established and developed under the constraints of anti-blackness. Perversely, planning could only see this form of settlement as a wasteful "choice," parasitic upon the economic lives of the broader population.

Similarly ignored in the regional planning process, finally, were a range of Black demands for better public spaces and "amenities." Demands like these, advanced at various public consultations, highlighted a whole series of actions that planners could have taken to improve the well-being of Black communities, including the installation of sidewalks, the improvement of roadways, and the construction of new community buildings and spaces of recreation. All of these demands, however, were judged to be unduly "local" in character and therefore out of place in a region-wide planning process. Explaining its dismissal of Black demands, the city wrote in 2005: "As has been stated throughout the regional planning process, the time for detailed discussions on specific and local community issues will come with the launch of a community visioning program once the Regional Plan is approved."[90] Black input, in other words, had been misdirected. It was insufficiently "regional" in character.

Drawing lines between local and regional concerns is commonplace in urban planning, and it undoubtedly helps to make decision making and public participation more manageable. However, the "local" and the "regional" are not so easy to disentangle, and their practical interconnections become plainly apparent when, in 2006, the local plans for East and North Preston were significantly modified to reflect the newly established goals and policies of the finalized Regional Plan.[91] A veritably *local* planning process was therefore encased within the regional planning project, and a set of community-specific changes were implemented without any meaningful input from the communities affected (their input having been judged misdirected). Clearly violated in this case was a principle specific to Black communities and not to the economic household to which planning devoted itself: the principle of Black self-determination. This principle, long advocated by Black activists, was finally accepted by the city as an official policy in its 1993 plan for East and North Preston.[92] Its purpose in this context was to shield Black communities from damaging state and market actions. Its purpose was to constitute Black communities as a zone apart from these actions, a zone in which Black decisions would hold sway. For the

Regional Plan, this Black-specific principle was evidently unrecognizable or unimportant. Oriented towards a universal and undifferentiated economic household, the plan ignored the various nonstandard, racially specific characteristics that Black communities and official planning policies asked to be recognized.

For Black communities, the regional planning process was a continuation of long-standing forms of exclusion and subjugation. Once pathologized, silenced, and deliberately targeted by planning projects, Black communities began in the 1960s to experience the effects of planning practices that professed to listen, that solicited their participation, and that seldom targeted them explicitly for displacement or political exclusion. These planning practices, however, achieved familiar effects through different means. Anti-blackness endured within the new practices not through explicit pathologization but through the centring of a figure of the human that seemed to be universal but actually departed significantly from the distinguishing features of Black life. The Regional Plan, reflecting the ascent of neoliberalism in the post-1960s period, catered to a pared-down, economistic rendering of this universality, the normative economic household. This figure, new in certain ways, entailed rather familiar consequences. Like the uniform political interests assumed in the planning events and movements of the 1960s and 1970s, the uniform economic dispositions assumed in the regional planning process made it harder to recognize the nonnormative situations of many Black residents: particular nonmarket home-building practices; particular racially inflected histories of community settlement; and particular policies and principles that had been developed to address the racial subjugation produced by public and private actors. Indifferent to these particularities, the Regional Plan ignored and indeed worsened the lives of those who had been most ill affected by the process of regional development that it aimed to regulate.

Effects like these are difficult to recognize within the dominant critical literature on neoliberalism (in general) or neoliberal planning (in particular). Foucault's analysis, for example, helpfully illuminates how the figure of *homo economicus* came to the centre of state and nonstate efforts to manage individuals and populations from the 1960s onward. His inattention to race, however, makes him unable to recognize how *homo economicus* became the new "normal" in a pre-existing normal/pathological continuum in which race, and specifically blackness, constituted the furthest reaches of pathology. He misses, as a result, how neoliberalism can preserve and intensify racial subjugation, not simply through overt racial pathologization but also through the codification as "economically rational" a set of supposedly universal and raceless dispositions that, in practice, most closely reflect those of privileged white individuals. In contrast, scholars of anti-blackness have frequently noted how seemingly raceless figures of the human, including *homo economicus*, conceal the white racial specificities that these figures actually encode. Sylvia Wynter, for example, describes the arrival of *homo economicus* as a modest alteration in the conception of the *normative* human.[93] From this perspective, the shift described by Foucauldian scholars of neoliberalism, a shift from a broadly multifaceted to a narrowly economistic conception of life, is a change confined primarily to the normative registers of life.[94] As the anti-Black effects of the Regional Plan demonstrate, neoliberalism's paring down of life's recognizable features, its fixation on economic rationality, is more or less relevant depending on the way one's life was recognized in an earlier period.

The approval of the Regional Plan in June 2006 was described as the beginning of a new era of regional development. In place of a patchwork of nonconforming development policies, a single plan was finally applied to the region as a whole. Future development, consequently, would finally occur according to a coherent, region-wide vision. Alongside the designation of specific growth centres, the plan also established a program of complementary public investments. Supporting the targeted development pattern was $150 million in transportation infrastructure (over twenty-five years); a commitment to the provision of municipal water, sewer, and public transportation in designated growth centres; and the creation of two new regional parks, situated in proximity to the new residential populations. For a normative, economically rational household, the plan might indeed make life better, especially when their municipal tax bill arrived. (The lower average service costs produced by the plan were expected to save the municipality $250 million over twenty-five years.) For Black communities, however, the plan could easily be seen as a calculated affront. Development targets would encourage home construction in some communities but would restrict construction in theirs. New funding for transportation and other infrastructure would be devoted to communities other than theirs. A pair of new parks would compensate for the natural areas eaten up by post-1960s development, but certainly not in their vicinity. If the haphazard, loosely regulated development of the last three decades had harmed living conditions in Black communities, the arrival of a coherent, region-wide vision would seem to undermine them further still.

Conclusion

The twenty-first century began in Halifax with a pair of planning initiatives that sought to recognize and respond to the exigencies of a new metropolitan and global context. Among the important changes brought about in the preceding three decades was a gradual transition towards "postindustrial" economic sectors; an increasingly regional pattern of residential and commercial development; and an imposed amalgamation of Halifax, Dartmouth, and two neighbouring municipalities, which finally enabled planning to be undertaken at a region-wide scale. The first of the two planning initiatives, HRM by Design, sought to address these new conditions in the particular setting of the Halifax downtown. This project, unfolding against the backdrop of incessant struggles over proposed downtown property developments, aimed to determine the acceptable form of future downtown development in advance. Assembling Halifax residents and translating their objectives into a set of form-based codes, the project hoped to pre-empt subsequent struggles over proposed developments and provide a relatively smooth mechanism through which footloose financial capital could settle into and gradually remake the central city. The second initiative, the Regional Plan, sought to shape development processes at the vaster scale of the amalgamated regional municipality. Addressing a terrain that had escaped coherent development controls for decades, this project sought to establish region-wide regulations that would mould future development into a form that was significantly less costly to the municipality, the region's taxpayers, and the natural environment. In 2009, after more than eight years of work, the city could boast of having a pair of new plans that would guide downtown and regional development into the twenty-first century.

In certain respects, the new initiatives entailed a significant break with the general form of twentieth-century planning. Earlier, decades-long efforts to sustain and nurture human life in a broad sense – a sense that included health, morality, welfare, and enjoyment – were clearly left behind in the initiatives' more narrow, economic focus. There was clearly nothing in the new initiatives resembling earlier periods' dramatic efforts to remake the lives of working-class residents through state-provided public housing. And yet, the most fundamental aspects of twentieth-century planning remained fully intact. At the centre of each initiative was a particular conception of the human being. In the case of HRM by Design, the focus was the "talented individual." In the case of the Regional Plan, it was the "economic household." In both cases, an economistic rendering of the human being, a particular version of *homo economicus*, provided the central logic and focus of the new planning practices. Making space for *homo economicus*, spatially supporting a particular kind of economic life, was the central aim of the new initiatives. The difference entailed in the new initiatives, therefore, was not their departure from earlier periods' efforts to sustain a particular form of life, but the sheer narrowness of their conception of life. Consistent with neoliberal policies more generally, the new initiatives sought largely to provide the spatial conditions in which (certain) residents could earn and buy a better life in the private market. Nonmarket aspects of life might be enhanced as well. But, if so, this would occur as a by-product of the economic effects – wealth, growth, and taxation – that neoliberal planning prioritized.

Narrowly economistic, the form of life envisioned by HRM by Design and the Regional Plan was also a singular, normative one – a conception of life that not all city residents were able to embody. In the case of HRM by Design, the focus on the talented individual noticeably sidelined the city's various heritage-supporting residents, especially the representatives of HTNS. In contrast to the talented individual whose entrepreneurial energies ostensibly benefited the entire city, heritage-supporting residents appeared moribund, state dependent, and irrelevant (if not obstructive) to the city's economic well-being. Their interests, consequently, had little effect on the resulting form-based codes, and the resulting development approvals process was clearly designed to limit the effect of these residents and their interests in the future. In the case of the Regional Plan, the focus on the economic household normalized a set of economic behaviours and objectives that contrasted with those of many Black residents. The plan's every effort to produce a less costly form of regional development, therefore, entailed *added* costs for peripheral Black communities. In each planning initiative, then, a version of *homo economicus* outlined the target and nontarget of planning practices: a normative form of life that planning would seek to recognize and support, as well as a form of existence that planning would neither recognize nor support. HTNS and peripheral Black communities, in different ways, were each cast beyond the sphere of economic normativity in this period. Their interests in planning processes, consequently, were isolated, ignored, and ultimately trampled upon.

Though similarly pathologized, heritage-supporting residents and peripheral Black communities would clearly be affected very differently by the new planning practices. The major effect of HRM by Design on local heritage supporters was to undercut their aesthetic claims upon the public realm of the city. It was to disparage and displace their interest in the preservation of heritage buildings, the view from Citadel Hill, and other aspects of the city's prevailing "look and feel." The effect of the Regional Plan on Black communities, in contrast, was to undercut their *every* claim. The plan, while it certainly sidelined Black residents' demands for better public transportation and public services, also introduced new prohibitions on their private lives, including their use of property and other economic practices that allowed them to sustain themselves. Differential consequences like these suggest, once again, the difference between the pathologization of certain white populations and the more fundamental, always- already pathological position of Black populations. These consequences suggest, as well, the finer differences within a broader neoliberal form of thought and practice that has usually been described in more monolithic terms: as a restoration of class power, for example, or a shift from "public values" to "economic values."[95] A shift from public values to economic values is perhaps descriptive of the marginalization of HTNS and its claims upon the public realm. The subjugation of Black communities, however, was something very different: a disregard for public values that were never *previously* respected and an assault on economic values that, departing from an anti-Black economic norm, were not respected as such. Supporting the rational economic activities of Black communities might indeed have been modestly helpful in this context.

As in earlier periods, the displacement of blackness from the field of planning's concerns had effects not just in Black communities but across the urban terrain. Post-1960s development, I have shown, significantly restructured the social geography of the Halifax region. The Halifax peninsula, in this period, became increasingly elite and unaffordable. Low-income and middle-income households, consequently, were pushed towards off-peninsula locations. HRM by Design, focused on the peninsula, did nothing to arrest this process and ultimately catered to the interests of residents that contemporary development processes were already favouring – the only residents, it seems, who could be imagined as inhabiting and possessing the peninsula in the future. The broader focus of the Regional Plan was thus essential, both socially and politically. Its efforts to produce a less costly form of residential development in the region would help to provide a home for low- and middle-income households increasingly barred from the peninsula and thereby contribute to an overall planning vision, constituted by HRM by Design and the Regional Plan together, which addressed the needs of a politically legitimate proportion of the population. Potentially impeding this broad vision, as certain planners recognized, were the region's Black communities, whose continued existence proved repellent to the "pride and prejudice" of many white residents.[96] Undermining the viability of these communities – a clear effect of the Regional Plan – was thus conducive to planning objectives in both the periphery and the peninsula. Planning, in the twenty-first century as in the twentieth, would locate the basis of its city-wide objectives in spaces that Black residents inhabited but could never, it seems, be imagined to possess.

8 Conclusion

Deep-rooted affiliations between planning, power, and race – the subject of this book – have significantly shaped the lives and spaces of twentieth-century Halifax. Planning in this period took human life as its primary object and concern. Assessments of individuals and collectivities were its starting point; the improvement of prevailing human health, happiness, prosperity, and well-being were its priorities; and the remaking of particular or city-wide living conditions was its method. The effects of twentieth-century planning were far-reaching and often astonishing. The city, in effect, became an organized extension of the mind and body. The making of the city came to shape, in profound ways, the making of people's lives. From the late nineteenth century onward, the characteristics of people's lives – whether people fell ill or remained in good health, whether their movement through space was convenient or frustrating, whether their experiences were enjoyable or dissatisfying – would depend significantly on the calculations and interventions of planning authorities. By planning's own standards, these efforts to shape people's lives were often successful. As the twentieth century wore on, the city undoubtedly became more healthy, more convenient, more prosperous, and more beautiful for many people. There is no question that the condition of many people's lives was improved and safeguarded through modern planning's enduring attention to the life-affecting qualities of the urban terrain.

The reach of these positive effects, however, was generally constrained to certain populations, and precisely the opposite effects were experienced by many individuals and subpopulations. Those most adversely affected by modern planning were those cast outside the normative conception of human life that guided planning's efforts. In some cases, the "pathological" were subjugated in order to improve them, to encase them forcibly within the realm of the normative. In other cases, these groups were exempted from planning's concerns altogether and rendered possible, through their exemption from these concerns, the delivery of life-aiding effects to the broader population. In all cases, blackness marked the horizon or outside of the life that planning sought to sustain and nurture. Displacing blackness, sometimes physically and always symbolically, provided an enduring coherence and orientation to twentieth-century city making. It brought the outlines of human life into relief, made it possible to discern prevailing degrees of normality and pathology among people, and helped to calibrate interventions that would produce more optimal forms of life through the improvement, containment, or elimination of the pathological. Displacing blackness from the field of planning's concerns, if not from the landscape itself, was integral to the remaking of lives and spaces in twentieth-century Halifax. Modern planning and the city that it sought to mould would be very different without this reiterated racial expulsion.

The structure of urban planning, while generally consistent across the twentieth century, assumed somewhat different forms in different contexts. Accordingly, each chapter of this book sought to illuminate some of the context-specific particularities of planning's enduring affiliation with power and race. At the turn of the twentieth century, I showed in chapter 2, the "moral and physical health" of poor and working-class individuals became a major preoccupation, and a new form of planning emerged in efforts to normalize these individuals through the remaking of their living conditions. These efforts, while oppressive primarily to poor and working-class white residents, gauged the supposed defects of these residents against the always-already pathological and therefore irreparable (nonnormalizable) lives of Black residents. Around the same time, as I showed in chapter 3, broader-scale initiatives, like sewer construction, street paving, and "efficient" land-use planning, began to be introduced and integrated into an early form of "comprehensive" planning. The aim of these initiatives was not to normalize individuals but to improve the overall health, contentedness, and prosperity of the local population. In the community of Africville, however, these initiatives produced the opposite effect: a marked worsening of life that ultimately enabled the pursuit and fulfilment of planning's life-sustaining objectives elsewhere in the city.

These early initiatives prefigured and partially enabled the wider-scale planning interventions of the post-World War II, urban renewal period. In this period, as I showed in chapter 4, improving the "welfare" of the overall population was planning's major objective. This involved initiatives, like slum clearance and the development of more efficient transportation infrastructure, that aimed to improve aggregate measures of human health, prosperity, and welfare. It also involved initiatives like the construction of public housing that, like the model tenements plan in 1905, sought to normalize particularly aberrant individuals. The effects of these manifold, welfare-improving efforts included the displacement of over five thousand Halifax residents, roughly 90 per cent of them white. Most seriously impacted, however, were the city's Black displacees, whose land- and community-based practices of survival were effaced and ultimately destroyed by a planning model that could imagine improvements in prevailing living conditions strictly from a white starting point. The improvement offered to Black displacees, when it was offered, was thus no improvement at all, but rather a top-down evisceration of the social and spatial practices that had allowed them to hold on in an anti-Black city.

The late 1960s brought new planning initiatives and priorities into circulation in Halifax, largely through the efforts of newly formed state institutions and newly emergent activist movements. The efforts of these new institutions and movements, as discussed in chapter 5, centred on demands for increased citizen involvement in planning processes and the creation of spatial conditions (i.e., amenity) that would create increased enjoyment for particular populations. These efforts led to a tense conflict over a potentially destructive expressway project called Harbour Drive North, which activists succeeded in halting in 1973. But they also freighted subtle forms of anti-blackness that operated less through the explicit targeting of Black populations than through the centring of implicitly white and middle-class conceptions of political struggle and urban amenity. A rather different vision of urban planning emerged from the activism of the Black United Front (BUF) between 1968 and 1974. As I discussed in chapter 6, BUF's activist efforts sought to recentre planning practices on the lives and self-determining capacities of Black individuals and communities. In seeking to enable Black self-determination, these efforts undercut dominant conceptions of normality and pathology, and produced modestly new genres of the human. These efforts, successful in many ways, were deemed unacceptable and were ultimately undermined by state institutions willing to listen to Black demands but unwilling to cede power to Black communities.

The first decade of the twenty-first century, finally, saw planning refocus on the economic lives of Halifax residents. This new focus, examined in chapter 7, reflected the ascent of neoliberal thinking in the post-1960s period and the gradual centring of state attention on the management of an economistic conception of the human, often termed *homo economicus*. This focus was reflected, in the early years of the twenty-first century, in the creation of new planning frameworks for the Halifax downtown and the greater urban region, respectively. Both of these new frameworks provided support to a particular conception of economic life, while subjugating other aspects of life and other forms of economic life. Their major effect was to sanction ongoing processes of displacement on the Halifax peninsula, as well as to outlaw the economic *and* noneconomic practices of the city's peripheral Black communities.

Tracking the connection between race and power across a century of modern planning initiatives provides a new and important perspective on contemporary city making. It illustrates, for one thing, how power and planning converge not just in efforts to facilitate capital accumulation or impose a rational order upon the city but also in efforts to secure and nurture human life through spatial means. Attending to efforts of this kind, it is possible to see how power circulates through seemingly benevolent and progressive planning proposals and how destruction is sometimes produced, paradoxically, in the name of protection, improvement, and well-being. The century-long perspective of this book also makes it possible to see how the circulation of power through urban planning changes over time and how it does not. There are important differences, for example, between the objectives of planning in the early, mid-, and late twentieth century. The forms of life that planning sought to cultivate in one period were not quite the same as the forms that it prioritized in a later period. What remained unchanged, however, was the role of context-specific norms in guiding planning's conception and management of life. No matter what form of life planning sought to cultivate, that is, specific norms made it possible to imagine this form of life and devise spatial interventions that would bring it into being through the proliferation of normative life, the diminution of pathological life, or both.

The perspective of this book, finally, makes it possible to see how race consistently secures the connection between power and planning. Blackness, I have shown, brings the outermost limits of the human into intelligibility and gives meaning to the opposed poles of normality and pathology that guide modern planning. This eviction of blackness from the realm of normative humanity – this specific form of racism – is thus integral to modern planning. The problem of racist planning, consequently, cannot be limited to the fact that racialized people often endure discrimination in venues like the job market and are therefore rendered vulnerable, due to their resulting poverty, to the predations of urban planning. Racism exists in the world outside of urban planning, to be sure, but it also operates within it. Nor is the problem simply that planning lacks the knowledge or resources to treat all groups equally. Planning, in twentieth-century Halifax, was usually quite well informed about the living conditions in Black communities but nevertheless ignored or worsened conditions that it endeavoured to improve elsewhere in the city. The resources available to planning, meanwhile, often encountered their limits precisely at the borders of Black life; they were cut off, that is, when further spending on infrastructure or services might benefit Black people. Nor, finally, is the issue simply the racial prejudices of planners and planning-involved actors. Efforts to unlearn racial prejudices, I showed, do not always disrupt the more fundamental role of anti-blackness in modernity: the constitution of a figure of the human that is decidedly anti-Black.

Viewing anti-blackness as integral to modern planning does not mean denying or dismissing the subjugation of certain non-Black populations. To the contrary, it is essential to recognize how various individuals and populations were, at one time or another, defined as pathological by modern planning and were therefore subjected to political exclusion, unwanted oversight, physical displacement, and other forms of spatialized subjugation. The effects of modern planning, for example, were frequently harmful to poor and working-class white residents. The twentieth century began, I showed, with a series of unaccountable interventions in the lives of the poor (and largely white) residents of the upper streets. As the century wore on, moreover, the land beneath poor people's homes was frequently sited for better uses, and poor people's bodies and behaviours were repeatedly marked for coercive correction through spatial means. And yet, the ostensible pathologies of white residents were frequently gauged in relation to those of Black residents and were most often presumed to be less grave. In many cases, this translated into planning interventions in which Black residents fared worse than white residents belonging to the same social class. The point, again, is not to discount the often brutal subjugation of non-Black populations on the grounds that another group had it worse.

The point, in the first instance, is to identify the subtle differences between different forms of oppression (e.g., race versus class). Beyond this, the point is to illuminate the role of anti-blackness in defining a conception of human pathology that ultimately contributes to the oppression of other groups.

What this book highlights, in the end, is the historic and ongoing role of anti-blackness within a system of power that extends well beyond the lives and spaces of Black people. Anti-blackness, I have argued, is not reducible to the mistreatment of Black communities. It exists and endures, more precisely, within a set of spatially and temporally differentiated relations, discourses, and practices that continually constitute gradations of the human. Blackness, in this schema, constitutes the always-already pathological pole of a spectrum of normality and pathology. Its effect, in producing this spectrum, is to render imaginable a whole series of planning interventions that promise to protect and improve human life, where this protection and improvement is implicitly or explicitly conceived as a form of individual or population-wide distancing from the pathology represented by blackness. Anti-blackness, in this sense, gives shape and orientation to a whole range of actions, including the pathologization and subjugation of many non-Black residents. Anti-blackness gives shape, as well, to more beneficial actions and outcomes. It provides the discursive means to imagine better forms of individual and collective life, as well as the material bases with which to create these better forms of life (e.g., dispossessed Black land). Anti-blackness, I have argued, shapes modern planning everywhere it operates. Displacing blackness, symbolically and physically, is essential to its operation.

Anti-Blackness and Planning Scholarship

The perspective advanced in this book is at odds with most scholarly discussions of urban planning today. Scholarly discussions, of course, have often been critical of urban planning. The work of David Harvey and James Scott, in particular, helpfully brings attention to the role of capitalist social relations and modernist state rationalities (respectively) in guiding planning practices and licensing various forms of social and physical destruction.[1] And yet, this work fails to critique (and often celebrates) planning's commitment to the improvement of human life. It fails, as a result, to grasp how racist ontologies consistently structure planning's conception of what life and its improvement entail.

The work of Michel Foucault, Paul Rabinow, and like-minded scholars holds more promise. This work approaches urban planning as part of a system of power centred on human life. The fostering of human life, for these authors, is the foremost task of modern planning. Abetting this task are a series of norms – social, biological, and spatial – that make it possible to assess the prevailing condition of life, distinguish optimal from suboptimal forms of life, and calibrate spatial interventions meant to promote a normative conception of human flourishing. This work, an example of critical ontology, is essential to my analysis in this book. And yet, it also has limitations. It fails, in particular, to recognize how conceptions of the human were shaped by the racial evictions constitutive of Euro-American colonialism, racial slavery, and their various afterlives.[2]

Addressing the limitations of Foucauldian critical ontology is an incisive and growing literature on anti-blackness. Exemplified by the work of Frantz Fanon, Saidiya Hartman, Sylvia Wynter, Katherine McKittrick, and Rinaldo Walcott, this line of analysis demonstrates that new European conceptions of "the human" emerged in tandem with, and depended upon, the eviction of colonized and enslaved people from this category. Blackness, in particular, marked the horizon or outside of the human as such. It signified an ever-present pathology that justified Black subjugation and enslavement, and that could subsequently be attributed, in lesser degrees, to subjugated Europeans and Euro-Americans.[3] This literature, though it pays little attention to urban planning, can be productively brought into discussions of the latter. An engagement with urban planning can, for one thing, reveal another venue in which anti-blackness is produced and maintained in the world. The continuation of slavery-era conceptions of Black pathology in the supposedly postslavery era, for example, can be linked not simply to well-recognized anti-Black institutions like the police and the prison system but also to the discourses and practices of postslavery urban planning. An engagement with planning can also deepen the analysis begun by Foucault, Rabinow, and other scholars who analyse planning as an effort to manage human life. If planning is part of a system of power centred on human life, and conceptions of the human are premised on anti-blackness, then how can planning *not* be an anti-Black endeavour?

Posing this question forces one to look for racialized power in less-than-obvious places and practices – not simply in planning's transactions with Black lives and spaces, that is, but in every effort through which planning seeks to nurture and sustain life. It forces one to reckon, in the end, with a form of racialized power that pervades urban life, that shapes, in every instance, the forms of individual and collective life that are possible in the modern city. A similar city-wide extensivity has frequently been attributed to other structures of power, such that it is possible, for example, to speak of "the capitalist city" or even "the sexist city." My aim in this book has been to put anti-blackness on a similar footing. Anti-blackness is an oppressive system that consistently shapes planning priorities and initiatives. It is a system, therefore, that inhabits every inch of the modern city and every aspect of modern life. My own life, as a white man, is produced within this system. The many ways that modern planning has indeed protected and improved my life are the intimate inscriptions of the system that this book critiques. To critique anti-Black planning is thus to put its many results, including the many lives it has actually improved, into question. It is to insist that another city and another form of life are necessary.

One of the limits of this book, it should be noted, is its relatively minimal discussion of settler colonialism. The historic dispossession of the Mi'kmaq from the shores of K'jipuktuk, as I noted in the introduction, was essential to the formation of modern urban planning in Halifax. This dispossession cleared, in gruesome manner, the area that came to be called Halifax from otherwise competing Indigenous territorial claims and allowed this area to be developed and regulated under the aegis of settler-state planners.[4] Also essential to modern planning were the various federal state policies that functioned to confine Mi'kmaw and other Indigenous people to designated reserves in nonurban locations, policies that helped to maintain cities like Halifax as relatively Indigenous-free spaces for much of the nineteenth and twentieth centuries. Beyond these basic connections, it is difficult to say much about how settler colonialism shaped modern urban planning, or how settler-colonial and anti-Black spatial logics may have intersected. Indigenous people, never accounting for more than 1 per cent of the Halifax population in the twentieth century, never attracted the explicit attention of planners in this period. Looking beyond the city, potentially important connections are visible. I noted at several points in the book how the actions of urban planners in Halifax paralleled the actions of federal institutions in nonurban Mi'kmaw reserves. A proper analysis of these connections, however, would require much more attention. It would require attention, in particular, to the material and discursive links between the operation power in different locations, through nominally distinct state institutions, and through subtly different logics of racialization.

The relationship between settler colonialism and anti-blackness has begun to receive more focused attention, both in critical scholarship and in political struggle. In Canada, discussions of this relationship have brought into conversation some of the most important Black and Indigenous activist-intellectuals of our time and have rendered conceivable radically new forms of political solidarity, collective struggle, and social-ecological existence.[5] In more than a few cases, discussions of anti-blackness and settler colonialism in Canada have invoked the story of Africville, a story that, in its interplay of racism and spatial dispossession, seems to mirror some of the forms of domination that Indigenous people have experienced on this continent.[6] To approach the intersection of anti-Black and settler-colonial power (partly) through the story of Africville is potentially productive. But, if so, it is important that the story be told as it has been by most African Nova Scotians: as a story about a particular place and a particular history, but also about a broader structure of anti-Black power that stretches across multiple places, time periods, and planning practices. The purpose of this book has been to trace this broader structure. Its primary contribution to discussions of anti-blackness and settler colonialism is thus to broaden the ways that the first of these two systems of power can be discussed.

Anti-Blackness and Planning Politics

A departure from current scholarly discussions of urban planning, this book also departs from many political discussions of the subject. In official venues, the connection between planning and racism is most often recognized – if it is recognized at all – in the form of state-conferred apologies for racist harms committed. In 2010, for example, the Halifax Regional Municipality (HRM) issued an official apology for the destruction of Africville in the 1960s. The apology, discussed in more detail below, expressed remorse for an action that, although never labelled "racist" in the text, uniquely and detrimentally affected racialized people. Similar apologies for similar incidents were issued around the same time in many North American cities. In the space of a few years, the City of Charlottesville, Virginia, apologized for the renewal-era destruction of the Black community of Vinegar Hill; the City of St Paul, Minnesota, issued an apology for the destruction of the Black community of Rondo in the same period; and Portland's Emanuel Medical Center apologized for the demolition of the Black community of Albina that, aided by the municipal and federal urban renewal funding, allowed the centre to expand.[7]

These apologies, specific to urban planning, are part of a broader and ongoing process through which state institutions express remorse for racist incidents. The Canadian federal government alone has issued at least ten official apologies since 1988, addressing racist incidents ranging from the expulsion of the Acadians in 1755 to the many injustices committed by Canada's Indigenous residential schools. As Henderson and Wakeham suggest, state-conferred apologies have become the dominant form through which racist actions gain attention and recompense in many white-majority countries.[8]

The HRM's apology for the destruction of Africville embodies the major features and limitations of state-conferred recognition of racist harms in general. The apology, issued in 2010, was expressed in a short text entitled, "Africville: Recognizing the Past, Present, and Future." In tandem with the written apology, the HRM committed $3 million towards the construction of a replica of Africville's Seaview Baptist Church in its original location and moved to create a new African Nova Scotian Affairs unit within the municipal bureaucracy. The written apology, though responding to decades of activism on the part of Africville displacees and other Black Nova Scotians, described the destruction of Africville in astonishingly narrow terms – much narrower than the terms typically adopted by Black activists. The apology asks for forgiveness for "what happened" in the 1960s. It apologizes, in particular, for the destruction of Africville homes and its church, as well as the resulting "disrupt[ion]" of Africville lives, feelings of "heartache," and other "distressing" consequences.[9] These consequences are attributed strictly to the city's decisions in the 1960s. No other decisions, earlier or later in time, are mentioned, and the only harms recognized outside the 1960s are indirect: the enduring "repercussions" and "lingering feelings of hurt and distrust" that the city's decisions in the 1960s spawned.

Although the apology was welcomed by some former Africville residents, it was seen as flawed and disingenuous by others. For Denise Allen, a Black activist and spokesperson for several Africville families, the apology was confined to an isolated action (i.e., the decision to demolish the community) and failed to address the broader, racist conditions that preceded and exceeded the action in question. For Allen, the narrowness of the official apology showed that the city, whatever its gestures towards the past, still did not "understand history." "They don't like history in Nova Scotia," she concluded.[10]

Without dismissing the favourable responses of some Africville residents to the municipal apology and associated measures – a response, however minuscule, to decades of struggle for *any* form of official recognition – it is important to trace the boundaries of the "recognition" that it provides. The work of the apology, like other recent apologies, was to isolate racism in space and time.[11] It was to treat the destruction of Africville in the 1960s as an event unique to this space and this time. There is no recognizable connection, as a result, between the destruction of Africville and the negation of Black lives in earlier periods, later periods, or elsewhere in the Halifax region. Nor is there any connection between anti-Black planning and the sustaining of other (white) lives. The work of the apology, in sum, was to create a minuscule injustice that could be recognized and, once recognized, transcended. "Our history cannot be rewritten," the apology concludes, "but, thankfully, the future is a blank page and, starting today, we hold the pen with which we can write a shared tomorrow."

The incredibly narrow terms through which racism gains recognition in official statements like this make it much harder, in the end, to address the perpetuation in the present of the problem recognized in the past. The imperative of official apologies, as Henderson and Wakeham suggest, is to express remorse and "move on," even as the conditions responsible for past harms generally persist. In Halifax, the persistence of anti-Black planning came to public attention a mere six months after the Africville apology. In this instance, a highway repair project in the Halifax periphery forced the Black residents of North Preston to endure a frustrating 7.6 kilometre detour, while the white residents of neighbouring Lake Major were provided special access to a shortcut that could have also served North Preston.[12] North Preston residents protested the decision and forced their municipal representative, Dave Hendsbee, to respond publicly. Speaking to the media, Hendsbee indicated how little he and the city had learned from the recent apology. He announced at this point that the city's decision to restrict access to the shortcut to the residents of Lake Major would be maintained and that the decision was a matter of "simple geography" and not "race."[13] "Geography" and "race" are thus two separate and distinct matters, despite everything the history of Africville should have taught Haligonians about the racist *shaping* of geography – lessons that Hendsbee, the political representative of the country's largest Black community, ought to have been well placed to learn.

Similar problems appeared in a host of other post-apology planning decisions. The official review of the Regional Plan, undertaken between 2012 and 2014, offered no greater recognition to the demands of peripheral Black communities, nor any attention to the role of historic and ongoing anti-Black racism in the creation of the landscape that the plan sought to regulate. Silenced during the 2001–6 regional planning process, the residents of Beechville, Upper Hammonds Plains, North Preston, and other Black communities were forced to repeat their earlier demands – to similarly unhearing planners.[14] The ongoing gentrification of the Halifax North End, meanwhile, is increasingly praised and actively promoted by city officials and bureaucrats. The displacement of the area's remaining Black residents, a process that ought to remind people of Africville, causes city officials no apparent concern. Nor has it cautioned them against suggesting that the ever-whitening North End is experiencing an all-encompassing "renaissance."[15] This, in sum, is what urban planning looks like in the aftermath of an apology that recognized racism as a particular incident and nothing more, an apology that located racism in a particular period and location, and then treated the city's future as a "blank" rather than racially inscribed "page."

The question, both scholarly and practical, is not only whether or not the effects of race and racism can be recognized but also *how* these effects are recognized. It takes no great strain, after all, to recognize that planning has committed harms against Black individuals and communities in certain moments. But what, precisely, is the material and discursive basis of these harms? How do these racial effects fit within a larger project? And what "positive" outcomes for other, non-Black lives might these harms enable and uphold?

To pose these questions is already to unsettle the narrow framework through which race and racism generally enter discussions of urban planning. Anti-blackness, I have argued in this book, may be observable in isolated incidents and locations, but its material basis and effects are much broader. There has never been a significant moment in which the lives of Black people have been recognized as full, normative lives by modern planning. There has never been a moment, moreover, in which the eviction of blackness from the sphere of recognized humanity has not given shape and purpose to planning's *general* operation, its operation across the entire surface and population of the city. The scope of anti-blackness has no clear temporal or geographical limits, and there is no apology, confined to a definable moment or location, that can make amends for it. Anti-blackness has helped to make the modern city and modern life. Recognizing this, viewing anti-blackness in these broader terms, forces a consideration of bigger, broader changes. And it might just make it possible to create a future that is something other than a repetition of the past.

Another Planning, Another Future

Visions of a different future are everywhere in prevailing discussions of urban planning. Not since the 1950s, indeed, has the imperative to revisit and radically remake accepted forms of city making been so widely trumpeted and accepted. For the most part, these imperatives are tied to the recognition of intensifying and potentially (human) extinction-causing ecological crises. Problems like climate change and resource depletion are partly urban problems, it is recognized, and efforts to address these problems are bound to be inadequate to the extent that urban living and urban planning are not radically reconfigured. The most prevalent future-oriented planning doctrines, consequently, seek to curtail the consumption of fossil fuels and other resources through more efficient and efficiency-inducing forms of development. At the regional scale, these efforts involve subtle variations on the growth-management strategies that informed the Halifax Regional Plan.[16] Denser, less dispersed forms of development are prioritized in these doctrines on the grounds that they consume less land; require less transportation between places of work, residence, and leisure; and enable various forms of public and shared transportation. At the central-city scale, these efforts generally include densification, mixed-use zoning, and the promotion of active (nonautomobile) transportation. In many cases, they also entail changes in urban design meant to attune cities to the fine grain of urban behaviour. The aim of these changes in design, as expressed in Jan Gehl's seminal planning treatise, is to produce physical forms that have been shown (through research) to promote more ecological, enjoyable, and convivial urban lifestyles.[17]

The problems that these planning doctrines seek to address are pressing ones. It is hard to imagine these problems being addressed, moreover, without implementing something like the physical changes they advocate. At their core, however, these doctrines are fully consistent with the form of planning I have critiqued in this book. In the first case, regional-scale ecological impacts are severed from the unequal social relations in which they are produced. The assumed source of these impacts is thus a standard, universal actor: an individual or household whose lifestyle choices ostensibly produce better or worse outcomes. Like the 2006 Regional Plan in Halifax, this perspective occludes the reasons that differently situated groups might make the same "choice" (e.g., living in dispersed, peripheral communities because, centuries earlier, there was no choice). It also leads to undifferentiated planning protocols that, while potentially reducing region-wide ecological impacts, may differentially harm already subjugated populations. In the second case, central-city lifestyles and *experiences* are severed from social relations. Jan Gehl's otherwise intriguing urban vision preserves the long-standing planning assumption that a single line can be drawn between spatial conditions and people's experience of these conditions. Like so many planning propositions since the 1960s, therefore, Gehl's work normalizes certain experiences of spatial conditions and occludes the ways that particular groups, due to their social position, may be barred from these conditions or experience them very differently. Thus, these future-oriented planning doctrines helpfully outline a physically different city but fail to move past the social forms and normative logics of the present.

The same failure occurs, ironically, in future-oriented visions that prioritize social transformation. Susan Fainstein's widely recognized vision of a "just city," for example, helpfully rebukes today's planners for overseeing the neoliberalization of urban regions and aiding in the creation of ever-vaster social inequalities. She also urges planners to recognize the "structural relationships" that exist between different groups and the differential access that groups might have to valued public spaces and venues (i.e., the lack of access available to certain groups).[18] Despite this attention to group-level specificities and inequalities, however, her vision ultimately attributes the same political form to all groups. All groups become, in effect, the bearers of shared interests or values that must somehow be reconciled with those of others. Like Saul Alinsky and the experts at Halifax's 1970 Encounter Week event, Fainstein explicitly pathologizes unduly narrow political interests; argues that all groups must "transcend their own narrow self-interest" to find common ground with other groups; and warns against political aims that would unduly deprive dominant groups of their privileges.[19] Indeed, her advice almost perfectly mirrors that of the Encounter Week expert Ed Logue – who intended to *quell* movements for social transformation – when she claims that the key "to moving toward greater equity … is to devise ways of mitigating the adverse effect on those forced to give up a great deal."[20] Fainstein's vision of the future, though helpfully prioritizing social justice, perpetuates the normalization of particular, common-ground-finding political behaviours and reaffirms the very questionable role that planners have often claimed since the 1960s: that of reconciling between normatively constituted interests and values.

For a vision of the future that is something more than the repetition of the past, I find it useful to look towards the long history of Black struggle and the handful of planning scholars and advocates who have sought to translate this history into a planning lexicon.[21] This entails a look towards the past, indeed. But it is a past that was never treated as legitimate and so, in a sense, was never incorporated into any present. Particularly instructive, I think, are BUF's efforts to articulate an urban future outside of prevailing political structures and ontologies. In the face of institutions and conceptions of the human that were developed to subjugate Black people, BUF did not seek inclusion or accommodation. Nor did it seek solidarity with more privileged groups on equal terms (i.e., on the basis of "common" interests that sidelined BUF's core interests). Rather, it insisted on the validity of Black lives and desires as they existed; it fought to diminish planning's control over Black communities; and it implemented a set of planning initiatives that allowed Black people to define their future and work with others to bring it into being. A major risk in this work was that a unitary Black subject, a blackened but still normalizing conception of the human, would become the focus of BUF's efforts. At its best, however, BUF recognized the differences, social inequalities, and power differentials that existed among Black people and devised planning initiatives, in at least a few cases, that explicitly favoured the more marginalized members of the Black population.

A similar vision of social transformation has been articulated many times since the early days of BUF. Most recently, the Black Lives Matter (BLM) movement has reconstituted some of the best elements of the Black radical tradition. BLM, though centred in the United States, has spawned formal chapters and BLM-inspired groups in cities around the world, including Halifax. The major focus of the movement is, of course, eradicating police violence. At the same time, it has organized around a much broader set of objectives, which include better housing, a guaranteed minimum income, free health care and postsecondary education, and radically demilitarized foreign policy.[22] In some cases, these objectives are directly relevant to urban planning. In other cases, the political logic behind the demands is relevant. BLM, like BUF in an earlier time, confronts anti-blackness with its un-incorporable antithesis: the resolute centring of Black lives and demands. It recognizes that to arrive at a future in which all lives matter equally, it is necessary to treat Black lives unequally (i.e., with greater priority than others) in the present. In doing so, importantly, BLM seeks to recognize and overturn a whole set of power differentials among Black people. It aims, in the words of a 2016 platform, to "elevat[e] the experiences and leadership of the most marginalized Black people, including but not limited to those who are women, queer, trans, femmes, gender nonconforming, Muslim, formerly or currently incarcerated, cash poor and working class, disabled, undocumented, and immigrant."[23] The liberation of all Black people, the platform claims, begins with the liberation of the most pathologized and subjugated Black people.

There are clear lessons here for today's urban planners and other municipal officials. The urban future envisioned by BUF and BLM is not reducible to a set of physical forms or quantifiable outcomes. Nor does it entail a universal conception of what human life is or should become. Instead, it shows how the process of city making, including the process through which the meaning of a viable life is defined, can be radically altered. In broad terms, these groups envision an almost total break with the prevailing form of modern planning and modern state power. Whereas modern planning has incessantly displaced blackness from the field of its concerns, and often from physical space as well, BUF and BLM seek to move blackness to the centre. White normativity, in this move, is dissolved both as the standard against which people's lives are evaluated and as the ideal condition that, through coercive planning interventions, people's lives might one day attain. In more practical terms, BUF and BLM call for existing authorities to cede the human and physical terrain they have claimed. They seek to end the ongoing process through which planning simultaneously assumes jurisdiction over Black lives, on the one hand, and evicts these lives from any desirable future, on the other. For state officials to heed these calls would mean moving immediately to redistribute existing planning authority and resources. This would involve, at a minimum, vesting decision-making authority in Black communities; diverting planning-related moneys and technical expertise towards Black decision-making processes; and treating as illegitimate any municipal planning decision *not* made by Black people that significantly impacts their lives.

There are lessons for planners here. But, then, there have always been lessons, and it has never been for lack of knowledge or clearly articulated Black demands that planners have produced the anti-Black outcomes that they have. More likely and ultimately more desirable than a self-directed change of perspective among professional planners and state officials is the creation of an extra-state movement that would bring about these changes through its own power. Indeed, BLM's vision of a radically different future is addressed less to state officials than to everyday people. Its vision is an invitation for people to join in a struggle that, while centring Black leadership and experiences, also seeks to eliminate all other forms of oppression. How BLM perceives the relationship between different forms of oppression is not entirely clear. What is clear is that BLM activists are not promoting an Alinsky-style alliance in which everyone's interests are seen as equivalent and the interests of more privileged groups are placed beyond challenge. Some forms of oppression, for BLM, are clearly graver than others, and they need to be prioritized in social struggle both because of their gravity and because of their symbolic role in sustaining other, less horrific forms of oppression (i.e., by defining a kind of pathology that can always be attributed, to a lesser extent, to other groups). Guided by this logic, BLM activists have forged their strongest relations of solidarity with groups whose experience of systemic oppression, dehumanization, and violence comes the closest to their own.[24]

What is most clear is that there cannot be a different future so long as relatively normative white people cling to their own status quo. This status quo, this life that modern planning has secured, is an obstruction to social transformation, even when its preservation is pursued in the context of a social movement that affirms non-white lives and interests as well. A different future, in other words, requires white people to do more than support or even prioritize others' interests. It requires them, it requires me, to leave our place within the boundaries of a humanity that has always depended for its coherence on the displacement and dehumanization of others. It requires us to refuse the ostensibly better life that planning and other technologies of power have offered us at enormous expense to others. The benefits of this life have never been, and can never be, universally distributed; they are predicted on exclusivity, violently defended.[25] For white people to act against anti-blackness, as Christina Sharpe suggests, is to leave the terrain of recognized humanity. "One must be willing to be more than uncomfortable," she writes. "One must be willing to be on the outside."[26] On the "outside," a place that Sharpe notes "some of us have never had any other choice" but to inhabit, an entirely different and genuinely better form of life might be created. A new form of urban planning, one released from its centuries-old connection to race and power, will be created here or nowhere.

Notes

1 Introduction

1 On the settlement of Halifax, see Jeffers Lennox, "An Empire on Paper: The Founding of Halifax and Conceptions of Imperial Space, 1744–55," *Canadian Historical Review* 88, no. 3 (2007): 373–412; Leslie Upton, *Mimacs and Colonists: Indian-White Relations in the Maritimes, 1713–1867* (Vancouver: University of British Columbia Press, 1979); Thomas Barnes, "'As Near As May Be Agreeable to the Laws of this Kingdom': Legal Birthright and Legal Baggage at Chebucto, 1749," *Dalhousie Law Journal* 8 (1984): 1–23.

2 Daniel Paul, *We Were Not the Savages: A Micmac Perspective on the Collision of European and Aboriginal Civilizations* (Halifax: Nimbus Press, 1993); Eric Adams, "Ghosts in the Court: Jonathan Belcher and the Proclamation of 1762," *Dalhousie Law Journal* 27, no. 2 (2004): 321–46.

3 The attack on Halifax is described in Barnes, "As Near As May Be Agreeable," 4. On later Mi'kmaq attacks on Halifax and Dartmouth, see Upton, *Micmacs and Colonists*. The quotes (from the Scalping Proclamation) appear in Paul, *We Were Not the Savages*, 108.

4 Adams, "Ghosts in the Court," 331.

5 The first significant use of the term "modern" by a Halifax mayor occurred in a 1901 address to city council, where councillors were urged to support municipal investments in infrastructure like sewerage and water mains. Thereafter, the term became increasingly used by the city, the business community, and citizens at large. City of Halifax, Minutes of the Council of the City of Halifax,, 8 May 1901, Halifax Regional Municipality Archives (HRMA), RG 102–1A, 7.

6 Halifax Local Council of Women (HCW), Minutes of the Local Council of Women, 1894–2002, 12 March 1906, Nova Scotia Archives and Records

Management (NSARM), MG 20, vol. 535, no. 5; Halifax, City Council Minutes, 30 April 1908, RG 102–1A, 365; City of Halifax, *The Master Plan for the City of Halifax As Prepared by the Civic Planning Commission* (Halifax: City of Halifax, 1945), 46.

7 A Foucauldian approach to urban planning is best exemplified in Paul Rabinow, *French Modern: Norms and Forms of the Social Environment* (Chicago: University of Chicago Press, 1995). I provide an extensive review and critique of the Foucauldian planning literature in Ted Rutland, "Enjoyable Life: Planning, Amenity, and the Contested Terrain of Urban Biopolitics," *Environment and Planning D: Society and Space* 24 (2015): 850–68.

8 The seminal literature on urban planning, focused on professional planners, includes Mel Scott, *American City Planning Since 1890: A History Commemorating the Fiftieth Anniversary of the American Institute of Planners* (Berkeley: University of California Press, 1971); Peter Hall, *Cities of Tomorrow: An Intellectual History of Urban Planning and Design in the Twentieth Century* (New York: Wiley-Blackwell, 2002). A broader approach to planning can be found in works of urban, social, and cultural history, as well as heterodox planning histories (that focus on the contributions of nondominant populations). See, for example, Mary Poovey, *Making a Social Body: British Cultural Formation, 1830–1864* (Chicago: University of Chicago Press, 1995), especially 75–99; June Manning Thomas and Marsha Ritzdorf, eds., *Urban Planning and the African American Community: In the Shadows* (Thousand Oaks: Sage Publications, 1997); Leonie Sandercock, ed., *Making the Invisible Visible: A Multicultural Planning History* (Berkeley: University of California Press, 1998).

9 Seminal contributions to the critical literature on urban planning that affirm the profession's role in creating a higher "quality of life" include Hall, *Cities of Tomorrow*, 424; Manuel Castells, *Crisis, Planning, and the Quality of Life* (Berkeley: Institute of Urban and Regional Development, 1982), 12, 19; Harvey Molotch, "The City as a Growth Machine: Toward a Political Economy of Place," *American Journal of Sociology* 82, no. 2 (1976): 320; David Harvey, "From Managerialism to Entrepreneurialism: The Transformation in Urban Governance in Late Capitalism," *Geografiska Annaler, Series B* 71, no. 1 (1989): 9; Leonie Sandercock, *Towards Cosmopolis: Planning for Multicultural Cities* (New York: Wiley, 1998), 146; Raphaël Fischler, "Planning for Social Betterment: From Standard of Living to Quality of Life," in *Urban Planning in a Changing World: The Twentieth Century Experience*, ed. Robert Freestone (New York: Taylor and Francis, 2000), 139–57.

10 The most instructive contributions to the literature on Africville include Donald Clairmont and Dennis Magill, *Africville Relocation Report* (Halifax: Institute of Public Affairs, 1971); Donald Clairmont and Dennis Magill,

Africville: The Life and Death of a Canadian Black Community (Toronto: Canadian Scholars' Press, 1999); Mount Saint Vincent Art Gallery, ed., *Africville: A Spirit That Lives On,* (Halifax: Black Cultural Centre for Nova Scotia, Africville Genealogy Society, and National Film Board, 1989); Jennifer Nelson, *Razing Africville: A Geography of Racism* (Toronto: University of Toronto Press, 2008); Mary Vincer, "A History of Marginalization – Africville: A Canadian Example of Forced Migration" (master's thesis, Ryerson University, 2008).

11 Clarke's most important poems, essays, and interviews include *Saltwater Spirituals and Deeper Blues* (Porter's Lake, NS: Pottersfield Press, 1983); *Whylah Falls* (Vancouver: Raincoast Books, 2000); "Treason of the Black Intellectuals?" (paper presented as the Third Annual Seagram Lecture, McGill Institute for the Study of Canada, Montréal, 4 November 1998); Christine McNair, "Boisterous, Raucous, Lush, and Colourful: An Interview with George Elliott Clarke," in *Omnibus: The Annual Gaspereau Press Reader* (Kentville, NS: Gaspereau Press, 2001), 18–21. Sylvia Hamilton, best known for her film-making, is the author of several important works on African Nova Scotian history, including "Naming Names, Naming Ourselves: A Survey of Early Black Women in Nova Scotia," in *We're Rooted Here and They Can't Pull Us Up: Essays in African Canadian Women's History,* ed. Peggy Bristow (Toronto: University of Toronto Press, 1994), 13–40; "African Baptist Women as Activists and Advocates in Adult Education in Nova Scotia" (master's thesis, Dalhousie University, 2000); "A Daughter's Journey," *Canadian Women's Studies* 23, no. 2 (2004): 6–12.

12 McNair, "Boisterous, Raucous, Lush, and Colourful," 18.

13 Estimates of Halifax's (and Nova Scotia's) Black population in the first two-thirds of the twentieth century vary widely; the Canadian Census figures are far from a reliable source. Walker suggests a total for Nova Scotia of twenty thousand in the 1960s, while the activists that appear in his work estimated the Black population of the greater Halifax area to be roughly fifteen thousand. James W. StG. Walker, "Black Confrontation in Sixties Halifax," in *Debating Dissent: Canada and the Sixties,* ed. Lara Campbell, Dominique Clément, and Gregory Kealey (Toronto: University of Toronto Press, 2012), 316n1. The Statistics Canada Census of the Population puts the total Black population in 2006 at 13,500, certainly an understatement.

14 The seminal contribution on the relationship between "the broad-based" and "the particular" is Cindy Katz, "On the Grounds of Globalization: A Topography for Feminist Political Engagements," *Signs* 26, no. 4 (2001): 1213–34. See also Doreen Massey, *Space, Place, and Gender* (Minneapolis: University of Minnesota Press, 1994); Geraldine Pratt and Victoria Rosner,

eds., *The Global and the Intimate: Feminism in Our Time* (New York: Columbia University Press, 2012).

15 These two tendencies are visible, respectively, in Nelson, *Razing Africville* and Donald Clairmont, "Review of Jennifer J. Nelson, *Razing Africville*," *Canadian Journal of Sociology* 34, no. 3 (2009): 920–2. The broader problem of reducing race to class in studies of urban renewal is discussed in Robert Gioielli, "'We Must Destroy You to Save You': Highway Construction and the City As a Modern Commons," *Radical History Review* 109 (2011): 67.

16 Estimates of the precontact Mi'kmaw population vary widely, from as low as three thousand to as high as one hundred thousand. See, regarding the lower figures, Wilson Wallis and Ruth Sawtell Wallis, *The Micmac Indians of Eastern Canada* (Minneapolis: University of Minnesota Press, 1955), 17; regarding the higher figures, Virginia Miller, "Aboriginal Micmac Population: A Review of the Evidence," *Ethnohistory* 23, no. 2 (1976): 117–27; Paul, *We Were Not the Savages*, 5. A general overview is provided in John Daniels, "The Indian Population of North America in 1492," *William and Mary Quarterly* 49, no. 2 (1992): 298–320.

17 Important restrictions on nonreserve Indigenous life are discussed in Paul, *We Were Not the Savages*, 221 (marriage), 211 (education), and 280 (employment). Other restrictions are discussed throughout the book.

18 Joy James, "Democracy and Captivity," in *The New Abolitionists: (Neo)Slave Narratives and Contemporary Prison Writings* (Albany: SUNY Press, 2005), xxv.

19 The seminal Marxist work on urban planning includes David Harvey, "On Planning the Ideology of Planning," in *Planning for the '80s: Challenge and Response*, ed. Robert Burchell and George Sternlieb (New Brunswick, NJ: Center for Urban Policy Research, 1978), 213–33; David Harvey, *The Condition of Postmodernity: An Enquiry into the Origins of Cultural Change* (New York: Blackwell, 1991); Michael Dear and Allen Scott, eds., *Urbanization and Urban Planning in Capitalist Society* (New York: Taylor and Francis, 1981); Robert Foglesong, *Planning the Capitalist City: American Urban Planning from the Colonial Era to the 1920s* (Princeton: Princeton University Press, 1986). For a review, see Kevin Gotham, "Urban Redevelopment: Past and Present," in *Critical Perspectives on Urban Redevelopment*, ed. Kevin Gotham (New York: Emerald Group Publishing, 2001), 1–31.

20 See James Scott, *Seeing Like a State: How Certain Schemes to Improve the Human Condition Have Failed* (New Haven: Yale University Press, 1999), 53–84. A similar view is outlined in Christine Boyer, *Dreaming the Rational City: The Myth of American City Planning* (Cambridge, MA: MIT Press, 1986). This foundational work informs many influential critiques of urban planning and propositions for its renovation, including Leonie Sandercock,

Cosmopolis II: Mongrel Cities of the 21st Century (New York: Continuum, 2003), especially 13–36; Robert Beauregard, "The Multiplicities of Planning," *Journal of Planning Education and Research* 20, no. 4 (2001): 437–9.

21 On the figure of the human in European thought, see Michel Foucault, *The Order of Things: An Archaeology of the Human Sciences* (New York: Routledge, 1970). The term "biopower" is introduced in *The History of Sexuality, Vol I: An Introduction* (New York: Random House, 1978). The term "critical ontology" is suggested in "What is Enlightenment?" in *The Foucault Reader*, ed. Paul Rabinow (New York: Pantheon Books, 1984), 50. Ian Hacking outlines this approach (substituting "historical" for "critical") in *Historical Ontology* (Cambridge, MA: Harvard University Press, 2004).

22 See Michel Foucault, *Birth of the Clinic: An Archaeology of Medical Perception* (New York: Routledge, 1973), 41; Nikolas Rose, "Identity, Genealogy, History," in *Questions of Cultural Identity*, ed. Stuart Hall and Paul du Gay (Thousand Oaks: Sage Publications, 1996), 128–50; Mary Beth Mader, *Sleights of Reason: Norm, Biosexuality, Development* (Albany: SUNY Press, 2011), 43–69.

23 Michel Foucault *"Society Must be Defended": Lectures at the Collège de France, 1975–1976* (New York: Picador, 2003), 239–64.

24 Michel Foucault, *Security, Territory, Population: Lectures at the Collège de France, 1977–1978* (New York: Picador, 2007), 22–3.

25 For a review of Foucauldian work on urban planning, see Rutland, "Enjoyable Life."

26 Rabinow, *French Modern*.

27 David Harvey, "From Managerialism to Entrepreneurialism," 16; *Condition of Postmodernity*, 70.

28 See, in particular, Sandercock, *Cosmopolis II*, 181–230. For a critique, see Kanishka Goonewardena, "Urban Studies, Critical Theory, Radical Politics: Eight Theses for Peter Marcuse," *City* 13, no. 2–3 (2009): 208–18.

29 This line of critique is developed in Anne Stoler, *Race and the Education of Desire: Foucault's History of Sexuality and the Colonial Order of Things* (Durham: Duke University Press, 1995); Brady Heiner, "Foucault and the Black Panthers," *City* 11, no. 3 (2007): 313–56; Alex Weheliye, *Habeas Viscus: Racializing Assemblages, Biopolitics, and Black Feminist Theories of the Human* (Durham: Duke University Press, 2014).

30 The seminal works in this extensive and fast-developing literature include Frantz Fanon, *Black Skin, White Masks* (New York: Grove Press, 1968); Katherine McKittrick, *Demonic Grounds: Black Women and the Cartographies of Struggle* (Minneapolis: University of Minnesota Press, 2006); Rinaldo Walcott, "The Problem of the Human: Black Ontologies and the 'Coloniality of Our Being,'" in *Postcoloniality – Decoloniality – Black Critique: Joints and Fissures*, ed.

Sabine Broeck and Carsten Junker (New York: Campus Verlag, 2014), 93–105; Sylvia Wynter, "Unsettling the Coloniality of Being/Power/Truth/Freedom: Towards the Human, After Man, Its Overrepresentation – An Argument," *New Centennial Review* 3, no. 3 (2003): 257–337; Saidiya Hartman, *Scenes of Subjection: Terror, Slavery, and Self-Making in Nineteenth-Century America* (Oxford: Oxford University Press, 1997); Jared Sexton, "The Social Life of Social Death: On Afro-Pessimism and Black Optimism," *InTensions* 5 (2011): 1–47; Frank Wilderson, *Red, White, and Black: Cinema and the Structure of US Antagonisms* (Durham: Duke University Press, 2010); Rashad Shabazz, *Spatializing Blackness: Architectures of Confinement and Black Masculinity in Chicago* (Chicago: University of Illinois Press, 2015).

31 This explanation is my synthesis of Hartman, *Scenes of Subjection*, 56–7; Ruth Wilson Gilmore, "Fatal Couplings of Power and Difference: Notes on Geography and Racism," *The Professional Geographer* 54, no. 1 (2002): 22; and Jared Sexton, *Amalgamation Schemes: Antiblackness and the Critique of Multiracialism* (Minneapolis: University of Minnesota Press, 2008), 1–42.

32 This history is most clearly traced in Wynter, "Unsettling the Coloniality of Being." The qualities of reason, conscience, and sentiment, and the denial that they existed among Black/enslaved people is emphasized in Hartman, *Scenes of Subjection*, 5.

33 Walcott, "Problem of the Human," 93 (emphasis mine). The insistence that Black people make social lives in and sometimes against enforced conditions of social, civic, and physical death appears throughout the literature on anti-blackness. See, for example, Clyde Woods, *Development Arrested: The Blues and Plantation Power in the Mississippi Delta* (New York: Verso, 1998); Wilson Gilmore, "Fatal Couplings," 15–24; Zenzele Isoke, *Urban Black Women and the Politics of Resistance* (New York: Palgrave Macmillan, 2013).

34 Sylvia Wynter, "On Disenchanting Discourse: 'Minority' Literary Criticism and Beyond," in *The Nature and Context of Minority Discourse*, ed. Abdul Jan Mohamed and David Loyd (Oxford: Oxford University Press, 1990), 222.

35 Lewis Gordon, *Existentia Africana: Understanding Africana Existential Thought* (New York: Routledge, 2000), 87.

36 An important exception is the work of Katherine McKittrick, which begins to interrogate anti-blackness not simply in the conception and management of Black spaces but also in dominant spatial representations writ large, a formation that she terms "rational cartographies of domination; *Demonic Grounds*, x. As I have suggested, the cartographies that guided planning in the twentieth century were not always "rational," but McKittrick's invitation to locate anti-blackness within dominant spatialities is a touchstone of this book.

37 On other "genres" of the human, see Wynter "Unsettling the Coloniality of Being" and Sylvia Wynter and Katherine McKittrick, "Unparalleled Catastrophe for Our Species? Or, to Give Humanness a Different Future: Conversations," in *Sylvia Wynter: On Being Human as Praxis*, ed. Katherine McKittrick (Durham: Duke University Press, 2015), 9–89.

2 "Higher Living through Environment": The Reformers, the Slums, and the Emergence of Modern Urban Planning

1 *Halifax Evening Mail*, 5 February 1905.

2 On the reform era and efforts to create a "higher" (healthier and more moral) form of life in Britain, see Anthony Wohl, *The Eternal Slum: Housing and Social Policy in Victorian London* (New Brunswick, NJ: Transaction Publishers, 2002); Robin Evans, "Rookeries and Model Dwellings: English Housing Reform and the Moralities of Private Space," *Architectural Association Quarterly* 10, no. 1 (1978): 24–35. In the United States, see Roy Lubove, *The Progressives and the Slums: Tenement House Reform in New York City, 1890–1917* (Pittsburgh: University of Pittsburgh Press, 1963). In Canada, see Mariana Valverde, "The City as a Moral Problem," in *The Age of Light, Soap, and Water: Moral Reform in English Canada, 1885–1925* (Toronto: University of Toronto Press, 2008); Alan Hunt, *Governing Morals: A Social History of Moral Regulation* (Cambridge: Cambridge University Press, 1999). The rise of environmentalism is discussed in Felix Driver "Moral Geographies: Social Science and the Urban Environment in Mid-Nineteenth Century England," *Transactions of the Institute of British Geographers* 13, no. 3 (1988): 275–87; Stephen Legg, "Planning Social Hygiene: From Contamination to Contagion in Interwar India," in *Imperial Contagions: Medicine, Hygiene, and Cultures of Planning in Asia*, ed. Robert Peckham and David Pomfret (Hong Kong: Hong Kong University Press, 2013), 105–22; Mitchell Dean, "'A Social Structure of Many Souls': Moral Regulation, Government, and Self-Formation," *Canadian Journal of Sociology* 19, no. 2 (2994): 145–68. The connection between environmentalism and urban planning, usually overlooked, receives a full treatment in Paul Rabinow, *French Modern: Norms and Forms of the Social Environment* (Chicago: University of Chicago Press, 1995).

3 The role of norms in structuring environmentalist perspectives and interventions is stressed in Rabinow, *French Modern*. Rabinow's analysis (and mine) draws significantly on Michel Foucault, *Birth of the Clinic: An Archaeology of Medical Perception* (New York: Routledge, 1973); Michel Foucault, *Discipline and Punish* (New York: Vintage, 1977).

4 On reform-era social transformation in US cities, see Lubove, *Progressives and the Slums*; S. Hays, "The Politics of Reform in Municipal Government in the Progressive Era," *The Pacific Northwest Quarterly*, 55 (1964): 157–69. In Canada, see Paul Rutherford, "Tomorrow's Metropolis: The Urban Reform Movement in Canada," *Historical Papers* 6, no. 1 (1971): 203–24; John Weaver, "Tomorrow's Metropolis Revisited: A Critical Assessment of Urban Reform in Canada, 1890–1920," in *The Canadian City: Essays in Urban History*, ed. Gilbert Stelter and Alan Artibise (Toronto: University of Toronto Press, 1977), 393–418; Valverde, *Age of Light*. Halifax population growth and the (limited) effects of immigration is outlined in Judith Fingard, Janet Guildford, and David Sutherland, *Halifax: The First 250 Years* (Halifax: Formac Press, 1999), 67–116; Larry McCann, "The 1890s: Fragmentation and the New Social Order," in *The Atlantic Provinces in Confederation*, ed. E.R. Forbes and D.A. Muise (Toronto: University of Toronto Press, 1993). Irish immigration to Halifax is discussed in Donald MacKay, *Flight from Famine: The Coming of the Irish to Canada* (Toronto: Dundurn Press, 1991), 321. The city's ethnic composition in 1871 is presented in Fingard et al., *Halifax*, 70. Its composition in 1901 is drawn from Government of Canada, *Fourth Census of Canada, Volume I: Population* (Ottawa: S.E. Dawson, 1902), 302–3.

5 The transformation of the Halifax (and Maritimes) economy in this period is discussed, seminally, in T.W. Acheson, "The National Policy and the Industrialization of the Maritimes, 1880–1910," *Acadiensis* 1, no. 2 (1972): 3–28; Gregory Marchildon, "John F. Stairs, Max Aitken, and the Scotia Group: Finance Capitalism and Industrial Decline in the Maritimes, 1890–1914," in *Farm, Factory, and Fortune: New Studies in the Economic History of the Maritime Provinces*, ed. Kris Inwood (Fredericton: Acadiensis Press, 1993), 197–218; David Sutherland, "Halifax 1815–1914: Colony to Colony," *Urban History Review* 4 (1975): 7–11. On the Sugar Refinery and Cotton Company, see Paul Erickson, *Halifax's North End: An Anthropologist Looks at the City* (Halifax: Lancelot Press, 1986), 47. On the shipyards, Victor Settie, "Halifax Shipyards, 1918–1978: An Historical Perspective" (master's thesis, Saint Mary's University, Halifax, 1994), 19–32. On industry in general, see Fingard et al. *Halifax*, 92–116.

6 The industrialization of Pictou, New Glasgow, and Sydney is detailed in Colin Howell, "The 1900s: Industry, Urbanization, and Reform," in *The Atlantic Provinces*, ed. E.R. Forbes and D.A. Muise (Toronto: University of Toronto Press, 1993), 155–91. On the development of the Halifax financial sector, see Christopher Armstrong, "Making a Market: Selling Securities in Atlantic Canada before World War I," *Canadian Journal of Economics* 13 (1980): 438–54; James Frost, *Merchant Princes: Halifax's First Family of*

Finance, Ships, and Steel (Toronto: James Lorimer and Company, 2003); Marchildon, "John F. Stairs."

7 Halifax Board of Trade, Annual Report 1899, MFM #12400, reel 6, Nova Scotia Archives and Records Management (NSARM), 7.

8 Ian McKay, "Class Struggle and Mercantile Capitalism: Craftsmen and Labourers on the Halifax Waterfront, 1850–1902," in *Working Men Who Got Wet: Proceedings of the Fourth Conference of the Atlantic Canada Shipping Project*, ed. Rosemary Ommer and Gerald Panting (St John's, NL: Maritime History Group, Memorial University of Newfoundland, 1980), 287–321. See Fingard, "From Sea to Rail: Black Transportation Workers and Their Families in Halifax, c. 1870–1916," *Acadiensis* 24, no. 2 (1995): 49–64; Suzanne Morton, "Separate Spheres in a Separate World: African-Nova Scotian Women in Late-19th-Century Halifax County," *Acadiensis* 12, no. 2 (1993): 61–83; Christina Simmons, "'Helping the Poorer Sisters': The Women of the Jost Mission, Halifax, 1905–1945," *Acadiensis* 14, no. 1 (1984): 3–27; Ian McKay, *The Craft Transformed: An Essay on the Carpenters of Halifax, 1885–1985* (Halifax: Lorimer and Company, 1985).

9 Sharon Myers, "'I Can Manage My Own Business Affairs': Female Industrial Workers in Halifax at the Turn of the Twentieth Century" (master's thesis, Saint Mary's University, 1989), 18, 41–2. See also Ian McKay, "Labour in the Halifax Baking and Confectionery Industry during the Last Half of the Nineteenth Century," *Labour/Le Travail* 3 (1978): 63–108; Simmons, "'Helping the Poorer Sisters.'"

10 Quoted in McKay, "Class Struggle," 293.

11 Myers, "I Can Manage," 31.

12 The construction of Georgian mansions in the South End is described in Susan Buggey, "Building Halifax, 1841–1871," *Acadiensis* 10, no. 1 (1980): 90–112. Reform-era social conditions in the upper streets are described in David Hood, *Down but Not Out: Community and the Upper Streets in Halifax, 1890–1914* (Halifax: Fernwood Publishing, 2010). The area's changing ethnic composition is traced in David Sutherland "Race Relations in Halifax, Nova Scotia, During the Mid-Victorian Quest for Reform," *Journal of the Canadian Historical Association* 7 (1996): 35–54; Owen Carrigan, "The Immigrant Experience in Halifax, 1881–1931," *Canadian Ethnic Studies* 20, no. 3 (1988): 28–41.

13 The middle-class character of the reform movement in Canada is emphasized in Rutherford, "Tomorrow's Metropolis"; Linda Kealy, *Enlisting Women for the Cause: Women, Labour, and the Left in Canada, 1890–1920* (Toronto: University of Toronto Press, 1998); Wayne Roberts, "'Rocking the Cradle for the World': The New Woman and Maternal Feminism, Toronto, 1877–1914," in *A Not Unreasonable Claim: Women and Reform in Canada, 1880s–1920s*, ed. Linda Kealey (Toronto: Women's Educational Press, 1979),

15–46. The reform efforts of the Board of Trade are documented in David Sutherland, "The Personnel and Policies of the Halifax Board of Trade, 1890–1914," in *The Enterprising Canadians: Entrepreneurs and Economic Development in Eastern Canada*, ed. L.R. Fischer and E.W. Sager (St John's, NL: Memorial University of Newfoundland, 1979), 203–29; Henry Roper, "The Halifax Board of Control: The Failure of Municipal Reform, 1906–1919," *Acadiensis* 14, no. 2 (1985): 46–65.

14 Armitage's career is described in Reginald Harris, *The Church of Saint Paul in Halifax, Nova Scotia, 1749–1949* (Toronto: Ryerson Press, 1949); Sarah Emsley, *St. Paul's in the Grand Parade, 1749–1999* (Halifax: Formac Publishing, 1999). On his contributions to the Evangelical movement in Canada, see George Rawlyk, *Aspects of the Canadian Evangelical Experience* (Montréal and Kingston: McGill-Queen's University Press, 1997), 176–7.

15 The HCW and its leadership in this period are described in Janet Guildford, *The Magnificent Services of Women: The Halifax Local Council of Women, 1894–2002* (Halifax: Oxford Street Press, 2002); Ernest Forbes, "Battles in Another War: Edith Archibald and the Halifax Feminist Movement," in *Challenging the Regional Stereotype: Essays on the 20th Century Maritimes* (Fredericton: University of New Brunswick Press, 1989), 67–90. Eliza Ritchie is discussed in Mary Creese and Thomas Creese, *Ladies in the Laboratory III: South African, Australian, New Zealand, and Canadian Women in Science* (Lanham, MD: Scarecrow Press, 2010), 192.

16 The HCW's dependence on domestic service was signalled frequently in its discussions, e.g., HCW, Minutes, 21 November 1907, NSARM, MG 20, vol. 535, no. 5. The share of domestic servants in the overall female workforce is stated in Simmons, "Helping the Poorer."

17 On the cholera outbreak, see Geoffrey Bilson and Patricia Bailey, "Cholera," in *Canadian Encyclopedia*, article published 18 May 1909, accessed 6 February 2016, http://www.thecanadianencyclopedia.ca/en/article/cholera. Tuberculosis cases are documented in Allan Mortan, *The Official Bicentennial Guide Book* (Halifax: City of Halifax, 1949). The 1890–1 diphtheria outbreak is documented in David Sutherland, "Diphtheria and the Doctors: The Halifax Epidemic of 1890–91," *Journal of the Royal Nova Scotia Historical Society* 15 (2012): 44–60.

18 The creation of the board of health was authorized by an act of the provincial legislature in 1888. The act, and the nomination of the board's first members, appears in City of Halifax, Minutes of the Council of the City of Halifax, 8 January 1889, Halifax Regional Municipality Archives (HRMA), RG 35-102A, 298.

19 Foucault's work on the development of modern medical knowledge is foundational here. See Foucault, *Birth of the Clinic*, 40–1, 183–213, 243; Thomas

Osborne, "Medicine and Epistemology: Michel Foucault and the Liberality of Clinical Reason," *History of the Human Sciences* 5, no. 2 (1992): 63–93. The phrase "physical and moral health" was common currency in anglophone reform movements in Canada. See Hunt, *Governing Morals;* Sean Purdy, "Industrial Efficiency, Social Order, and Moral Purity: Housing Reform Thought in English Canada, 1900–1950," *Urban History Review* 25, no. 2 (1997): 30–40.

20 Rabinow, *French Modern,* 30–8.

21 On the 1832 outbreak in Britain, see Mary Poovey, *Making a Social Body: British Cultural Formation, 1830–1864* (Chicago: University of Chicago Press, 1995), 75–99. On New York City, see Dolores Greenberg, "Reconstructing Race and Protest: Environmental Justice in New York City," *Environmental History* 5, no. 2 (2000): 223–50. On Montréal, see Geoffrey Bilson, "The First Epidemic of Asiatic Cholera in Lower Canada, 1832," *Medical History* 21 (1977): 411–33. On the ascent of a normative perspective on public health in the second half of the nineteenth century, see Wohl, *Eternal Slum;* Thomas Osborne, "Security and Vitality: Drains, Liberalism, and Power in the Nineteenth Century," in *Foucault and Political Reason: Liberalism, Neo-Liberalism, and Rationalities of Government,* ed. Andrew Barry, Thomas Osborne, and Nikolas Rose (Chicago: University of Chicago Press, 1996), 99–122.

22 Halifax, City Council Minutes, 7 October 1890, 194.

23 The board's early actions appear in Halifax, City Council Minutes, 27 May 1898, 19 (closure of business); 17 August 1892, 22; 22 February 1899, 131 (containment of animal slaughter); 30 April 1898, 42; 26 July 1898, 42 (repair of residences); 7 November 1899, 98 (demolition of residences).

24 Significant progress reports on the board's home-to-home inspections appear in the *Halifax Evening Mail* between 1905 and 1911. See, in particular, *Evening Mail,* 15 March 1906; 18 May 1906; 6 June 1907; 8 October 1901. Reports that focus on the upper streets appear in *Evening Mail,* 18 August 1908; 22 November 1911. The details of the new inspection form are discussed in *Evening Mail,* 18 August 1908.

25 *Evening Mail,* 6 June 1907.

26 See, in particular, *Evening Mail,* 15 March 1906.

27 *Evening Mail,* 22 November 1911.

28 Hattie's career is summarized in Franklin Boyer, "Dr. William Harop Hattie (Obituary)," *Canadian Medical Association Journal* 26, no. 1 (1932): 121–2.

29 *Evening Mail,* 28 March 1906.

30 Ibid.

31 Ibid. Hattie's support for the model tenements was also vocalized at an annual meeting of the HCW. See HCW, Minutes, 16 April 1907, NSARM, MG 20, vol. 535, no. 3.

32 The case is described in *Evening Mail*, 28 March 1906.

33 On Armitage's tenure at St Paul's, see Reginald Harris, *The Church of Saint Paul in Halifax, Nova Scotia, 1749–1949* (Toronto: Ryerson Press, 1949); Sarah Emsley, *St. Paul's in the Grand Parade, 1749–1999* (Halifax: Formac Publishing, 1999). On his contributions to the Evangelical movement in Canada, see George Rawlyk, *Aspects of the Canadian Evangelical Experience* (Montréal and Kingston: McGill-Queen's University Press, 1997), 176–7; William Katerberg, *Modernity and the Dilemma of North American Anglican Identities, 1880–1950* (Montréal and Kingston: McGill-Queen's Press, 2001), 44, 233; William Armitage, *The Story of the Canadian Revision of the Prayer Book* (Toronto: McClelland and Stewart, 1922).

34 Emsley notes that St Paul's Sunday-school program was attended by "poor children in rags"; *St. Paul's in the Grand Parade*, 63. The charitable efforts of St Paul's parishioners are enumerated in Harris, *Church of Saint Paul*, 248. Some of the city's most influential reformers included Charles Blackadar (chairman of the local Association for Improving the Condition of the Poor); George Wright (a prominent businessman and philanthropist); and Bessie Egan (HCW member and relief worker). Emsley notes Blackadar and Wright were parishioners at St Paul's; *St. Paul's in the Grand Parade*, 34, 35. Egan's life and connection to St Paul's is documented in Judith Fingard, "Bessie Egan," in *The Haligonians: 100 Fascinating Lives from the Halifax Region* (Halifax: Formac Publishing, 2005), 48–9.

35 *Evening Mail*, 5 February 1905. As in other statements quoted in this chapter, the author of the *Evening Mail* article employs the sexist language of the time, using the word "man" to refer to people of all genders. On Armitage's career, see n14 above.

36 On nineteenth-century Evangelism, see Boyd Hilton, *The Age of Atonement: The Influence of Evangelicalism on Social and Economic Thought, 1785–1865* (Oxford: Oxford University Press, 1992). The social-reform work of Evangelicals is best analysed in Richard Allen, *The Social Passion: Religion and Social Reform in Canada, 1914–1928* (Toronto: University of Toronto Press, 1990); Wohl, *Eternal Slum*, 52–5, 74–8.

37 See Wohl, *Eternal Slum*, 74–8; Edwin Hodder, *The Life and Work of the Seventh Earl of Shaftesbury* (London: Cassell and Company, 1886); Geoffrey Finlayson, *The Seventh Earl of Shaftesbury, 1801–1885* (Vancouver: Regent College Publishing, 1981).

38 Hodder, *Seventh Earl of Shaftesbury*, 434.

39 Ibid.

40 William Armitage, *Cities of Refuge* (London: Marshall Bros., 1900), 19.

41 Armitage, *Cities of Refuge*, 84.

42 George Wright, "Better Housing for the People," n.d., HCW Scrapbook, 1908–17, NSARM, MG 20, no. 204.
43 *Evening Mail*, 4 April 1906.
44 *Evening Mail*, 16 May 1907.
45 The quote is from Charles Blackadar, the associate of Armitage's and St Paul's parishioner. Victorian Order of Nurses (VON), Minutes, 1909, NSARM, MG 20, vol. 765, no. 1.
46 *Evening Mail*, 16 May 1907.
47 Armitage quotes from *Evening Mail*, 5 February 1905; 16 May 1907. The final quote is from Wright, "Better Housing."
48 The HCW's early years are documented in Guildford, *Magnificent Services*; Forbes, "Battles in Another War." On Egan's involvement, see Fingard, "Bessie Egan." A broad perspective on the work of the VON in Canada is provided in Beverley Boutilier, "Nursing Nation Builders: The 'Council Idea,' Western Women, and the Founding of the Victorian Order of Nurses, 1896–1900," in *Telling Tales: Essays in Western Women's History*, ed. Catherine Cavanaugh and Randi Warne (Vancouver: University of British Columbia Press). VON's home visits in Halifax and the quote appear in VON, "Work of the Victorian Order of Nurses Commended," VON Minutes, 1909, NSARM, MG 20, vol. 765, no. 1.
49 On Lady Aberdeen and maternal feminism, see Forbes, "Battles in Another War"; Veronica Strong-Boag, *The Parliament of Women: The National Council of Women of Canada, 1893–1929* (Ottawa: National Museums of Canada, 1976); Valverde, *Age of Light*, 61–3; Roberts, "'Rocking the Cradle.'" I consider the stakes in this strategy in more detail in Ted Rutland, "'Where the Little Life Unfolds': Women's Citizenship, Moral Regulation, and the Production of Scale in Early Twentieth-Century Halifax, Nova Scotia," *Journal of Historical Geography* 42 (2013): 167–79.
50 Quotes are from M. Stead, "Opinions from Representative People as to Women's Work as Members of School Boards," HCW Scrapbook, 11 March 1911; E. Ritchie, "Should Women Be on School Boards?" HCW Scrapbook, 26 October 1909; M. Stead, "Criticism of School Board Not Intended, HCW Scrapbook, 25 March 1911.
51 Elizabeth Murray, "What Women are Doing in Nova Scotia," HCW Scrapbook, 19 June 1912.
52 E. Ritchie, "White Slave Trade Must Be Stopped," HCW Scrapbook, 12 January 1910; M. Sexton, "The Local Council of Women and Its Work," HCW Scrapbook, 17 July 1908.
53 E. Ritchie, "Supervised Playgrounds," HCW Scrapbook, 30 May 1908; A. Houston, "Duty of the Public to the Children," HCW Scrapbook, 22 June 1912; Mary Ellen McNab, "Vacation Playgrounds," HCW Scrapbook, 17 July 1909; Sexton, "Local Council of Women."

54 M. Stead, "When Will Philanthropy Take This Wide Direction," HCW Scrapbook, 1 February 1910.
55 McNab, "Vacation Playgrounds."
56 Ibid.
57 All quotes from HCW, Minutes, 12 March 1906. Housing surveys became a nation-wide priority of the NCWC in 1906 on the urging of Halifax's Eliza Ritchie. See HCW, Minutes, 12 March 1906; National Council of Women, *Yearbook, 1906* (Ottawa: NCWC), 30.
58 The exposés appears in *Evening Mail*, 29 January 1905; 13 February 1905; 17 February 1905. The newspaper was owned, incidentally, by the husband of HCW president Agnes Dennis. The two HCW members were also VON nurses. See VON, "Work of the Victorian Order."
59 All quotes from the three-part exposé (n58).
60 White supremacy was, by this time, well established in Canada. Feelings of white insecurity, nevertheless, are well documented. See, for example, Valverde, *Age of Light*.
61 The HCW's segregated approach to adoption is discussed in "A Home for Neglected Colored Children," HCW Scrapbook, 1917. On social services, the HCW discussed the prevalence of segregated free-lunch counters (operated by the city) in a 1916 meeting; one member suggested that the policy should be opposed, but another argued that segregation was not the same as "discrimination," and the matter was dropped; HCW, Minutes, 19 August 1916. The idea that proximity to blackness would impede white normalization was most clearly expressed in the groups' campaign on "feeble-mindedness." See Stephen Ellis, "'Modern Science Has It Well in Hand': Nova Scotia's 'Experiment' in Eugenics," *Shunpiking*, 30 April 2004, 83.
62 Stead, "When Will Philanthropy."
63 Friedrich Engels, *The Condition of the Working-Class in England in 1844* (London: Allen and Unwin, 1892).
64 W.E.B. DuBois, *The Philadelphia Negro* (New York: Lippincott, 1899).
65 *Evening Mail*, 28 March 1906.
66 *Evening Mail*, 5 February 1905 (emphasis mine).
67 VON, "Work of the Victorian Order" (emphasis mine).
68 See Poovey, *Making a Social Body*; Hodder, *Seventh Earl of Shaftesbury*; Chris Otter, *The Victorian Eye: A Political History of Light and Vision in Britain, 1800–1910* (Chicago: University of Chicago Press, 2008).
69 See ch. 3 and Ted Rutland, "'The City Is an Apartment House': Property, Improvement, and Dispossession in Early Twentieth-Century Halifax, Nova Scotia," *Urban Geography* 36, no. 3 (2015): 359–84.

70 Poovey, *Making a Social Body*, 83.
71 *Evening Mail*, 22 November 1911; "The Board of Health Should Act," HCW Scrapbook, 19 July 1916; VON, "The Work of the Victorian Order."
72 *Evening Mail*, 17 February 1905.
73 *Evening Mail*, 28 October 1910.
74 *Evening Mail*, 29 January 1905 (emphasis mine).
75 On mothers' refusal to send their children to the playgrounds, see the article by E. Ritchie, , HCW Scrapbook, n.d. (but around July 1908). The destruction of the exhibit is noted in *Evening Mail*, 8 September 1910. Residents' refusal to leave an unsanitary dwelling is indicated in *Evening Mail*, 15 March 1906.
76 *Evening Mail*, 15 March 1906.
77 Quote is from "Young Girls Who Frequent Thoroughfares of Halifax in Evenings," HCW Scrapbook, 8 January 1908.
78 The model tenements movement in Britain is documented in John Tarn, *Five Per Cent Philanthropy: An Account of Housing in Urban Areas Between 1840 and 1914* (Cambridge: Cambridge University Press, 1973); Evans, "Rookeries and Model Dwellings." The figure one hundred thousand is cited in Wohl, *Eternal Slum*, 147–9.
79 North American model tenements projects are discussed in Lubove, *Progressives and the Slums*; Cynthia Zaitzevsky, "Housing Boston's Poor: The First Philanthropic Experiments," *Journal of the Society of Architectural Historians* 42, no. 2 (1983): 157–67; Lorna Hurl, "The Toronto Housing Company, 1912–1923: The Pitfalls of Painless Philanthropy," *Canadian Historical Review* 65, no. 1 (1984): 28–53. Armitage's visit to Britain and study of British blueprints is mentioned in *Evening Mail*, 5 February 1905; 28 March 1906.
80 Foucault, *Discipline and Punish*, 172.
81 Ibid., 207. A similar normalizing architecture, for Foucault, was expressed in other nineteenth-century enclosures, including hospitals, asylums, schools, and (notably) "working class housing estates." Ibid., 171, 298.
82 These tactics are introduced in ibid., 141–3, 170–7.
83 The Model Houses for Families building is discussed in Tarn, *Five Per Cent*, 15–25; Wohl, *Eternal Slum*, 176–7.
84 Cited in Wohl, *Eternal Slum*, 165.
85 *Evening Mail*, 11 June 1906.
86 The details of the proposed tenements, including all quotes, appear in *Evening Mail*, 24 February 1906; 28 March 1906; 4 April 1906; 11 June 1906; Halifax, City Council Minutes, 10 March 1909, 375.

87 The major investors are listed in *Evening Mail,* 24 February 1906. The purchase of property is mentioned in *Evening Mail,* 6 June 1908; Halifax, City Council Minutes, 10 March 1909, 375.

88 The quotes appear in *Evening Mail,* 26 March 1912; 16 May 1907. A count of 150 people per block in the targeted area was reported in *Evening Mail,* 26 March 1912. A summary of weekly rents paid by the area's tenants appears in Halifax, Report – Re: Armitage Building Scheme, 26 March 1909, HRMA, RG 35–102(1B), box 7, no. 75.

89 A block-by-block approach is stressed in *Evening Mail,* 26 March 1912. This approach was not favoured by all model tenements supporters. A city councillor otherwise supportive of Armitage's plan argued that the city should "expropriate the entire area and raze all buildings thereon excepting only such as I have referred to above [i.e., some business premises]. After the cleaning of the expropriated area, the city should undertake the replanning of the entire district." Halifax, City Council Minutes, 8 February 1912, 293. The Board of Trade's support appears in Halifax Board of Trade, Minutes, 19 March 1912.

90 *Evening Mail,* 6 June 1908.

91 *Evening Mail,* 16 May 1907.

92 "Abolition of the Slums," HCW Scrapbook, 26 March 1912.

93 Armstrong, "Making a Market"; Frost, *Merchant Princes,* 256–7; Marchildon, "John F. Stairs," 216.

94 Acheson, "National Policy"; Sutherland, "Halifax 1815–1914"; James Frost, "The 'Nationalization' of the Bank of Nova Scotia, 1880–1910," *Acadiensis* 12, no. 1 (1982): 3–38.

95 The five initial investors were William Stairs, John Payzant, Richard Henry Brown, Jr, Thomas Ritchie, and Charles Blackadar. William Stairs was closely associated with RSC, as well as with Eastern Trust (acquired by Bank of Montréal in 1905) and the Union Bank of Halifax (acquired by Royal Bank in 1910). He died unexpectedly in 1904. Frost, *Merchant Princes.* Richard Henry Brown, Jr was the manager of the Sydney-based General Mining Association from 1866 to 1901, when the company was sold to Nova Scotia Steel (a Scotia Group company). His capital was therefore tied into Scotia Group and RSC from 1901 onward. Marilyn Gerriets, "The Rise and Fall of a Free-Standing Company in Nova Scotia: The General Mining Association," in *Canadian Multinationals and International Finance,* ed. Gregory Marchildon and Duncan McDowall (New York: Routledge, 1992), 42. John Payzant was president of Bank of Nova Scotia from 1899 to 1918; the bank moved its headquarters to Toronto in

1901. Frost, "'Nationalization.'" Thomas Ritchie was a part of a law firm that represented Merchants Bank of Halifax (later Royal Bank); in 1891, he left the firm to serve as vice-president of Merchants Bank. David Flaherty and Carol Wilton, ed. *Inside the Law: Canadian Law Firms in Historical Perspective* (Toronto: University of Toronto Press, 1996), 281, 299. Charles Blackadar was also tied into fleeing financial capital. His primary occupation was proprietor of the *Acadian Reporter* newspaper; he also served as a director of the Union Bank of Halifax (acquired by Royal Bank in 1910). As a close associate of Armitage and chairman of the Association for Improving the Condition of the Poor, it is unlikely that he would have wanted to back out of the model tenements plan. His newspaper came on very hard times in the early 1900s, however, and it could be that he lacked the capital to contribute as he had planned. Henry Morgan, ed., *The Canadian Men and Women of the Time: A Handbook of Canadian Biography* (Toronto: William Briggs, 1912), 107; Murray Beck, "Blackadar, Henry Dugwell," in *Dictionary of Canadian Biography, 1901–1910,* vol. 13, ed. Ramsay Cook (Toronto: University of Toronto Press, 1994).

96 Armitage's proposal is outlined in Halifax, City Council Minutes, 7 January 1909, 301. Council's response appears in City Council Minutes, 10 March 1909, 375.

97 Wohl, *Eternal Slum,* 155

98 Halifax, City Council Minutes, 10 March 1909, 376.

99 The last public discussion appears in HCW, Minutes, 26 March 1912.

100 The costliness, or inefficiency, of the model tenements is in fact a central characteristic of normalizing (or "disciplinary") power in general. As Foucault remarks, the dependence of disciplinary power upon the creation of wholly new, "artificial" spaces entailed an expense that was eventually seen as prohibitive, especially with the eventual conception of "biopolitical" technologies of power that could work with *existing* material spaces and processes. See Michel Foucault, *Security, Territory, Population: Lectures at the Collège de France, 1977–1978* (New York: Picador, 2007), 72. Comprehensive planning, I argue, is an expression of more efficient, biopolitical power.

3 Planning the Town White: Comprehensive Planning, Scientific Racism, and the Destruction of Africville

1 City of Halifax, Minutes of the Council of the City of Halifax, 9 June 1914, Halifax Regional Municipality Archives (HRMA), RG 102–1A, 48.

2 The first comprehensive plan is generally considered to be Harland Bartholomew's *A Plan for the City of Vancouver British Columbia* (Vancouver: City of Vancouver, 1930). On the influence of Bartholomew and his plan on the planning profession, see Norman Johnson, "Harland Bartholomew: Precedent for the Profession," *Journal of the American Institute of Planners* 29, no. 2 (1973): 115–24; Joseph Heathcott, ""The Whole City is Our Laboratory': Harland Bartholomew and the Production of Urban Knowledge," *Journal of Planning History* 4, no. 4 (2005): 322–55. Notably, Bartholomew's emphasis on city-wide knowledge and objectives carried into seminal articulations of comprehensive planning in the 1950s and 1960s – the heyday of comprehensive planning in practice. See Alan Altshuler, "The Goals of Comprehensive Planning," *Journal of the American Institute of Planners* 31, no. 3 (1965): 186–95. These elements, city-wide knowledge and objectives, certainly came into being before the publication of Bartholomew's plan, and they are central to the form of power that Foucault calls biopolitics. See Michel Foucault, *"Society Must Be Defended": Lectures at the Collège de France, 1975–1976* (New York: Picador, 2003); Ted Rutland, "Enjoyable Life: Planning, Amenity, and the Contested Terrain of Urban Biopolitics," *Environment and Planning D: Society and Space* 33, no. 5 (2015): 850–68.

3 The rise of the planning profession in the United States is documented in Mel Scott, *American City Planning Since 1890: A History Commemorating the Fiftieth Anniversary of the American Institute of Planners* (Berkeley: University of California Press, 1971). The Canadian profession has no equivalent to Scott's treatise. A more cursory history is traced in Gerald Hodge, *Planning Canadian Communities: An Introduction to Its Principles, Practice, and Participants* (Vancouver: Nelson Thomas Learning, 2003).

4 The history of racism, including the period of its emergence, is subject to wide-ranging debate. Some scholars tie racism rigidly to biological notions of racial difference and therefore locate its origins in the works of eighteenth-century natural historians (proto-biologists). See, for example, Hannah Augstein, *Race: The Origins of an Idea, 1760–1850* (Bristol: Thoemmes Press, 1996). Other scholars, while acknowledging the importance of early natural historians, argue that racism emerged much earlier and rested (in these earlier periods) on not-yet-biological foundations. See Sylvia Wynter, "Unsettling the Coloniality of Being/Power/Truth/Freedom: Towards the Human, After Man, Its Overrepresentation – An Argument," *New Centennial Review* 3, no. 3 (2003): 257–337; David Theo Goldberg, *Racist Culture: Philosophy and the Politics of Meaning* (New York: Wiley, 1993); Nell Irvin Painter, *The History of White People* (New York: W.W. Norton, 2011).

The stakes in these different accounts are partly traced in David Macey, "Rethinking Biopolitics, Race, and Power in the Wake of Foucault," *Theory, Culture, Society* 26, no. 6 (2009): 186–205.

5 The structure of scientific racism is outlined in Martin Barker, "Biology and the New Racism," in *Anatomy of Racism*, ed. David Theo Goldberg (Minneapolis: University of Minnesota Press, 1990), 18–37; Nancy Leys Stepan and Sander Gilman, "Appropriating the Idioms of Science: The Rejection of Scientific Racism," in *The "Racial" Economy of Science: Toward a Democratic Future* (Bloomington and Indianapolis: Indiana University Press, 1993), 72–103; Foucault, *"Society Must Be Defended."* (Note that Foucault uses the unconventional term "state racism" to describe a configuration that the broader literature calls scientific racism.)

6 The influence of scientific racism on immigration policy is traced in Franca Iacovetta, Michael Quinlan, and Ian Radforth, "Immigration and Labour: Australia and Canada Compared," *Labour/Le Travail* 38 (1996): 90–115; David Matas, "Racism in Canadian Immigration Policy," in *Perspectives on Racism and the Human Services Sector*, ed. C.E. James (Toronto: University of Toronto Press, 1996), 93–103; Ninette Kelley and Michael Trebilcock, *Making the Mosaic: A History of Canadian Immigration Policy* (Toronto: University of Toronto Press, 2010), 132; Nandita Sharma, "Anti-Trafficking Rhetoric and the Making of a Global Apartheid," *NWSA Journal* 17, no. 3 (2005): 88–111. The influence of racism on reform-era public health is diagnosed in Kay Anderson, *Vancouver's Chinatown: Racial Discourse in Canada, 1875–1980* (Montréal and Kingston: McGill-Queen's University Press, 1991); Nayan Shah, *Contagious Divides: Epidemics and Race in San Francisco's Chinatown* (Berkeley: University of California Press, 2001).

7 The development of Halifax from its founding to the mid-nineteenth century is traced in Judith Fingard, Janet Guildford, and David Sutherland, *Halifax: The First 250 Years* (Halifax: Formac Publishing, 1999), 8–91; Paul Erickson, *Halifax's North End: An Anthropologist Looks at the City* (Halifax: Lancelot Press, 1986); Paul Erickson, *Historic North End Halifax* (Halifax: Nimbus, 2004). The claim that the South End was originally more homogeneously working class than the North End is stressed in Erickson, but contradicted by Susan Buggey, "Building Halifax, 1841–1871," *Acadiensis* 10, no. 1 (1980): 95.

8 This section of the Intercolonial Railway was originally called the Nova Scotia Railroad. See Erickson, *Halifax's North End*, 42–5.

9 The industrialization of Richmond is documented in ibid., 34–47; Erickson, *Historic North End*, 79–90.

10 See Buggey, "Building Halifax," 95; Erickson, *Halifax's North End*, 32–4.

11 Erickson, *Halifax's North End*, 32–9. The claim that the upper streets were populated by Black residents until the arrival of significant Irish migration is advanced in David Sutherland, "Race Relations in Halifax, Nova Scotia, During the Mid-Victorian Quest for Reform," *Journal of the Canadian Historical Association* 7, no. 1 (1996): 42.

12 Bridglal Pachai, *The Nova Scotia Black Experience through the Centuries* (Halifax: Nimbus Press, 2007), 97.

13 See Harvey Amani Whitfield, "Slavery in English Nova Scotia," *Journal of the Royal Nova Scotia Historical Society* 13 (2010): 28.

14 See ibid., 23; Harvey Amani Whitfield, "African and New World African Immigration to Mainland Nova Scotia, 1749–1816," *Journal of the Royal Nova Scotia Historical Society* 7 (2004): 10. On the trade with the West Indies, see Julian Gwyn, *Excessive Expectations: Maritime Commerce and the Economic Development of Nova Scotia* (Montréal and Kingston: McGill-Queen's Press, 1998), 54–6.

15 See Harvey Amani Whitfield, "The Struggle over Slavery in the Maritime Colonies," *Acadiensis* 41, no. 2 (Summer / Autumn 2012): 17–44.

16 Black enslavement in Nova Scotia is detailed in ibid. Black migration to Nova Scotia is documented in James Walker, *The Black Loyalists: The Search for a Promised Land in Nova Scotia and Sierra Leone, 1783–1870* (Toronto: University of Toronto Press, 1992); Harvey Amani Whitfield, *Blacks on the Border: The Black Refugees in British North America, 1815–1860* (Burlington: University of Vermont Press, 2006); Pachai, *Nova Scotia Black Experience.*

17 The scholarship on land (mal)distribution is summarized in Pachai, *Nova Scotia Black Experience*; Mary Vincer, "A History of Marginalization – Africville: A Canadian Example of Forced Migration" (master's thesis, Ryerson University, 2008), 16–31.

18 Black employment in central Halifax is documented in Pachai, *Nova Scotia Black Experience*; Suzanne Morton, "Separate Spheres in a Separate World: African-Nova Scotian Women in Late-19th-Century Halifax County," *Acadiensis* 12, no. 2 (1993): 61–83. The figure for Black settlement in the Old North End is an estimate derived from the 1901 Canadian Census, which lists 336 Black residents in Ward 5 (roughly the North End). Census-makers, it is recognized by historians, consistently undercounted Black individuals and households in Nova Scotia; thus, the high end of my estimate is higher than the census count. The settlement of fifty residents on Campbell Road in the 1840s and 1850s is cited in most scholarship on Africville, including the seminal work Donald Clairmont and Dennis Magill, *Africville: The Life and Death of a Canadian Black Community* (Toronto: Canadian Scholars' Press, 1999).

19 The debate on the origins of Africville is helpfully summarized in Vincer, "History of Marginalization," 35.

20 The early years of Africville are traced in Clairmont and Magill, *Africville;* Angel Nieves, "Memories of Africville: Urban Renewal, Reparations, and the Africadian Diaspora," in *Black Geographies and the Politics of Place,* ed. Katherine McKittrick and Clyde Woods (Toronto: Between the Lines, 2007), 82–96; Jennifer Nelson, *Razing Africville: A Geography of Racism* (Toronto: University of Toronto Press, 2008).

21 Quoted in Clairmont and Magill, *Africville,* 91.

22 Pachai, *Nova Scotia Black Experience,* 159.

23 A general history of infrastructure improvements is provided in Halifax, City Council Minutes, 26 April 1895, 234–6; 3 May 1897, 206–7; and especially 8 May 1901, 7–9.

24 Halifax, City Council Minutes, 8 May 1901, 8.

25 Halifax, City Council Minutes, 26 April 1895, 234

26 Halifax, City Council Minutes, 26 April 1895, 234–6; 30 December 1901, 138–9.

27 Both quotes are from Halifax, City Council Minutes, 20 December 1901, 138–9.

28 Halifax, City Council Minutes, 10 May 1905, 23; 16 May 1907, 31; 7 May 1908, 10.

29 See Foucault, *"Society Must Be Defended,"* 239–64; Michel Foucault, *Security, Territory, Population: Lectures at the Collège de France, 1977–1978* (New York: Picador, 2007), 29–54. Biopolitics, it should be noted, is generally said to have emerged later than the normalizing form of knowledge and power that I investigated in the last chapter. It is not unusual, however, to observe both configurations operating in tandem and/or emerging roughly in parallel.

30 *Halifax Evening Mail,* 28 March 1906.

31 Halifax, City Council Minutes, 15 May 1906, 24; also 12 May 1897, 4–5.

32 Halifax, City Council Minutes, 8 May 1901, 7–9. On the paving of sidewalks and streets, see City Council Minutes, 10 May 1905, 22–6; 15 May 1906, 20–6.

33 For the term "public convenience" used to describe the positive effects of investments in surface paving and street lighting, see Halifax, City Council Minutes, 15 May 1906, 21–2; 7 May 1908, 10. For other descriptions of the expected effects of paving and street lighting, see City Council Minutes, 12 May 1897, 3–7; 14 May 1902, 3; 15 May 1906, 21–2; 7 May 1908, 10. Convenience is linked to the absence of mud by Mayor Adam Crosby in City Council Minutes, 7 May 1908, 10. For an early description of the importance of "convenience" to urban planning, see Thomas Adams, *Municipal*

and Real Estate Finance in Canada (Ottawa: Commission of Conservation, 1921).

34 See Foucault, *Security, Territory, Population*, 326–7; Adams, *Municipal and Real Estate Finance*, 5–6. I detail the importance of happiness to nineteenth- and early twentieth-century urban planning in Rutland, "Enjoyable Life."

35 Halifax, City Council Minutes, 10 May 1899, 13.

36 Halifax, City Council Minutes, 14 May 1902, 3. A similar sentiment is expressed in City Council Minutes, 15 May 1906, 21. The lack of progress in pleasing citizens in this way is discussed in City Council Minutes, 7 May 1908, 10.

37 Halifax, City Council Minutes, 30 April 1908, 365.

38 Halifax, City Council Minutes, 15 May 1906, 21–2; 30 April 1908, 364–73.

39 For a similar argument about modern planning, see Paul Rabinow, *French Modern* (Chicago: University of Chicago Press, 1995); Foucault, *Security, Territory, Population*, 21.

40 Halifax, City Council Minutes, 7 May 1908, 10.

41 Halifax, City Council Minutes, 12 May 1897, 3. An analogous opposition was drawn by many mayors in this period; see City Council Minutes, 10 May 1899, 13; 15 May 1906, 20.

42 Both quotes are from Halifax, City Council Minutes, 30 December 1901, 138–9.

43 Donald Clairmont and Dennis Magill, *Africville Relocation Report* (Halifax: Institute of Public Affairs, 1971), 74–7.

44 Mount Saint Vincent Art Gallery, ed., *Africville: A Spirit that Lives on* (Halifax: Black Cultural Centre for Nova Scotia, Africville Genealogy Society, and National Film Board, 1989).

45 These planning decisions and their effects are charted in Clairmont and Magill, *Africville*, 93–6, 109.

46 Clairmont and Magill, *Relocation Report*, 75, 106, 190, 255.

47 Nelson, *Razing Africville*, 81.

48 The board's first effects to reform municipal taxation are discussed in Halifax Board of Trade, Discussion by the Halifax Board of Trade on the Tax Reform Proposed by the Halifax Tax Reform Association, 23 March 1892, Nova Scotia Archives and Records Management (NSARM), 5. The minutes of the 1901 forum on municipal taxation appear in Halifax, Special Committee Meeting Books, vol. 1, 1898–1902, 18 October 1901, 22 October 1901, 11 November 1901, 27 February 1902, HRMA, 102–1G. I discuss the struggle over municipal taxation and its implication for modern planning in more detail in Ted Rutland, ""The City Is an Apartment House': Property, Improvement, and Dispossession in Early Twentieth-Century Halifax, Nova Scotia," *Urban Geography* 36, no. 3 (2015): 359–84.

49 David Ricardo, *On the Principles of Political Economy and Taxation* (London: John Murray, 1817), 33.
50 Ricardo's elimination of a value-creating role for land is emphasized in Michel Foucault, *The Order of Things: An Archeology of the Human Sciences* (New York: Vintage Books, 1970), 279–80.
51 See Henry George, *Progress and Poverty* (New York: Appleton, 1880), 120.
52 Henry George, "Land and People," in *Henry George's Writings on the United Kingdom*, ed. Kenneth Wenzer (Oxford: Elsevier Science, 2002), 123.
53 George's political career is documented in George Geiger, *The Philosophy of Henry George* (New York: Hyperion Press, 1975). His influence on North American cities is traced in Ramsay Cook, "Henry George and the Poverty of Canadian Progress," *Historical Papers* 12, no. 1 (1977): 142–56; Gregory Levine, "The Single Tax in Montreal and Toronto, 1880 to 1920: Successes, Failures, and the Transformation of an Idea," *American Journal of Economics and Sociology* 52, no. 4 (1993): 417–32; Mason Gaffney, "Two Centuries of Economic Thought on Taxation of Land Rents," in *Land Value Taxation*, ed. Richard Lindholm and Arthur Lynn (Madison: University of Wisconsin Press, 1982), 151–96.
54 City of Halifax, Special Committee Meeting Books, 27 February 1902, HRMA.
55 *Evening Mail*, 10 February 1912. See also *Evening Mail*, 17 September 1910.
56 Sexton made these comments at the meeting of the Halifax Local Council of Women (HCW). See HCW, Minutes, 26 March 1912, NSARM, MG 20, vol. 535, no. 3. The HCW's own endorsement of the single tax appears in Halifax, City Council Minutes, 3 March 1921, 755.
57 All quotes from City of Halifax, "Tax Act of the City of Halifax," contained in Report Special Committee on Tax Exemptions, 13 March 1924, HRMA, RG 35-102-1B. The passage of the new tax regime by the city council appears in Halifax, City Council Minutes, 13 May 1914, 33.
58 Halifax, "Tax Act of the City of Halifax."
59 William Somers's approach to taxation is outlined in William Somers, *The Valuation of Real Estate for the Purpose of Taxation* (St Paul, MN: Rich and Clymer, 1901). For discussion of the effects of Somers's approach on North American cities, see Charles Barker, *Henry George* (Westport, CT: Greenwood Press, 1974); Robert Bremner, "The Civic Revival in Ohio: Tax Equalization in Cleveland," *American Journal of Economics and Sociology* 10, no. 3 (1951): 301–12; Mason Gaffney, "Two Centuries of Economic Thought"; H.W. Batt, "Land Value Maps Are Not New, but Their Utility Needs to Be Re-discovered," *International Journal of Transdisiplinary Research* 4, no. 1 (2009): 108–58. Somers's approach was eventually codified and marketed by Manufacturers' Appraisal Company of Cleveland, a representative of

which visited Halifax to lecture the public and city council in 1914. This visit and the city's adoption of a new approach based on Somers's work (but developed locally rather than through the services of Manufacturers' Appraisal) are discussed in Halifax, City Council Minutes, 22 July 1914, 138; 5 October 1916, 262; 7 March 1918, 449.

60 The formation of the city's first "town planning board," with Doane as its executive officer is discussed in Halifax, City Council Minutes, 10 February 1916, 415. Doane's pre-1916 planning activities are outlined in City Council Minutes, 16 May 1912, 67; 5 September 1912, 225; 17 October 1912, 276. Discussion of Doane's trip to the National Town Planning Conference appears in City Council Minutes, 22 April 1914, 493; 9 June 1914, 48.

61 The role of planning within the "conservation of life" is discussed in Alan Artibise and Gilbert Stelter, "Conservation Planning and Urban Planning: The Canadian Commission of Conservation in Historical Perspective," in *Planning for Conservation: An International Perspective*, ed. Roger Kain (London: Mansell, 1981), 17–36. The trajectory of Adams's career, including his years with the Commission of Conservation, is documented in Michael Simpson, *Thomas Adams and the Modern Town Planning Movement: Britain, Canada, and the United States, 1900–1940* (New York: Mansell, 1985); Alan Armstrong, "Thomas Adams and the Commission of Conservation," *Plan Canada* 1, no. 1 (1959): 16–32. Adams's visit to Halifax in 1915 and his role in the drafting of the Nova Scotia Planning Act are discussed in Leifka Vissers and Jill Grant, "Planning Experts and Local Reformers: The 1915 Town Planning Act in Nova Scotia" (paper presented to the Annual Conference of the IPHS, Istanbul, Turkey, July 2010). The city's efforts to bring Adams to Halifax in 1917 to replan the area destroyed by the 1917 Halifax Explosion are discussed in Halifax, City Council Minutes, 12 December 1917, 286; 20 December 1917, 305.

62 Daniel Rogers documents that Adams and George travelled in similar circles when the latter visited Britain in the 1890s. Daniel Rogers, *Atlantic Crossings: Social Politics in a Progressive Age* (Cambridge, MA: Harvard University Press). Adams credits George in his seminal 1917 publication for the insight that a "community" ought to "obtain ... as much as possible of the value which is socially created [i.e., land value]." Thomas Adams, *Rural Planning and Development* (Ottawa: Commission of Conservation, 1917), 17. For a discussion of this point, see Harlod Buttenheim et al., "Urban Development: The Pattern and the Background," *Planners Journal* 1, no. 4 (1935), 83–4.

63 Adams, *Municipal and Real Estate Finance*, 3, 7, 12.

64 Ibid.,14.

65 Ibid., 8–10, 14.
66 On the presumed sanctity of private property and the challenge it posed to the formation of modern planning, see Ian Mckay, "The Liberal Order Framework: A Prospectus for a Reconnaissance of Canadian History," *Canadian Historical Review* 81, no. 4 (2000): 616–78; Rogers, "Civic Ambitions," in *Atlantic Crossings;* Paul Rutherford, "Tomorrow's Metropolis: The Urban Reform Movement in Canada, 1880–1920," *Historical Papers* 6, no. 1 (1971): 203–24.
67 Adams, *Municipal and Real Estate Finance,* 15.
68 All quotes from Halifax, City Council Minutes, 9 June 1914, 48–50.
69 Halifax, City Council Minutes, 23 March 1915, 484.
70 Clairmont and Magill, *Africville,* 77.
71 Clairmont and Magill, *Relocation Report,* 104–5.
72 Halifax, City Council Minutes, 9 September 1915, 211.
73 Ibid., 217–18. The capitalization of "City" in this passage might confusingly suggest that the referent is not the local population but the municipality. In this context, however, state and nonstate officials frequently capitalized the word when referring to the population, as well as the municipality. For example, the city solicitor's claim in 1916 that "the City may be regarded as a huge combination of a market and apartment house in which one pays for the space occupied, and in which the City has no more concern with the means or income or gains or losses of the occupier ... than the owner of a market or apartment house" capitalizes both senses of the word "city." (Halifax, "Tax Act of the City of Halifax.") The possible meanings of the 1915 claim about Africville, then, are twofold. However, it is far more likely, given all the efforts at the time to attract industry and grow the city numerically, that the passage refers to the population.
74 Halifax, City Council Minutes, 27 April 1916, 569.
75 Clairmont and Magill, *Relocation Report,* 95–7.
76 Halifax, City Council Minutes, 11 January 1907, 252. The expropriation is later discussed in City Council Minutes, 10 December 1903, 175.
77 Cited in Clairmont and Magill, *Relocation Report,* 148.
78 Clairmont and Magill, *Relocation Report,* 100.
79 Ibid., 122 (emphasis mine).
80 The campaign against the Mi'kmaq and the enslavement of African people both preceded the arrival of biologically defined racial categories. For some scholars, this means that these processes preceded the arrival of racism (the assumption being that racism requires biologically defined racial categories). Other scholars, upon whose work my analysis is based, locate racism in prebiological racial categories. See n4 above.

81 The term "afterlife of slavery" is introduced in Saidiya Hartman, *Loose Your Mother: A Journey Along the Atlantic Slave Route* (New York: Macmillan, 2008), 6. Though the term itself is not used, the afterlife of slavery is a central concern in her earlier work, *Scenes of Subjection: Terror, Slavery, and Self-Making in Nineteenth-Century America* (Oxford: Oxford University Press, 1997).

82 The transition from an understanding of race based on geography to one based on biology (or prebiological conceptions of heredity) is traced in David Theo Goldberg, *Racist Culture: Philosophy and the Politics of Meaning* (New York: Wiley, 1993); Foucault, *"Society Must Be Defended."* The importance of Buffon (Georges-Louis Leclerc, Compte de Buffon, a French natural historian) to this transition is stressed in many histories, including Andrew Curran, *The Anatomy of Blackness: Science and Slavery in the Age of Enlightenment* (Baltimore: John's Hopkins University Press, 2011). The importance of Cornelius de Pauw (a Dutch geographer) is discussed in Kay Anderson, *Race and the Crisis of Humanism* (New York: Routledge, 2007); Curran, *Anatomy of Blackness;* Augstein, *Race.* Less often linked to this transition (in critical scholarship on the latter) is Friedrich Sigmund Merkel, a German anatomist; however, his contributions to the nascent science of heredity are frequently underscored in the scientific literature itself. See John Hunter and Karl Holubar, "Freidrich Sigmund Merkel: The Man Behind the Eponym," *American Journal of Dermatopathology* 4, no. 6 (1982): 521–6.

83 See n5 above. The importance of not expliclity racial distinctions, such as "feeble-mindedness," is explored by Foucault and Stepan in particular.

84 See Noel Ignatiev, *How the Irish Became White* (New York: Routledge, 1995); Theodore Allen, *The Invention of the White Race, Volume 1: Racial Oppression and Social Control* (New York: Verso, 1994).

85 Ignatiev, *How the Irish Became White,* 2.

86 Sutherland, "Race Relations."

87 Ibid.

88 Owen Carrigan, "The Immigrant Experience in Halifax, 1881–1931," *Canadian Ethnic Studies* 20, no. 3 (1988): 28–41.

89 Stephen Poole notes that the superintendent of the garden was Ricard Power, who had gardened for the Duke of Devonshire in Ireland. He devised a plan, Poole suggests, "that remains remarkably intact." Stephen Poole, *Halifax: Discovering its Heritage* (Halifax: Formac Publishing, 2000), 41. Patrick Keane documents the early activities of the Nova Scotia Horticultural Society, the initial developer of the Public Garden. In 1836, the society lamented that "we have few or no professional gardeners." The society cited Massachusetts horticultural societies as examples worth emulating and thought that public gardens in Halifax would "promote

an exercise of domestic affection, and create a more refined taste for social pleasures." Patrick Keane, "Joseph Howe and Adult Education," *Acadiensis* 3, no. 1 (1973): 35–49.

90 See Ladelle McWhorter, *Racism and Sexual Oppression in Anglo-America* (Bloomington: University of Indiana Press, 2009), 43–4; Audrey Smedley, *Race in North America: Origin and Evolution of a Worldview* (Boulder: Westview Press, 1993), 178–81, 237–9.

91 The Canadian state's belief in Indigenous improvement/normalization, never uncontested, is analysed in Renisa Mawani, *Colonial Proximities: Crossracial Encounters and Juridical Truths in British Columbia, 1871–1921* (Vancouver: UBC Press, 2009), 136–42. On changing conceptions of Indigenous inferiority in present-day Canada, see Saliha Belmessous, "Assimilation and Racialism in Seventeenth- and Eighteenth-Century French Colonial Policy," *American Historical Review* 110, no. 2 (2005): 322–49. On the logic of elimination through assimilation, see Patrick Wolfe, "Settler Colonialism and the Elimination of the Native," *Journal of Genocide Research* 8, no. 4 (2006): 387–409.

92 Cited in Neil MacMaster, *Racism in Europe: 1870–2000* (New York: Palgrave Macmillan, 2001), 63.

93 Cited in Smedley, *Race in North America*, 241.

94 Quoted in Sutherland, "Race Relations," 52–3.

95 Robin Winks, *The Blacks in Canada* (Montréal and Kingston: McGill-Queen's University Press, 1971), 292.

96 Quoted in Sutherland, "Race Relations," 47.

97 Sutherland, "Race Relations." See also John Garner, *The Franchise and Politics in British North America, 1755–1867* (Toronto: University of Toronto Press, 1969), 30–3.

98 Sutherland, "Race Relations."

99 Quoted in ibid., 42.

100 Quoted in ibid., 52.

101 Quoted in Michael Boudreau, *City of Order: Crime and Society in Halifax, 1918–35* (Vancouver: UBC Press, 2012), 167. On similar events in the Jim Crow South, see Sarah Haley, *No Mercy Here: Gender, Punishment, and the Making of Jim Crow Modernity* (Chapel Hill: University of North Carolina Press, 2016), 17–57.

102 Nelson, *Razing Africville*, 71; Clairmont and Magill, *Africville*, 120–5.

103 On immigration policies see n6 above. On miscegenation policies and eugenics in Canada, see Carolyn Strange and Jennifer Stephen, "Eugenics in Canada: A Checkered History, 1850s–1990s," in *The Oxford Handbook of Eugenics*, ed. Alison Bashford and Philippa Levine (Oxford: Oxford University Press, 2010), 522–38.

104 Renisa Mawani, "Genealogies of the Land: Aboriginality, Law, and Territory in Vancouver's Stanley Park," *Social and Legal Studies* 14, no. 3 (2005): 315–39; Jordan Stanger-Ross, "Municipal Colonialism in Vancouver: City Planning and the Conflict over Indian Reserves, 1928–1950s," *Canadian Historical Review* 89, no. 4 (2008): 541–80; Penelope Edmonds, *Urbanizing Frontiers: Indigenous Peoples and Settlers in 19th-Century Pacific Rim Cities* (Vancouver: UBC Press, 2010); Glen Coulthard, *Red Skin, White Masks* (Minneapolis: University of Minnesota Press, 2014).

105 Daniel Paul, *We Were Not the Savages: A Micmac Perspective on the Collision of European and Aboriginal Civilizations* (Halifax: Nimbus Press, 1993), 217–19; Jacob Remes, "Mi'kmaq in the Halifax Explosion of 1917: Leadership, Transience, and the Struggle for Land Rights," *Ethnohistory* 61, no. 3 (2014): 445–66. Population figures are from Government of Canada, *Fourth Census of Canada, 1901* (Ottawa: S.E. Dawson, 1902), 302–3.

106 Sylvia Hamilton, *And I Alone Escaped to Tell You* (Kentville, NS: Gaspereau Press, 2014), 22.

107 Katherine McKittrick, "On Plantations, Prisons, and a Black Sense of Place," *Social and Cultural Geography* 12, no. 8 (2011): 949.

108 Nicolas Brady, "Looking for Azealia's Harlem Shake, or How We Mistake the Politics of Obliteration for Appropriation," *Out of Nowhere: Black Meditations at the Cutting Edge*, 7 March 2013, accessed 2 February 2015, https://outofnowhereblog.wordpress.com/2013/03/07/looking-for-azealias-harlem-shake-or-how-we-mistake-the-politics-of-obliteration-for-appropriation.

4 A Calibrated Rush for Progress: Urban Renewal, Anti-Blackness, and the Diverse Effects of a Totalizing Planning Project

1 Quoted in Marcus Patterson, "Slum Clearance in Halifax: The Role of Gordon Stephenson" (master's thesis, Dalhousie University, 2009), 16.

2 The literature on urban renewal is vast. For a broad view, see Martin Anderson, *The Federal Bulldozer: A Critical Analysis of Urban Renewal, 1949–1962* (Cambridge, MA: MIT Press, 1964); Christopher Klemek, *The Transatlantic Collapse of Urban Renewal: Postwar Urbanism from New York to Berlin* (Chicago: University of Chicago Press, 2011). On the Canadian experience, see John Bacher, *Keeping to the Marketplace: The Evolution of Canadian Housing Policy* (Montréal and Kingston: McGill-Queen's University Press, 1993); John Miron, *Housing Postwar Canada: Demographic Change, Household Formation, and Housing Demand* (Montréal and Kingston: McGill-Queen's Press, 1988); Margaret Rockwell, "The Facelift

and the Wrecking Ball: Urban Renewal and Hamilton's King Street West, 1957–1971," *Urban History Review* 37, no. 2 (2009): 53–61; Roger Picton "Selling National Urban Renewal: The National Film Board, the National Capital Commission, and Post-War Planning in Ottawa, Canada," *Urban History* 37, no. 2 (2010): 301–21; Sean Purdy, "Framing Regent Park: The National Film Board of Canada and the Construction of 'Outcast Spaces' in the Inner City, 1953 to 1994," *Media, Culture, and Society* 27, no. 4 (2005): 523–49. The best work on Halifax is Donald Clairmont and Dennis Magill, *Africville: The Life and Death of a Canadian Black Community* (Toronto: Canadian Scholars' Press, 1999); Jill Grant, *The Drama of Democracy: Contention and Dispute in Community Planning* (Toronto: University of Toronto Press, 1994).

3 Quoted in Elizabeth Pacey, *The Battle of Citadel Hill* (Halifax: Lancelot Press, 1979), 7.

4 The Census of Canada puts Halifax's population at 67,726 in 1921 and 79,352 in 1931. The wartime census of 1941 put the city's population at 96,636 in 1941, a 40 per cent jump from the 1921 figure.

5 The World War II years in Halifax, including its economic effects, are documented in Judith Fingard, Janet Guildford, and David Sutherland, *Halifax: The First 250 Years* (Halifax: Formac Press, 1999), 138–59. The city's habitual (wartime) boom and (postwar) bust cycle is often mentioned. See, for example, Jill Grant and Marcus Patterson, "Scientific Cloak/Romantic Heart: Gordon Stephenson and the Redevelopment Study of Halifax, 1957," *Town Planning Review* 83, no. 3 (2012): 4.

6 See David Harvey, *The Condition of Postmodernity: An Enquiry into the Origins of Cultural Change* (New York: Blackwell, 1991); Jane Jenson, "Different but Not 'Exceptional': Canada's Permeable Fordism," *Canadian Review of Sociology and Anthropology*, 26, no. 1 (1989): 69–93.

7 Postwar efforts to relocate nonurban Canadians to more populous agglomerations are discussed in Bryant Fairley, "The Struggle for Capitalism in the Fishing Industry in Newfoundland," *Studies in Political Economy* 17, no. 1 (1985), 47–8; Daniel Paul, *We Were Not the Savages* (Halifax: Nimbus Publishing, 1993), 264–98; Tina Loo, "Africville and the Dynamics of State Power in Postwar Canada," *Acadiensis* 39, no. 2 (2010): 23–47.

8 See Roger Keil and Stefan Kipfer, "The Urban Experience and Globalization," in *Changing Canada: Political Economy as Transformation*, ed. Wallace Clement and Leah Vosko (Montréal and Kingston: McGill-Queen's University Press, 2003), 335–62. The history of the NHA and CMHC is best documented by Bacher, *Keeping to the Marketplace*.

9 City of Halifax, *The Master Plan for the City of Halifax as Prepared by the Civic Planning Commission* (Halifax: City of Halifax, 1945), 1.

10 Ibid., 36.
11 Ibid., 52.
12 All three quotes from ibid., 49, 53.
13 The support of Halifax community organizations is detailed in Patterson, "Slum Clearance in Halifax," 21–9.
14 The quote is from a 1964 newspaper article cited in Jennifer Nelson, *Razing Africville: A Geography of Racism* (Toronto: University of Toronto Press, 2008), 75.
15 City of Halifax, Minutes of the Council of the City of Halifax, 21 January 1954, Halifax Regional Municipality Archives (HRMA), RG 102–1A, 64. The plan and citizen opposition to it is outlined in Patterson, "Slum Clearance in Halifax," 26–9.
16 Quoted in Patterson, "Slum Clearance in Halifax," 29.
17 The 1944 NHA provisions and their limited effect (their usage by Toronto, exclusively) are discussed in Purdy, "Framing Regent Park"; Ryan James, "From 'Slum Clearance' to 'Revitalization': Planning, Expertise, and Moral Regulation in Toronto's Regent Park," *Planning Perspectives* 25, no. 1 (2010): 69–86.
18 See the Canadian-focused literature in n2 above.
19 Gordon Stephenson, *A Redevelopment Study of Halifax, Nova Scotia* (Halifax: City of Halifax, 1957). Stephenson's career, including the influence of Le Corbusier, is documented in Patterson, "Slum Clearance in Halifax."
20 Stephenson, *Redevelopment Study*, 52.
21 The quote is from Stephenson, *Redevelopment Study*, 26. City council's consideration of the report and its approval of Scheme 9 is discussed in City of Halifax, Housing and Redevelopment Committee Minutes, 15 October 1957, HRMA, 102–42A.
22 The gradually worked-out details of the agreement and Diefenbaker's arrival in Halifax to sign are recorded in Redevelopment Committee Minutes, 13 January 1958; 17 January 1958; 23 January 1958.
23 In some cases, tenants were given two weeks' notice to vacate; in other cases, they received as much as two months. See City of Halifax, "174–178 Grafton St, 12 and 14 Poplar Grove, 1961," Redevelopment Committee – Special Expropriation Submissions, HRMA, 102–42.E4; Redevelopment Committee Minutes, 16 April 1958, 102–42A, 14.
24 The quotation, emanating from CMHC policy, was often repeated in planning discussions. See, for example, Redevelopment Committee Minutes, 3 April 1959.
25 The passing of Ordinance 50 and its effects are discussed in City of Halifax, Progress Report on Blight Removal and Public Housing, Housing and Redevelopment Committee Minutes, 19 December 1961. The report lists 207 families displaced by the application of Ordinance 50 and 175 families

displaced by landlords' anticipation of its application. These figures exclude nonfamily members (e.g., individuals living alone or with other, nonrelated individuals). Assuming the same ratio of families to housing units prevailed in these areas as in the CRA (where there were 267 families and 385 housing units), then 298 housing units were destroyed through the application of Ordinance 50 and 252 through landlords' anticipation. A minimum of 250 units (Ordinance 50) and 200 units (landlords' anticipation) seems reasonable. Further assuming a similar ratio of housing units to residents prevailed in these areas as in the CRA (where there were 1,620 residents and 385 units), a total of 1,893 residents were displaced through these actions. Assuming, finally, a similar ratio of family members to nonfamily members prevailed in these areas as in the CRA (where there were 1,180 family members and 440 nonfamily members), 1,379 of these displacees were family members and 514 were nonfamily members. The breakdown of family members, nonfamily members, and housing units in the CRA is presented in Redevelopment Committee Minutes, 14 November 1957, 6. These estimates are consistent with those of the city early in the application of Ordinance 50 (1,500 displacees). See Redevelopment Committee Minutes, 16 April 1958, 10.

26 Redevelopment Committee Minutes, 16 April 1958, 10.

27 Ibid., 1.

28 Ibid., 8.

29 The approval of the first two (new) phases is discussed in Redevelopment Committee Minutes, 23 May 1958. A third phase is discussed (but not clearly approved) in the Minutes, 23 March 1959. The acquisition of properties for the third phase began in May 1958. See Redevelopment Committee Minutes, 23 May 1958. Using the same assumptions as in n25 above, the destruction of these ninety-two housing units resulted in the displacement of 386 residents, 281 of them family members and 105 nonfamily members.

30 Negotiations with thirteen CRA-located businesses are specifically mentioned in Redevelopment Committee Minutes between 15 October 1957 and 23 January 1962.

31 The first contact with the tavern owner is noted in Redevelopment Committee Minutes, 5 December 1958, 102–42A. The details of the case appear in Redevelopment Committee – Special Expropriation Submissions, Grafton Street, 11 March 1959–18 January 1962, HRMA, 102–42-E1. The quote is from 11 March 1959.

32 Redevelopment Committee – Special Expropriation Submissions, Grafton Street, 18 January 1962.

33 Redevelopment Committee Minutes, 4 July 1958, 14.
34 Redevelopment Committee minutes, 4 March 1960, 5.
35 The story of the Fleet family, including all quotes, appears in Eviction – Mr. Elmer Fleet – 3-A Wellington Court, Housing and Redevelopment Committee Minutes, 21 November 1961, 8–9.
36 Pacey, *Battle of Citadel Hill*, 25–6.
37 See Progress Report on Blight Removal and Public Housing. My estimates from nn25 and 29 above put the total displaced persons at 3,899 (1,620 from the CRA, 386 from the additional three phases, and 1,893 from Ordinance 50-related "blight removal").
38 Ibid., 13.
39 Redevelopment Committee Minutes, 14 November 1957, 6.
40 My estimates in nn24 and 28 above put the total displaced nonfamily members at 1,059 (440 from the CRA, 105 from the additional three phases, and 514 from Ordinance 50-related "blight removal").
41 Redevelopment Committee Minutes, 21 November 1961, 7; Progress Report on Blight Removal and Public Housing, 4.
42 In the initial plans, low income was not to be a barrier to tenancy in Mulgrave Park. A council decision on 25 May 1959 set the maximum income for tenant households at $3,900 per year, but no minimum. Low income became a barrier to tenancy when the project opened, in part because the Housing Authority targeted a particular average rent – and rents were geared to tenants' incomes. On 21 November 1961 it was reported that the aim of the Housing Authority was to achieve an overall average rent of $58/month, and that it had "deviated from the priority list [of displaced residents] in an attempt to raise the average rent on the project by allocations to higher income families." See Halifax, City Council Minutes, 25 May 1959, 385; Redevelopment Committee Minutes, 21 November 1961, 6 and 4 June 1962.
43 Both quotes from Progress Report on Blight Removal and Public Housing, 7, 1.
44 Stephenson, *Redevelopment Study*, 25–6.
45 City of Halifax, Central Redevelopment Area Advisory Committee Records, 11 February 1963, HRMA, 102–42.D16, 4. Grant's career and authoritarian style are discussed in Donald Clairmont and Dennis Magill, *Africville Relocation Report* (Halifax: Institute of Public Affairs, 1971), 116.
46 James Lorimer, *The Developers* (Toronto: James Lorimer and Company, 1978).
47 The events that led to the creation of Halifax Developments Inc. are discussed in Pacey, *Battle of Citadel Hill*, 28–9; Robert Collier, *Contemporary*

Cathedrals: Large-Scale Developments in Canadian Cities (Toronto: Harvest House, 1975), 160.

48 See the discussion of the three proposals in Development Department Records – Central Redevelopment Area – Call for Development Proposals, 1966, HRMA, 102–41 D.6, 29.

49 HDI's original choice, as architect, was the modernist luminary I.M. Pei, who refused the offer. See Collier, *Contemporary Cathedrals.* Koch's career and style are discussed in Douglass Shand-Tucci, *Built in Boston: City and Suburb, 1800–2000* (Amherst, MA: University of Massachusetts Press, 1999), 260.

50 The construction of Scotia Square is analysed in Paul Erickson, *Halifax's North End: An Anthropologist Looks at the City* (Halifax: Lancelot Press, 1986), 80; Pacey, *Battle of Citadel Hill;* Claire Renwick, "City Building and Architectural Renewal: A Historical Study of Five Buildings in Halifax, Nova Scotia" (master's thesis, Concordia University, 2010).

51 The new developers are discussed in Pacey, *Battle of Citadel Hill.* Campeau's comment appears in Collier, *Contemporary Cathedrals.*

52 Halifax, *Master Plan,* 52–3.

53 See Fairley, "Struggle for Capitalism," 47–8.

54 The figures are from Lisa Patterson, "Indian Affairs and the Nova Scotia Centralization project" (master's thesis, Dalhousie University, 1985), 64, 84; Anita Tobin, "The Effects of Centralization on the Social and Political Systems of the Mainland Nova Scotia Mi'kmaq" (master's thesis, Saint Mary's University, 1999), 52. The migration of the Mi'kmaq outside Nova Scotia is noted in Daniel Paul, *We Were Not the Savages: A Micmac Perspective on the Collision of European and Aboriginal Civilizations* (Halifax: Nimbus Press, 1993), 297.

55 These assumptions and the quoted section can be found in a Department of Indian Affairs memo from 1945, quoted in Paul, *We Were Not the Savages,* 286–7.

56 Quoted in Paul, *We Were Not the Savages,* 293–7.

57 Housing policymakers' concerns about social justice are best documented in Humphrey Carver, *A Compassionate Landscape* (Toronto: University of Toronto Press, 1975), 56; Albert Rose, *Regent Park: A Study in Slum Clearance* (Toronto: University of Toronto Press, 1958); John Miron, "On Progress in Housing Canadians," in *Progress in Housing Canadians,* ed. John Miron (Montréal and Kingston: McGill-Queen's Press, 1993), 7–21. On the normative, population-managing dimensions of public housing, see Sean Purdy, "Industrial Efficiency, Social Order, and Moral Purity: Housing Reform Thought in English Canada, 1900–1950," *Urban History Review* 25, no. 2

(1997): 30–40; Sean Purdy, "Scaffolding Citizenship: Housing Reform and Nation Formation in Canada, 1900–1950," in *Contesting Canadian Citizenship: Historical Readings*, ed. Robert Adamoski, Dorothy Chunn, and Robert Menzies (Peterborough, ON: Broadview Press, 2002), 141–7.

58 Redevelopment Committee Minutes, 13 January 1958, 4.

59 The initial tenant-selection criteria for Mulgrave Park are established in Halifax, City Council Minutes, 15 September 1960, 1043. Concerns about Mulgrave tenants' behaviour, including criminality, immorality, and hanging clothes lines, are registered frequently in the minutes of city council and the Housing and Redevelopment Committee. See, for example, City Council Minutes, 26 April 1962, 303. The top-down character of Canadian public housing in general is discussed in Purdy, "Scaffolding Citizenship," 146–7.

60 Early efforts to build public housing in Halifax, including the Bayers Road project, are detailed in John Bacher, "From Study to Reality: The Establishment of Public Housing in Halifax, 1930–1953," *Acadiensis* 18, no. 1 (1988): 120–35.

61 The Stephenson Report called for the construction of public housing for 4,500 inhabitants, without specifying the number of units this would involve. The figure I cite (1,100) is based on the ratio of inhabitants/housing units that the report recommends for the Mulgrave Park project (330 units and 1,200 inhabits). See Stephenson, *Redevelopment Study*, 24, 58. The history of the Mulgrave Park site is traced in Garry Shutlak, "The Governor's North Farm and Mulgrave Park, Halifax," *The Griffin: A Publication of Heritage Trust of Nova Scotia* 30, no. 3 (September 2005): 1–4. The approval of the Mulgrave project and the eventual funding arrangements appear in Redevelopment Committee Minutes, 16 December 1957; Halifax, City Council Minutes, 16 October 1958, 536. The allocation of Mulgrave units to CRA and blight-removal displacees, respectively, was debated for several months. The final decision appears in City Council Minutes, 12 January 1961, 23. The quote from Mayor Kitz appears in City Council Minutes, 16 October 1958, 548.

62 The city's working definition of overcrowding (inhabitants per room) is set out in Stephenson, *Redevelopment Study*, 46–7. The Mulgrave project contained 349 units on 11.5 acres (for 30 units/acre). Bacher, *Keeping to the Marketplace*, 216. The CRA contained 385 units on 14 acres (for 27.5 units/acre); it was thus slightly less dense than Mulgrave Park on a unit/acre basis. Figures for the CRA are provided in Redevelopment Committee Minutes, 14 November 1957, 6.

63 The two quotes are from Halifax, City Council Minutes, 16 October 1958, 538, 546. The number and layout of the units is outlined in ibid., 536–51.

64 On income and rent levels, see n42 above. Concerns that Mulgrave might become a slum were expressed in Halifax, City Council Minutes, 16 October 1958, 546; they appear again, after the opening of the project, in City Council Minutes, 26 April 1962, 303. The eviction of "immoral" tenants, supplemented by police action, is ordered in City Council Minutes, 17 May 1962, 338. The rate of two evictions per day is cited in Bacher, *Keeping to the Marketplace*, 217.

65 Recreation programs, the study groups, and the quote appear in Redevelopment Committee Minutes, 2 January 1962, 4.

66 The original intention, expressed at a November 1957 meeting of the Housing and Redevelopment Committee, was that the clearing of the CRA proceed in an "orderly fashion from block to block as rehousing was available to those diplaced." Redevelopment Committee Minutes, 14 Nov 1957, 12. Given the February 1958 start of the CRA redevelopment, the completion of the first Mulgrave Park units in November 1961 suggests a thirty-three-month delay. The agreement with the CMHC and the province, finally reached in April 1958, is discussed in Halifax, City Council Minutes, 13 March 1958, 133; 17 April 1958, 225. The tendering of the construction contract appears in Redevelopment Committee Minutes, 22 October 1959, 1–7. The partial opening of one hundred units (in November 1961) is discussed in Redevelopment Committee Minutes, 21 November 1961, 3–6. The $5.2 million cost appears in Redevelopment Committee Minutes, 5 December 1961, 4.

67 Carver, *Compassionate Landscape*, 142.

68 Redevelopment Committee Minutes, 9 December 1957, 4.

69 The transfer of the property to Halifax is discussed frequently by the Housing and Redevelopment Committee between 1958 and 61. The prospect of the transfer first appears in Redevelopment Committee Minutes, 12 June 1958, 3. The conditions under which it will be transferred are stipulated in Redevelopment Committee Minutes, 1 February 1961. Early plans for the property are discussed in Redevelopment Committee Minutes, 4 July 1958; 1 May 1958; 29 April 1960. A vaster project, exceeding the terrain of the School for the Deaf property, is articulated in Redevelopment Committee Minutes, 11 March 1960; 29 April 1960.

70 City of Halifax, Uniacke Square Redevelopment Project Report, 1962, HRMA, 102–105–3, box 23. The quote appears in Redevelopment Committee Minutes, 29 April 1960, 20.

71 Halifax, City Council Minutes, 14 June 1962. Small amendments appear in City Council Minutes, 13 September 1962, 531.

72 Uniacke Square Redevelopment Report, 24 April 1963, HRMA, 102–42.D4. The figure for permanent displacement (two thousand residents) is also signalled in Uniacke Square Redevelopment Report, 1962, 14.

73 The rejection of the homes' "blighted" status appears in Uniacke Square Redevelopment Report, 1963, 18. The quote is from Halifax, City Council Minutes, 13 June 1963, 260. Similar concerns are raised in City Council Minutes, 23 October 1963, 465.
74 Uniacke Square Redevelopment Report, 1963, 3.
75 The details of the project are outlined in Central Mortgage and Housing Company, "Uniacke Aquare, Phase I" (Ottawa: CMHC, 1964). The quote is from "Second Stage of Uniacke Square Completed," *Halifax Mail-Star*, 13 October 1967.
76 Halifax, *Master Plan*, 55.
77 Stephenson, *Redevelopment Study*, 56.
78 See Halifax, *Master Plan*, 56; Clairmont and Magill, *Relocation Report*, 115–16.
79 Quoted in Clairmont and Magill, *Relocation Report*, 69.
80 Community life in Africville in this period is outlined in Mount Saint Vincent Art Gallery, ed., *Africville: A Spirit that Lives on* (Halifax: Black Cultural Centre for Nova Scotia, Africville Genealogy Society, and National Film Board, 1989); Clairmont and Magill, *Relocation Report*; Clairmont and Magill, *Africville*. The survey results are presented in Institute of Public Affairs, *The Condition of the Negroes of Halifax City, Nova Scotia: A Study* (Halifax: Institute of Public Affairs, 1962).
81 The quote is from an interview with Rose conducted for, and cited in, Clairmont and Magill, *Relocation Report*, 160–1. Rose's 1963 report is contained in an appendix to this report. Albert Rose, "Report of a Visit to Halifax with Particular Respect to Africville," in Clairmont and Magill, *Relocation Report*, appendix F.
82 Quoted in Nelson, *Razing Africville*, 75.
83 The amounts paid by the city to Africville residents are presented in Clairmont and Magill, *Africville*, 189. On the relocation itself, see ibid., 190–203. The potential illegalities in the expropriation proceedings came to light in the 1990s and were evaluated by the Nova Scotia Supreme Court in 2015. See "Ex-Africville Residents Seek to Be Re-Included in Lawsuit Against City," *Halifax Chronicle-Herald*, 25 February 2015.
84 Residents granted tenancy to Mulgrave Park are discussed in Clairmont and Magill, *Africville*, 222–9. The racism of Halifax landlords, which would have to be faced by displacees not granted public housing tenancy, is outlined in Institute of Public Affairs, *Condition of Negroes*. The problems with the promised social services are outlined in Clairmont and Magill, *Africville*, 193–7.

85 David Woods, *Native Song: Poetry and Paintings* (Halifax: Nimbus Publishing, 2008), 93.

86 Donald Clairmont provides a signature example of this class-centred analysis in his critique of Jennifer Nelson's race-focused book on Africville. Racism, for Clairmont, exists in places like the job market and political system, and enters urban planning only through its effects (e.g., poverty and lack of political power) that racism elsewhere induces. Donald Clairmont, "Review of Jennifer J. Nelson, *Razing Africville: A Geography of Racism*," *Canadian Journal of Sociology* 34, no. 3 (2009): 920–2. On the broader ascription of urban renewal displacement to social class rather than to race, see Robert Gioielli, "'We Must Destroy You to Save You': Highway Construction and the City as a Modern Commons," *Radical History Review* 109 (2011): 67.

87 Stephenson mentions "Negro" home ownership in *Redevelopment Study*, 46. Homeownership was outlined in detail in Institute for Public Affairs, *Condition of Negroes.*

88 Joy James, *Resisting State Violence: Radicalism, Gender, and Race in US Culture* (Minneapolis: University of Minnesota, 1996). This analysis, minus the critique of Foucault, is elaborated in Joy James, "Afrarealism and the Black Matrix: Maroon Philosophy at Democracy's Border," *The Black Scholar* 43, no. 4 (2013): 124–31.

89 Halifax, *Master Plan*, 29.

90 Robert Caro, *The Power Broker: Robert Moses and the Fall of New York* (New York: Vintage Books, 1975), 837–94.

91 Andrew Giguere, "'… And the Twain Shall Meet': Baltimore's East-West Expressway and the Construction of the 'Highway to Nowhere'" (master's thesis, Ohio University, 2009); Nicholas Brady, "Spring in Baltimore," *Gawker* (blog), 11 July 2015, http://gawker.com/spring-in-baltimore-1717209805.

92 For a broad view of expressway construction, see Christopher Leo, *The Politics of Urban Development: Canadian Urban Expressway Disputes* (Toronto: Institute of Public Administration of Canada, 1977). On Saint John and London, see, respectively, Greg Marquis, "Uneven Renaissance: Urban Development in Saint John 1955–1976," *Journal of New Brunswick Studies* 1 (2010): 91–112; Danielle Robinson, "Modernism at a Crossroad: The Spadina Expressway Controversy, Toronto, ON, 1960–1971," *Canadian Historical Review* 92, no. 2 (2011): 301. Jean Drapeau's view of expressway construction is presented in *Circulation à Montréal*, directed by Bernard Devlin (Montréal: Office National de Film, 1955), DVD. The Ville-Marie expressway and its effects on the Saint-Antoine district (also known as Little Burgundy) have never been treated in detail. Parts of the story are

presented in Myer Negru, "'Little Burgundy' Plan Progresses," *Montreal Gazette*, 30 September 1966; "'Little Burgundy'... The Second Project," *Montreal Gazette*, 17 December 1966; Dorothy Williams, *Blacks in Montreal, 1628–1986: An Urban Demography* (Cowansville, QC: Éditions Yvon Blais, 1989), 72–3.

93 Halifax, *Master Plan*, 14, 8.

94 The design of the expressway and the quote are from City of Halifax, "A Functional Planning Report for Harbour Drive," 1965, HRMA, 102–40. D3, 15–16. The expected social costs of the expressway are presented in "What Kind of City Do We Want?," *MOVE Magazine* 1, no. 1 (1971): 3.

95 The promise of an expressway to Halifax Developments Inc. (for Scotia Square) is mentioned in Collier, *Contemporary Cathedrals*, 152. The company expressed its entitlement to an expressway in City Council Minutes, 20 December 1967, 1059–60. The city's acquisition of properties for the expressway is discussed in City of Halifax, Byars to Mayor and Development Committee, 5 March 1965, Development Department Records, HRMA, 102–41. The approval of phase 1 of the Cogswell Interchange project after a lengthy debate appears in City Council Minutes, 19 July 1967, 661. The beginning of the second phase is discussed in "Interchange on Schedule: Ready in One Month," *Halifax Mail-Star*, 1 August 1968. The first concrete plan for Harbour Drive South is City of Halifax, *Harbour Drive Series, Report 1: Harbour Drive General* (Halifax: City of Halifax, 1966). In council meetings, the discussion of Harbour Drive was frequently entwined with the discussion of the Cogswell Interchange in 1967–8.

96 On the struggle over expressways in the United States, see Richard Baumbach and William Borah, *The Second Battle of New Orleans: A History of the Vieux Carré Riverfront Expressway Controversy* (Tuscaloosa: University of Alabama Press, 1981); Alan Lupo, Frank Colcord, and Edmund Fowler, *Rites of Way: The Politics of Transportation in Boston and the US City* (New York: Little, Brown, 1971); John Seley, *Development of a Sophisticated Opposition: The Lower Manhattan Expressway Issue* (Princeton: Princeton University Press, 1970); William Issel, "'Land Values, Human Values, and the Preservation of the City's Treasured Appearance': Environmentalism, Politics, and the San Francisco Freeway Revolt," *Pacific Historical Review* 68, no. 4 (1999): 611–46; Raymond Mohl, "Stop the Road: Freeway Revolts in American Cities," *Journal of Urban History* 30, no. 5 (2004): 674–706. In Canada, see Leo, *Politics of Urban Development*; Kay Anderson, *Vancouver's Chinatown: Racial Discourse in Canada, 1875–1980* (Montréal and Kingston: McGill-Queen's University Press, 1995); Robinson, "Modernism at a Crossroad."

97 Luc Boltanski and Eve Chiapello, *The New Spirit of Capitalism* (London: Verso, 2005). The involvement of the New Left in expressway politics is

charted in Klemek, *Transatlantic Collapse*; David Ley, "Liberal Ideology and the Postindustrial City," *Annals of the Association of American Geographers* 70, no. 2 (1980): 238–58. The quote is from Mohl, "Stop the Road," 678.

98 On the involvement of Black Power activists in anti-expressway movements, see Robert Self, "To Plan our Liberation: Black Power and the Politics of Place in Oakland, California, 1965–1977," *Journal of Urban History* 26 (2000): 759–92; Jeanne Theoharis and Komozi Woodard, *Groundwork: Local Black Freedom Movements in America* (New York: NYU Press, 2005); Peniel Joseph, ed., *Neighborhood Rebels: Black Power at the Local Level* (New York: Palgrave Macmillan, 2010).

99 The struggle to preserve the waterfront buildings is described in detail (but with errors on some of the dates) in A.F. Duffus, "Heritage Properties – Halifax," in *Rehabilitation of Buildings: Second Canadian Building Congress, 17 October 1979, Toronto* (Ottawa: National Research Council Canada, 1980), 179–85; Renwick, "City Building and Architectural Renewal." The seven buildings designated as a heritage site comprised Privateers' Warehouse, Collins Bank and Warehouse, Pickford and Black Shipping Office and Warehouse, Simon's Warehouse, The Red Store, Wooden Store, and Carpenter Shop. The first four are early 1800s stone buildings, while the latter three are late 1800s wooden structures. See Peter John Stokes, *Waterfront Buildings of Halifax, Nova Scotia* (Ottawa: Historic Sites and Monuments Board of Canada, 1963).

100 See Pacey, *Battle of Citadel Hill*, 8–10; Heritage Trust, *Preservation for Use* (Halifax: Heritage Trust, 1972), 3.

101 Pacey, *Battle of Citadel Hill*, 21.

102 Halifax, City Council Minutes, 14 March 1968, 232–3.

103 Fingard, Guildford, and Sutherland, *Halifax*, 178.

104 Collins's most important early intervention was L.W. Collins, A Brief Concerning the Preservation and Restoration of Certain Waterfront Buildings in Halifax, Nova Scotia - Submitted to the Mayor and Aldermen, Halifax City Council, 3 August 1964, Heritage Trust Fonds, Nova Scotia Archives and Records Management (NSARM), MG 30, series L, vol. 1. The mission of the advisory committee is quoted in Renwick, "City Building and Architectural Renewal," 67.

105 Halifax, City Council Minutes, 14 March 1968.

106 A.M. Margison and Associates, Evaluation of Alternate Proposals for the Connection of Upper Water Street to the Cogswell Street Interchange, July 1968, HRMA, 625.725E. The document is improperly dated "July, 1969" by the archives. Discussion of the document appears in Halifax, City Council Minutes, 19 March 1968, 246; Peter Meerburg, "Harbour Drive to Bury History," *Halifax Mail-Star*, 20 March 1968.

107 Halifax, City Council Minutes, 19 June 1969.

108 "Council Will Reconsider Decision," *Halifax Mail-Star*, 27 June 1969; Halifax, City Council Minutes, 31 July 1969, 695.

109 O'Brien's touring of W.A. Stewart through the waterfront buildings is mentioned in Halifax, City Council Minutes, 2 July 1969. Rumours of interested developers were discussed at the same meeting, as well as on 31 July 1969.

110 The decision to reconsider the plan is discussed in "Council Will Reconsider Decision," *Halifax Mail-Star*, 27 June 1969. The discussion of the new scenario occurred at a meeting on 31 July 1969. The quote is from Halifax, City Council Minutes, 31 July 1969, 691.

111 Halifax, City Council Minutes, 31 July 1969, 697.

112 The rehabilitation project is discussed in "City Gets Chance to Look Ahead," *Halifax Mail-Star*, 14 August 1972.

113 For African Nova Scotians, writes Clarke, "the advent of modernity ... was marked, not by the founding of a university or the election of a premier, but by the bulldozers of *'progress' destroying* the Seaview United Baptist Church and the entire community of Africville at the end of the 1960s in the name of *integration* and urban development" (my emphasis). George Elliott Clarke, "Towards a Conservative Modernity: Cultural Nationalism in Contemporary Acadian and Africadian Poetry," *Frontenac Review* 9 (1992): 45–63.

5 "A Place to Enjoy Oneself": Anti-Renewal Activism, Citizen Involvement, and the Limits of Urban Amenity

1 "What Kind of City Do We Want?," *MOVE Magazine* 1, no. 1 (1971): 3.

2 On the meaning and history of amenity in urban planning, see Mariana Valverde, "Taking Land Use seriously: Toward an Ontology of Municipal Law" *Law Text Culture* 9 (2005): 34–58; Peter Smith, "The Principle of Utility and the Origins of Planning Legislation in Alberta, 1912–1975," in *The Usable Urban Past: Planning and Politics in the Modern Canadian City*, ed. Alan Artibise and Gilbert Stelter (Toronto: Macmillan, 1979), 196–225; Leo Kuper, "Social Science Research and the Planning of Urban Neighbourhoods," *Social Forces* 29, no. 3 (1951): 237–43.

3 Early discussions of amenity are reviewed in Mel Scott, *American City Planning Since 1890* (Berkeley: University of California, 1971), 11, 107, 118. The renewed interest in amenity among anti-renewal activists is discussed most centrally in David Ley, "Liberal Ideology and the Postindustrial City," *Annals of the Association of American Geographers* 70, no. 2 (1980): 238–58; Christopher Klemek, *The Transatlantic Collapse of Urban Renewal: Postwar Urbanism from New York to Berlin* (Chicago: University of Chicago Press, 2011).

4 On the importance of citizen involvement in struggles over 1960s public policies, including urban renewal, see Edmund Burke, "Citizen Participation Strategies," *Journal of the American Institute of Planners* 34, no. 5 (1968): 287–94; Lillian Rubin, "Maximum Feasible Participation: The Origins, Implications, and Present Status," *Annals of the American Academy of Political and Social Science* 385, no. 1 (1969): 14–29; Leslie Pal, *Interest of State: The Politics of Language, Multiculturalism, and Feminism in Canada* (Montréal and Kingston: McGill-Queen's Press, 1993).

5 For a broad review of 1960s social movements in Canada, see Lara Campbell, Gregory Kealey, and Dominique Clément, eds., *Debating Dissent: Canada and the Sixties* (Toronto: University of Toronto Press, 2012). Canadian Black Power and Red Power movements (and their connections to movements elsewhere) are discussed in David Austin, *Fear of a Black Nation: Race, Sex, and Security in Sixties Montreal* (Toronto: Between the Lines Press, 2013); Sean Mills, *The Empire Within: Postcolonial Thought and Political Activism in Sixties Montreal* (Montréal and Kingston: McGill-Queen's University Press, 2010); Glen Coulthard, *Red Skin, White Masks: Rejecting the Colonial Politics of Recognition* (Minneapolis: University of Minnesota Press, 2014); Scott Rutherford, "The Anicinabe Park Occupation and Indigenous Decolonization," in *The Hidden 1970s: Histories of Radicalism*, ed. Dan Berger (Rutgers, NJ: Rutgers University Press, 2010), 77–94. The distinction between "artistic" and "social" critiques is most clearly elaborated in Luc Boltanski and Eve Chiapello, *The New Spirit of Capitalism* (London: Verso, 2005). On the urban politics of Black Power, see Robert Self, "To Plan Our Liberation: Black Power and the Politics of Place in Oakland, California, 1965–1977," *Journal of Urban History* 26 (2000): 759–92; Jeanne Theoharis and Komozi Woodard, *Groundwork: Local Black Freedom Movements in America* (New York: NYU Press, 2005); Peniel Joseph, ed., *Neighborhood Rebels: Black Power at the Local Level* (New York: Palgrave Macmillan, 2010). On the urban politics of the counterculture and New Left, see Manuel Castells, *The City and the Grassroots: A Cross-Cultural Theory of Urban Social Movements* (Berkeley: University of California Press, 1983); Klemek, *Transatlantic Collapse*.

6 See Judith Fingard, Janet Guildford, and David Sutherland, *Halifax: The First 250 Years* (Halifax: Formac Publishing, 1999), 160–78; James Walker, "Black Confrontation in Sixties Halifax," in *Debating Dissent: Canada and the Sixties*, ed. Lara Campbell, Gregory Kealey, and Dominique Clément (Toronto: University of Toronto Press, 2012), 173–92; Margaret Gall, "Movement for Citizens Voice and Action: A Case Study on Citizen Participation" (master's thesis, Dalhousie University, 1974).

7 See Elizabeth Pacey, *The Battle of Citadel Hill* (Halifax: Lancelot Press, 1979); Lachlan Barber, "Making Meaning of Heritage Landscapes: The Politics of Redevelopment in Halifax, NS," *Canadian Geographer* 57, no. 1 (2012): 90–112.
8 Pacey, *Battle of Citadel Hill*, 8, 10.
9 City of Halifax, *Views Citadel Hill – Progress Reports 1 and 2* (Halifax: City of Halifax, 1972), 5, 3.
10 An example of the HDBA's revived political activities appears in City of Halifax, Minutes of the Council of the City of Halifax, 25 June 1970, Halifax Regional Municipality Archives (HRMA), RG 102–1A, 402. Ironically, the group had earlier petitioned council in support of the Stephenson Report. See City of Halifax, J.B. Ashbourne to Mayor and Council, Downtown Business and Professional Men's Association, Halifax, City Council Minutes, 27 September 1960, 1138.
11 Changes in Halifax retailing are documented in Hugh Millward, "Twentieth-Century Retail Change in the Halifax Central Business District," *Canadian Geographer* 41, no. 2 (1997): 194–201; Joan Doehler, "Scotia Square: Its Impact on the Downtown Core" (master's thesis, Dalhousie University, 2001).
12 Halifax, City Council Minutes, 23 July 1965, 497a.
13 Halifax, City Council Minutes, 17 June 1971, 374; 16 September 1971, 561; 10 November 1971, 650; C.E. Babb, Director of Planning, to Members of the Downtown Committee, 18 September 1971, Town Planning Board Reports, HRMA, RG 102–40 (D.15); City of Halifax, *What Kind of Downtown Do We Want?* (Halifax: City of Halifax, 1972).
14 Halifax, *What Kind of Downtown*, n.p.
15 The latter quote, resonant with the vision of *What Kind of Downtown*, is from the objectives of the Downtown Committee, outlined in Halifax, City Council Minutes, 16 September 1971, 561.
16 I trace Foucault's discussion of enjoyment in Ted Rutland, "Enjoyable Life: Planning, Amenity, and the Contested Terrain of Urban Biopolitics," *Environment and Planning D: Society and Space* 33, no. 5 (2015): 850–68. Other work in this vein includes Ben Anderson, "Affect and Biopower: Towards a Politics of Life," *Transactions of the Institute of British Geographers* 37, no. 1 (2011): 28–43; Daniel Andrade, "Governing 'Emotional' Life: Passions, Moral Sentiments, and Emotion," *International Review of Sociology* 24, no. 1 (2014): 110–29; and Eric Olund, "'Disreputable Life': Race, Sex, and Intimacy," *Environment and Planning D: Society and Space* 28, no. 1 (2010): 142–57. Foucault's discussion of vitalpolitics appears in Michel Foucault, *The Birth of Biopolitics: Lectures at the Collège de France, 1978–1979* (New York: Picador, 2010).

17 Alexander Rüstow, "Organic Policy (Vitalpolitik) Versus Mass Regimentation," in *Freedom and Serfdom: An Anthology of Western Thought*, ed. Arnold Hunold (Dordrecht: D. Reidel Publishing, 1967), 187.
18 Foucault, *Birth of Biopolitics*.
19 See n2 above.
20 A.L. Murray, "Frederick Law Olmsted and the Design of Mount Royal Park, Montreal," *Journal of the Society of Architectural Historians* 26, no. 3 (1967): 163. The term "amenity," though not yet widely used in nineteenth-century planning discussions, is employed by Olmsted at several points in his written work. See, for example, Frederick Law Olmsted, *Plans and Views of Public Parks* (Baltimore: John's Hopkins University Press, 2015), xiii, 297.
21 Scott, *American City Planning*, 11, 107.
22 Halifax, City Council Minutes, 30 April 1908, 365.
23 On the integration of amenity into a larger planning framework, see Thomas Adams, *Municipal and Real Estate Finance in Canada* (Ottawa: Thomas Mulvey, 1921), 5–6. Gordon Stephenson's 1957 plan for Halifax was also exemplary in this regard, extolling the psychologically pleasing effects of the city's physical setting and "human"-scale downtown. These qualities, of course, tended to be overlooked in a planning report geared so heavily to the "best use" of land and the normalization of low-income populations. Gordon Stephenson, *A Redevelopment Study of Halifax, Nova Scotia* (Halifax: City of Halifax, 1957), 24–5.
24 Smith, "Principle of Utility."
25 Kuper, "Social Science Research."
26 Ley, "Liberal Ideology."
27 See Humphrey Carver, *A Compassionate Landscape* (Toronto: University of Toronto Press, 1975), 180–94; Pamela Stern and Peter V. Hall, *The Proposal Economy: Neoliberal Citizenship in "Ontario's Most Historic Town"* (Vancouver: University of British Columbia Press, 2015), 44.
28 See Gerald Hodge and Ira Robinson, "Regional Economic Development Planning," in *Planning Canadian Regions* (Vancouver: University of British Columbia Press, 2001), 161–89; Michael Bradfield, *Regional Economics: Analysis and Policies in Canada* (Toronto: McGraw-Hill Ryerson, 1988).
29 The NSPS is briefly discussed in Gall, "Movement for Citizens Voice"; Dimitry Anastakis, "Building a 'New Nova Scotia': State Intervention, the Auto Industry, and the Case of Volvo in Halifax, 1963–1998," *Acadiensis* 34, no. 1 (2004): 3–30.
30 Interview with Leonard Poetschke, 22 July 2009. "Dull Jargon Kills Enthusiasm," n.d., Metropolitan Area Planning Council (MAPC) Records, HRMA, RG 102 (S2.3).

31 Daniel Bell, "Notes on the Post-Industrial Society – Part One," *Public Interest* 6 (Winter 1967): 24–35; Daniel Bell, "Notes on the Post-Industrial Society – Part Two," *Public Interest* 6 (Spring 1967): 102–18.
32 Bell, "Notes – Part One," 35.
33 Rüstow, "Organic Policy." On the connection to the New Left, see Foucault, *Birth of Biopolitics*, 129–58.
34 See Howard Brick, *Daniel Bell and the Decline of Intellectual Radicalism: Social Theory and Political Reconciliation in the 1940s* (Madison: University of Wisconsin Press, 1986).
35 Benjamin Higgins, "Towards a Science of Community Planning," *Journal of the American Institute of Planners* 15, no. 3 (1949): 12.
36 Benjamin Higgins, "Search for a Welfare Function," *Growth and Change* 5, no. 4 (1974): 5.
37 These views are best expressed in the NSPS-funded report, MAPC, "New Directions for Development: Outline of a Development Strategy for the Halifax Dartmouth Metropolitan Area," 2 February 1971, HRMA, MAPC Records, RG 102 (S2.3).
38 Ibid., 5.
39 Ibid., 6.
40 Ibid., 6.
41 See James DeFilippis, *Unmaking Goliath: Community Control in the Face of Global Capital* (New York: Routledge, 2004), 37–60; Self, "To Plan Our Liberation"; Michael Orsini, "From 'Community Run' to 'Community Based'? Exploring the Dynamics of Civil Society-State Transformation in Urban Montreal," in *Forgotten Families: Globalization and the Health of Canadians*, ed. Ronald Labonté (Ottawa: Institute for Population Health, 2010), 169–84; Mills, *Empire Within*.
42 See n4 above.
43 Interview with Leonard Poetschke.
44 On MAPC, see Hugh Millward, "Peri-urban Residential Development in the Halifax Region 1960–2000: Magnets, Constraints, and Planning Policies," *Canadian Geographer* 46, no. 1 (2002): 33–47; Jill Grant, "Hard Luck: The Failure of Regional Planning in Nova Scotia," *Canadian Journal of Regional Science* 12, no. 2 (1989): 273–84.
45 "Major Role for Metro Area Planning Group," 19 June 1970, MAPC Records, HRMA, RG 102 (S2.3).
46 "Kentville Huddle Huge Success," 4 March 1971, MAPC Records, HRMA, RG 102 (S2.3).
47 See Saul Alinsky, *Reveille for Radicals* (New York: Vintage, 1946); Douglas Rossinow, *Visions of Progress: The Left-Liberal Tradition in America* (Philadelphia: University of Pennsylvania Press, 2008).

48 Saul Alinsky, *Rules for Radicals: A Practical Primer for Realistic Radicals* (New York: Vintage, 1972), 53.

49 Ibid., 120.

50 Lawrence Engel, "Saul Alinsky and the Chicago School," *Speculative Philosophy* 16, no. 1 (2002): 50–66.

51 The twelve experts were: Ed Logue (chief of the New York Urban Development Corporation); Martin Rein (Centre for Environmental Studies, University of London); Wilbur Thompson (urban economist, Wayne State University); Benjamin Higgins (economist, Université de Montréal); Lucius Walker (Interreligious Foundation); Clare Gunn (expert on tourism, Texas A&M); David Kirkbride (vice president of Canadian Industries Ltd); T.J. (Joe) Scanlon (journalist and professor at Carleton University); Frank Steggart (specialist in governmental structure, Atlanta); Konrad Studnicki-Gizbert (transport economist, York University); Dennis McDermott (head of Canadian Auto Workers); and Scott Greer (sociologist, Northwestern University). See Nova Scotia Voluntary Planning Board (NSVPB), *Encounter on Urban Environment, Vol. 3: Historian's Report* (Halifax: NSVPB, 1970).

52 See Fingard, Guildford, and Sutherland, *Halifax*, 160–78; *Encounter on Urban Environment*, directed by Roger Hart (Toronto: National Film Board, 1971), DVD.

53 See NSVPB, *Encounter on Urban Environment, vol. 5: Transcript of Final Session* (Halifax: NSVPB, 1970), 3–5.

54 NSVPB, *Historian's Report*, 67.

55 NSVPB, *Encounter on Urban Environment, vol. 12: Structure of Decision-Making* (Halifax: NSVPB, 1970), 30–1 (emphasis mine).

56 NSVPB, *Historian's Report*, 41 (emphasis mine).

57 Michel Foucault, *Security, Territory, Population: Lectures at the Collège de France, 1977–1978* (New York: Picador, 2004), 55–66; Mary Beth Mader, *Sleights of Reason: Norm, Biosexuality, Development* (Albany: SUNY Press, 2011), 43–69.

58 NSVPB, *Historian's Report*, 64.

59 Ibid., 41.

60 NSVPB, *Encounter on Urban Environment: Transcript of Daily Sessions, Wednesday, February 25, 1970* (Halifax: NSVPB, 1970), 259–60.

61 On BUF, see ch. 6; Walker, "Black Confrontation"; Daniel McNeil, "Afro(Americo)centricity in Black (American) Nova Scotia," *Canadian Review of American Studies* 35, no. 1 (2005): 57–85; Jennifer Smith, *An International History of the Black Panther Party* (New York: Garland, 1999); Robert Ashe, *Halifax Champion: Black Power in Gloves* (Halifax: Formac Publishing, 2004). Estimates of Nova Scotia's Black population in this period vary; the Canadian Census figures are far from a reliable source. The figure eighteen

thousand was often cited by BUF. Walker suggests a total of twenty thousand; "Black Confrontation," 316n1.

62 NSVPB, *Transcript of Daily Sessions,* 276–7.

63 See, for example, Julissa Reynoso, "The Impact of Identity Politics and Public Sector Reform on Organizing and the Practice of Democracy," *Columbia Human Rights Law Review* 37 (2005): 149–87.

64 NSVPB, *Structure of Decision-Making,* 29.

65 Quoted in "In the Panther's Wake," *Globe Magazine,* 15 February 1969, 43.

66 Analysis of racial discrimination cases is based on Case and Special Assignment Officer: Reports, Correspondence, 1971–4, BUF Fonds, Nova Scotia Records and Archives Management (NSARM), vol. 9, no. 12; Case Files: Human Rights Commission (N.S.), 1972–9, BUF Fonds, NSARM, vol. 19, no. 6.

67 Quote is from "Kentville Huddle a Success."

68 MOVE staff levels are traced in MOVE Progress Report, 21 March 1972, Dalhousie University Archives (DUA), MOVE Collection, MS 11–1, box 2. Funding is charted in Gall, "Movement for Citizens Voice"; Presentation, n.d., DUA, MOVE Collection, box 10; MOVE Core funding proposal to the Ministry of State for Urban Affairs, September 1974, DUA, MOVE Collection, MS 11–1, box 1, 6.

69 Exhaustive efforts were made to locate the rights holder to *figures 5.2* and *5.3* for permission to use these images, but to no avail. Please contact the author if you hold rights to these.

70 *MOVE Magazine* 1, no. 1 (1971): 3.

71 Cross-class alliances were perhaps especially common in anti-expressway movements. See Richard Baumbach and William Borah, *The Second Battle of New Orleans: A History of the Vieux Carré Riverfront Expressway Controversy* (Tuscaloosa: University of Alabama Press, 1981); Alan Lupo, Frank Colcord, and Edmund Fowler, *Rites of Way: The Politics of Transportation in Boston and the US City* (New York: Little, Brown, 1971); John Seley, *Development of a Sophisticated Opposition: The Lower Manhattan Expressway Issue* (Princeton: Princeton University Press, 1970); Raymond Mohl, "Stop the Road: Freeway Revolts in American Cities," *Journal of Urban History* 30, no. 5 (2004): 674–706.

72 Frances Early, "'A Grandly Subversive Time': The Halifax Branch of the Voice of Women in the 1960s," in *Mothers of the Municipality: Women, Work, and Social Policy in Post-1945 Halifax,* ed. Judith Fingard and Janet Guildford (Toronto: University of Toronto Press, 2005), 265.

73 See Saidiya Hartman, *Scenes of Subjection: Slavery, Terror, and Self-Making in Nineteenth-Century America* (Oxford: Oxford University Press, 1997), 56–7.

74 "Kentville Opening Session Feb/71," MOVE Collection, DUA, MS 11–1, box 15, 50.

75 These conflicts are traced in Gall, "Movement for Citizens Voice," 23, 27–30.
76 Jackie Barkley, "MOVE: An Analysis," DUA, MOVE Collection, MS 11–1, box 14, 15.
77 Interview with Leonard Poetschke; Interview with Fred Lennarson, 14 September 2009.
78 The workshop with Alinsky is mentioned in "History of the Organization," n.d., DUA, MOVE Collection, MS 11–1, box 14, 1. For an Alinsky-inspired training manual, see "What Happens in Groups: An Analysis to Help you Organize," DUA, MOVE Collection, MS 11–1, box 14. Alinsky's books, the National Film Board documentary, and the expectation that activists join groups on the basis of their interests was discussed in interviews with four MOVE activists.
79 MOVE, "What We Talked About," DUA, MOVE Collection, MS 11–1, box 1.
80 City of Halifax, Central Redevelopment Area – Call for Development Proposals, 1966, Development Department Records, HRMA, RG 35–102–41 (D.6), 6; City of Halifax, A Functional Planning Report for Harbour Drive, November 1965, RG 35–102 (40 D.3), 4.
81 *MOVE Magazine* 1, no. 1 (1971): 3.
82 MOVE's research at City Hall was discussed in interview with Alan Ruffman, 27 July 2009. MOVE's criticism of Harbour Drive is outlined in *MOVE Magazine* 1, no. 1 (1971); MOVE, Submission of Harbour Drive North Committee to the Public Hearing on Draft Halifax Municipal Development Plan, HRMA, RG 102–1B.
83 City of Halifax, Municipal Development Plan, 16 November 1972, HRMA, RG 102–1B.
84 City of Halifax, Henderson to Mayor and City Planning Committee, 13 March 1973, HRMA, Town Planning Board Records, RG 35–102 (40 D.1).
85 Halifax, City Council Minutes, 26 October 1972, 483.
86 One MOVE activist remembers there being eighty questions; an archived MOVE press release indicates forty-five questions. See MOVE, Press release, 18 January 1973, DUA, box 13F.
87 MOVE, Submission of Harbour Drive North Committee, 6.
88 Mayor O'Brien's commitment to respond to the forty-five questions in writing appears in MOVE, Press release.
89 City of Halifax, Discussions of Public Participation and Planning for Halifax, 1973, Town Planning Board Records, HRMA, RG 35–102 (40 D.1), 24.
90 City of Halifax, *Municipal Development Plan* (Halifax: City of Halifax, 1980).
91 The firing of Leonard Poetsche and his twelve-person NSPS team is discussed in Dulcie Conrad, "How Federal Planner Tom Kent Is Killing the Maritimes," *The 4th Estate*, 20 January 1971. The NSPS's Fred Lennarson informed activists at the February 1971 Kentville meeting that the agency

had earmarked $200,000 in its 1970–1 budget for community groups and that this money could be used to support the soon-to-be-formed activist alliance. Ironically, the NSPS was already being disbanded at this point. See MOVE, "Kentville Opening Session Feb/71," MOVE Collection, DUA, MS 11–1, box 15, 50.

92 MOVE's funding sources and Fitzgerald's efforts to cut them off are discussed in Gall, "Movement for Citizens Voice."

93 Internal discussion of the alliance's divisions appears in Ecology Action Centre, "Position Re: MOVE Adopted in Principle February 26 and in Detail March 21," March 1973, MOVE Records, DUA, MS 11–1, box 14, 1; Barkley, "MOVE: An Analysis"; Mollie Gallagher, "Another Bit of Paper," MOVE Records, DUA, MS 11–1, box 14.

94 *The 4th Estate*, 7 February 1974. The same claims are made in Gall, "Movement for Citizens Voice," 24–5.

95 *MOVE Magazine* 1, no. 1 (1971): 3–4.

96 Barkley, "MOVE: An Analysis," 20, 22.

97 See Hartman, *Scenes of Subjection*, 17–48. Christina Sharpe, *Monstrous Intimacies: Making Post-Slavery Subjects* (Durham: Duke University Press, 2009), 111–52.

98 Lewis Gordon, *Bad Faith and Antiblack Racism* (Atlantic Highlands, NJ: Humanities Press, 1995), 99–100.

99 See Hartman, *Scenes of Subjection*, 17–48; Sharpe, *Monstrous Intimacies*, 111–52.

100 Halifax "race riots" are discussed in Donald Clairmont, "Policing the Uptown: Inner-City Community Policing Challenges and the Halifax 'Race Riot' of 1991" (Halifax: Atlantic Institute of Criminology, 1992); Christopher McCormick, "The Halifax Race Riot: Extralocality and Racism in the News," in *Constructing Danger: Emotions and Mis/representation of Crime in the News* (Halifax: Fernwood Publishing, 2010), 118–35; George Elliott Clarke, "White Cops, Black Corpses," *National Post*, 10 April 2015.

6 Planning by Other Means: The Black United Front and the Struggle for Self-Determination

1 The diverse perspectives and their eventual influence on the Black United Front (BUF) are discussed in Frank Boyd, "The Politics of the Minority Game: The Decline and Fall of the Black United Front," *New Maritimes*, March 1985, 10–12; Jules Oliver, "Formation of BUF," keynote address to the Canada Custom and Revenue Agency, Ottawa, 19 February 2004; James Walker, "Black Confrontation in Sixties Halifax," in *Debating Dissent: Canada and the Sixties*, ed. Lara Campbell, Gregory Kealey, and Dominique Clément (Toronto: University of Toronto Press, 2012), 173–92.

2 Contrasts with earlier Black organizations were frequently drawn by members of the BUF. Black resistance in Nova Scotia, by this point, had existed for more than two centuries, and it had taken many forms. Its *organizational* forms, however, had been relatively consistent. It tended to involve white people in leadership positions (alongside Black people) and tended to communicate demands to dominant institutions rather than challenge the latter from a position of power. For broad reviews of Black resistance in Nova Scotia, see Bridglal Pachai, *Beneath the Clouds of the Promised Land, 1800–1989* (Halifax: Black Educators Society of Nova Scotia, 1991); Sheridan Hay, "The Black Protest Tradition in Nova Scotia, 1783–1964" (master's thesis, Saint Mary's University, 1997).

3 Quoted in Barbara Hinds, "Black Power: Has Halifax Found the Answer?" *Atlantic Advocate*, January 1969, 9–15.

4 For a broad history of Black self-determination, see V.P. Franklin, *Black Self-Determination: A Cultural History of the Faith of Our Fathers* (Westport, CT: Lawrence Hill and Company, 1984); Jonathan Fenderson, "Towards the Gentrification of Black Power(?)," *Race and Class* 55, no. 1 (2013): 1–22. The significance of self-determination to the 1960s/70s Black Power movement (especially its urban-focused dimensions) is outlined in Rhonda Williams, "The Pursuit of Audacious Power: Rebel Reformers and Neighbourhood Politics in Baltimore, 1966–1968," in *Neighborhood Rebels: Black Power at the Local Level*, ed. Peniel Joseph (New York: Palgrave Macmillan, 2010), 215–42; Karen Ferguson, "Organizing the Ghetto: The Ford Foundation, CORE, and White Power in the Black Power Era, 1967–1969," *Journal of Urban History* 34, no. 1 (2007): 67–100. The Black Power movement in Canada is documented in David Austin, "All Roads Led to Montreal: Black Power, the Caribbean, and the Black Radical Tradition in Canada," *Journal of African American History* 92, no. 4 (2007): 516–39; David Austin, *Fear of a Black Nation: Race, Sex, and Security in Sixties Montreal* (Toronto: Between the Lines Press, 2013); Chris Harris, "The Development of Working-Class Organic Intellectuals in the Canadian Black Left Tradition: Historical Roots and Contemporary Expressions, Future Directions" (PhD diss., University of Toronto, 2011). BUF's definition of self-determination (Black people defining "their own destiny") appears frequently in its annual reports and executive director's reports. See, for example, BUF, Executive Director's Report, Annual Meeting, 25–6 October 1974, BUF Fonds, Nova Scotia Records and Archives Management (NSARM), vol. 7, no. 5, 3.

5 On the connection between Black Power and urban planning/renewal, see Williams, "Pursuit of Audacious Power"; Robert Self, "To Plan Our Liberation: Black Power and the Politics of Place in Oakland, California,

1965–1977," *Journal of Urban History* 26 (2000): 759–92; Jeanne Theoharis and Komozi Woodard, *Groundwork: Local Black Freedom Movements in America* (New York: NYU Press, 2005); Peniel Joseph, ed., *Neighborhood Rebels: Black Power at the Local Level* (New York: Palgrave Macmillan, 2010).

6 The rejection of white norms within the Black Power movement is emphasized in Nikhil Pal Singh, *Black Is a Country: Race and the Unfinished Struggle for Democracy* (Cambridge, MA: Harvard University Press, 2005), 128; Sylvia Wynter, "Unsettling the Coloniality of Being/Power/Truth/Freedom: Towards the Human, After Man, Its Overrepresentation – An Argument," *New Centennial Review* 3, no. 3 (2003): 257–337. The geographical implications of this antinormativity are explored in Katherine McKittrick, "On Plantations, Prisons, and a Black Sense of Place," *Social and Cultural Geography* 12, no. 8 (2011): 947–63.

7 This critique has been advanced in many places and forms, and resonates with a broader critique of essentialism in the post-1960s period. For a critique that singles out the Black Power movement (though, notably, without mentioning the Black Panther Party), see Cedric Johnson, *Revolutionaries to Race Leaders: Black Power and the Making of African American Politics* (Minneapolis: University of Minnesota Press, 2007).

8 The resistance of enslaved Black Nova Scotians (including resistance against re-enslavement) is discussed in Harvey Amani Whitfield, "The Struggle over Slavery in the Maritime Colonies," *Acadiensis* 41, no. 2 (Summer/Autumn 2012): 17–44. The history of the Black Loyalists and Black Refugees is documented in James Walker, *The Black Loyalists: The Search for a Promised Land in Nova Scotia and Sierra Leone, 1783–1870* (Toronto: University of Toronto Press, 1992); Harvey Amani Whitfield, *Blacks on the Border: The Black Refugees in British North America, 1815–1860* (Burlington: University of Vermont Press, 2006). El Jones's argument about self-liberation has been made in spoken-word poetry and political speeches; its essence flows through *Live From the Afrikan Resistance!* (Halifax: Fernwood Publishing, 2014). A more general treatment of Black resistance in Nova Scotia, including the struggle for better living conditions, appears in Pachai, *Beneath the Clouds*; Hay, "Black Protest Tradition; James Walker, *Identity: The Black Experience in Canada* (Toronto: Ontario Educational Communications Authority, 1979); David Sutherland, "Race Relations in Halifax, Nova Scotia, During the Mid-Victorian Quest for Reform," *Journal of the Canadian Historical Association* 7, no. 1 (1996): 35–54.

9 Saidiya Hartman, *Scenes of Subjection: Slavery, Terror, and Self-Making in Nineteenth-Century America* (Oxford: Oxford University Press, 1997), 76.

10 Sylvia Hamilton, "Naming Names, Naming Ourselves: A Survey of Early Black Women in Nova Scotia," in *We're Rooted Here and They Can't Pull Us*

Up: Essays in African Canadian Women's History, ed. Peggy Bristow (Toronto: University of Toronto Press, 1994), 13–40.

11 Sarah Haley, *No Mercy Here: Gender, Punishment, and the Making of Jim Crow Modernity* (Durham: University of North Carolina Press, 2016), 200.

12 On the Halifax branch of the Brotherhood of Sleeping Car Porters, see Hay, "Black Protest Tradition," 117. On the Home for Coloured Children, see ibid.; Charles Saunders, *Share and Care: The Story of the Nova Scotia Home for Colored Children* (Halifax: Nimbus Publishing, 1994). On the Nova Scotia branches of the Universal Negro Improvement Association, see Carla Marano, "'Rising Strongly and Rapidly': The Universal Negro Improvement Association in Canada, 1919–1940," *Canadian Historical Review*, 91, no. 2 (2010): 250; Marcus Garvey, *The Marcus Garvey and Universal Negro Improvement Association Papers*, vol. 4, ed. Robert Hill (Berkeley: University of California Press, 1985), 794–803.

13 The political importance of the Baptist Church is detailed in Pachai, *Beneath the Clouds*; Colin Thomson, *Born with a Call: A Biography of Dr. William Pearly Oliver* (Cherry Brook, NS: Black Cultural Centre for Nova Scotia, 1986).

14 Fred Moten, "The Case of Blackness," *Criticism* 50, no. 2 (2008): 178.

15 Judith Fingard, "Race and Respectability in Victorian Halifax," *Journal of Imperial and Commonwealth History* 20, no. 2 (1992): 183.

16 City of Halifax, Minutes of the Council of the City of Halifax, 19 June 1919, Halifax Regional Municipality Archives (HRMA), RG 102–1A, 72.

17 Ibid., 21 January 1954, 64.

18 See Fingard, "Race and Respectability."

19 On the Black Power movement, see n4 above. The movement's rejection of white norms is most clearly highlighted by Singh, *Black Is a Country*. Its cultivation of new "genres" of the human is described by Wynter, "Unsettling the Coloniality of Being" and Sylvia Wynter and Katherine McKittrick, "Unparalleled Catastrophe for Our Species? Or, to Give Humanness a Different Future: Conversations," in *Sylvia Wynter: On Being Human as Praxis*, ed. Katherine McKittrick (Durham: Duke University Press, 2015), 9–89.

20 "Called Racist by Black, White Radicals Cheer," *Globe and Mail*, 14 December 1968, 11. Jones's biography, until recently, had not been written. The core of my account draws from the partial biographies that appear in the film *Hymn to Freedom Part II: Nova Scotia – Against the Tides*, directed by Sylvia Hamilton (Mississauga: International Tele-Film, 1994), VHS; Daniel McNeil, "Afro(Americo)centricity in Black (American) Nova Scotia," *Canadian Review of American Studies* 35, no. 1 (2005): 57–85; Jon Tattrie, *The Hermit of Africville: The Life of Eddie Carvery* (Lawrencetown Beach, NS: Pottersfield

Press, 2010); *Encounter at Kwacha House – Halifax*, directed by Rex Tasker (Toronto: National Film Board, 1967), DVD. A rich, book-length biography finally arrived, with Burnley "Rocky" Jones and James W. StG. Walker, *Burnley "Rocky" Jones – Revolutionary* (Halifax: Roseway Publishing, 2016).

21 *Encounter at Kwacha House.*

22 Walker, "Black Confrontation," 179.

23 Austin, "All Roads Led to Montreal," 524.

24 Jones's appearance at the Black Writers Congress is discussed in Austin, "All Roads Led to Montreal." The postcongress visits of Black radicals to Halifax is documented in Jennifer Smith, *An International History of the Black Panther Party* (New York: Garland, 1999), 97–9; Walker, "Black Confrontation"; Tattrie, *Hermit of Africville.*

25 Quoted in Peniel Joseph, "Revolution in Babylon: Stokely Carmichael and America in the 1960s," *Souls* 9, no. 4 (2007): 290. On other occasions, Carmichael would express a more muted (nonviolent, nonrevolutionary) version of Black Power. In the 1966 speech that is often credited for introducing the concept, he defined Black Power in terms that closely express the vision of the (soon to be formed) Black United Front: "It is a call for black people in this country to unite, to recognize their heritage, to build a sense of community. It is a call for black people to define their own goals, to lead their own organizations." Peniel Joseph, *Dark Days, Bright Nights: From Black Power to Barack Obama* (New York: Basic Books, 2010), 26. His 1967 co-authored book expressed a similar vision; see Stokely Carmichael and Charles Hamilton, *Black Power: The Politics of Liberation in America* (New York: Vintage Books, 1967).

26 Quoted in Walker, "Black Confrontation," 175.

27 Tattrie, *Hermit of Africville.*

28 Quoted in Hinds, "Black Power," 13.

29 George Sams's visit to Halifax is traced in Walker, "Black Confrontation," 175–7; Smith, *International History*, 97–9. Sams was later revealed to be an informant of the US Federal Bureau of Investitation (FBI). He played a crucial role in setting up Black Panther chairman Bobby Seale on murder charges. See Paul Bass and Douglas Rae, *Murder in the Model City: The Black Panthers, Yale, and the Redemption of a Killer* (New York: Basic Books, 2009).

30 Walker, "Black Confrontation," 176.

31 See Sunera Thobani, *Exalted Subjects: Studies in the Making of Race and Nation in Canada* (Toronto: University of Toronto Press, 2007), 143–78.

32 Quoted in Walker, "Black Confrontation," 186.

33 The appointment of Jules Oliver as executive director (starting 20 April 1970) is noted in BUF, Minutes, Board of Directors Meeting, 25 April 1970, BUF Fonds, NSARM, vol. 3, no. 11.

34 The quote is from BUF, Executive Director's Report, 25–6 October 1974, 3. Earlier discussions of self-determination appear in many annual reports and director's reports. See, for example, BUF, Director's Report, 30 January 1971, BUF Fonds, NSARM, vol. 3, no. 11, 7.

35 See n4 above. The idea of linking First and Third World struggles through the pursuit of self-determination was influentially expressed by Malcolm X. See Malcolm X, "Linking the Problem," in *Malcolm X Speaks: Selected Speeches and Statements*, ed. George Breitman (New York: Grove Weidenfeld, 1965), 218.

36 On 1960s articulations of Black self-determination (including the reduced importance of establishing Black nation-states), see Rod Bush, *We Are Not What We Seem: Black Nationalism and Class Struggle* (New York: NYU Press, 2000), 7. The Black Panthers' vision of a decentralized society of self-governing communities is traced in Kathleen Cleaver and George Katsiaficas, *Liberation, Imagination, and the Black Panther Party: A New Look at the Black Panthers and their Legacy* (New York: Routledge, 2014). CORE and its conception of self-determination is finely traced in Williams, "Pursuit of Audacious Power."

37 BUF, "Declaration for Demonstration on 25 January 1971," BUF Fonds, NSARM, vol. 16, no. 10.

38 *GRASP*, July–August 1971, BUF Fonds, NSARM, O/S F90/G76.

39 BUF, Annual Progress Report, April 1972–March 1973, BUF Fonds, NSARM, vol. 7, no. 4, 46–7.

40 Ibid.; BUF, "Declaration for Demonstration on 25 January 1971."

41 See "Halifax Inquiry Set for Prejudice Case," *Globe and Mail*, 24 March 1970, 8; BUF, "Warner, Carlyle – Human Rights Case," BUF Fonds, NSARM, vol. 22, no. 20.

42 BUF, Minutes, Meeting of the Board of BUF and the Exec of the NSAACP, 19 May 1971, BUF Fonds, NSARM, vol. 3, no. 12.

43 BUF, Housing Survey of Black Communities, 1973, BUF Fonds, NSARM, vol. 8, no. 20, 2. Plans for the housing survey are discussed in BUF, Director's Report, 23 May 1970, BUF Fonds, NSARM, vol. 3, no. 11, 7; *GRASP*, June 1972, BUF Fonds, NSARM, O/S F90/G76.

44 BUF, "Tri-Function Convention, 1970–1," BUF Fonds, NSARM, vol. 2, no. 11, 4.

45 *GRASP*, December 1971, BUF Fonds, NSARM, O/S F90/G76, 4.

46 BUF, Cherry Brook Development, Meeting Minutes, 1970s, BUF Fonds, NSARM, vol. 17, no. 2, 2.

47 Quoted in "In the Panther's Wake," *Globe Magazine*, 15 February 1969, 43.

48 Quoted in Hinds, "Black Power."

49 In July 1970, one Black Haligonian reported being shut out of employment in the downtown; she had recently applied for two jobs in Scotia Square

and one on Barrington Street, and had been discriminated against in all three cases. BUF, Minutes, Board of Directors Meeting, 18 July 1970, BUF Fonds, NSARM, vol. 3, no. 11, 3. Analysis of racial discrimination cases based on BUF, Case and Special Assignment Officer: Reports, Correspondence, 1971–4, BUF Fonds, NSARM, vol. 9, no. 12; BUF, Case Files: Human Rights Commission (NS), 1972–9, BUF Fonds, NSARM, vol. 19, no. 6.

50 BUF, Minutes, Board of Directors Meeting, 18 July 1970, 3.

51 Quoted in *GRASP*, May 1971, BUF Fonds, NSARM, vol. 23, F90/G76.

52 Ibid.; BUF, Annual Progress Report, April 1970–March 1971, BUF Fonds, NSARM, vol. 7, no. 2, 35; BUF, Director's Report, 30 January 1971; BUF, Annual Progress report, April 1971–March 1972, BUF Fonds, NSARM, vol. 7, no. 3.

53 BUF, Director's Report, 26 September 1970, BUF Fonds, NSARM, vol. 3, no. 11, 4.

54 Harold Cruse, *The Crisis of the Negro Intellectual: A Historical Analysis of the Failure of Black Leadership* (New York: New York Review of Books, 1967), 7–8.

55 See James Smethurst, *The Black Arts Movement: Literary Nationalism in the 1960s and 1970s* (Chapel Hill: University of North Carolina Press, 2006); Daniel Widener, *Black Arts West: Culture an Struggle in Postwar Los Angeles* (Durham: Duke University Press, 2009).

56 BUF, Executive Director's Report, Annual Meeting, 25–6 October 1974, 3.

57 BUF, Outline of Brief to Graham Commission, 1971, BUF Fonds, NSARM, vol. 3, no. 12.

58 *GRASP* ran monthly from September 1970 until May 1971 and then semimonthly until 1978. BUF's first television program, a one-off spot, appeared in mid-1970. A four-part series aired in October 1972 and was repeated in April–May 1973; two more parts were produced in 1973 and aired as a six-part series in the fall of 1972. See BUF, Director's Report, 18 July 1970, BUF Fonds, NSARM, vol. 3, no. 11; BUF Newsletter, November 1972, vol. 23, no. 16.

59 BUF, Brief to Dalhousie University, 9 July 1971, BUF Fonds, NSARM, vol. 3, no. 3, 2–3.

60 BUF, Director's Report, 30 January 1971, 2.

61 The community recreation committees and the total amount fundraised are discussed in BUF, "History and Need of Black United Front," n.d. (but likely in 1971), BUF Fonds, NSARM, vol. 8, no. 2, 9; "Community Recreation and Development," vol. 17, no. 13. The quote is from Director's Report, 20 June 1970, vol. 3, no. 11, 7.

62 BUF, Director's Report, 23 May 1970.

63 On the 1974 program targeting single-family households, see ibid. The Beechville model community program is discussed in ibid.; Director's Report, 26 September 1970, 4–5. On the 1975 "winter warmth" program, see BUF, Executive Director's Report, Annual Meeting, 25–6 October 1974, 19.
64 BUF, "Annual Progress Report, April 1970–March 1971, 48.
65 BUF, Minutes, Board of Directors Meeting, 12 December 1970, vol. 3, no. 11, 2.
66 BUF, Director's Report, 30 January 1971, 7.
67 Quoted in Walker, "Black Confrontation," 189.
68 BUF, Report on Liaison Committee Meeting, 31 May 1971, vol. 18, no. 3.
69 BUF, Report on Liaison Committee Meeting, 1 March 1971, vol. 18, no. 3.
70 *GRASP*, December 1971, 4.
71 See BUF, Director's Report, 26 September 1970, 2–3.
72 BUF, Report on Liaison Committee Meeting, 30 November 1970, vol. 18, no. 3.
73 See, in particular, BUF's demand that the province channel "reparations" in the form of $10,000 for every Black Nova Scotian towards projects and programs devised by the Black community (through BUF). *GRASP*, July–August 1971.
74 The first convention occurred in November 1970, the second in June 1971, and the third in June 1972. A fourth meeting occurred in June 1974 but was termed a "retreat" rather than a "convention," and did not involve government representatives. See BUF, Director's Report, 12 December 1970, vol. 3, no. 11, 1–2; BUF, "Tri-Function Conventions, 1970–71," vol. 2, no. 11; *GRASP*, July–August, 1971; *GRASP*, July 1972; A.E. Criss, "CAP Funding," 12 September 1974, BUF Fonds, NSARM, vol. 16, no. 11.
75 See, for example, BUF, "Tri-Function Conventions, 1970–71," 4–5.
76 The first and second conventions were credited with achieving small changes, but the demands presented at the events were very seldom accepted. A series of demands stemming from the first convention – none of them granted – are outlined in BUF, Proposal Presented to the Premier of Nova Scotia, 9 March 1971, vol. 3, no. 12. The second convention is credited for the appointment of George McCurdy (a Black man) to the head of the Nova Scotia Human Rights Commission in BUF, Minutes, Board of Directors Meeting, 31 October 1971, vol. 3, no. 12. A summary of Premier Regan's promises stemming from the second convention (promises, effectively, to attend future, more specific meetings) are discussed in BUF, Director's Report, 25 September 1971, vol. 3, no. 12, 6. The third tri-function convention, BUF noted, was attended by only one of the invited government ministers, and the event's second day was devoted to "blast[ing] the

NS government, citing its unwillingness to participate as exemplary of [the] historical attitude of racism in the province." See *GRASP*, July 1972, 1.

77 Private meetings with state officials expanded in number and importance as the period of BUF's original grant came towards its end. See, for example, BUF, Report of Ottawa Delegation, 1974, vol. 16, no. 4; A.E. Criss to P.A. Best, Winston Ruck, J.E. Burdley, and W. Follock [*sic*], 31 August 1975, vol. 16, no. 11.

78 BUF, Director's Report, 26 September 1970, 4.

79 BUF, Carrie M. Best to Chairman, 28 February 1971, vol. 3, no. 12, 3.

80 See Ward Chirchill and Jim Vander Wall, *Agents of Repression: The FBI's Secret War against the Black Panther Party and the American Indian Movement* (Boston: South End Press, 1988).

81 As Donald Freed points out, Sams travelled widely in the late 1960s, and his visit to a location was often followed by a round-up of Black activists by municipal, state, and federal police. "Sams," however, "was never caught; he always managed to leave before the raids were made." Donald Freed, *Agony in New Haven* (New York: Simon and Schuster, 1973), 24–25. Sams's connection to the FBI is also discussed in detail in Bass and Rae, *Murder in the Model City*.

82 Quoted in Charles Saunders, "RCMP Snooping No Surprise," *Halifax Daily News*, 17 April 1994. In addition to surveillance, Rocky Jones maintained that the RCMP were "advocating the funding of [Black] moderates so that so-called militants would lose favour." See McNeil, "Afro(Americo)centricity," 61.

83 The moves of the Halifax police are discussed in Tattrie, *Hermit of Africville*. The pattern of Sams's activities is best described in Freed, *Agony in New Haven*; Bass and Rae, *Murder in the Model City*.

84 Tim Mitchell, "Black Rights Advocate Refuses to Quit," *Dalhousie Gazette*, 1 March 2009. For more on the RCMP's surveillance of Jones, see Saunders, "RCMP Snooping."

85 Saunders, "RCMP Snooping."

86 Daye's jaywalking ticket is discussed in BUF, Minutes, Board of Directors Meeting, 20 June 1970, vol. 3, no. 11, 2–3. The "threat" of Black visibility and agency is analysed in Austin, *Fear of a Black Nation*, 157–76.

87 Both quotes appear in Walker, "Black Confrontation," 186–7.

88 BUF, Minutes, Board of Directors Meeting, 25 April 1970.

89 Smith, *International History*, 102.

90 BUF, Brief to Dalhousie University, 9 July 1971, 1–2.

91 BUF, Submission for Developmental Phase – Demonstration Project, vol. 16, no. 4, 1 (emphasis mine).

92 Both quotes appear in Walker, "Black Confrontation," 186–7.

93 Ibid., 183–4.
94 Boyd's position is articulated in his "Politics of the Minority Game." Jones's investments in other political projects are evidenced in his participation at Encounter Week, where he is identified as a member of the Dalhousie Black Students Union. *Encounter on Urban Environment*, directed by Roger Hart (Toronto: National Film Board, 1971), DVD.
95 J.A. MacKenzie to Mike Keyes, 9 December 1974, BUF Fonds, NSARM, vol. 16, no. 11.
96 See for example, J.A. MacKenzie to Art Chriss [*sic*], 8 January 1975, vol. 18, no. 8; C.A. Black to Art Chriss [*sic*], 27 February 1976, BUF Fonds, NSARM, vol. 18, no. 8.
97 The ten-year funding request is discussed in A.E. Criss to BUF Board, 13 January 1975, vol. 16, no. 11. The government response is discussed in BUF, Report of Ottawa Delegation, 1974.
98 Letter from R.J. Stoddard (city clerk) to A.E. Criss, 2 May 1974, vol. 4, no. 13.
99 See P.A. Best and Art Criss, "Guidelines for Delegation to Ottawa," BUF Fonds, NSARM, vol. 16, no. 4.
100 This and other stipulations of CAP funding are outlined in Harold Huskilson to Winston Ruck, 26 June 1975, BUF Fonds, NSARM, vol. 16, no. 11.
101 Quote appears in BUF, Minutes, Executive Committee Meeting, 23 March 1974, vol. 2, no. 16, 8. The discussion of CAP funding appears in Best and Criss, "Guidelines for Delegation to Ottawa"; BUF, Working Paper Re: Meeting with Harold Huskilson, 1975, vol. 16, no. 11.
102 See the letters between BUF and provincial officials in Case Files: Department of Social Services, 1974–1983, BUF Fonds, NSARM, vol. 18, no. 8. Concerns about BUF's travel budget (tied to these high-level meetings) are registered in *Halifax Daily News*, 28 November 1984, BUF Fonds, NSARM, vol. 16, no. 5.
103 "Better Communication the Key to Survival," 1984, BUF Fonds, NSARM, vol. 16, no. 5.
104 Quoted in *Halifax Daily News*, 4 February 1989; second article, undated (but around 4 February 1989); both in BUF Fonds, NSARM, vol. 16, no. 5.
105 The prospect of Jones's hiring and BUF members' (quoted) responses to it are detailed in *Halifax Daily News*, 6 June 1988; 4 February 1989, BUF Fonds, NSARM, vol. 16, no. 5.
106 Thobani, *Exalted Subjects*, 180–1.
107 Quoted in Ted Rutland, "African People Pulling Together: Black Nova Scotian Community to Join African Union," *Halifax Media Co-Op*, 30 September 2011.
108 Haley, *No Mercy Here*, 200.

7 Making Space for Homo economicus: Neoliberalism, Regional Planning, and the Boundaries of Economic Life

1 HRM stands for Halifax Regional Municipality.

2 On the rise of neoliberal thinking and policies around the world, see Bob Jessop, "Fordism and Post-Fordism: A Critical Reformulation," in *Pathways to Industrialization and Regional Development*, ed. Allen Scott and Michael Storper (London: Routledge, 1992), 46–69; David Harvey, *A Brief History of Neoliberalism* (Oxford: Oxford University Press, 2007); Jamie Peck, *Constructions of Neoliberal Reason* (Oxford: Oxford University Press, 2010). On the urban dimensions of neoliberalism, see Stefan Kipfer and Roger Keil, "Toronto Inc.? Planning the Competitive City in New Toronto," *Antipode* 34, no. 2 (2002): 227–64; Helga Leitner, Jamie Peck, and Eric Sheppard, eds., *Contesting Neoliberalism: Urban Frontiers* (New York: Guilford Press, 2007). On the annulment of funding for public housing, see Jeanne Wolfe, "Canadian Housing Policy in the Nineties," *Housing Studies* 13, no. 1 (1998): 121–34.

3 On *homo economicus* as a normative rendering of the human, see Wendy Brown, "Neoliberalism and the End of Liberal Democracy," in *Edgework: Critical Essays on Knowledge and Politics* (Princeton: Princeton University Press, 2009), 37–59. Brown's work extends Michel Foucault's provisional analysis of neoliberalism in *The Birth of Biopolitics: Lectures at the Collège de France, 1978–1979* (New York: Palgrave Macmillan, 2008). The link between neoliberalism and anti-blackness, overlooked in nearly all work on neoliberalism, is most helpfully sketched in Jared Sexton, "Captivity, by Turns: A Comment on the Work of Ashley Hunt," *Art Journal* 66, no. 3 (2007): 74–9.

4 Economic restructuring and private-sector job losses are detailed in Thom Workman, "The Decaying Social Compact in Atlantic Canada," in *From the Net to the 'Net': Atlantic Canada and the Global Economy*, ed. Henry Veltmeyer and James Sacouman (Toronto: University of Toronto Press, 2005), 85–98; Judith Fingard, Janet Guildford, and David Sutherland, *Halifax: The First 250 Years* (Halifax: Formac Publishing, 1999), 179–92.

5 Greater Halifax Partnership, *Economic Profile of Greater Halifax – Chart Book* (Halifax: Greater Halifax Partnership, 2005), 12; Gardner Pinfold Consulting, *Economic Potential of HRM and Halifax Harbour* (Halifax: Gardner Pinfold, 2004), 11, 18.

6 Greater Halifax Partnership, *Economic Profile*, 7. See also Gardner Pinfold, *Economic Potential*, 2–3.

7 Andrew Sancton, "Reducing Costs by Consolidating Municipalities: New Brunswick, Nova Scotia, and Ontario," *Canadian Public Administration* 39,

no. 3 (1996): 267–89. Figures from Igor Vojnovic, "The Fiscal Distribution of the Provincial-Municipal Service Exchange in Nova Scotia," *Canadian Public Administration* 42, no. 4 (1999): 512–41.

8 Spreading the burden of service costs is emphasized in Vojnovic, "Fiscal Distribution"; Wayne Adams, "HRM's Two Solitudes," *Halifax Daily News*, 28 September 2004. Overall efficiencies are underlined in Sancton, "Reducing Costs."

9 Figures from Stantec Consulting, *Quantifying the Costs and Benefits to HRM, Residents, and the Environment of Alternate Growth Scenarios* (Halifax: Stantec Consulting, 2013), 2.3.

10 Hugh Millward, "Peri-Urban Residential Development in the Halifax region 1960–2000: Magnets, Constraints, and Planning Policies," *Canadian Geographer* 46, no. 1 (2002): 33–47; Turner Drake and Partners, *Market Survey of Downtown Halifax* (Halifax: Turner Drake, 2008).

11 Millward, "Peri-Urban Residential Development."

12 Figures are from Victoria Prouse et al., *Neighbourhood Change in the Halifax Regional Municipality, 1970 to 2010: Applying the "Three Cities" Model* (Halifax: Dalhousie University, 2014), 22. The category that I am calling "poorest" includes census tracts where the average individual income is 80 per cent or less than the region-wide (Census Metropolitan Area) average. The category that I am calling "richest" includes census tracts were the average individual income is 120 per cent or more than the region-wide average.

13 Figures from Statistics Canada, *Census of Canada, 1971* (Ottawa: Statistics Canada, 1971); *Census of Canada, 2001* (Ottawa: Statistics Canada, 2001). Locations of off-peninsula poverty are named in Prouse et al., *Neighbourhood Change*, 19.

14 City of Halifax, *Downtown Halifax Secondary Municipal Planning Strategy* (Halifax: HRM, 2008), 15. Property values in this area are discussed in Lis van Berkel, "Where Goes the Neighbourhood?" *The Coast* (Halifax), 12 April 2007.

15 The gentrification of Gottingen Street is described in Chris Benjamin, "Rebuilding Halifax's Most Feared Neighbourhood, One Project at a Time," *Globe and Mail*, 24 September 2010; Jim Silver, *Public Housing Risks and Alternatives: Uniacke Square in North End Halifax* (Halifax: Canadian Centre for Policy Alternatives, 2008); Ingrid Waldron, *North End Matters: Using the People Assessing their Health Process (PATH) to Explore the Social Determinants of Health in the Black Community in the North End* (Halifax: Dalhousie University, 2015). The price of a Gottingen condominium is cited in Carsten Knox, "Why Buying a Condo in Halifax is a Good Idea – and Selling One Might Be Even Better," *The Coast* (Halifax), 19 April 2012. Statistics Canada's 1911 National Household Survey puts the median value of a home in the same census tract at $299,571.

16 Turner Drake, *Market Survey,* 13–14.
17 See Knox, "Why Buying a Condo."
18 Interview with Halifax developer, 9 April 2008.
19 I describe this process, from global financial flows to local property development, in Ted Rutland, "The Financialization of Urban Redevelopment," *Geography Compass* 4, no. 8 (2010): 1167–78.
20 The quote is from "Highrise Project No 'Disneyfication' of Halifax: Architect," CBC News, 28 March 2006, http://www.cbc.ca/news/canada/nova-scotia/highrise-project-no-disneyfication-of-halifax-architect-1.611517. The contest over the property development in this period is detailed in Lachlan Barber, "Making Meaning of Heritage Landscapes: The Politics of Redevelopment in Halifax, Nova Scotia," *Canadian Geographer* 57, no. 2 (2013): 90–11.
21 An overview of major suburban developers is provided in "Digging into Development; Major Players," *Halifax Chronicle-Herald,* 24 October 2003. The incomes targeted by development is suggested in Prouse et al., *Neighbourhood Change.*
22 The figure refers to the wealthiest 10 per cent of Halifax (Census Metropolitan Area) census tracts in 2001 in terms of median household income. Statistics Canada, *Census of Canada.*
23 See Millward, "Peri-Urban Residential Development"; Kirk Brewer, *Densifying Dartmouth? Emerging Land Use Patterns in Suburban Development* (Halifax: Trends in the Suburbs Project, 2013).
24 Prouse et al., *Neighbourhood Change,* 22.
25 See Alex Kawchuk, "Exploring the Condition of Rental Housing in Spryfield, Nova Scotia" (master's project, Dalhousie University, 2014); Jeremy Murphy, "The Viability of Converting Public Housing Projects into Tenant-Managed Housing in Spryfield" (master's project, Dalhousie University, 2006).
26 See David Hulchanski, *The Three Cities Within Toronto: Income Polarization Among Toronto's Neighbourhoods, 1970–2005* (Toronto: Cities Centre, 2010); Vanessa Parlette and Deborah Cowen, "Dead Malls: Suburban Activism, Local Spaces, Global Logistics," *Journal of Urban and Regional Research* 35, no. 4 (2011): 794–811.
27 Millward, "Peri-Urban Residential Development," 43.
28 Chris Lambie, "Residents Disagree Over Role of Racism in Boundary Dispute," *Halifax Daily News,* 7 February 1997; "East Preston Group Denounces Area Councilor," *Halifax Daily News,* 19 March 1997. The quote appears in Amy Smeltzer, "Neighbourhood Segregation Traditional, but Changing," *Halifax Commoner,* 15 February 2002.

29 Progress on Beechville Estates, including profits on land sales, is discussed in Armco's annual reports between 1998 and 2004. See, in particular, Armco Capital, *Annual Report 2004* (Halifax, Armco Capital, 2004). The new 306-unit subdivision was announced in 2012 and was approved in 2014. Sherry Borden, "Lovett Lake Proposal Worries Beechville Residents," *Halifax Chronicle-Herald*, 9 August 2014.

30 Althea Tolliver and James Francois, *From Africville to New Road: How Four Communities Planned their Development* (Dartmouth, NS: Watershed Joint Action Committee/BUF, 1983), 18.

31 Brynn Kelly, *Brief Overview of Policy Issues Related to Rural Nova Scotia's Black Community* (Halifax: Rural Communities Impacting Policy, 2003), 8.

32 See Richard Dooley, "Dirty Water Ignored Because of Discrimination," *Halifax Daily News*, 15 April 1999; Keith Bonnell, "A Long Wait For a Good Drink; Upper Hammonds Plains Taps in," *Halifax Chronicle-Herald*, 15 December 1999; Sherri Borden, "Upper Hammonds Plains Water Trial Begins," *Halifax Chronicle-Herald*, 26 November 2002; Rachel Boomer, "Residents Win Water Hookup Battle with City," *Halifax Daily News*, 29 April 2005.

33 Bob Nauss to Mayor Kelly and Members of Halifax Regional Council, HRM by Design Information Report, 5 September 2006, 3.

34 The details and aims of the process are outlined in Nauss, HRM by Design.

35 HRM, *HRM by Design: The Downtown Halifax Plan – CIP 2010 Awards for Planning Excellence* (Halifax: HRM, 2010), 9.

36 The six phases are outlined in Nauss, HRM by Design. The consultants' presentations include HRM, "HRM by Design: Vision Statement + Principles," 27 February 2007; HRM, "Urban Design Concepts and Strategies," 31 July 2007; HRM, "The Downtown Halifax Plan," 16 April 2008.

37 Unless otherwise noted, the details of HRM by Design public events stem from my own observations as a participant.

38 Dan English to Mayor Kelly and Members of Halifax Regional Council, "HRM by Design: Urban Design Vision and Principles *and* Increase to Contract," 19 February 2007, 3; Andy Fillmore to Jennifer Keesmaat and Harold Madi, "Expansion of Scope – HRM by Design," 13 February 2007, included as attachment to Dan English letter of 19 February 2007.

39 HRM, Urban Design Task Force Minutes, 7 February 2007; HRM, Committee of the Whole Minutes, 27 February 2007. Notably, the expanded scope of the project was explained to the urban-design task force (by head planner Andy Fillmore) as a means to protect architectural heritage rather than to streamline the approvals process.

40 HRM, "Development Approvals and Economic Development," September 2007.
41 Richard Florida, *The Rise of the Creative Class, Revisited* (New York: Basic Books, 2012), 238.
42 See Jane M. Jacobs, "Staging Difference: Aestheticization and the Politics of Difference in Contemporary Cities" in *Cities of Difference*, ed. Ruth Fincher and Jane M. Jacobs (New York: The Guilford Press, 1998), 252–78; Sunera Thobani, *Exalted Subjects: Studies in the Making of Race and Nation in Canada* (Toronto: University of Toronto Press, 2007), 143–75.
43 The effect is evident in Florida's ranking of cities' innovation and ethnic diversity in Richard Florida, *Cities and the Creative Class* (New York: Routledge, 2005), 136. At the bottom of both rankings are a series of Black-majority cities like Memphis and New Orleans, as well as cities with large (but not majority) Black populations like Buffalo, Richmond, Rochester, and Cleveland. These cities, because of their relatively small foreign-born populations, register as ethnically undiverse.
44 Richard Florida, *The Rise of the Creative Class* (New York: Basic Books, 2002), 229.
45 See Michel Foucault, *Birth of Biopolitics*. This book is most often read as a departure from Foucault's work on biopolitics. While the term itself appears very seldom in the book (aside from the title), Foucault makes clear that he sees liberalism (the overt focus of the book/lectures) as the "general framework of biopolitics" (22).
46 Florida, *Rise of the Creative Class*, xxii.
47 Ibid., 10.
48 Meric Gertler and Tara Vinodrai, *Competing on Creativity: Focus on Halifax* (Halifax: GHP, 2004); HRM, *Strategies for Success: Halifax Regional Municipality's Economic Development Strategy, 2005–2010* (Halifax: HRM, 2005).
49 For more on Fusion, see Gladys Leung, "The Role of Fusion Halifax in the Halifax Urban Development Dialogue" (master's project, Dalhousie University, 2013).
50 Quote is from Peter Moorhouse and Cheryl Stewart, "Cities That Act Attract Young People," *Halifax Chronicle-Herald*, 9 June 2008. The need for a talent-representing organization was identified in the GHP-commissioned study, Next Generation Consulting, *Attracting and Retaining Talent to Greater Halifax* (Halifax: Next Generation Consulting, 2007), 7. The activities of Fusion Halifax are explored in Leung, "Role of Fusion Halifax."
51 HRM, *Strategies for Success*, 8, 9, 15, 38; Moorhouse and Stewart, "Cities That Act."

52 HRM, *Strategies for Success*, 20.
53 All quotes from HRM, "Development Approvals."
54 HRM, "Downtown Halifax Secondary Planning Strategy, vol. 1 – Draft for Public Review," 7 April 2008. The public release / circulation of the document is discussed in HRM, Urban Design Task Force Minutes, 26 March 2008. For clarification regarding the ability of downtown property owners to contest development approvals, see HRM, Response to councillor comments, 12 May 2009 (updated 27 May 2009).
55 Turner Drake, *Market Study*. The study was delivered to council in Paul Dunphy to Mayor Kelly and Members of Halifax Regional Council, "HRM by Design: Demand, Capacity, and Baseline Indicators Study," 13 March 2009. Discussion of the report by HRM by Design opponents appears in "Halifax Development Report Misconstrued: Consultant," CBC News, 7 May 2009, http://www.cbc.ca/news/canada/nova-scotia/halifax-development-report-misconstrued-consultant-1.813768; Rebecca Jamieson to Halifax Regional Council, re: HRMbyDesign, submitted to city council on 5 May 2009, available from City Clerk's Office.
56 HTNS, *Ten Reasons HRM by Design Puts Halifax at Risk* (Halifax: Heritage Trust, 2008).
57 Ron Burdock to Halifax Regional Council, re: HRMbyDesign, submitted to city council on 5 May 2009, available from City Clerk's Office.
58 Jean Chard to Halifax Regional Council, re: HRMbyDesign, submitted to city council on 5 May 2009, available from City Clerk's Office.
59 HTNS to Halifax Regional Council, re: HRMbyDesign, submitted to city council on 5 May 2009, available from City Clerk's Office.
60 See HRM, Regional Council Minutes, 5–6 May 2009, 30.
61 Ibid., 20–1, 36.
62 Quoted in Ted Rutland, "Designs on Downtown Halifax," *Halifax Media Co-op*, 9 May 2009, http://halifax.mediacoop.ca/story/1508.
63 HRM, "Regional Council Approved HRMbyDesign Downtown Plan," news release, 16 June 2009.
64 Quoted in Amy Pugsley Fraser, "Developing Story: Halifax Region Creates Plan to Tackle Mushrooming Growth," *Halifax Chronicle-Herald*, 16 May 2005.
65 HRM, *Regional Municipal Planning Strategy* (Halifax: HRM, 2006), 15–16. The details of the planning process are also described in this document.
66 See G.C. Hufbauer and B.W. Severn, "Municipal Costs and Urban Area," *Journal of Urban Economics* 2, no. 3 (1975): 199–211; Richard Peiser, "Does It Pay to Plan Suburban Growth?" *Journal of the American Planning Association*

50, no. 4 (1984): 419–33; John Roseth, "Infrastructure Pricing and Urban Settlement," *Australian Planner* 30, no. 3 (1992): 162–6. A critical history of these ideas is provided by Rob Krueger and David Gibbs, "'Third Wave' Sustainability? Smart Growth and Regional Development in the USA," *Regional Studies* 42, no. 9 (2008): 1263–74.

67 Brett Hulsey, *How Uncontrolled Sprawl Increases Your Property Taxes and Threatens Your Quality of Life* (Madison, WI: Sierra Club, 1996). The seminal study on the combined economic and ecological costs of sprawl is Robert Burchell et al., *Costs of Sprawl – 2000* (Washington, DC: National Academy Press, 2002).

68 This research is surveyed in Michael Neuman, "The Compact City Fallacy," *Journal of Planning Education and Research* 25, no. 1 (2005): 11–26.

69 See Krueger and Gibbs, "'Third Wave' Sustainability."

70 HRM, *Settlement Pattern and Form with Service Cost Analysis* (Halifax: HRM, 2005), 11.

71 Ibid., 3.

72 HRM, *Regional Municipal Planning Strategy*, 110–11.

73 Cantwell and Company, *Land Use and Transportation Plan for Wrights Cove – Final Report* (Halifax: Cantwell and Company, 2006).

74 Shane MacKinlay, "Council Gives Black Rocky Ride," *Halifax Daily News*, 1 December 2004.

75 Kim Moar, "Planner: Urban Sprawl Taking Toll on Halifax," *Halifax Daily News*, 21 October 2001.

76 Pugsley Fraser, "Developing Story."

77 "HRM Building Ban Angers Developers," CBC News, 23 January 2004 (cached version available at http://www.oocities.org/waverleywest/HRMbuildingbanangersdevelopers.html).

78 Amy Pugsley, "HRM Planning to Shape its Future," *Halifax Chronicle-Herald*, 14 May 2004. The GHP's position is mentioned in Shane MacKinlay, "Big Thinkers to Plot Ways for Growth," *Halifax Daily News*, 23 June 2005.

79 These assumptions are evident in all major city-produced documents submitted to the regional planning process. See, in particular, HRM, *Regional Municipal Planning Strategy*, 6 (taxation), 59 (residents' choice of location).

80 Data provided by Property Valuation Services, Dartmouth, NS.

81 George McLellan to Mayor Peter Kelly and Members of Halifax Regional Council, "Interim Growth Management: Plan Amendments," 5 March 2004, 2.

82 HRM, "HRM, Water Commission Support Temporary Moratorium on New Housing Projects," news release, 22 January 2004. Lot estimates from Kim Moar, "Builders Still Dispute City's 'Bogus Figures,'" *Halifax Daily News*, 31 January 2004.

83 Quoted in Amy Pugsley, "HRM Accepts Growth Plan Amendment," *Halifax Chronicle-Herald*, 5 May 2004.
84 HRM, Regional Council Minutes, 5 May 2004, 10.
85 McLellan "Interim Growth Management."
86 The specifics are detailed in HRM, *Regional Municipal Planning Strategy*, 36–62. Outside the eight growth centres, the construction of new private roads was prohibited, while the construction of new public roads and the creation of up to eight new lots on these roads was allowed under certain circumstances. The creation of up to three flag lots in these areas was also permitted. These restrictions, the same as the amended temporary restrictions, applied to all peripheral Black communities. In addition to these restrictions, the community of Upper Hammonds Plains was also prohibited from undertaking residential development on any new road, public or private.
87 Quoted in HRM, *Regional Plan 5 Year Review, Phase II: Response to Public Input* (Halifax: HRM, 2012), 15.
88 The demands of East Preston residents are outlined in HRM, *Draft Regional Plan – East Preston Workshop – June 1, 2005* (Halifax: HRM, 2005). Planners' dismissal of these (and other) demands appears in HRM, *Response to Regional Plan Public Hearing* (Halifax: HRM, 2005).
89 Katherine McKittrick, *Demonic Grounds: Black Women and the Cartographies of Struggle* (Minneapolis: University of Minnesota Press, 2006), x.
90 HRM, *Response to Regional Plan Public Hearing*, 151–2. Black demands appear in ibid. and HRM, *Draft Regional Plan – East Preston Workshop*; HRM, *Draft Regional Plan – Cole Harbour Workshop* (Halifax: HRM, 2005).
91 HRM, *Municipal Planning Strategy for North Preston/Lake Major, Lake Loon/Cherrybrook, and East Preston* (Halifax: HRM, 2006).
92 Ibid., 3, 11.
93 Sylvia Wynter and Katherine McKittrick, "Unparalleld Catastrophe for Our Species? Or, to Give Humanness a Different Future: Conversations," in *Sylvia Wynter: On Being Human as Praxis*, ed. Katherine McKittrick (Durham: Duke University Press, 2014), 9–89.
94 See Wendy Brown's (otherwise excellent) Foucauldian analysis of neoliberalism in *Undoing the Demos: Neoliberalism's Stealth Revolution* (Cambridge, MA: MIT Press, 2015), 110; Brown, *Edgework*, 37–59.
95 See Harvey, *Brief History of Neoliberalism*, 15–16; Brown, *Undoing the Demos*, 110; Brown, *Edgework*, 37–59.
96 Millward, "Peri-Urban Residential Development,"43.

8 Conclusion

1 David Harvey, "On Planning the Ideology of Planning," in *Planning Theory in the 1980s: Challenge and Response*, ed. Robert Burchell and George Sternlieb (New Brunswick, NJ: Center for Urban Policy Research, 1978), 213–34; David Harvey, *The Condition of Postmodernity: An Enquiry into the Origins of Cultural Change* (New York: Blackwell, 1991); James Scott, *Seeing Like a State: How Certain Schemes to Improve the Human Condition Have Failed* (New Haven: Yale University Press, 1999), 53–84. A similar approach to Scott's appears in Christine Boyer, *Dreaming the Rational City: The Myth of American City Planning* (Cambridge, MA: MIT Press, 1986); Leonie Sandercock, *Cosmopolis II: Mongrel Cities of the 21st Century* (New York: Continuum, 2003).

2 Michel Foucault, *The Order of Things: An Archaeology of the Human Sciences* (New York: Routledge, 1970); Michel Foucault, *Security, Territory, Population: Lectures at the Collège de France, 1977–1978* (New York: Picador, 2007), 22–3; Michel Foucault, "What is Enlightenment?" in *The Foucault Reader*, ed. Paul Rabinow (New York: Pantheon Books, 1984), 32–50; Paul Rabinow, *French Modern: Norms and Forms of the Social Environment* (Chicago: University of Chicago Press, 1995). Foucault's blindness to race is outlined in Anne Stoler, *Race and the Education of Desire: Foucault's History of Sexuality and the Colonial Order of Things* (Durham: Duke University Press, 1995); Brady Heiner, "Foucault and the Black Panthers," *City* 11, no. 3 (2007): 313–56.

3 Frantz Fanon, *Black Skin, White Masks* (New York: Grove Press, 1968); Katherine McKittrick, *Demonic Grounds: Black Women and the Cartographies of Struggle* (Minneapolis: University of Minnesota Press, 2006); Rinaldo Walcott, "The Problem of the Human: Black Ontologies and the 'Coloniality of Our Being,'" in *Postcoloniality – Decoloniality – Black Critique: Joints and Fissures*, ed. Sabine Broeck and Carsten Junker (New York: Campus Verlag, 2014), 93–105; Sylvia Wynter, "Unsettling the Coloniality of Being/Power/Truth/Freedom: Towards the Human, After Man, Its Overrepresentation – An Argument," *New Centennial Review* 3, no. 3 (2003): 257–337; Saidiya Hartman, *Scenes of Subjection: Terror, Slavery, and Self-Making in Nineteenth-Century America* (Oxford: Oxford University Press, 1997).

4 See Glen Coulthard, *Red Skin, White Masks: Rejecting the Colonial Politics of Recognition* (Minneapolis: University of Minnesota Press, 2014), 173–6; Libby Porter, *Unlearning the Colonial Cultures of Planning* (Burlington, VT: Ashgate Publishing, 2010).

5 See, for example, Leanne Simpson, "Indict the System: Indigenous and Black Connected Resistance," *Leanne Betasamosake Simpson* (blog), 28 November 2014, https://www.leannesimpson.ca/writings/

indict-the-system-indigenous-black-connected-resistance; Tiffany Lethabo King, "Interview with Dr. Tiffany Lethabo King," *Feral Feminisms* 4 (Summer 2015): 64–8.

6 See Cindy Holmes, Sarah Hunt, and Amy Piedalue, "Violence, Colonialism, and Space: Towards a Decolonizing Dialogue," *ACME: An International E-Journal for Critical Geographies* 14, no. 2 (2014): 539–70, https://www.acme-journal.org/index.php/acme/article/view/1102.

7 HRM, "Africville: Recognizing the Past, Present, and Future," Halifax (municipal government website), 24 February 2010, https://www.halifax.ca/about-halifax/diversity-inclusion/african-nova-scotian-affairs/africville/apology; Brandon Collins, "Ferguson and Charlottesville: A Comparison of Racist Histories," Brandon Collins for Charlottesville, 23 August 2014, https://votebrandoncollins.wordpress.com/2014/08/23/ferguson-and-charlottesville-a-comparison-of-racist-histories; Jane Eastwood, "Apology Offered for Destruction of African American Neighborhood," Local and Regional Government Alliance for Race and Equity, 11 August 2015, http://www.racialequityalliance.org/2015/08/11/apology-offered-for-destruction-of-historic-african-american-neighborhood; Casey Parks, "Fifty Years Later, Legacy Emanuel Medical Center Attempts to Make Amends for Razing Neighborhood," *The Oregonian*, 21 September 2012.

8 Jennifer Henderson and Pauline Wakeham, introduction to *Reconciling Canada: Critical Perspectives on the Culture of Redress*, ed. Jennifer Henderson and Pauline Wakeham (Toronto: University of Toronto Press, 2013). See also Rinaldo Walcott, "Into the Ranks of Man: Vicious Modernism and the Politics of Reconciliation," in *Cultivating Canada: Reconciliation through the Lens of Cultural Diversity*, ed. Ashok Mathur, Jonathan Dewar, and Mike DeGagné (Ottawa: Aboriginal Healing Foundation, 2011), 341–50.

9 HRM, "Africville."

10 Quoted in Dalal Razzaq, "Refusing to Forget," *Halifax Media Co-Op*, 14 April 2010.

11 See Henderson and Wakeham, introduction.

12 Katherine Laidlaw, "Bridge Jobs Fuels Tensions in 'Mississippi of the North,'" *National Post*, 9 August 2010.

13 "Road Restriction Prompts Racism Allegations," CBC News, 9 August 2010, http://www.cbc.ca/news/canada/nova-scotia/road-restriction-prompts-racism-allegation-1.879697.

14 See HRM, *Regional Plan 5 Year Review, Phase II: Response to Public Input* (Halifax: HRM, 2012).

15 The city's role in promoting North End gentrification is discussed in Hilary Beaumont, "Pushed Out by Gentrification?" *The Coast* (Halifax), 8 August 2013. The response of Black North Enders, including Lindell

Smith and Rodney Small, is discussed in Phillis McGregor, "Halifax: A City with Two North Ends – Part I," CBC News, 14 April 2015, http://www.cbc.ca/news/canada/nova-scotia/halifax-a-city-with-two-north-ends-part-1-1.3031005; Ingrid Waldron, *North End Matters: Using the People Assessing their Health Process (PATH) to Explore the Social Determinants of Health in the Black Community in the North End* (Halifax: Dalhousie University, 2015).

16 Peter Newman, Timothy Beatley, and Heather Boyer, *Resilient Cities: Responding to Peak Oil and Climate Change* (Washington, DC: Island Press, 2009); Richard Register, *Ecocities: Building Cities in Balance with Nature* (Gabriola Island, BC: New Society Publishers, 2013); Peter Timothy Beatley, *Green Urbanism: Learning from European Cities* (Washington, DC: Island Press, 2012).

17 Jan Gehl, *Cities for People* (Washington, DC: Island Press, 2013); Mike Lydon and Anthony Garcia, *Tactical Urbanism: Short Term Action for Long Term Change* (Washington, DC: Island Press, 2015).

18 Susain Faintein, "Planning and the Just City," in *Searching for the Just City: Debates in Urban Theory and Practice*, ed. Peter Marcuse et al. (New York: Routledge, 2009), 29.

19 Ibid., 34–5.

20 Ibid., 29.

21 Promising visions of urban planning that look towards the history of radical Black struggle include June Manning Thomas and Marsha Ritzdorf, eds., *Urban Planning and the African American Community: In the Shadows* (Thousand Oaks: Sage Publications, 1997); Marisa Zapata and Lisa Bates, "Equity Planning Revisited," *Journal of Planning Education and Research* 35, no. 3 (2015): 245–8.

22 Movement for Black Lives, *A Vision for Black Lives: Policy Demands for Black Power, Freedom, and Justice,* Movement for Black Lives, accessed 6 December 2016, https://policy.m4bl.org/wp-content/uploads/2016/07/20160726-m4bl-Vision-Booklet-V3.pdf. Robin D.G. Kelley situates the M4BL platform within the broader Black radical tradition in "What Does Black Lives Matter Want?" *Boston Review*, 17 August 2016.

23 Movement for Black Lives, *A Vision for Black Lives*, 3.

24 BLM's strongest relations of solidarity, thus far, have been forged with Indigenous people in North America and with Palestinians. See Movement for Black Lives, *Vision for Black Lives*, 4; Leanne Simpson, "An Indigenous View on #BlackLivesMatter," *Yes! Magazine,* 5 December 2014, http://www.yesmagazine.org/peace-justice/indigenous-view-black-lives-matter-leanne-simpson; Kelly Hayes, "Where Movements Meet: Black Lives Matter Organizers Visit #NoDAPL," *Truthout*, 2

September 2016, http://www.truth-out.org/news/item/37468-where-movements-meet-black-lives-matter-organizers-visit-nodapl; Emma Green, "Why Do Black Activists Care about Palestine?" *The Atlantic*, 18 August 2016; Nora Barrows-Friedman, "Palestinians Welcome Movement for Black Lives Platform," *Electronic Intifada*, 9 August 2016, https://electronicintifada.net/blogs/nora-barrows-friedman/palestinians-welcome-movement-black-lives-platform.

25 Hartman, *Scenes of Subjection*, 118.

26 Christina Sharpe, "Lose Your Kin," *The New Inquiry*, 16 November 2016.

Index

www.ingramcontent.com/pod-product-compliance
Lightning Source LLC
LaVergne TN
LVHW090801070826
844660LV00022B/1052

* 9 7 8 1 4 8 7 5 2 2 7 2 8 *